The Development of the Nominal Plural Forms
in Early Middle English

Hituzi Linguistics in English

No.1	Lexical Borrowing and its Impact on English	Makimi Kimura-Kano
No.2	From a Subordinate Clause to an Independent Clause	Yuko Higashiizumi
No.3	ModalP and Subjunctive Present	Tadao Nomura
No.4	A Historical Study of Referent Honorifics in Japanese	Takashi Nagata
No.5	Communicating Skills of Intention	Tsutomu Sakamoto
No.6	A Pragmatic Approach to the Generation and Gender Gap in Japanese Politeness Strategies	Toshihiko Suzuki
No.7	Japanese Women's Listening Behavior in Face-to-face Conversation	Sachie Miyazaki
No.8	An Enterprise in the Cognitive Science of Language	Tetsuya Sano et al.
No.9	Syntactic Structure and Silence	Hisao Tokisaki
No.10	The Development of the Nominal Plural Forms in Early Middle English	Ryuichi Hotta
No.11	Chunking and Instruction	Takayuki Nakamori
No.12	Detecting and Sharing Perspectives Using Causals in Japanese	Ryoko Uno
No.13	Discourse Representation of Temporal Relations in the So-Called Head-Internal Relatives	Kuniyoshi Ishikawa
No.14	Features and Roles of Filled Pauses in Speech Communication	Michiko Watanabe
No.15	Japanese Loanword Phonology	Masahiko Mutsukawa

Hituzi Linguistics in English No. 10

The Development of the Nominal Plural Forms in Early Middle English

Ryuichi Hotta

Hituzi Syobo Publishing

Copyright © Ryuichi Hotta 2009
First published 2009

Author: Ryuichi Hotta

All rights reserved. Except for the quotation of short passages for the purposes of criticism and review, no part of this publication may be reproduced, stored in a retrieval system, or transmitted in any form or by any means, electronic, mechanical, photocopying, recording or otherwise, without the written prior permission of the publisher.
In case of photocopying and electronic copying and retrieval from network personally, permission will be given on receipts of payment and making inquiries. For details please contact us through e-mail. Our e-mail address is given below.

Book Design © Hirokazu Mukai (glyph)

Hituzi Syobo Publishing
Yamato bldg. 2F, 2-1-2 Sengoku Bunkyo-ku Tokyo, Japan
112-0011

phone +81-3-5319-4916 fax +81-3-5319-4917
e-mail: toiawase@hituzi.co.jp
http://www.hituzi.co.jp/
postal transfer 00120-8-142852

ISBN978-4-89476-403-3
Printed in Japan

Contents

List of Tables	vii
List of Figures	xi
Preface	xiii
Acknowledgements	xv
Abbreviations	xviii

1 Introduction   1
    1.1 Aim of Study 1
    1.2 Scope of Study 5

2 Preliminary Discussions   7
    2.1 Review of Roedler's Study 7
       2.1.1 Northern 9
       2.1.2 North-East Midland 9
       2.1.3 South-East Midland 10
       2.1.4 North-West Midland 11
       2.1.5 South-West Midland 11
       2.1.6 Southwestern 12
       2.1.7 Southeastern 14
       2.1.8 Cause of the Development 15
       2.1.9 Critical Comments on Roedler's Study 17
    2.2 Review of Classen's Study 19
    2.3 Germanic Backgrounds 20
       2.3.1 Introduction to Germanic Backgrounds 20
       2.3.2 East Germanic 22
       2.3.3 West Germanic 24
       2.3.4 North Germanic 29
       2.3.5 Summary of Germanic Backgrounds 35

3	**Textual Evidence**		**37**
3.1	Principles of Treating Textual Evidence		37
	3.1.1 Where Textual Evidence Comes From		37
	3.1.2 Collecting Plural Forms		38
	3.1.3 Case Syncretism		40
	3.1.4 Plural Forms Reference System		43
	3.1.5 Plural Forms Profiles		51
	3.1.6 Comparing Texts at Various Levels		52
3.2	Dialect-by-Dialect Study of Plural Formation Transfer		54
	3.2.1 Text Groups		54
	3.2.2 Northern Text Group		57
	3.2.3 North-East Midland Text Group		58
	3.2.4 South-East Midland Text Group		59
	3.2.5 North-West Midland Text Group		61
	3.2.6 South-West Midland Text Group		62
	3.2.7 Southwestern Text Group		67
	3.2.8 Southeastern Text Group		68
	3.2.9 Panchronic Summary of Plural Formation Transfer . . .		70
3.3	Item-Based Study		73
	3.3.1 Masc-S Nouns		74
	3.3.2 Masc-N Nouns		74
	3.3.3 Neut-N Nouns		75
	3.3.4 Fem-N Nouns		75
	3.3.5 Masc-V Nouns		75
	3.3.6 Neut-V Nouns		75
	3.3.7 Fem-V Nouns		76
	3.3.8 Masc-Ø Nouns		77
	3.3.9 Neut-Ø Nouns		77
	3.3.10 Fem-Ø Nouns		78
	3.3.11 Masc-M Nouns		78
	3.3.12 Neut-M Nouns		78
	3.3.13 Fem-M Nouns		79
	3.3.14 Summary of Item-Based Study		79

4	**Study of Selected Texts**	81
	4.1 The *Lambeth Homilies*	82
	4.2 *The Owl and the Nightingale*	86
	4.3 The *Ancrene Wisse/Riwle*	91
	4.4 The *Poema Morale*	98
	4.5 *The Peterborough Chronicle*	109
5	**HOW: Lexical Diffusion**	117
	5.1 Introduction to Lexical Diffusion	117
	5.2 Advantages of Lexical Diffusion	121
	5.3 Applicability of Lexical Diffusion to Morphological Change	123
	5.4 Lexical Diffusion and the Early Middle English Plural System	126
6	**WHY: Language-Internal Motivation**	133
	6.1 Mobility across Classes	133
	6.2 Levelling of Inflectional Endings	134
	6.3 Systemic Reorganisation of the Nominal Morphology	135
	6.4 Loss of Gender	137
	6.5 Phonetic and Phonological Conditions	138
	6.6 Syntactic Agreement	141
	6.7 Semantic and Lexical Considerations	144
	6.8 Case Syncretism and the Spread of *-s*	147
	6.9 Summary of Language-Internal Motivation	148
7	**WHY: Language-External Motivation**	153
	7.1 Language Contact	153
	7.2 Contact with Old Norse	154
	7.3 Theoretical Assumptions	157
	7.4 Old Norse Contact Hypothesis	161
	7.5 Illustration of Forms	169
	7.6 Contact between Dialects	174
8	**Conclusion**	177
	Appendices	181

A	Text List by ID		181
B	PFPs of Period/Dialect Text Groups		194
B.1	PFPs of Northern Text Group		195
	B.1.1 PFP 100000 (C10a Northern)	. . . .	195
	B.1.2 PFP 110000 (C13a Northern)	. . . .	196
	B.1.3 PFP 120000 (C13b Northern)	. . . .	196
	B.1.4 PFP 130000 (C14a Northern)	. . . .	197
B.2	PFPs of North-East Midland Text Group		197
	B.2.1 PFP 140000 (C12b North-East Midland)	. . . .	197
	B.2.2 PFP 150000 (C13b North-East Midland)	. . . .	198
	B.2.3 PFP 160000 (C14a North-East Midland)	. . . .	199
B.3	PFPs of South-East Midland Text Group		199
	B.3.1 PFP 170000 (C12a South-East Midland)	. . . .	199
	B.3.2 PFP 180000 (C12b South-East Midland)	. . . .	200
	B.3.3 PFP 190000 (C13a South-East Midland)	. . . .	201
	B.3.4 PFP 200000 (C13b South-East Midland)	. . . .	201
	B.3.5 PFP 210000 (C14a South-East Midland)	. . . .	202
B.4	PFPs of North-West Midland Text Group		203
	B.4.1 PFP 220000 (C13a North-West Midland)	. . . .	203
	B.4.2 PFP 230000 (C13b North-West Midland)	. . . .	204
B.5	PFPs of South-West Midland Text Group		204
	B.5.1 PFP 240000 (C9a South-West Midland)	. . . .	204
	B.5.2 PFP 250000 (C9b South-West Midland)	. . . .	205
	B.5.3 PFP 260000 (C10a South-West Midland)	. . . .	205
	B.5.4 PFP 270000 (C12b South-West Midland)	. . . .	206
	B.5.5 PFP 280000 (C13a South-West Midland)	. . . .	207
	B.5.6 PFP 290000 (C13b South-West Midland)	. . . .	208
	B.5.7 PFP 300000 (C14a South-West Midland)	. . . .	209
B.6	PFPs of Southwestern Text Group		210
	B.6.1 PFP 310000 (C12b Southwestern)	. . . .	210
	B.6.2 PFP 320000 (C13a Southwestern)	. . . .	210
	B.6.3 PFP 330000 (C13b Southwestern)	. . . .	211
	B.6.4 PFP 340000 (C14a Southwestern)	. . . .	211
	B.6.5 PFP 350000 (C14b Southwestern)	. . . .	212

		B.6.6	PFP 360000 (C15a Southwestern)	213
	B.7	PFPs of Southeastern Text Group		213
		B.7.1	PFP 370000 (C13a Southeastern)	213
		B.7.2	PFP 380000 (C14a Southeastern)	214
		B.7.3	PFP 390000 (C15a Southeastern)	215
C	Panchronic Summary of Plural Formation Transfer			216
D	PFPs of Selected Texts			227
	D.1	PFPs of the *Lambeth Homilies*		227
		D.1.1	PFP 2000 (Lang 1)	227
		D.1.2	PFP 2001 (Lang 2)	228
		D.1.3	PFP 5 (L)	229
	D.2	PFPs of *The Owl and the Nightingale*		229
		D.2.1	PFP 1 (J)	229
		D.2.2	PFP 2 (C1)	229
		D.2.3	PFP 3 (C2)	230
	D.3	PFPs of the *Ancrene Wisse/Riwle*		230
		D.3.1	PFP 272 (A)	230
		D.3.2	PFP 273 (C)	231
		D.3.3	PFP 245 (N)	232
		D.3.4	PFP 118 (T)	233
	D.4	PFPs of the *Poema Morale*		233
		D.4.1	PFP 5 (L)	233
		D.4.2	PFP 6 (e)	234
		D.4.3	PFP 7 (E)	235
		D.4.4	PFP 9 (J)	235
		D.4.5	PFP 10 (M)	236
		D.4.6	PFP 4 (T)	236
		D.4.7	PFP 8 (D)	237
	D.5	PFPs of *The Peterborough Chronicle*		237
		D.5.1	PFP 15000 (CA)	237
		D.5.2	PFP 16000 (1C)	238
		D.5.3	PFP 149 (FC)	239
E	Item Profiles			240
F	Old Norse Declensions			258

Notes 260

Bibliography 272
    Primary Sources 272
    Secondary Sources 274

Index 286

List of Tables

2.1	Paradigm of Proto-Germanic	23
2.2	Paradigm of Gothic	23
2.3	Paradigm of Old High German	26
2.4	Paradigm of Old Saxon	30
2.5	Paradigm of Proto-Scandinavian	30
2.6	Paradigm of Common Scandinavian	32
2.7	Paradigm of Old Danish	33
3.1	Text Groups according to Period/Dialect	56
3.2	Statistical Summary for Northern	57
3.3	Statistical Summary for North-East Midland	58
3.4	Statistical Summary for South-East Midland	59
3.5	Statistical Summary for North-West Midland	61
3.6	Statistical Summary for South-West Midland	62
3.7	Statistical Summary for Southwestern	67
3.8	Statistical Summary for Southeastern	68
3.9	Spread Rate for *-s*	71
3.10	Spread Rate for *-n*	72
4.1	Statistical Summary for the *Lambeth Homilies*	82
4.2	Statistical Summary for *The Owl and the Nightingale*	86
4.3	Statistical Summary for the *Ancrene Wisse/Riwle*	91
4.4	Plural Forms Comparison for the *Ancrene Wisse/Riwle*: 1	94
4.5	Smith's Phonological Comparison for the *Ancrene Wisse/Riwle*	95
4.6	Plural Forms Comparison for the *Ancrene Wisse/Riwle*: 2	96
4.7	Plural Forms Comparison for the *Ancrene Wisse/Riwle*: 3	96
4.8	Statistical Summary for the *Poema Morale*	98

4.9	Diachronic and Diatopic Assignment of the Seven *Poema Morale* Texts	100
4.10	Statistical Summary for *The Peterborough Chronicle*	109
6.1	Distribution of Plural Types by Gender and Declension	136
6.2	Transfer Rates of Heavy- and Light-Syllabic *a*-Stem Neuters	139
6.3	Transfer Rates of Heavy- and Light-Syllabic Strong Feminines	139
7.1	Distribution of Old English Declensions	161
7.2	Old Norse Weak and Old English Strong Declensions	164
7.3	Old Norse Strong Declensions	166
C.1	Rate for *-s*	217
C.2	Rate for *-n*	218
C.3	Rate for *-V*	219
C.4	Rate for *-ø*	220
C.5	Rate for Minor Plural Types	221
C.6	Spread Rate for *-s*	222
C.7	Spread Rate for *-n*	223
C.8	Spread Rate for *-V*	224
C.9	Spread Rate for *-ø*	225
C.10	Spread Rate for Minor Plural Types	226
E.1	Item Profile for *blōstm* (Masc-S)	241
E.2	Item Profile for *dēofol* (Masc-S)	241
E.3	Item Profile for *sīþ* (Masc-S)	241
E.4	Item Profile for *fāh* (Masc-N)	241
E.5	Item Profile for *fēolaga* (Masc-N)	242
E.6	Item Profile for *fēra* (Masc-N)	242
E.7	Item Profile for *hālga* (Masc-N)	242
E.8	Item Profile for *hīwan* (Masc-N)	242
E.9	Item Profile for *nama* (Masc-N)	243
E.10	Item Profile for *steorra* (Masc-N)	243
E.11	Item Profile for *tīma* (Masc-N)	243
E.12	Item Profile for *wræcca* (Masc-N)	243

E.13 Item Profile for *ēage* (Neut-N) 244

E.14 Item Profile for *ēare* (Neut-N) 244

E.15 Item Profile for *cirice* (Fem-N) 244

E.16 Item Profile for *heorte* (Fem-N) 244

E.17 Item Profile for *hlǣfdige* (Fem-N) 245

E.18 Item Profile for *mæsse* (Fem-N) 245

E.19 Item Profile for *nǣdre* (Fem-N) 245

E.20 Item Profile for *sunu* (Masc-V) 245

E.21 Item Profile for *bed* (Neut-V) 246

E.22 Item Profile for *bod* (Neut-V) 246

E.23 Item Profile for *geat* (Neut-V) 246

E.24 Item Profile for *lim* (Neut-V) 246

E.25 Item Profile for *mægden* (Neut-V) 247

E.26 Item Profile for *writ* (Neut-V) 247

E.27 Item Profile for *yfel* (Neut-V) 247

E.28 Item Profile for *-ung* (Fem-V) 247

E.29 Item Profile for *bēn* (Fem-V) 248

E.30 Item Profile for *bliss* (Fem-V) 248

E.31 Item Profile for *dǣd* (Fem-V) 248

E.32 Item Profile for *giefu* (Fem-V) 248

E.33 Item Profile for *hǣs* (Fem-V) 249

E.34 Item Profile for *hand* (Fem-V) 249

E.35 Item Profile for *lagu* (Fem-V) 249

E.36 Item Profile for *lufu* (Fem-V) 249

E.37 Item Profile for *miht* (Fem-V) 250

E.38 Item Profile for *pīn* (Fem-V) 250

E.39 Item Profile for *sāwol* (Fem-V) 250

E.40 Item Profile for *synn* (Fem-V) 250

E.41 Item Profile for *wund* (Fem-V) 251

E.42 Item Profile for *brōþor* (Masc-Ø) 251

E.43 Item Profile for *bān* (Neut-Ø) 251

E.44 Item Profile for *bearn* (Neut-Ø) 251

E.45 Item Profile for *cynn* (Neut-Ø) 252

E.46 Item Profile for *dēor* (Neut-Ø) 252

E.47 Item Profile for *gēar* (Neut-Ø) 252

E.48 Item Profile for *gōd* (Neut-Ø) 252

E.49 Item Profile for *hors* (Neut-Ø) 253

E.50 Item Profile for *hundred* (Neut-Ø) 253

E.51 Item Profile for *land* (Neut-Ø) 253

E.52 Item Profile for *scēap* (Neut-Ø) 253

E.53 Item Profile for *trēow* (Neut-Ø) 254

E.54 Item Profile for *þing* (Neut-Ø) 254

E.55 Item Profile for *wǣpen* (Neut-Ø) 254

E.56 Item Profile for *wæter* (Neut-Ø) 254

E.57 Item Profile for *weorc* (Neut-Ø) 255

E.58 Item Profile for *wīf* (Neut-Ø) 255

E.59 Item Profile for *winter* (Neut-Ø) 255

E.60 Item Profile for *witt* (Neut-Ø) 255

E.61 Item Profile for *word* (Neut-Ø) 256

E.62 Item Profile for *sweostor* (Fem-Ø) 256

E.63 Item Profile for *fēond* (Masc-M) 256

E.64 Item Profile for *frēond* (Masc-M) 256

E.65 Item Profile for *cild* (Neut-M) 257

E.66 Item Profile for *niht* (Fem-M) 257

List of Figures

2.1	Middle English Dialect Map	8
3.1	Localisation of Examined Texts	55
3.2	Rate for Northern	57
3.3	Rate for North-East Midland	59
3.4	Rate for South-East Midland	60
3.5	Rate for North-West Midland	61
3.6	Rate for South-West Midland	62
3.7	Rate for Southwestern	68
3.8	Rate for Southeastern	69
3.9	Spread Rate for -s	71
3.10	Spread Rate for -n	72
4.1	Rate for the *Lambeth Homilies*	82
4.2	Rate for *The Owl and the Nightingale*	86
4.3	Rate for the *Ancrene Wisse/Riwle*	91
4.4	Rate for the *Poema Morale*	98
4.5	Rate for *The Peterborough Chronicle*	109
5.1	Characteristic S-Curve of Lexical Diffusion	119
5.2	Rate for -s	127
5.3	Rate for -n	127
6.1	Rate of Case Syncretism	147
6.2	Rate for -s	148
7.1	Illustration of Old Norse Contact Hypothesis	169
C.1	Rate for -s	217
C.2	Rate for -n	218

C.3	Rate for -V	219
C.4	Rate for -$\emptyset$	220
C.5	Rate for Minor Plural Types	221
C.6	Spread Rate for -s	222
C.7	Spread Rate for -n	223
C.8	Spread Rate for -V	224
C.9	Spread Rate for -$\emptyset$	225
C.10	Spread Rate for Minor Plural Types	226

Preface

The development of the nominal plural has long been a forgotten subject. The first and last dedicated study was made nearly a century ago as a dissertation by Roedler, and since then there has been a silence with the exception of a few sporadic considerations, as if the subject had already been exhaustively examined.

It is true that an overview picture of the development of plural formation is sufficiently well-known to be mentioned in any introduction to the history of the English language; however, the detailed description and explanation of what happened in the critical Early Middle English period, and how and why it occurred in that particular period have hardly been questioned. The shortage of literature on such a fundamental issue was a natural motive for my research.

Another source of motivation for me to address the issue was the availability of the text database resulting from the *LAEME* project at the Institute for Historical Dialectology, University of Edinburgh. Thanks to the generosity of the staff of the project, particularly of Drs Margaret Laing and Keith Williamson, I had access to part of the *LAEME* text database more than two years prior to its official publication in electronic forms. Of the 247 scribal texts I examined for the study, 134 were analysed from the *LAEME* text database. The present study is therefore partly based on a version of *LAEME* as it was still under preparation, and not on the officially published online version available now; there is no doubt, however, that the present study will prove to be one of the earliest attempts at making use of the achievements of the *LAEME* project.

Yet another motivation for my undertaking this research is the recent development of language change theories including contact linguistics and lexical diffusion theory. The subject of the nominal plurals may not be new, but with these recently developed theories as well as with *LAEME*, it can be addressed from a fresh viewpoint, which, I hope, will apply to related areas of research on the history of English.

Lastly, I believe that the subject is one of those which non-native speakers of English, including the present author, a native speaker of Japanese, might well be more sensitive to and therefore more readily dedicate themselves to. Here is an anecdote from the days when I was researching at the University of Glasgow. My supervisor, a distinguished philologist/linguist, took up the topic of grammatical number in an undergraduate seminar where I happened to be present. He invited me to describe how the number category is represented in Japanese. When I said that there is no obligatory number category in Japanese, it aroused interest in the seminar. The singular/plural distinction comes so naturally to speakers of a language that has it as a built-in grammatical category that they have little dreamt that some languages lack number distinction. To the present author, in contrast, the number category has never come naturally, and therefore is a matter worthy of serious study.

An advantage given to foreign students of a language is that they are likely to pose a kind of question that might hardly occur to native speakers of the language. I hope the reader will find in the present study the long-held interest of a student whose mother tongue is not English but who is fascinated by the question of how the medium of the number category has developed in the language.

Acknowledgements

The present monograph is a revised version of my doctoral dissertation submitted under the same title to the University of Glasgow, Graduate School of Arts and Humanities, in September, 2005. The publication of this book was only made possible through the support I have received from many people to this day.

First of all, I wish to express my sincere gratitude to Professor Jeremy J. Smith, my supervisor when I was conducting this research at Glasgow. Without his thoughtful and helpful advice, I could not have completed the research. I owe to him much of the insight into the present subject. It is through his tutorship that I have come to see how philological and linguistic approaches can be reconciled.

My special thanks are due to Professor Hiroshi Ogawa of Showa Women's University, who was one of my supervisors while studying in the master's and doctoral courses at the University of Tokyo, Graduate School of Arts and Sciences. His tutorship provided me with countless insights leading to the main idea of the present work particularly in the earlier stages of research.

Professor Jun Terasawa, the other supervisor of mine at the University of Tokyo, offered me no less assistance in his tutorship, infusing me with the key theoretical concepts and making countless helpful suggestions on the subject.

I am indebted to Professor Kiyoaki Kikuchi of Rikkyo University for his constructive criticisms of certain sections of the book and his general advice for publication. I also thank Professor John D. Scahill of Keio University for his critical suggestions and proofreading at the final stage of my writing. Thanks also go to Professor John Matthews of Chuo University for his closest proofreading, which must have been painstaking work because of countless errors and mistakes in the manuscript.

There are a number of professors in Scotland, particularly from the University of Glasgow, whom I wish to thank for supporting me during my research. I would like to thank Dr Simon Horobin for reading my original dissertation carefully to make critical comments. I am most grateful to Dr Kathryn A. Lowe, who gave me an accessible introduction to Old Norse. I would also like to express my thanks to Dr Robert McColl Millar of the University of Aberdeen for his inspiring discussion on the subject.

I gratefully acknowledge dedicated teachings of professors who in my bachelor's course provided me with academic foundations for the research. Professor Emeritus Nobuyuki Higashi, my supervisor for my undergraduate course at Tokyo University of Foreign Studies, aroused my initial interest in the history of English. Professor Akira Baba's lectures in English linguistics also lay the linguistic foundation for the research.

Professor Osamu Fukushima of Tokyo Woman's Christian University, with his unlimited curiosity about languages, has had a strong impact on my attitude toward the English language as a multilingual composite. The late Professor Tateo Kimura introduced me to the fascinating world of Middle English. My interest in Scandinavian languages goes back to an undergraduate course of Modern Danish by Professor Koichi Jin of Teikyo University, who gave me vital comments on related studies of mine on several occasions.

I am no less grateful to those who gave me academic advice particularly for my postgraduate studies. I learnt from Professor Tadao Kubouchi of Komazawa University how to deal with early English writings with academic rigour. Professor Yoshiko Kobayashi of the University of Tokyo not only taught me to read medieval texts with literary interests but also gave me helpful comments on my master's thesis, which formed the basis for the doctoral dissertation. Professor Harumi Tanabe of Seikei University not only encouraged me to do the research in Glasgow but also provided me with a number of helpful suggestions on many occasions when I read research papers in academic meetings. To Professor Michiko Ogura of Chiba University I owe my gratitude for many valuable comments on some related studies of mine at academic conferences. Professor Mieko Ogura of Tsurumi University offered me encouraging advice on the theoretical issues addressed in the present study.

I am most grateful to the staff of the Institute for Historical Dialectology, University of Edinburgh, for permission to consult the text database and its related linguistic atlas more than two years prior to publication. Among others, I wish to express special thanks to Drs Margaret Laing and Keith Williamson, who encouraged me to take advantage of the latest achievements of theirs.

The research was supported largely through grants from Rotary International, without whose financial support my research at Glasgow would not have been so fruitful. I would also like to convey my gratitude to the Japan Society for the Promotion of Science (JSPS) for awarding a Grant-in-Aid for Young Scientists (Start-up) for 2007–08 (No. 19820038). It enabled me to remain dedicated to the study after the dissertation was submitted. Once again I owe the present publication to financial support from the JSPS, who awarded a Grant-in-Aid for Publication of Scientific Research Results (No. 205949).

I extend my gratitude to Hituzi Syobo, especially Chief Editor Isao Matsumoto and Mr Takashi Moriwaki for all their cooperation from the planning stages through to the completion of this volume.

Last but definitely not least, I have to give many thanks to my family, especially my wife, Makiko, for their unlimited patience and unfailing support all the time. Without their cooperation, I could not have written this book.

Abbreviations

~		fluctuate(s) with
acc.		acccusative (case)
C		century, as in the following examples:
	C11	the eleventh century
	C12a	the first half of the twelfth century
	C12b	the second half of the twelfth century
	C13a1	the first quarter of the thirteenth century
	C13b2	the last quarter of the thirteenth century
ca.		about (*circa*)
dat.		dative (case)
EME		Early Middle English
fem.		feminine
fol(s).		folio(s)
gen.		genitive (case)
LAEME		*A Linguistic Atlas of Early Middle English* (ed. Margaret Laing and Roger Lass)
LALME		*A Linguistic Atlas of Late Mediaeval English* (ed. Angus McIntosh et al.)
M		minor plural type
masc.		masculine
ME-I		"Middle English Innovation" as a type of the noun (see page 47)
MS		manuscript
N		Northern (dialect)
n		*n*-plural or *n*-ending
NEM		North-East Midland (dialect)
neut.		neuter

nom.	nominative (case)
NWM	North-West Midland (dialect)
O&N	*The Owl and the Nightingale*
OE	Old English
ø	ø-plural or ø-ending
PFP	Plural Forms Profile
pl.	plural
PMor	the *Poema Morale*
Ru1	*The Rushworth Gloss to the Gospel according to Saint Matthew*
s	*s*-plural or *s*-ending
SE	Southeastern (dialect)
SEM	South-East Midland (dialect)
sg.	singular
str.	strong (declension)
SW	Southwestern (dialect)
SWM	South-West Midland (dialect)
V	vowel-plural or vowel-ending
wk.	weak (declension)

Chapter 1 Introduction

1.1 Aim of Study

The present study investigates how different nominal plural forms were distributed geographically and developed diachronically during the Early Middle English period. It also enquires into why the plural systems developed in the way they did.

The broad history of the nominal plural forms in English has long been known. As a result of system-destructive phonological processes such as the levelling of vowels and the loss of n in inflectional endings, the Old English plural system was reorganised into new Early Middle English systems where s- and/or n-plurals prevailed.

In Early Middle English each dialect had a different plural system. To put it roughly, in the North and East of England -s was effectively the only plural ending, while in the South and West there was a tripartite competition among -s, -n, and vowels, aside from minor plural formations such as non-inflectional and i-mutated plurals.

Any discussion of Early Middle English grammar must address inflectional levelling. The development of the nominal plural formation is just one aspect of the global inflectional levelling taking place in Early Middle English and should be seen as part of the whole dynamic change of the time. Moore characterises the period as follows:

> The period from 1050 to 1300, on the other hand, was characterised by very extensive morphological changes that transformed English from a rather highly inflected language to one having the relatively few and simple inflections of late Middle English. All distinctions of case were lost except the genitive singular of nouns and the distinctions of grammatical gender were lost altogether. And even the grammatical categories that

remained were more simply expressed, for in late Middle English the single ending -*es* had replaced the variety of endings that had expressed the genitive singular and plural of nouns in Old English. ("Earliest" 238)

Thus the history of nominal plurals has been regarded as an aspect of arguably the most dynamic changes in the history of the English language; however, there has been little detailed study made on the subject.

One of the few studies ever made on the topic is Roedler's dissertation on the development of the *s*-plural. He examined a wide range of periods and dialects based on a large collection of actual examples, and tried to describe the development of the nominal plural system diachronically. It was indeed a dedicated study for its time, but nearly a century later, it is now considerably outdated in many ways. There is still much left to be done to unravel the process of the systemic change. New attempts must be made not only to present individual facts as individual points but also to connect them into a line so that a bird's-eye view of the chronological and geographical continuum of the plural system can be had. My goal in this book is to describe closely "how" the plural system developed in the periods centring around Early Middle English in special consideration of diachronic and diatopic aspects. Once the question of "how" is answered, the next question to ask is "why" different configurations of the plural system developed in different dialects and what motives underlay the development in individual dialects. The question of "why" is particularly worth posing, since surprisingly few attempts have thus far been made at identifying the causation of the development. To be fair, Roedler addressed the causation for the spread of -*s*, but his answer to the question of "why" was too language-internally motivated to be accepted as a tenable account.

In historical linguistics, the importance of asking not only the "how" but also the "why" of development must be stressed. In my view the question of "why" should be a natural step that follows the question of "how," but linguists have long refrained from asking "why" through academic modesty. I believe, however, that it is allowable to speak less ambitiously of *conditioning factors*, rather than *absolute causes*, of language change. On this belief I agree with Smith when he says:

> it is held here that an adequate history of English must attempt at least to

take account of the 'why' as well as the 'how' of the changes the language has undergone; problems of causation must therefore be confronted in any historical account, however provisional the resulting explanations might be. (*Historical* 12)

It is to be admitted that any answers for "how" and "why" will only be plausible or provisional because historical linguistics is an abductive discipline (Andersen; Anttila 196–98, 285–86). This means that the suggested description and explanation of the language change is a reasoned inference made with reference to universals such as human experience, human nature, and culture, and to observed facts. The number of possible inferences made in this way is theoretically infinite, and therefore the best that historical linguists can offer is a subset of the theoretically possible descriptions and explanations. Being methodologically abductive, historical linguistics is different from natural science; it is no less tempting, however, to make such inferences in historical linguistics since it allows for different interpretations for a phenomenon.

In this study I address the questions of "how" and, with special emphasis, "why" not as a review of the previous studies but in light of the latest methodologies developed for English historical linguistics. First of all, there has recently been a growing interest in the dialectological approach to Middle English. Immediately relevant to the present study is the ongoing project for *A Linguistic Atlas of Early Middle English* (ed. Laing and Lass; hereafter cited as *LAEME*) at the Institute for Historical Dialectology, University of Edinburgh. Inspired and motivated by its predecessor, *A Linguistic Atlas of Late Mediaeval English* (ed. McIntosh, Samuels, and Benskin; hereafter cited as *LALME*), the *LAEME* project is seen as a great encouragement for the study not only of Early Middle English but also of the general history of English.[1]

The present study in fact took advantage of the *LAEME* text database. Thanks to the generosity of the editing staff, particularly of Dr Margaret Laing, I had access to part of the *LAEME* text database prior to its official publication in electronic forms. Of the 247 scribal texts I examined for the study, 134 were analysed from the *LAEME* text database. I have to add that the present study is therefore partly based on a version of *LAEME* as it was still under preparation, and not on the officially published online version available at the time of the publication of this book.

Secondly, the last few decades have seen development in general theories of language change. One of the most promising theories on language change is the lexical diffusion model, which theorises the way language change proceeds in the system, in the vocabulary and in the population. According to the lexical diffusion model, the diffusion of linguistic innovation starts slowly, affecting only a handful of words at first. Some time later, there comes a moment when the diffusion gathers momentum and quickens through the majority of the lexicon. This quick diffusion continues until it affects most of the lexicon, and then tapers off toward the end, leaving a handful of words unaffected by change. If charted in a graph, the diffusion shows a characteristic slow-quick-quick-slow S-curve along the time axis. The lexical diffusion model will be fully introduced in Chapter 5.

The third of the latest theories recognised in the present study is contact linguistics. It provides a theoretical framework in which to interpret the development of plural formations in Early Middle English. It also gives us an insight into the question of "why" the northern and the southern dialects differed so much in plural formation transfer. Language contact that existed between Old English and Old Norse is the key to an understanding of the gap. The topic, fully taken up in Chapter 7, constitutes one of the major points of discussion in the book.

To summarise, the main goals of the present study are:

1. to describe "how" nominal plural formations were distributed diatopically and developed diachronically in the periods centring around Early Middle English;

2. to explain "why" the development took place at the time, in the place and in the way that it did.

To pursue these goals, I take advantage of the latest achievements of English historical linguistics.

1.2 Scope of Study

The present study focuses on the Early Middle English period instead of covering a longer time range. There are reasons for this focus. First of all, while Roedler's study covered a wide span of time from Proto-Germanic to Modern English, its attention to individual periods was limited. What I need to do now is to make a close enquiry into individual periods, particularly the period of Early Middle English.

I take up the Early Middle English period because it is surely the most dynamic period in terms of plural formation transfer. The relatively stable Old English system was dramatically disturbed as the Early Middle English period began, and most of the systemic restructuring went on during the period. By the Late Middle English period, the plural system was largely stabilised in the North and East. In the South and West, frequent variation in plural formation continued indeed well into Late Middle English, but the direction of the development was already determined. By the Modern English period, every dialect had an essentially standardised plural system, which has continued to this day with only slight modification. In hindsight, therefore, the core period of the dynamic change was the Early Middle English period without doubt. Changes that occurred before and after were relatively marginal.

Next, what makes a study of Early Middle English especially interesting is that the ongoing *LAEME* project is sure to open a new era in English historical linguistics by providing us with a helpful tool to investigate Early Middle English dialects. The digital text database and dialect maps that it offers will not only make the period more worthy of study than ever but also make diachronic comparison easier, especially between Early Middle English and Late Middle English as well.

In the above I may have given the impression that whereas the Early Middle English period is worth examining, other periods are of minor importance. I only meant this in a relative sense. It should not be forgotten that the reorganisation process of the plural system was never at rest at any time in history. The development was underway continuously, and each period deserves investigation in its own right. Although I give preference for the Early Middle English period over other periods, I find it still important not to ignore a diachronically wider perspective. In this view, I extend the time range to be covered slightly backward and forward; that is, I take account of part of Late Old English and Late Middle English.

How far the time range should be extended backward and forward from Early Middle English is, as I admit, rather arbitrarily decided from dialect to dialect. This is because the development of the plural system varied considerably across dialects. In the North and East, the spread of the *s*-plural started as early as the mid-tenth century and nearly finished perhaps before 1200, whereas in the South and West it started later and proceeded more slowly, continuing into the beginning of the Modern English period.

Considering the difference between the North and East on the one hand and the South and West on the other, it will be sensible to set up an earlier and shorter time range for the more northern and eastern dialects and a later and longer one for the more southern and western. A reasonable diachronic scope might be from 1100 to 1300 for the North and East and from 1150 to 1400 for the South and West.

The time range proposed here, however, has to be slightly adjusted in accord with the availability of texts from each period or dialect. For example, the Northern dialect hardly provides a significant amount of surviving linguistic evidence from C12 (the twelfth century), so the proposed time range cannot practically apply. Likewise, there is not much textual evidence of the Southeastern dialect from C12b (the second half of the twelfth century) and C13b (the second half of the thirteenth century), which creates an unfortunate gap in the proposed time range.

Given these circumstances, the time range for the present study can practically be defined as between C12b and C14a, give or take a few decades or perhaps even a century depending upon the availability of evidence.

Chapter 2 Preliminary Discussions

Elementary histories of the English language normally describe the development of the nominal plural system in this way: the s-ending first showed its tendency to spread in the Northern dialect as early as C10b; the development was then followed by the Midlands, where it was fighting against the rival n-ending in Early Middle English; finally the southern dialects joined the movement only in Late Middle English or even later.

There are surprisingly few accounts that provide a more detailed description than this, and Roedler's and Classen's studies are among the few. In what follows, I first review Roedler's study and then go on to see what Classen says about the change in the plural system. Then I provide the Germanic backgrounds of the nominal plural system with a view to comparing the English development with those of related languages.

2.1 Review of Roedler's Study

The most important study ever made on the present subject is Roedler's. He surveyed the spread of -s both diachronically and diatopically, covering the periods from Proto-Germanic to Modern English and the dialects from Northern through Midland to Southern. His research was indeed based on a large collection of evidence, but nearly a century later, we cannot deny that his approach appears antiquated in many ways. As we will see in Section 2.1.9, several points of his study need serious reconsideration.

Below I summarise Roedler's findings with the main focus on the transitional period from Late Old English to Late Middle English. In his study as well as the present one, the conventional division of Middle English dialects is assumed, that is, Middle English is divided into seven dialects, as shown in the map of Figure 2.1 on page 8: Northern (N), North-East Midland (NEM), South-East Midland (SEM), North-West Midland (NWM), South-West Midland (SWM),

Figure 2.1: Middle English Dialect Map

Southwestern (SW), and Southeastern (SE).[2]

In the present book, the Northern, North-East Midland and North-West Midland dialects taken together are referred to as the northern dialects in its relative sense, while on the other hand the South-West Midland, Southwestern, and Southeastern dialects are referred to as the southern dialects. I will use these terms of convenience frequently, but they should be understood loosely and relatively.[3]

It should be remembered that these divisions are somewhat arbitrary, as any dialect boundaries necessarily are. In fact, as we will see below, Roedler's division is somewhat different from what has been traditionally accepted.

2.1.1 Northern

In Northern -*s* had long been established by the beginning of Early Middle English. This is suggested, for example, by evidence from the C10b Northumbrian gloss to the *Lindisfarne Gospels*. This Late Old English text already shows a striking tendency to extend -*s* to nouns of historically unexpected classes. Roedler also examined the *Cursor Mundi* of ca. 1300 and the *North English Legendary* presumably of C13b2 (the last quarter of the thirteenth century).

The development between C10b and C13b is not known in detail, but the period would certainly be critical to the establishment of the *s*-dominant plural system in the dialect.

Most of the remaining non-*s*-plurals historically belonged either to the endingless long-syllabic neuters (e.g. Old English *þing*) or to the weak nouns with -*n* (e.g. Old English *ēage*). Some endingless forms fluctuated with *s*-forms, e.g. forms for "things," "works," "words," "wives," and "maids." Most of the historical weak nouns took -*n* but could also occur with -*s*.

2.1.2 North-East Midland

Like the Northern dialect, the North-East Midland dialect represents a well-developed stage in terms of the spread of -*s*. Roedler examined *The Peterborough Chronicle*, which he divided into two parts on linguistic and scribal grounds.[4] The first part consists of the annals up to the year 1131, representing a transitional stage between Old and Middle English. The second part constitutes the rest of the text, the annals from 1132 to 1154, representing a more innovative language.

The first part largely shows the inflections of the Late West-Saxon *Schriftsprache*, but provides some evidence of the *s*-plural spreading over to unhistorical classes, especially to the long-syllabic neuters. In contrast, the second part, composed only about a few decades after the first part, shows a great step forward to the dominance of -*s*.

Roedler also examined *The Ormulum* (ca. 1200), in which -*s* is already an established rule with few exceptions. The relatively early dominance of -*s* in North-East Midland is further confirmed by evidence from later texts such as the *Debate between Body and Soul* (C13b), the *Harrowing of Hell* (the end of C13), and *Havelok* (ca. 1270).[5]

Roedler summarised the North-East Midland development as follows:

> . . . in the North-East Midland already about 1200—perhaps already in the second half of the 12th century, according to whether or not one will generalise the results obtained from the 2nd part of *The Peterborough Chronicle*—the spread of the *s*-plural reached the Modern English standpoint in principle. (1: 31) (translation mine)[6]

2.1.3 South-East Midland

For this dialect, Roedler examined the *Genesis and Exodus* and the *Bestiary*, both from C13a. Being the earliest Middle English evidence of this dialect, they show some growth of the *s*-plural while still keeping a considerable number of old inflections. There are some new *n*-plurals such as *weden, treen, sunen,* and *steden*.

Roedler went on to look at later Middle English texts of this dialect: the *Floris and Blauncheflur* (ca. 1250); the *Assumption of Our Lady* (C12b); the *Magdalenen-legende* of Laud Misc. 108 (ca. C13b2); *Canticum de Creatione*; and the *Seven Sins* (C13). In these texts, in addition to surviving *n*-plurals such as *asshen, been, cupen, fleen, heortene, pesen,* and *steorrene*, there are some newly developed *n*-plurals, including *cleen, honden, serwen, soreʒen, wounden, children, kyen,* and *lambron* (the last three as double plurals).

Roedler concluded that in this dialect the spread of -*s* was nearly accomplished by C13a, whereas non-*s*-plurals, though still attested widely well into

Late Middle English, should be interpreted as exceptions.

2.1.4 North-West Midland

Roedler investigated this dialect as represented by the *Earliest Complete English Prose Psalter* (C14a) and *Sir Gawain and the Green Knight* (C14b). In both texts -*s* is established as the dominant plural ending. Another potential representative of the dialect, the *Ancrene Riwle* of BL Cotton Titus D xviii (C13a1), was analysed separately because it was strongly influenced by southern dialectal characteristics.

This dialect suffers from a shortage of evidence compared to the Northern and North-East Midland counterparts, so the details are hard to obtain. On the basis of the available evidence culled from the texts and the careful consideration of evidence from the *Ancrene Riwle*, Roedler summarised:

> Perhaps, however, the development took the same process in the North-West Midland as in the North-East Midland neighbour dialect, so that we can go back even to 1200. (1: 47) (translation mine)[7]

2.1.5 South-West Midland

Before starting to review Roedler's study of the South-West Midland dialect, I must say a few words about his dialectal division of Middle English. The traditional grouping in Middle English dialectology breaks down the Midlands into four dialects: North-East, South-East, North-West, and South-West. Opinion varies, however, on the exact area covered by South-West Midlands.

The more traditional view is that South-West Midland covers the area west of the *mon/man* line as far north as the *-en/-eth* line divides it from North-West Midland, as in the dialect map in Figure 2.1 on page 8. This means that a large number of texts including the so-called AB group should be assigned to this dialect. On the other hand, some, including Kurath et al. (8), assume that the area defined above is just part of a large Southwestern dialectal area.

Roedler's South-West Midlands is based on the latter interpretation. In his terms the South-West Midlands covers a relatively narrow area north of the South-West Midlands as defined in the traditional division. In this and the following sections that review Roedler's research, I adopt his definition of the

South-West Midlands for the sake of discussion, but elsewhere in this book I will use the term "South-West Midlands" as defined in the traditional division.[8]

For the dialectal area of the South-West Midlands (in Roedler's terms), Roedler first examined the B-text of *Piers Plowman* (1377). The text shows the prevalence of the *s*-plural. He then examined the B-text of Laʒamon's *Brut*, which he dated *ca.* 1250.[9] From the distribution of the plural endings he suggested the assignment of the text to South-West Midland.[10] Aside from a number of old inflections that have perhaps survived through the scribe's mechanical copying, the *s*-plurals already dominate the plural system of the text language.

Roedler concluded that the *s*-plural was prevalent in South-West Midland in C13a although, as in South-East Midland, the use of the *n*-plural was also growing alongside it.

2.1.6 Southwestern

In Roedler's terms the Southwest was distinguished from the Middle South. The former roughly corresponds to what we traditionally call the Southwest Midlands, while the latter to the Southwest. In this section I will follow Roedler's dialectal grouping, although I follow the traditional division elsewhere.

Plural forms in the southern dialects of Early Middle English were marked mostly by one of the three endings, -*es*, -*en*, and -*e*. Once -*e* ceased to be used regularly because of its morphophonological unreliability, the option was then between -*es* and -*en*.

Many of the historical non-*s*-plurals transferred either to -*s* or -*n*, but more than a few still kept old forms, resulting in frequent fluctuation between traditional and innovative forms. This situation lasted until Late Middle English in the southern dialects.

Roedler investigated the following texts from *his* Southwestern dialect, or *our* traditional South-West Midland dialect: the *Poema Morale* (*ca.* 1170); the fragments of the *Debate between Body and Soul* (MS from C12); the *Lambeth Homilies* (C12b2); and the A-text of Laʒamon's *Brut* (*ca.* 1200).[11]

The texts from *his* Middle South, or *our* Southwestern, are: the *Ancrene Riwle*, Cotton Nero A xiv (the beginning of C13); *Hali Meiðhad* (1225); Verses in Jesus College 29 (the middle of C13); some pieces in Morris's *Old English Homilies*, including *On God Ureison of ure Lefdi*, the *Lofsong of ure Louerde*, *Sawles Warde*, etc.; the *Life of St Katherine*; and the *Life of St Juliana* (C13a).

The *Poema Morale* retains old inflections, but there are a number of innovative formations. In the fragments of the *Debate between Body and Soul*, there are some new *s*-plurals from the neuters and some new *n*-plurals from the feminines and the short-syllabic neuters.

In the *Lambeth Homilies* a systematic extension of -*s* and -*n* is observed. The long-syllabic neuters mostly take -*s*, but occasionally -*n*. A few disyllabic or polysyllabic neuters also take -*s*, while the short-syllabic neuters, the strong feminines and the kinship nouns tend to take -*n*.

Laʒamon's *Brut* represents a little more developed stage than the *Lambeth Homilies* in its distribution of -*s*. There are many innovative *n*-plurals, but it may not be that all of them represent genuine innovation because most of them occur in post-prepositional positions. *N*-forms in post-prepositional positions may only represent reduced vestiges derived from the old dative plural *um*-ending. Even so, the *n*-plural was thus still productive to some extent around 1200, while -*s* was clearly becoming dominant.

As for Roedler's Middle South, the *Ancrene Riwle* represents a slightly more advanced stage for -*s* than *Brut*. The long-syllabic neuters take -*s* while the short-syllabic neuters waver between -*s* and -*n*. The strong feminines and the weak nouns regularly take -*n* except for long-syllabic feminines such as -*ung*, -*ing*, and -*nis*, all of which regularly take -*s*. A similar picture is observed in the other texts named in the list above, all belonging to the so-called AB group along with the *Ancrene Riwle*.

Roedler further investigated three later Middle English texts: Robert of Gloucester's *Chronicle* (*ca.* 1300); Southern pieces in Harley 2253 (*ca.* 1310; in the dialect of northern Herefordshire); and Trevisa's translation of *Polychronicon* (*ca.* 1387). Evidence from these texts shows that in this dialect -*s* was not yet established as the single dominant ending by Late Middle English. He summarised the situation:

> The *es*-ending is the rule for a great number of the strong masculines and the strong neuters; however, most of the other formations in these classes

are also still found. In the other classes, strong fluctuation between the *en*-ending and the *es*-ending still predominates, even though the *s*-plural has been adopted on a large scale by the strong feminines and the masculine *n*-stems. The weak feminines seem to have maintained the old formation most persistently. (1: 71) (translation mine)[12]

We may note that although in this dialect the spread of -*s* was fairly slow, the spread never stopped during the Middle English period.

2.1.7 Southeastern

This dialect is like the Southwestern in that the plural system was balanced between the *s*- and *n*-endings for most of the Middle English period. One characteristic of the Southeastern dialect is that innovative *s*-plurals appeared from the earliest Middle English period on, affecting not only the strong feminines and the short-syllabic strong neuters but also the weak nouns. *N*-plurals did not spread as remarkably as in Southwestern, but they were fairly productive.

Roedler divided the dialect into Southeast Saxon and Kentish. He examined Southeast Saxon with the following texts: *Vices and Virtues* (*ca.* 1200); the *Poema Morale*, Trinity College B. 14. 52 (the beginning of C13); the *Vespasian Homilies* (*ca.* 1200); and the *Trinity Homilies*.[13] For the Late Middle English development, he examined the Southern version of *Octavian*.

The survey of the Southeast Saxon texts showed that the earlier competition between -*s* and -*n* resolved into the dominance of -*s* toward the end of C14.

Roedler investigated the Kentish dialect with the following texts: the *Kentish Gospels* in Royal 1 A xiv and Hatton 38 (C12b); the *Poema Morale*, Digby 4 (the beginning of C13); the *Kentish Sermons* (C13a); the Winteney version of the Benedictine rule (C13a1); Dan Michel's *Ayenbite of Inwyt* (1340); and William of Shoreham's poems (C14a). The development of Kentish was similar to that of Southeast Saxon, but the fluctuation between -*s* and -*n* was greater for the weak and strong feminine nouns.

All in all, the Southeastern development was slightly earlier and faster than the Southwestern.

2.1.8 Cause of the Development

Roedler's dialect-by-dialect investigation may be summarised as follows. The spread of -*s* was accomplished earliest in C12b for Northern and North Midland. Then South Midland followed in C13a, though non-*s*-plurals were far more common and persistent there than in the northern dialects. Then Southeastern became more or less *s*-dominant in C14, but in Southwestern and Kentish, -*n* and -*s* remained in competition until C14 or even later.

Roedler explained why -*s* (and -*n* where relevant) spread more quickly in some dialects than in others. His explanation was functionalistic throughout, that is, he ascribed the development to the therapeutic power or systemic regulation inherent in language. His functionalistic attitude is best expressed in his own phrase in English, "the survival of the fittest" (2: 491).

Roedler's discussion about the cause of the development centres around the five key linguistic processes.

1. analogical attraction by the major declensions
2. analogical processes motivated by inflectional indistinction in the nominative singular among different stem classes
3. the levelling of vowels in inflectional endings
4. the loss of *n* in inflectional endings
5. the loss of grammatical gender

The earliest merger between different stem classes dates as far back as the pre-Old English period, when the *i*- and *u*-stem feminines were gradually merged into the major *ō*-stem feminines for lack of inflectional distinction in the nominative singular. Likewise, lack of formal distinction in the nominative singular explains the early assimilation of the long-syllabic *i*- and *u*-stem masculines into the major *a*-stem masculines.

The levelling of vowels in inflectional endings occurred in the late Old English period.[14] Since number distinction among many classes of nouns heavily depended on the value of these vowels, the levelling necessarily blurred the number distinction.

Another crucial factor that contributed to the spread of -*s* was the loss of the *n*-ending from the *n*-stem nouns. Although the loss was not regular, it certainly affected the *n*-stem nouns and quickened their transfer to the dominant *s*-plural. Since -*n* was effectively the only rival to -*s*, its decrease meant the relative growth of -*s*.

As a result of the levelling of vowels and the loss of *n* in inflectional endings, nouns of different classes now took -*e* in many inflections, singular and plural. In consequence, -*e* alone was no longer reliable to distinguish number. What was confusing, there was another phonological process underway in which "inorganic -*e*" was often added to the stem of nouns in the nominative singular. The result was a confused situation where a vowel and *n* switched on and off as if at random in many inflections, singular and plural. Consequently, the number distinction for many nouns was not effectively made either by a vowel or by *n*. The easy remedy was naturally to transfer to the dominant *s*-plural.

Yet another factor that contributed to the spread of -*s* was the loss of grammatical gender. If the linguistic sense of grammatical gender had remained strong in a speaker's mind, the transfer of the *s*-plural across genders would have been unlikely because -*s* was strongly associated with the masculine, and the masculine alone. The weakening of grammatical gender made cross-gender transfers easy.

In the southern dialects, the development was rather different because the levelling of vowels, the loss of *n* and the loss of grammatical gender were all slow. There the *n*-plural competed with the *s*-plural for a long time. One reason for the *n*-plural to have become productive in the southern dialects was that the *e*-ending in the nominative singular of many nouns was associated with the weak nouns (note that the vowel ending was characteristic of the nominative singular of weak nouns of any gender, e.g. *guma*, *tunge*, and *ēage*). By this association, many nouns ending in -*e* in the nominative singular was open to weakening, no matter what its historical class or gender.

According to Roedler, while the short-syllabic strong feminines tended to take an "inorganic -*e*" and therefore to weaken, the long-syllabic counterparts tended to occur without an "inorganic -*e*" (perhaps because they were long enough to begin with) and therefore to transfer to -*s*, in the negative line, along with the strong neuters and so on.

The rest of the nouns that had long refused -*s* accepted it only when the levelling of vowels, the loss of *n* and the loss of grammatical gender were all completed. In the southern dialects, this happened only in the later period of Middle English.

Roedler proposed these correlated processes as contributing factors to the development of the plural system. Let us note that his proposal for the cause of the development was functionalistic throughout, admitting of no extralinguistic considerations.

2.1.9 Critical Comments on Roedler's Study

Roedler's research was a substantial contribution to the study of the development of plural forms. It was indeed *for his time*, but now it appears too outdated to be accepted without reconsideration.

Thanks to the accumulated scholarship on English historical dialectology since Roedler's time, we have a more detailed understanding of Early Middle English texts: more precise dating and localisation have become available for many texts; more philological studies of individual texts have been made; and many more printed editions and even digitised text databases have come within our reach. I can thus take advantage of these later achievements in English philology as well as the recent theories in historical linguistics to examine Roedler's findings critically. There are six points to be made.

First, although the North-West Midland and northern South-West Midland dialects were poorly represented in Roedler's study, Laing's localisation in her *Catalogue* allows us to add some texts as representative of the dialects (e.g. *Stabat iuxta crucem Christi* [Text ID #124] and alliterative lyrics [Text ID #136]).

Secondly, Roedler's localisation of some texts is dubious. While Roedler assigned *The Peterborough Chronicle*, *Havelok*, and the *Harrowing of Hell* to the North-East Midland dialect, the first two should be assigned, based on *LAEME*, to South-East Midland and the last one to South-West Midland. His assignment of *Vices and Virtues*, the *Poema Morale*, and the *Trinity Homilies* to Southeastern is likewise questionable. Based on *LAEME*, I assign them to South-East Midland.

Thirdly, although Roedler enumerated a large number of plural forms from various periods and dialects, he did not quantify them as modern dialectologists would do. In other words, he did not provide us with statistical statements on the development and distribution of plural endings. For example, when he mentioned that -*s* was "established" as a rule at a particular time in a particular dialect, it is not clear by what measure he judged it as established.

Fourthly, Roedler did not deal with linguistic variation systematically. He indeed enumerated examples of morphological variation, but failed to discuss what kind of variation was characteristic of each dialect or how variants were distributed across dialects. The development of the plural formations would be better understood from a variationist viewpoint, which is now a widely accepted approach to language and language change.

Fifthly, Roedler's study gives the misleading impression that individual dialects underwent independent developments. To be fair, he implicitly assumed that linguistic change would diffuse from dialect to dialect; he should have been explicit about it, however, in so far as he took a dialectological approach. In the present study, I put explicit emphasis on the diatopically mobile nature of linguistic diffusion. In Section 7.6, I will show that neighbouring dialects formed linguistic continua.

Finally, and most importantly, Roedler's attitude to the question of "why" the plural system developed in the way it did was dogmatically functionalistic. He explained the development of the plural system almost exclusively by language-internal systemic regulation. His persistence in a functionalistic approach was such that extralinguistic factors hardly entered his argument. In fact he explicitly dismissed language-external explanation (as in the influence of French) as "unnötig" (2: 499).

I disagree with him on his exclusively functionalistic attitude. First, since any linguistic development should be multi-factorial in nature, both intra- and extralinguistic points of view have to be assumed a priori. Next, the fact that -*s* spread first in Northern, then in Midland and finally in Southern points to a north-to-south diffusion of the linguistic change. Besides, differences in the speed with which the -*s* spread between the northern and the southern dialects strongly suggest a sociolinguistic pressure on the North, especially one associated with Norse-English contact in the Danelaw.

Thus, in opposition to Roedler, I assume both intra- and extralinguistic factors in discussing the cause of the development of the plural system. I will return to this issue in Chapter 7.

2.2 Review of Classen's Study

Whereas Roedler's approach was almost exclusively language-internal, Classen took a language-external approach in his short article, "-s and -n Plurals in Middle English." He proposed the idea that Norse-English contact had a significant effect on the development of the *s*-plural. In this section I will summarise Classen's Old Norse contact hypothesis.

Classen argued that the northern liking for the *s*-plural in Middle English was due to Norse-English contact. First, he considered that the growth of the *n*-plural, as in the southern dialects, should represent the normal course of development, whereas the growth of the *s*-ending in the North should need special explanation.

Classen's view of the "normal development" is based on the ubiquity of weak nouns, as he said: "Doubtless the Old English weak declension contained more nouns, masculine, feminine and neuter, than any single strong declension" (*Outlines* 94).[15] He argued that the ubiquity of weak nouns set up the analogical ground for the extension of the *n*-ending in the southern dialects of Middle English.

On the other hand, he found it necessary to provide special accounts for the Northern growth of the *s*-plural in Middle English. Given the period and dialect, the obvious point he looked to was the possible effect of Old Norse.

The possibility of an Old Norse effect on the English plural system would have been easy to imagine if Old Norse had had the very *s*-plural corresponding to the English *s*-plural; the fact is, however, that no *s*-plural existed in Old Norse. Then how could Classen ever advance such a hypothesis?

He looked to inflectional similarity between the Old Norse weak declension and the Old English strong declension. In the singular, both declensions show rather similar inflections, so his reasoning was that where linguistic contact was closest, Old Norse weak nouns came to decline as if they were strong.

There is also some similarity in the plural inflections. For example, the two paradigms are very close in the nominative plural of the neuter, the accusative plural, the dative plural and the majority of the genitive plural. The only outstanding difference is in the nominative plural of the masculine and the feminine.

Moreover, Old Norse inflections generally lacked the *n*-ending, so the English weak *n*-plurals must have been unfamiliar to Old Norse speakers in the Danelaw. This situation prevented the *n*-ending from growing in the northern dialects. Classen even considered it likely that in the plural Old English speakers substituted their familiar -*as* for the corresponding Old Norse -*ar* and consequently the *s*-plural became dominant.

On this matter Jespersen has the following to say:

> . . . I incline to think that E. Classen is right in thinking that the Danes count for something in bringing about the final victory of -*s* over its competitor -*n*, for the Danes had no plural in -*n*, and -*s* reminded them of their own -*r*. (*Language* 214)

When Jespersen said that -*s* "reminded" the Danes of their own -*r*, he meant it not phonetically but in terms of the morphological functions carried by these consonants. -*r* and -*s* are phonetically distinct, but their inflectional functions between the two languages were remarkably parallel.

As far as I know, no one except Jespersen has reacted to Classen's hypothesis. I will give a full discussion on this issue in Section 7.4.

2.3 Germanic Backgrounds

2.3.1 Introduction to Germanic Backgrounds

To understand better how plural endings developed in English, it will be useful to take an overview of the developments of other Germanic languages. First, comparison between cognate languages will bring into relief the peculiarities in the development of English. Comparison will throw new light not only on how the English plural system developed as it did but also on where the development in English was different from those in its cognate languages. We should note that it is important to ask why some changes did *not* take place as well. As Milroy remarks:

> Therefore, as a historical linguist, I thought that we might get a better understanding of what linguistic change actually is, and how and why it happens, if we could also come closer to specifying the conditions under

which it does not happen—the conditions under which 'states' and forms of language are maintained and changes resisted. (*Linguistic* 11–12)

Secondly, as we will see, most Germanic developments were motivated by both language-internal and -external forces. Some similarities between the languages may be due to the so-called Germanic drift, that is, the diachronic tendency that the Germanic languages have had toward (particularly morphological) simplification; but others may better be explained as due to independent developments or as a result of language contact with the neighbouring languages or dialects. In fact, the large part of the so-called drift of the Germanic can be seen as a result of the long-term mutual contact. Comparison of the cognate languages, therefore, should give us an opportunity to consider both language-internal and -external forces in language change.

Thirdly, Old Norse is a particularly important Germanic language for the present study, and I will argue in Chapter 7 that it may have had an important effect on the English plural system. Therefore, it is of particular importance to examine here how Old Norse developed its plural system in comparison with English and other Germanic languages.

I will not go into the highly debated issue of the Germanic macro-grouping, but in the argument below I accept the traditional view that the Germanic languages are divided into three main branches, East, West, and North.[16] Despite the apparently distinct division between the three branches, linguistic contact between neighbouring dialects could have readily allowed features to move from one branch to another. Therefore, based on their genetic relationship, cross-group contact generated an intricate network of the Germanic isoglosses, within which the developments in individual languages must be placed.

Before going into individual Germanic languages, let us take an overview of the Proto-Germanic nominal inflections, which provides the hypothetical base on which its daughter languages developed their own inflectional systems.

The Proto-Germanic system, as in Table 2.1 on page 23, is a theoretical reconstruction. I depend upon Prokosch's *Comparative Germanic Grammar* for the sets of paradigms below. Germanic comparative linguists set up the following stem classes of nouns: *a*-stem (or *o*-stem in Indo-European terms), $\bar{o}$-stem (or $\bar{a}$-stem in Indo-European terms), *i*-stem, *u*-stem, *n*-stem, *s*-stem, athematic stem, *r*-stem, and *nt*-stem. In addition there are a few minor stems such as the heteroclitic stem and *t*-stem. Some stems are subcategorised: the *wa*- and *ja*-stems branch from the *a*-stem; the *wō*- and *jō*-stem from the *ō*-stem; and the *īn*-stem from the *n*-stem.

To take account of all these stems would obscure our central argument, so let us focus on the four major vowel stem classes (the strong declension) and the one consonant stem class (the weak declension), that is, *a*-, *ō*-, *i*-, *u*- and *n*- stems. The paradigms below leave out the ablative, locative and instrumental cases because of their minor role in the later development of Germanic.

The first thing to note about the Proto-Germanic paradigm is that the accusative plural is differentiated from the nominative plural in all stem classes except the neuter. This contrasts with later West Germanic languages including Old English, in which the two plural cases always took the same form. The fact that the nominative plural was thus different from the accusative plural at the Proto-Germanic stage had a far-reaching effect on the ways in which Germanic languages were differentiated from one another in their later development.

In Proto-Germanic, while the two case forms were distinct, each of the two case forms took the same ending across different classes, strong or weak, except for the neuter, that is, *-es* for the nominative plural and *-ns* for the accusative plural. We may note that Old English had distinct sets of the nominative/accusative plural endings according to gender and the strong/weak class opposition (e.g. *stānas* "stones", *giefa* "gifts", *hūs* "houses", and *guman* "men").

2.3.2 East Germanic

As Gothic is effectively the only language available that represents East Germanic, I take up the Gothic paradigm (Table 2.2 on page 23). It retains Proto-Germanic inflections better than any Germanic language of which we have a good knowledge.

The paradigm shows general similarity to the Proto-Germanic paradigm, but there are a few differences arising from phonological and morphological changes. In some declensions the nominative plural and accusative plural forms were effectively merged, e.g. *gumans* and *tuggōns* for the *n*-stem. Other declensions, however, kept the two case forms distinct, e.g. *wulfōs/wulfans*.

Table 2.1: Paradigm of Proto-Germanic

	a-stem masc.	a-stem neut.	ō-stem fem.	i-stem masc.	i-stem fem.	u-stem masc.	u-stem fem.	n-stem masc.	n-stem neut.	n-stem fem.
nom. sg.	-s	-s	-ø	-s	-ø	-s	-s	-ø	-ø	-ø
acc. sg.	-m	-s	-ø	-ø	-ø	-ø	-ø	-ø	-ø	-ø
gen. sg.	-so	-so	-es/-os	-es/-os	-es/-os	-es/-os	-es/-os	-es/-os	-es/-os	-es/-os
dat. sg	-ai	-ai	-ai	-i	-i	-i	-i	-i	-i	-i
nom. pl.	-es	-ā	-es	-es	-es	-es	-es	-es	-ā	-es
acc. pl.	-ns	-ā	-ns	-ns	-ns	-ns	-ns	-ns	-ā	-ns
gen. pl.	-om	-om	-om	-om	-om	-om	-om	-om	-om	-om
dat. pl.	-mis	-mis	-mis	-mis	-mis	-mis	-mis	-mis	-mis	-mis

Table 2.2: Paradigm of Gothic

	a-stem masc.	a-stem neut.	ō-stem fem.	i-stem masc.	i-stem fem.	u-stem masc.	u-stem fem.	n-stem masc.	n-stem neut.	n-stem fem.
nom. sg.	wulfs	barn	giba	gasts	dēþs	sunus	handus	guma	augō	tuggō
acc. sg.	wulf	barn	giba	gast	dēþ	sunu	handu	guman	augō	tuggōn
gen. sg.	wulfis	barnis	gibōs	gastis	dēþais	sunaus	handaus	gumins	augins	tuggōns
dat. sg	wulfa	barna	gibai	gasta	dēþai	sunau	handau	gumin	augin	tuggōn
nom. pl.	wulfōs	barna	gibōs	gasteis	dēþeis	sunōs	handōs	gumans	augōna	tuggōns
acc. pl.	wulfans	barna	gibōns	gastins	dēþins	sununs	handuns	gumans	augōna	tuggōns
gen. pl.	wulfē	barnē	gibō	gastē	dēþē	suniwē	handiwē	gumanē	auganē	tuggōnō
dat. pl.	wulfam	barnam	gibōm	gastim	dēþim	sunum	handum	gumam	augam	tuggōm

Prokosch proposed that Gothic *a*-stem masculine nominative plural forms like *wulfōs* might have affected the *s*-ending of the Old English and Old Saxon nominative/accusative plural (*Comparative* 237).[17] Underlying this proposal is the fact that Old English and Old Saxon were the only West Germanic languages that preserved the Proto-Germanic *s*-ending in the nominative/accusative plural. The other West Germanic languages commonly lost -*s* in these case forms (e.g. *wolfā* in Old High German).

Prokosch's reasoning goes like this: the original Anglo-Frisian speaking area was adjacent to that of Gothic and other East Germanic speakers, and the likely language contact there encouraged Old English and Old Saxon speakers to adopt the nominative/accusative plural form in -*s* on the model of the Gothic nominative plural suffix -*ōs*.

Although this proposal cannot go beyond speculation and there is some doubt as to whether the proposed contact could be geographically possible to start with, yet the proposal is intriguing particularly because it could provide a reasonable account (in consideration of extralinguistic factors) for why some West Germanic languages retained certain case endings whereas others did not.

2.3.3 West Germanic

High German

The development from Old High German to New High German is somewhat comparable to that from Old English to Middle English in that a number of morphological distinctions were levelled as a consequence of sound reduction. The High German development, however, was more modest than the English. New High German has evolved with a much more "colourful" inflectional system than Modern English. Studying the High German development, therefore, may help us to see how English might have developed if the Old English inflectional system had not collapsed in the destructive way that it did.

The history of High German is conventionally divided into the following periods: Old High German (750?–1050), Middle High German (1050–1350), Early New High German (1350–1650), and New High German (1650–). I follow the development of the same five major declensions as before, but I add the *s*-stem declension to the table (Table 2.3 on page 26), because it was an input to later

-*er*, one of the most important High German plural endings.

The paradigm shows a number of changes from the Proto-Germanic stage. I will focus on the changes relevant to the later development of the High German inflectional system or those that may give a hint to an understanding of the development of English.

First, the nominative/accusative plural forms were merged in all declensions. As for the *a*-stem masc., this is because the nominative plural form came from the accusative plural, which had no consonantal ending at the North-West Germanic stage (Voyles 228). The resultant lack of the *s*-ending in the nominative/accusative plural is in a stark contrast with other West Germanic languages, including Old English and Old Saxon.

Next, in Old High German the nominative/accusative plural endings in the *ā*- and *i*-stem declensions were each shared by the masculine and the feminine. This agreement partly resulted from analogical attraction between the masculine and the feminine endings, which had been different earlier (Voyles 228). Such agreement was not always found in Old English and Old Saxon, where the nominative/accusative plural forms of the strong masculines and the strong feminines were normally distinct (typically, -*s* for the masculine and a vowel ending for the feminine).

Furthermore, in Old High German *i*-mutation was functional in certain inflections of the *i*-, *u*-, and *s*-stem classes, as in *gesti*, *henti*, and *lembir*. According to Prokosch, the long vowel in *tāti* of the *i*-stem also had an *i*-mutated value though not represented in spelling (*Comparative* 247).

The functional role of *i*-mutation in these inflections is clear when we look at such words as *gast* of the *i*-stem masculine. The noun distinguished the plural series of inflections from the singular by *i*-mutation as well as by inflectional endings. At a later stage of the development, *i*-mutation became tied up with plurality. In English, such an association between *i*-mutation and plurality was weaker, and the device was utilised only for the *r*-stem and athematic stems but not for the *i*-, *u*-, or *s*-stems.

One final point to note is the distinct -*ir*- element in the *s*-stem plural inflections. This element was later to develop into one of the most productive plural suffixes in New High German: -*er*.

The following Middle High German period is characterised by inflectional

Table 2.3: Paradigm of Old High German

	a-stem masc.	a-stem neut.	ō-stem fem.	i-stem masc.	i-stem masc.	u-stem masc.	u-stem masc.	n-stem fem.	n-stem neut.	n-stem fem.	s-stem neut.
nom. sg.	wolf	barn	[geba]	gast	tāt	fridu	hant	gumo	ouga	zunga	lamb
acc. sg.	wolf	barn	geba	gast	tāt	fridu	hant	gumon	ouga	zungun	lamb
gen. sg.	wolfes	barnes	geba	gastes	tāti	frides	henti	gumen	ougen	zungūn	lambes
dat. sg.	wolfe	barne	gebu	gaste	tāti	fride	henti	gumen	ougen	zungūn	lambe
nom. pl.	wolfā	barn	gebā	gesti	tāti	fridi	henti	gumon	ougun	zungūn	lembir
acc. pl.	wolfā	barn	gebā	gesti	tāti	fridi	henti	gumon	ougun	zungūn	lembir
gen. pl.	wolfo	barno	[gebōno]	gest(e)o	tāt(e)o	frid(e)o	hent(e)o	gumōno	ougono	zungōno	lembiro
dat. pl.	wolfum	barnum	gebōm	gestim	tātim	fridim	hantum	gumōm	ougōm	zungōm	lembirum

variation and systematic restructuring. By this period the language had experienced the levelling of vowels and the apocopy of final *e* in inflectional endings. As a result, many inflectional endings were merged and an increasing number of nouns were incapable of making number distinctions. Under these circumstances, Middle High German had to seek alternative ways of marking nominal plurality.

There were five solutions: retention of the *e*-ending in the plural as opposed to the ø-ending in the singular; *i*-mutation of the stem vowel in combination with the *e*-ending in the plural; the extended use of the *er*-plural derived from Old High German *-ir-*; the continued use of unmarked plurals; and the continued use of the *n*-plural.

Having started as a purely phonological process, *i*-mutation became functionalised as a morphological device to mark plurality. The reason that this device was particularly favoured in High German seems, as Prokosch notes, to be that in High German the phonological process of *i*-mutation started later than in other languages and failed to work so regularly (*Comparative* 247). The partial implementation of *i*-mutation induced its reinterpretation as a morphological device to distinguish the plural from the singular.

The extension of the *er*-plural may also be explained from a functional point of view. Originally in Proto-Germanic, the *s*-stem nouns taking the *-ir*-plural counted only half a dozen or so. Later, however, they began to attract ø-ending neuter nouns, which had failed to distinguish number. In addition, the *r*-ending was phonetically more robust than vowels or *-n*. Consequently, New High German has by now acquired more than a hundred *er*-plurals (Prokosch, *Sounds* 183).

The inflectional system remained unstable during the following Early New High German period. One of the major factors for the instability was ironically the growing standardisation of written language. To quote R. Keller, "the growth of a written standard language spread regional features to other areas and by making them supra-regional increased variation and thus morphological confusion" (410).[18]

Not only did most neuters continue to take the *er*-plural but also some masculines transferred to *-er*, presumably because once the *e*-plural lost ground as a result of apocopy, the gender barrier between the masculine and the neuter became weaker.

Meanwhile, the *n*-plural became gradually associated with the feminine, especially with those unaffected by *i*-mutation. The *n*-ending was also associated with animate nouns, so the masculine *n*-plurals managed to survive if they denoted animate beings. Otherwise, the historical masculine *n*-plurals changed over to other declensions.

The unmarked plural was still available but limited to the masculine and the neuter. The absence of unmarked feminine plurals may be connected with the functionality of the feminine definite articles. The masculine and neuter definite articles had distinct forms for the singular and the plural: *der* (nom. sg. masc.) / *die* (nom. pl. masc.), and *das* (nom. sg. neut.) / *die* (nom. pl. neut.). In contrast, the feminine definite articles did not have distinct forms: *die* (nom. sg. fem.) / *die* (nom. pl. fem.). The feminine nouns therefore would have to have some device other than the definite article for clear plural marking.

The instability of the inflectional system in Early New High German was gradually resolved toward the end of the New High German period. In addition to the surviving plural endings and *i*-mutation, the new foreign suffix *-s* was now introduced from Low German, French, and English. The *s*-plural spread even to native German words.

The emerging New High German number system was highly functional. Various morphological devices to mark plurality were available, and even where they failed to work, there was another device available to mark number, i.e. morphosyntactic agreement with determiners, adjectives and verbs.

As I mentioned earlier, Early Middle English and Middle High German commonly underwent destructive sound processes in inflectional endings. In English, this resulted in a systemic shift from the tripartite plural system of *-s*, *-n*, and *-e* into the dichotomic system of *-s* and *-n*, which was later to develop into the *s*-dominant plural system in Modern English. Unlike High German, English hardly developed *i*-mutation or *-er*. On the other hand, High German developed several alternative devices to mark plurality. The contrast between German and English is best observed in the way the two languages reacted to unmarked neuter plurals. In English most of them finally changed over to the *s*-ending, while Middle High German introduced the new *er*-ending.

Despite the apparently different courses the two languages took, they had a rather similar experience in fact. As described above, Middle High German made use of devices such as the definite article agreement and the animacy/inanimacy opposition to mark number. In Sections 6.6 and 6.7 I will discuss that these devices were taken advantage of in English as well though to a limited extent.

Low German
Old Saxon shared an important characteristic with Old English, that is, the *s*-suffix in the nominative/accusative plural. Otherwise, it was more similar to Old High German than to Old English. For example, Old Saxon shared with Old High German *i*-mutation for *i*- and *u*-stem classes. Otherwise there is not much to mention, and I simply give the Old Saxon paradigm in Table 2.4 on page 30.

2.3.4 North Germanic
North Germanic or Scandinavian is conventionally periodised into Proto-Scandinavian (–550), Common Scandinavian (550–1050), Old Scandinavian (1050–1350), Middle Scandinavian (1350–1550), and Modern Scandinavian (1550–). The inflectional paradigms that appear below are taken mostly from Haugen (*Scandinavian*) and Noreen (*Altisländische* and *Altschwedische*).

Proto-Scandinavian (–550)
Let us start with the Proto-Scandinavian inflections as theoretically reconstructed (see Table 2.5 on page 30). In this and the following sections, by convention <R> represents a sound of *r*-coloured [z] developed from its Proto-Germanic ancestor.

If we compare Proto-Scandinavian and Old English, the former distinguished the nominative and accusative forms for the masculine both in the singular and the plural, whereas the latter did not (e.g. *stān/stān* in the singular and *stānas/stānas* in the plural). This is an important feature of Proto-Scandinavian because it was the accusative plural form, not the nominative plural form, of the masculine that later developed into the *e*-ending, one of the two major plural endings as in Modern Danish (the other being -*er*).

Table 2.4: Paradigm of Old Saxon

	a-stem masc.	a-stem neut.	$\bar{o}$-stem fem.	i-stem masc.	u-stem masc.	u-stem fem.	n-stem masc.	n-stem neut.	n-stem fem.
nom. sg.	wulf	barn	[geba]	gast	sunu	hand	gumo	ōga	tunga
acc. sg.	wulf	barn	geba	gast	sunu	hand	gumon	ōga	tungun
gen. sg.	wulfes	barnes	geba	gastes	suno	hendo	gumen	ōgen	tungun
dat. sg	wulfe	barne	gebu	gaste	suno	hendi	gumen	ōgen	tungun
nom. pl.	wulfos	barn	geba	gesti	suni	hendi	gumon	ōgun	tungun
acc. pl.	wulfos	barn	geba	gesti	suni	hendi	gumon	ōgun	tungun
gen. pl.	wulfo	barno	[gebono]	gestio	sunio	hando	gumono	ōgono	tungono
dat. pl.	wulfum	barnum	[gebun]	gestium	sunun	handum	gumun	ōgun	tungun

Table 2.5: Paradigm of Proto-Scandinavian

	a-stem masc.	a-stem neut.	$\bar{o}$-stem fem.	i-stem masc. / fem.	u-stem masc. / neut.	n-stem masc.	n-stem neut.	n-stem fem.
nom. sg.	-aR	-a	-ō	-iR	-uR	-a	-ō	-ō
acc. sg.	-a	-a	-ō	-i	-u	-an	-ō	-un, -ūn
gen. sg.	-ass	-ass	-ōR	-iR	-ōR	-an	-an	-un
dat. sg.	-ē, -ø, -ō	-ē, -ø, -ō	-ō	-ī	-iu	-an, -in	-an, -in	-ōn
nom. pl.	-ōR	-ō	-ōR	-iR	-iR(masc.) / -ō(neut.)	-an	-un, -u, -ō	-un
acc. pl.	-an	-ō	-ōR	-in(masc.) / -iR(fem.)	-u(masc.) / -ō(neut.)	—	-un, -u, -ō	-un
gen. pl.	-ō	-ō	-ō	-ō	-ō	-no	-no	-na
dat. pl.	-om(i)R	-om(i)R	-om(i)R	-om(i)R	-om(i)R	—	—	—

We may note that the strong feminines of the $\bar{o}$- and i-stems had the vowel plus R-ending in the nominative/accusative plural just as the strong masculines did. The presence of the R-ending in the feminines as well as the masculines was critical in that the r-ending (derived from the R-ending) became a common plural marker at later stages of the Scandinavian languages. In general, morphological differences across gender were less distinctive in Scandinavian than in English.

Another point to make is that the Proto-Scandinavian strong feminines took the R-ending in the genitive singular as well, while the Old English strong feminines did not take the corresponding s-ending. This is another sharp contrast, considering that in both languages the genitive singular form developed hand in hand with the nominative/accusative plural.

Common Scandinavian (550–1050)

After several sound changes from the Proto-Scandinavian stage, the Common Scandinavian system appeared as in Table 2.6 on page 32.

At this stage, the earlier endings and the earlier inflectional classes were somewhat levelled. Let us note particularly the near-total absence of the n-ending in weak inflections. The loss of the nasals occurred in two steps: first, vowels preceding nasals were nasalised, and then the nasalised vowels were denasalised into a long vowel by a principle of compensatory lengthening (Haugen, *Scandinavian* 155; Voyles 122).

When -n was lost, the weak nouns became incapable of making number distinctions in many cases. The solution then was to bring the vowel plus R-ending from the strong declensions into the historical weak declensions. Interestingly, this draws a striking parallel with the English development, for toward Early Middle English n in inflectional endings was increasingly lost in many dialects, so that weak nouns had to work out alternative ways to make number distinctions. The northern dialects brought the s-ending into the weak plural slot, whereas the southern dialects revitalised the weakening n-ending by virtue of analogy.

Another point to make on the Common Scandinavian inflectional system is the centripetal force of the a- and $\bar{o}$-stem declensions. These two major declensions "swallowed" other minor declensions after vowel syncope in unstressed

Table 2.6: Paradigm of Common Scandinavian

	a-stem masc.	a-stem neut.	$\bar{o}$-stem fem.	i-stem masc. / fem.	u-stem masc. / neut.	n-stem masc.	n-stem neut.	n-stem fem.
nom. sg.	-R	-ø	-ø	-R(masc.)	-R(masc.)	-i, -e	-a	-a
acc. sg.	-ø	-ø	-ø	-ø	-ø	-a	-a	-u
gen. sg.	-ss	-ss	-aR	-iR, -ss(masc.) / -aR(fem.)	-aR	-a	-a	-u
dat. sg.	-i, -ø, -u	-i, -ø, -u	-u, -ø	-ø	-i, -ø	-a, -i	-a, -i	-u
nom. pl.	-aR	-ø	-aR	-iR	-iR(masc.) / -ø(neut.)	-aR	-um, -u, -a	-uR
acc. pl.	-a	-ø	-aR	-i(masc.) / -iR(fem.)	-u, -i(masc.) / -ø(neut.)	-a	-um, -u, -a	-uR
gen. pl.	-a	-a	-a	-a	-a	-a	-na	-na, -a
dat. pl.	-um	-um	-um	-um	-um	-um	-um	-um

syllables, and the number of distinct declensions decreased. For example, the *i*- and *u*-stem masculines lost their distinct vowels before the *R*-ending in the nominative singular and were merged into the major *a*-stem declension.

In this levelling process, various strong declensions were integrated into the major *a*- and *ō*-stem declensions. Both in Scandinavian and English, it was the centripetal force of the two major declensions that contributed to the generation of the simplified plural system.

Old Scandinavian (Paradigm of Danish) (1050–1350)

By 1350 several linguistic innovations broke down the Scandinavian languages into West and East branches. In this and the following sections I will focus on the East branch, particularly Danish. I choose Danish because the development in Danish is particularly interesting as Haugen says that it "stands out as the most advanced, with a distinctive development that separates it from the other Sc languages" (*Scandinavian* 208). It should be instructive to compare the Middle and Modern Danish developments with the Early Middle English one since they shared a comparable level of simplification in history. The Old Danish paradigm is given in Table 2.7.

There was gender and case syncretism in the Common Scandinavian period, so by the Old Danish period a new simplified plural system had come into being in which plurality was expressed by either -*e* (derived from -*a* of the *a*-stem masculine accusative plural) or -*er* (derived from -*aR* of the *ō*-stem feminine nominative/accusative plural).[19] The neuter nouns, on the other hand, formed the plural either in -*ø* or -*e*. Distinction between the strong and weak declensions was no longer made.

The simplification of the paradigm was mostly due to the loss of *R*.[20] Since

Table 2.7: Paradigm of Old Danish

	masc. / fem.	neut.
nom. /acc. / dat. sg.	-(e)	-(e)
gen. sg.	-s	-s
nom. / acc. / dat. pl.	-e(r)	-ø, -e(r)
gen. pl.	-s	-s

the R-ending used to play a variety of morphophonological roles, its loss necessarily caused a restructuring of the whole paradigm. In the a-stem masculine singular, the loss of $-R$ caused the merger of the nominative and accusative forms in favour of the latter. Likewise, the loss of $-R$ affected the a-stem masculine plural in such a way that the R-less accusative plural $-a$ (later $-e$) was chosen as a new common plural. $-R$ did not disappear everywhere, however, as $-er$ (developed from $-aR$ of the $\bar{o}$-stem feminine nominative/accusative plural) was later revived as another viable plural marker in the language.

Let us note another Old Danish innovation. Old Danish generalised $-s$ as the genitive singular marker at the expense of historical $-aR$, which used to be primarily for the feminine nouns. This s-ending was taken from $-ss$ of the a-stem masculine genitive singular, and it even came to function as the genitive plural marker. This development of $-s$ in Old Danish corresponds exactly to the generalisation of the s-genitive in English.

An equally drastic simplification took place in other mainland Scandinavian varieties as well. Haugen's following remark is suggestive from a contact linguistic point of view:

> External influence, e.g. from the LG [Low German] speech community, probably played a major role, as suggested by the way in which the changes spread into those areas most easily accessible to Germans and often failed to touch the more remote dialects (Ic [Icelandic] Fa [Faroese] Dal[arna] Sw[edish]). MLG [Middle Low German], ME [Middle English] and MSc [Middle Scandinavian] formed part of a central, innovating area, with intense communication, while Ic [Icelandic] in the north and MHG [Middle High German] in the south were marginal and (hence?) conservative. (*Scandinavian* 285)

If we follow Haugen, the northern dialects of English had the closest contact with the Scandinavian people. Probably because of this sociolinguistic conditions, the morphological reorganisation proceeded earlier and faster in the northern parts of England than in the rest of the country.

Middle and Modern Scandinavian (Paradigm of Danish) (1350–1550 and 1550–)

The nominal system of Old Danish came down almost unchanged into the following period, so I will treat Middle and Modern Danish together. Danish based its plural system on the two endings -*e* and -*er*, except that in the East Jutland dialect -*er* was generalised at the expense of -*e*.

Many nouns of common gender fluctuated between -*e* and -*er* until C18 and C19, but the general rule was that -*e* was attached to either native monosyllabics (e.g. *drenge* "boys") or disyllabics whose stem ended in -*er* (e.g. *døtre* "daughters"), while -*er* was more productively suffixed to loanwords, derivatives and many others (e.g. *stater* "states," *venskaber* "friendships," and *skyer* "clouds"). Unlike English, Danish has kept the vowel suffix alive to this day.

As for the neuter, fluctuation between -*ø* and -*e(r)* continued until the former was generalised as a rule in C18.

2.3.5 Summary of Germanic Backgrounds

In the preceding sections I compared several Germanic plural systems with the following intentions in mind.

1. to provide reference points against which the development in English can be compared
2. to bring into relief the characteristics of the development in English
3. to stress the importance of addressing the subject from both intra- and extralinguistic points of view
4. to introduce the Old Norse paradigm and its development before discussing the Old Norse contact hypothesis in Section 7.4

Germanic languages have had much in common with one another in the development of their inflectional systems. Each language drifted away from the fully inflected Proto-Germanic system to a more or less simplified system. In many languages, grammatical categories such as case and gender were reduced if not completely lost. Interestingly enough, all the languages have retained the number distinction to this day.

Listed below are summarised features of the various Germanic developments seen above which may throw light on the development in English.

1. Some (stages) of the languages distinguished between the nominative plural and the accusative plural form while others did not. English belongs to the latter group.

2. Some (stages) of the languages made a sharper distinction between the strong masculine and the strong feminine inflections than others. While the distinction was present in Old English, it was lost in Middle English according as gender was lost.

3. In many of the languages, the number of distinct declensions decreased over time, largely due to the levelling and loss of sounds in inflectional endings. From Old English to Middle English, various strong declension types were integrated into the a-stem or $\bar{o}$-stem types.

4. In many of the languages, the nominative plural and the genitive singular showed a parallel development. English has developed -s for both case forms.

5. Some languages lost consonants such as -n in weak inflectional endings but made up for the loss in some ways. In the northern dialects of Middle English, -s was brought into the emptied slot while in the southern dialects the half lost n came back to life through analogy.

6. Contact between the neighbouring languages seems to underlie the development (mostly simplification) of the inflectional system in many languages. Pre-Old English was possibly in contact with Old Saxon and Gothic on the continent; Old English with Old Norse; and Old Danish with Low German.

Sharing a common proto-language, all Germanic languages drifted toward morphological simplification. They were in close contact with one another, mutually affecting the direction of language change.

Chapter 3   Textual Evidence

3.1   Principles of Treating Textual Evidence

3.1.1   Where Textual Evidence Comes From

This chapter analyses actual data from many Early Middle English texts and from a few Late Old English and Late Middle English texts. Before studying texts I will set up a number of principles to which I keep in handling texts.

First of all, I need to define where textual evidence comes from. Textual evidence should of course come from individual texts, but what are individual texts? When I speak of texts in the present study, I assume scribal texts as distinct from literary texts. The concept of scribal text was developed through the production of *LALME*, one of the main aims of which was to identify scribes who contributed to separate parts in the same or different manuscripts.

Each scribal text is considered unique with respect to language, and therefore must be analysed in its own right for linguistic purposes. In a number of cases, however, separate parts of text copied by a scribe may be sufficiently linguistically consistent to be reasonably "conflated" as if they made up one contiguous scribal text. The unit of text I use in this study is either a scribal text or a conflated set of scribal texts as defined here.

The Early Middle English text database is now electronically available as the online *LAEME*. *LAEME* attempts to localise surviving Early Middle English texts as precisely as possible. All the localisation and dating of individual texts assumed in the present study are therefore based on the information achieved for the *LAEME* project.

It is worth a mention that the central concern of *LAEME* as well as its predecessor *LALME* has been to identify anonymous scribes graphemically and morphologically and then, based on this identification, to attempt to localise a text language in relation to another by means of a "fit technique" (see Benskin and Laing). For this purpose, each text is given a Linguistic Profile.

For the present study I developed tailored profiles for the purpose of studying plurals, inspired by Linguistic Profiles. I will call them Plural Forms Profiles (PFPs). PFPs aim neither to identify scribes nor localise text language as the Linguistic Profile does, but to situate the plural system of a scribal text in relation to that of another in a diachronic and diatopic network with a view to describing the development of the Early Middle English plural system as a whole. I will introduce PFPs in Section 3.1.5.

Of the 247 scribal texts that I analysed in full or in part, 113 were manually analysed from printed editions, while 134 were analysed on the computer from the *LAEME* text database (for the list of texts, see Appendix A). The computational approach is particularly useful in analysing longer texts. In contrast, when it comes to close analysis of a text or close comparison across texts, the manual approach is necessary.

3.1.2 Collecting Plural Forms

Having defined where to find textual evidence, I will define what linguistic elements should be collected from texts. First of all, focus should be on the plural forms of nouns as opposed to those of pronominals and adjectives. Accordingly, plural forms such as *oðres* (pronominal as in *of alle þe oðres*) and *flesliches* (adjectival as in *ðe flesliches lustes*) are left outside the scope of study, even if they might prove to be an interesting study of the morphological relationship between nominals, pronominals, and adjectives.

Adjective-derived nouns and numerals as opposed to adjectives proper come within our scope (e.g. *guodes, halȝen, hundredis, ðhusenz, uueles,* and *wreches*). On the other hand, nominally used adjectives are left out of account (e.g. *þa heðene, þe cristine,* and *te ontfule*). However, judgement is often in doubt as to whether a given case is a full-fledged noun of adjectival origin or just a nominally used adjective. In uncertain cases, my position is to stand on the conservative side by leaving them out of consideration.[21]

In the second place, nominal plurals must be collected in their nominative and accusative cases as opposed to the dative and genitive cases. There is reason for leaving the latter two cases out of account. In Old English the four cases were fairly well distinct, but during the run-up to the Middle English period, this four-case system began to collapse as a result of morphophonological processes.

By Early Middle English, the nominative and accusative cases first fell together as the common case, which was later joined by the dative case.

In most cases, the genitive case also fell together morphologically with the other cases during the Middle English period, but it was functionally, if not formally, so distinct from the other cases that it was not totally "swallowed up" by the common nominative/accusative case. Therefore, it is reasonable first to separate the genitive case from the other three.

The reason why I give preference to the nominative/accusative case over the dative case is that the former morphologically "swallowed up" the latter rather than the other way around. In order to follow the diachronically continuous development of the nominal plural forms, we must focus on the case forms which promise diachronic comparability rather than those which fail to do so. Seeing that the dative case was to be displaced by the nominative/accusative case toward Late Middle English, the "swallowing" side should be examined.

It is often difficult, however, to distinguish whether a given form represents a nominative/accusative or a dative since the case system was unstable in the transitional Early Middle English period. In those positions where Old English syntax should require dative plural forms, Early Middle English could show either a common nominative/accusative case form or a dative case form, apparently interchangeably.[22]

To illustrate a case that is difficult to judge, if we come across nominal plurals which end with -*en* in dative environments, say, after a preposition, how could we tell whether we are looking at a reduced reflex of the old dative plural ending -*um* or at an innovative *n*-plural as a new common case plural form? If the former, the form has to be dismissed out of consideration because it is considered a dative example; if the latter, it has to be counted in our records as relevant, because it is considered a common case example.

The linguistic process of case distinction being lost from Late Old English to Early Middle English is known as case syncretism. The general rule is that in earlier Early Middle English texts case syncretism was only halfway through, whereas in later Early Middle English texts it was more or less complete. We must always keep case syncretism in mind when reading text because it directly affects the way that nominal plural data should be collected for this study. This issue will be taken up more closely in the next section.

The third limitation I impose on the "plural forms" is to dismiss those that occur in rhyming positions in verse. The following is what Benskin and Laing have to say on this matter:

> ... in general the rhyming usage of later M.E. texts can be expected to differ sharply from the line-internal usage. The resulting *Mischsprache* is easily recognised for what it is, and in constructing a profile of a given scribal dialect, rhyming usage must either be recorded separately, or ignored. (70)

In this quotation they speak of Late Middle English texts, but the same should be true of Early Middle English texts. In theory it is possible to assume what they call "scribal diglossia" (71) in which a scribe confuses and exchanges rhyming usages with in-line usages; however, even if some scribal diglossia is involved, most rhyming usages will be distinct from in-line usages, so should be recorded separately if not ignored altogether.

In the above, I defined what I mean by the "plural forms" in the present study. To recapitulate, the target is "common case plural forms of prototypical nouns that occur outside rhyming positions."

3.1.3 Case Syncretism

Case syncretism is a morphological process in which a number of distinct case forms are merged. As was introduced in the preceding section, the case syncretism we are particularly concerned with is one that gradually proceeded from Late Old English to Early Middle English where the earlier four-case system was restructured first to a three-case system (the common nom./acc, the gen., and the dat.) and then to a two-case system (the common nom./acc./dat. and the gen.) primarily as a result of phonological levelling and loss in unstressed inflectional syllables. In the history of English, it is without doubt one of the most significant factors that contributed to the morphological simplification of the language.

Since case syncretism was a gradual process, the extent to which it proceeded varied with periods, dialects, and texts. It is important to make sure again why we should take account of the extent to which case syncretism is completed in individual texts. For one thing, the completion level of case syncretism is a rough indicator of how "modern" the text language is. As the *s*-dominant plural system is another rough indicator of how "modern" the language is, it is likely that the process of case syncretism and the generalisation of the *s*-plural are correlated (see Section 6.8 on this issue).

Another reason to consider case syncretism is that the process can be considered to be a kind of language-internal diffusion in that the nominative/accusative case forms "diffused" into dative environments. The process of case syncretism may thus be seen as an interesting example of linguistic diffusion just like the spread of the *s*-plural itself, in which *-s* "diffused" into historical non-*s* slots.

Moreover, there is practical need to take case syncretism into account. As I defined in the preceding section, nominal plurals are collected only in their nominative and accusative case forms for fear that inclusion of dative forms, typically in *-en*, would result in an unduly high frequency of the *n*-plural, for example. There are, however, many instances that show case syncretism is surely working in dative environments. They would provide additional examples of what are effectively nominative/accusative plural forms. Thus, if we are able to distinguish in dative environments between syncretism-affected forms and syncretism-unaffected forms, the former may be granted effectively the same status as genuine common nominative/accusative forms. This practical approach will help to increase examples relevant to the study. Since surviving Early Middle English materials are not particularly abundant, any measure to increase usable data should be welcome.

For example, let us suppose that we have recorded all plural forms occurring in dative environments in a text. If this text represents a language in which case syncretism has already proceeded a long way, most of the recorded forms should be formally identical to their corresponding nominative/accusative forms. This would be convenient for us because they would provide more plural examples for analysis than if we were only to extract plurals in syntactically nominative/accusative positions.

If, conversely, the text represents a language which shows a low level of case syncretism, most of the recorded forms from dative environments should have endings such as *-en* and *-e*, derived from the Old English *-um*. By taking a large number of these forms into account, we would run the risk of reporting a misleadingly high rate of the *n*- or vowel-plural against, say, the *s*-plural.

Let us suppose, on the other hand, that we dismissed all plural forms occurring in dative environments in a text. If this text happens to show a high level of case syncretism, most of the dismissed forms would have been additional evidence of innovative plural forms since they should be formally identical to their corresponding nominative/accusative forms. Unfortunately, however, they were left out of account to start with, so we could not benefit from these examples.

If, conversely, the text happens to show a low level of syncretism, most of the dismissed forms should have *um*-derived endings perhaps distinct from their corresponding nominative/accusative forms. In this case, we may be able to make a reasonable report of the distribution of common case plural forms in the text, though it is still likely that we will have missed a relatively small number of innovative plural forms of interest from dative environments.

As the reasoning above shows, neither categorical inclusion nor exclusion of plural forms in dative environments seems to be a good solution when we wish to obtain as many relevant plurals as possible from the finite corpus, but only those that can safely be considered nominative/accusative plurals.

I will treat plurals in dative environments in the following manner. If a plural in a dative environment is *s*-ending, ø-ending, or of minor plural formation types such as *i*-mutation and *r*-ending, it can with fair certainty be interpreted as effectively the same form as the corresponding nominative/accusative form since syncretism-unaffected dative plurals should be either *n*-ending or *V*-ending, derived from the older -*um*.[23]

Uncertainty arises over the *n*- or *V*-plural. If a plural in a dative environment takes either -*n* or -*V*, there are few clues as to whether the form represents a genuine innovation with that ending or just a reduced reflex of the older dative plural -*um*. If we are fortunate enough, we may encounter examples which regularly take an *n*- or *V*-ending in dative environments but which take an *s*-ending in nominative/accusative environments. In such cases, we can safely conclude that these *n*- or *V*-forms in dative environments are reflexes of the old dative plurals, and thus leave them out of account. When, however, such a clear clue is not available, as is most often the case, we simply cannot judge.

From the consideration above, the working principle I should take with regard to the *n*- and *V*-endings in dative environments is to stand on the conservative side by dismissing, or at best separately recording, them as irrelevant evidence for fear of running the potential risk of overestimating n- or V-plurals. I take this stance throughout, but always bear in mind that a (hopefully small) number of potentially relevant examples in dative environments may have been discarded.[24]

I close this section by defining how to figure out the extent to which case syncretism is completed in a text language (hereafter cited as the syncretism rate). It is defined as the token-based ratio of plurals in dative environments that can be accepted as relevant to the present analysis as just explained, to all plurals in dative environments in a text. Thus, in a hypothetical text that has a total of 100 nominal plural forms in dative environments (by the token counting), if 60 of them can be accepted as morphologically identical to their counterparts in nominative/accusative environments, the syncretism rate of this text language will be 0.6.

The calculated rate is a minimum possible rate since it should by definition underestimate possible innovation in -n or -V in dative environments. In addition, the syncretism rate is only calculated on plurals, taking no account of singulars. I believe, however, that the syncretism rate so calculated is fairly representative and useful as an index of a text language.

3.1.4 Plural Forms Reference System

After plural forms are collected from the text in the manner explained above, I check whether they have had any plural formation changeover since Old English. Because this involves diachronic comparison, it is essential to establish a reference system to make it possible to associate a given Early Middle English plural form with its Old English equivalent. Such a reference system could be based on any Old English or Early Middle English dialect, but in practice it is convenient to base the reference system on the well-known paradigm of the West-Saxon dialect of Old English.

What we must bear in mind in adopting the West-Saxon paradigm as a base for an Old English to Early Middle English reference system is that given Early Middle English forms may not be direct reflexes of their associated West-Saxon forms. For example, plural forms collected from the Final Continuation of *The Peterborough Chronicle* are descendants of the corresponding East Mercian forms rather than West-Saxon, so using the West-Saxon based reference system must be seen as misguided, strictly speaking. I stress that the West-Saxon reference system only provides a working base to associate a given Early Middle English plural form of any dialect with a West-Saxon Old English plural form.

Most handbooks on Old English grammar such as Campbell focus on the West-Saxon dialect and display nominal paradigms according to the conventions of Germanic comparative linguistics. They are classified in terms of stem ending, gender, morphological category, syllable weight, and phonological category. Such a detailed classification, however, would be unsuitable to the present study. Since I am just trying to establish a reference system between Old English and Early Middle English plural forms, a less detailed and more synchronically oriented description of the West-Saxon paradigm will do.

For example, although from a Germanic point of view it is meaningful to distinguish, say, between the a-stem masculines and the ja-stem masculines or between the $\bar{o}$-stem feminines and the i-stem feminines, this distinction hardly enlightens us with regard to the later development of plural formation, for each pair inflected in almost the same way in Old and Middle English.

Now, how much less detailed should our classification be? I propose two morphological categories, gender and plural type, as the most important keys to help to describe the Old English to Early Middle English development of the plural system.

There is evidence in plenty that gender affected the way Early Middle English nouns pluralised. For example, many Old English strong masculines that pluralised without -s (e.g. Old English u-stem *sunu* and n-stem *stēda*) transferred to s-plurals earlier than the strong neuters (e.g. Old English a-stem *þing* and wa-stem *trēow*), many of which in turn transferred to s-plurals earlier than the strong feminines.

There is also evidence that the historical plural type played a role in the way plural formation transfer occurred. Old English n- and V-plurals were, whatever their gender, more changeable than Old English s- and $\emptyset$-plurals. It is also known that i-mutated plurals were among the slowest to transfer to the other plural types.

The two key categories are closely related: s-plurals were always masculines, $\emptyset$-plurals were normally neuters, V-plurals were largely feminines or neuters, and so on.

There are other categories which played a role in directing plural formation changeover in Early Middle English. For example, there are a number of cases of plural formation transfer that can be well explained in terms of syllable weight, morphophonology, morphosyntax or semantics. These categories are, however, less functional than gender and the plural type. Although they are not fully covered in the present study, related discussions are made in Chapter 6.

I introduce below a classification of the West-Saxon nouns based on the two key categories. Each of the thirteen classes is exemplified by the traditional stem-type with typical nouns given in their nominative singular and nominative plural forms in parentheses.[25]

Masc-S (masculine *s*-plurals):
    a-stems (*stān-stānas*), *ja*-stems (*here-hergas, secg-secgas, ende-endas*), *wa*-stems (*bearu-bearwas, þēaw-þēawas*), *i*-stems (*wine-winas, giest-giestas*), kinship nouns (*fæder-fædras*)

Masc-N (masculine *n*-plurals):
    n-stems (*guma-guman, gefēa-gefēan*)

Neut-N (neuter *n*-plurals):
    n-stems (*ēage-ēagan*)

Fem-N (feminine *n*-plurals):
    n-stems (*tunge-tungan*)

Masc-V (masculine vowel-plurals):
    u-stems (*sunu-suna, feld-felda*)

Neut-V (neuter vowel-plurals):
    a-stems (*scip-scipu*), *ja*-stems (*wīte-wītu*), *wa*-stems (*searu-searu*), *i*-stems (*spere-speru*)

Fem-V (feminine vowel-plurals):
    ō-stems (*giefu-giefa, lār-lāra*), *jō*-stems (*synn-synna, gierd-gierda*), *wō*-stems (*sinu-sinwa, lǣs-lǣswa*), *i*-stems (*dǣd-dǣda*), *u*-stems (*duru-dura, hand-handa*)

Masc-Ø (masculine zero-plurals):
> kinship nouns (*brōþor-brōþor*), dental stems (*mōnaþ-mōnaþ*)

Neut-Ø (neuter zero-plurals):
> *a*-stems (*word-word*), *ja*-stems (*cynn-cynn*), *wa*-stems (*cnēow-cnēow*), *i*-stems (*geswinc-geswinc*)

Fem-Ø (feminine zero-plurals):
> kinship nouns (*dohtor-dohtor*), dental stems (*mægþ-mægþ*)

Masc-M (masculines with minor plural formations):
> athematic nouns (*fōt-fēt, mann-menn*), /-nd-/ stems (*frēond-friend*)

Neut-M (neuters with minor plural formations):
> Indo-European *es/os*-stems (*cealf-cealfru, cild-cildru*)

Fem-M (feminines with minor plural formations):
> athematic nouns (*studu-styde, bōc-bēc*)

Hereafter, each of these classes is referred to as an Old English reference class, and each referenced West-Saxon plural form is referred to as an Old English reference form. Thus, when we encounter the plural form *stones* in an Early Middle English text, we say that it is an Early Middle English reflex of the Old English reference form *stānas* belonging to the Old English reference class "Masc-S." Likewise, the Early Middle English plural form *synnes* can be described as an Early Middle English reflex of the Old English reference form *synna* belonging to the Old English reference class "Fem-V." This reference system is used to describe plural formation transfers. In the first example *stones* is an instance of an Old English Masc-S noun having experienced no plural formation transfer, while in the second *synnes* is an instance of an Old English Fem-V noun having transferred to the *s*-plural.

As for nouns that are only attested in Early Middle English and have no exact Old English equivalent, they may be referred to in either of the two ways. First, if these nouns are compounds or derivatives based on known Old English elements, their word-final morpheme may well have an Old English counterpart. If this is the case, they may be assigned to an Old English reference class together with the other Old English nouns with that morpheme.

For example, there are no Old English reference forms exactly corresponding to Early Middle English compounds *largemen*, *beggares*, and *cluppunges*, but they can be treated in the same way as other attested Old English compounds with *-man*, *-ere*, and *-ung*.

Alternatively, if Early Middle English nouns carry no element associable with any Old English morpheme, as in foreign loanwords, they are simply referred to as having no Old English reference form and grouped into the special class "Middle English Innovation" (abbreviated as ME-I). This class also includes Early Middle English nouns which have been converted from Old English non-substantives and have no exact Old English *nominal* equivalents. For example, in Early Middle English the forms *selcuðes* and *tigðes* occur as full-fledged nouns, but they were originally adjectives (Old English *seldcūþ* and *tēoþa* respectively). Since the Early Middle English forms have no Old English *nominal* equivalent, they are treated as Middle English innovations.

I have thus far classified Old English nouns rather categorically into thirteen classes (plus one special ME-I class). Many Old English nouns fit in one of the thirteen classes, but there are not a small number that fail to. Some nouns belong to more than one gender, and others alternate their plural types.

Such linguistic variation is difficult to handle when I try to establish a working reference system between Old English and Early Middle English. Take the Old English noun for "love" for example. In Old English the noun inflected either as an *ō*-stem feminine with its nominative/accusative plural *lufa* or as an *n*-stem feminine with its nominative/accusative plural *lufan*.[26] By the classification proposed it belongs either to Fem-V or Fem-N. Now, if I encounter the plural form *luues* in an Early Middle English text, I am surely looking at an instance of plural formation transfer, but should I count it as an instance of transfer from Fem-V to the *s*-plural or from Fem-N to the *s*-plural? Such a situation is hard to deal with when I try to classify every instance of plural formation transfer in order to tell which type of transfer was possible or common and which was not.

Inflectional variability in Old English nouns indicates that some plural formation changeover had already taken place before the Old English period. This fact cannot be overemphasised when we discuss the development of plural formation from Late Old English to Early Middle English. To take Old English "love" again, if we encounter *luuen* in an Early Middle English text, it is uncertain whether we should infer that any plural formation changeover was involved at all, because the *n*-plural was possible, to start with, in Old English alongside the more common vowel-ending plural. In this case, should I interpret *luuen* as an instance of an Old English Fem-V noun shifting to an *n*-plural or an instance of an Old English Fem-N noun having come down unchanged?

Given such inflectional variability, it is perhaps misleading to assign the Old English noun "love" categorically either to the Fem-V class or to the Fem-N class. Leaving the matter undecided, however, is inadeguate for working purposes; therefore I set up the following principle. I assign each variable noun to one of the possible classes as if no inflectional variation were involved, decision on assignment being made according to how variants are treated in such references as Campbell and C. Hall.

Although a large number of nouns show inflectional variation, this working principle will work without causing serious practical problems. I stress that I take this approach only for working purposes, mostly for computer processing. Otherwise, I would rather respect instances of variation and draw attention to them when necessary, as this study is meant to be variationist in orientation.

To see where the variation problem can arise, I give an alphabetical list of West-Saxon nouns that display inflectional variation in the plural. For the present study, I assigned each noun in the list to the first of the possible classes given in parentheses.

-waru (Fem-V, Fem-N, Masc-S)
ǣdr, ǣdre (Fem-V, Fem-N)
ǣt (Masc-S, Fem-V, Neut-Ø)
āncor, āncora (Masc-S, Masc-N)
bend (Fem-V, Masc-S)
berie, berig (Fem-N, Neut-Ø)
bīleofa, bīleofen (Masc-N, Fem-V)
bisen (Fem-V, Neut-V, Neut-Ø)
bīwist (Fem-V, Masc-S)
blōstm, blōstma (Masc-S, Fem-V, Masc-N)
brēost (Neut-Ø, Masc-S, Fem-V)
byrd, byrdu (Fem-V, Neut-Ø)
byrele (Masc-S, Fem-N)
candel (Fem-V, Neut-Ø)

cealf (Neut-M, Neut-Ø, Masc-S)
cild (Neut-M, Neut-Ø)
clūs, clūse (Fem-V, Fem-N)
crāwa, crāwe (Masc-N, Fem-N)
culfer, culfre (Fem-V, Fem-N)
cynd (Neut-Ø, Fem-V)
cyrnel (Masc-S, Neut-V)
dēaw (Masc-S, Neut-Ø)
dēofol (Masc-S, Neut-V)
dīc (Masc-S, Fem-V)
earc, earce (Fem-V, Fem-N)
efeta, efete (Masc-N, Fem-N)
ele (Masc-S, Neut-V)
ellen (Masc-S, Neut-V)
ēst (Fem-V, Masc-S)

ēþel (Masc-S, Neut-V)
fǣtels, fǣtel (Masc-S)
fæþm, fæþme (Masc-S, Fem-N)
felg, felge (Fem-V, Fem-N)
fenn (Neut-Ø, Masc-S)
feoht, feohte (Neut-Ø, Fem-N)
fēond (Masc-M, Masc-S)
fers (Neut-Ø, Masc-S)
fiell (Masc-S, Neut-Ø)
fiþere (Neut-V, Masc-S)
flōd (Masc-S, Neut-Ø)
force, forca (Fem-N, Masc-N)
foreweard (Fem-V, Neut-Ø)
frēond (Masc-M, Masc-S)
frōfor (Fem-V, Masc-S, Neut-Ø)
gærsum, gærsuma (Masc-S, Neut-Ø, Fem-N)
gift (Neut-Ø, Fem-V)
god (Masc-S, Neut-V)
grād, grāde (Masc-S, Fem-N)
grǣfa, grǣfe (Masc-N, Fem-N)
grīn, grin (Fem-V, Neut-Ø, Neut-V)
gyrn (Masc-S, Neut-Ø)
hēap (Masc-S, Fem-V)
help (Fem-V, Masc-S)
heofon (Masc-S, Fem-V)
heorr (Masc-S, Fem-V)
hlǣw (Masc-S, Neut-Ø)
hord (Neut-Ø, Masc-S)
hund (Neut-Ø, Neut-V)
hundred (Neut-Ø, Neut-V)
impa, impe (Masc-N, Fem-N)
lāc (Neut-Ø, Fem-V)
lǣl, lǣla (Fem-V, Masc-N)
lǣn (Neut-Ø, Fem-V)
lāttēow, lātteowa (Masc-S, Masc-N)
lēo (Masc-N, Fem-N)
līeg (Masc-S, Neut-Ø)
līget, līgetu (Neut-V, Masc-S, Fem-V)
list (Masc-S, Fem-V)
liþ (Neut-V, Masc-S)
lufu (Fem-V, Fem-N)
lyft (Masc-S, Fem-V, Neut-Ø)
mete (Masc-S, Masc-V)
mitta, mitte (Masc-N, Fem-N)
morþor (Neut-Ø, Masc-S)
mynd (Fem-V, Neut-Ø)

netel, netele (Fem-V, Fem-N)
olfend, olfenda, olfende (Masc-S, Masc-N, Fem-N)
onweald (Masc-S, Fem-V, Neut-Ø)
palm, palma (Masc-S, Masc-N)
prica, price (Masc-N, Fem-N)
sācerd (Masc-S, Fem-V)
sǣ (Masc-S, Fem-V)
sǣl (Masc-S, Fem-V)
sagu, saga (Fem-V, Masc-N)
sand (Masc-S, Fem-V)
sceaft (Fem-V, Masc-S, Neut-Ø)
scyld (Fem-V, Masc-S)
seht (Masc-S, Fem-V)
steall (Masc-S, Neut-Ø)
stede (Masc-S, Masc-V)
stīg (Fem-V, Masc-S)
strǣl (Masc-S, Fem-V)
tilþ, tilþe (Fem-V, Fem-N)
timbre, timbru (Neut-V, Fem-V)
tintreg, tintrega (Neut-Ø, Masc-N)
toll (Masc-S, Neut-Ø)
trod, trodu (Neut-V, Fem-V)
tungol (Neut-Ø, Neut-V, Masc-N)
þēod, þēode (Fem-V, Neut-V)
þēostru, þēostre (Fem-V, Neut-V)
þrēa (Masc-S, Masc-N)
þrote, þrotu (Fem-N, Fem-V)
þūsend (Neut-Ø, Neut-V)
þwang (Masc-S, Fem-V)
uncyst, uncyste (Fem-V, Fem-N)
ungelimp (Neut-Ø, Masc-S)
wæcc, wæcce (Fem-V, Fem-N)
wæstm, wæstme (Masc-S, Neut-V, Fem-V)
weard (Fem-V, Masc-S)
weler (Masc-S, Fem-V)
wīc (Neut-Ø, Fem-V)
wiell, wiella, wielle (Masc-S, Masc-N, Fem-N)
wiht (Fem-V, Neut-V)
willa, will (Masc-N, Neut-Ø)
winter (Neut-Ø, Masc-V)
wolcen (Neut-Ø, Neut-V)
wyrd (Fem-V, Neut-Ø)
wyrht (Fem-V, Neut-Ø)
ysl, ysle (Fem-V, Fem-N)

The list is not meant to be exhaustive, but it should cover most of the variable nouns appearing in the texts analysed. We may recognise some common types of variation from the list. The most common fluctuations are: Masc-S ~ Neut-Ø; Masc-S ~ Fem-V; and Masc-N ~ Fem-N. In addition, frequent variation is displayed by many nouns of the "minor declensions," including the kinship nouns, the /-nd-/ stem, the Indo-European *es/os*-stem and the dental stem.

Another common source of variation is the strong neuters, which pluralised either with -ø or -u. As a rule, the choice of the ending was controlled by the number of syllables and the syllable weight of the stem, but what we commonly notice in Old English text is interchangeability between the two endings for polysyllabic nouns. Examples of Neut-Ø ~ Neut-V include: *hēafod* ~ *hēafdu*; *tācen* ~ *tācnu*; *wǣpen* ~ *wǣpnu*; and *wundor* ~ *wundru*.

In the above I set up Old English reference classes with a view to establishing a plural forms reference system between Old English and Early Middle English. However, establishing a clear-cut classification was sometimes problematic. By way of summary, the following points must be borne in mind.

First, the given Early Middle English plural forms may not necessarily be direct Early Middle English reflexes of the West-Saxon based reference forms. Secondly, categorical classification could be misleading because some Old English nouns made plurals in more than one way and could not fit within rigid classification. Thirdly, there was variation and changeover in plural formation already in Old English or even before, so some instances of the Early Middle English variation and changeover may be better interpreted as continuations from Old English than as Early Middle English innovations.

Now that I have classified the Old English West-Saxon plurals, I go on to classify Early Middle English plurals. Five plural formations are recognised: *s*, *n*, *V* (vowel-endings), *ø* (zero-endings), and *M* (minor plural formations). The *n*-ending type may include not only common *n*-plurals but also the *ne*-plurals, as in *ehne* (Old English *ēage*) and *hesne* (Old English *hǣs*). Double plurals such as *ehnen* also fall in this type.

The minor plural formations include nouns which pluralised not by adding a certain ending but by stem alternation (e.g. *men* "men" and *bec* "books"). The -*r*- infix to such nouns as *ǣg*, *cealf*, *cild*, and *lamb* might be considered another type of stem alternation, but since this *r* was mostly frozen as part of the plural stem, it makes more sense to focus on the ending type than on the -r- itself. Accordingly, *children* and *childre*, for example, are taken as a *n*- and a *V*-ending type respectively. If, however, the plural form ends with -r as a result of metathesis, as in *childer* and *calfur*, the -r- with its preceding vowel is considered morphologically significant, so it is specially interpreted as a minor plural type.

3.1.5 Plural Forms Profiles

In the present study, I analyse the plural system in Early Middle English texts in terms of the Plural Forms Profile (hereafter cited as PFP), as mentioned earlier. This approach makes it easier not only to investigate the plural system of individual texts but also to compare the plural systems of different texts. I have made up a PFP for each of the scribal texts examined, but space does not allow me to reproduce each of them in the present book. What I can present in this book are a subset of the PFPs (see Appendices B and D).

The following is the procedure for making the PFP of a text. When each plural form is encountered in a text, it is recorded with information such as page/line reference in the edition, grammatical case, Old English reference class like Masc-S, Old English reference form, Early Middle English plural type, whether in a rhyming position or not and, sometimes for later consideration, context in which the form occurs.

Compounds and derivatives are granted the same status as the stem morpheme they carry, and are treated together with other compounds or derivatives with that morpheme. For example, *men*, *leofemen*, *wepmen*, and *wimmen*, all attested in the hand A part of the *Lambeth Homilies*, are treated together as one type, because they are all based on the morpheme *-men* and belong to the Old English Masc-M class, or the Early Middle English minor plural type.

To take another example, the *Poema Morale* of Lambeth MS (Text ID #5) witnesses the plurals *dede*, *misdede*, and *deden*. They all go back to Old English *dǣd* and belong to the Old English Fem-V class. From an Early Middle English point of view, the first two forms are of the *V*-ending type, while the third is of the *n*-ending type.

After all the plurals in a text are recorded this way, they are put to analysis. Data may be counted either by token or by type. Token counting is normally used when we are interested in the total number of occurrences or calculate the syncretism rate, but in most other cases type counting is preferred. This is because token counting is likely to overestimate the influence of frequent irregular plurals. For example, in a text which contains a large number of *men* and *men*-compounds, token counting would produce an unduly high rate of plurals of the minor plural formation. In type counting, no matter how many times *men* occurs in the text, they are counted as one type, and their share is fairly reflected in numerical statements.

The two important figures calculated on the type count are the (type) rate and the spread rate for the plural formation. The (type) rate represents the share that a given plural formation, like the *s*-plural, has in all the type-counted plural examples in text. On the other hand, the spread rate requires additional calculation. To obtain the spread rate of, say, the *s*-plural, the first step is to get (1) the type-count frequency of Old English Masc-S class nouns in text, no matter what plural type they actually take. The next step is to type-count (2) the frequency of the *s*-plurals actually occurring in text. The spread rate of the *s*-plural can now be obtained by dividing (2) by (1). If the historically expected frequency equals the actual frequency, whether because no plural formation transfer is involved or because some plural formation transfers offset each other, the spread rate will be 1.0.[27]

Finally, the analysed data are all presented in a PFP format as described in the explanatory note in Appendix B.

3.1.6 Comparing Texts at Various Levels

Once a text is analysed for plural forms, the text language is ready to be compared to other text languages. We cannot compare text languages at random, however. We need to choose texts which can be compared meaningfully from a diachronic and diatopic viewpoint. Since there are a large number of analysed texts, let us first group them according to period and dialect.

As illustrated on the dialect map in Figure 2.1 on page 8, Early Middle English is conventionally broken down into seven dialects: Northern (N), North-East Midland (NEM), South-East Midland (SEM), North-West Midland (NWM), South-West Midland (SWM), Southwestern (SW), and Southeastern (SE). Chronologically, the Early Middle English period may be sectioned by the half century, that is, C12a is followed by C12b, C13a, and so forth.[28]

When Early Middle English texts are thus grouped by period/dialect, diachronic and diatopic comparison can be made by the group. For example, we may first look at the situation for the C12b South-West Midland group of texts, then compare it with that for the C13a South-West Midland group, and further with those for the C13b and C14a South-West Midland group. We can easily apply the procedures to other dialects, and with this work done we will get a diachronic summary for each dialect.

When individual dialects have thus been summarised diachronically, it is then possible to see how differently the plural system developed from dialect to dialect. In this way, we can see the diachronic development and diatopic distribution of all the plural systems available in Early Middle English.

What is achieved this way, however, will be a rough overview rather than a detailed description of the complex linguistic reality, because individual texts have been bundled simply according to period/dialect, without philological consideration of individual texts. Therefore, we need to come back to individual texts later in order to balance the gained overview with actual evidence from texts.

I have made a PFP for each analysed scribal text, but it makes no sense to compare all the PFPs at random. I selected a few texts of philological interest, that is, texts that survive in more than one version and/or can be compared meaningfully from a diachronic/diatopic point of view. They are put to comparative analysis in Chapter 4.

Another way of investigating plural forms in Early Middle English is to look at the distribution of individual items across dialects and across periods. The schedule of plural formation transfer may differ greatly not only from dialect to dialect but also from item to item. In order to understand the development of the plural system in detail, it is essential to see how individual nouns changed their plural formation. An item-based investigation is made in Section 3.3.

3.2 Dialect-by-Dialect Study of Plural Formation Transfer

3.2.1 Text Groups

As I explained in the preceding section, texts are analysed by period/dialect group. Each period/dialect is treated as if it constituted one long text. Such a bundling of texts can admittedly be problematic since individual texts must have their own linguistic characteristics even if they were written in roughly the same period and dialect. However, there is adequate reason to advocate the bundling of texts.

First, the bundling of the texts of (roughly) the same period/dialect enables us to capture the average linguistic picture of that particular period/dialect. In addition, such a picture can provide a point of departure for closer study of individual texts. Moreover, while each individual text may provide only a handful of examples of the plurals, texts bundled together may provide many more examples.

Table 3.1 on page 56 shows the period/dialect-arranged text groups. Each scribal text is represented by its ID (for which see Appendix A). On the other hand, the map in Figure 3.1 on page 55 represents the localisation of the texts I analysed for the present study to give a rough idea of dialectal coverage.

Hereafter, to refer to particular text groups, I use expressions such as the C12b North-East Midland group and the C13a South-West Midland group. Each period/dialect text group is given a single PFP as if it were one long text. These PFPs are printed in Appendix B, and should be referred to as we go along the following sections. The following sections summarise the dialect-by-dialect developments.

3 Textual Evidence   55

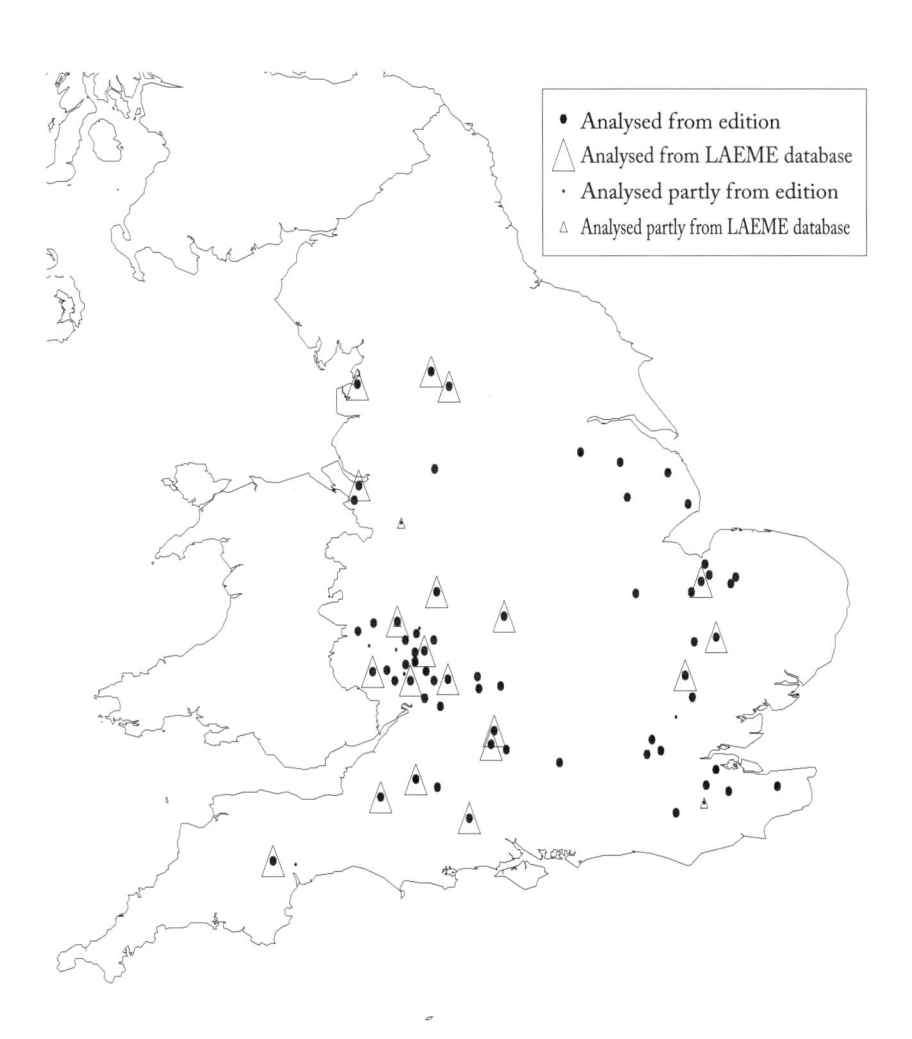

Figure 3.1: Localisation of Examined Texts

Table 3.1: Text Groups according to Period/Dialect

	C9a	C9b	C10a	C10b	C11a	C11b	C12a	C12b	C13a	C13b	C14a	C14b	C15a	TOTAL
N			#17000						#231	#296 #297	#298			5
NEM								#29000		#15 #128 #159	#129			5
SEM							#16000	#4 #149 #1200 #1300	#13 #64 #138	#11 #137 #150 #155 #175 #269 #270 #285 #1400	#25000			18
NWM									#16 #118 #122 #124	#136				5
SWM	#12000	#13000	#11000					#5 #170 #189 #2000 #2001 #10000 #14000	#6 #7 #20 #146 #245 #260 #261 #262 #272 #273 #1800 #1900	#2 #3 #10 #126 #158 #187 #214 #218 #220 #222 #229 #238 #246 #247 #248 #249 #264 #271 #278 #1100 #2002	#125 #27000			45
SW								#63	#144 #156 #157 #26000	#163 #263	#140 #258 #286	#24000	#23000	12
SE									#8 #17 #67 #142		#291 #21000		#20000	7
TOTAL	1	1	2	0	0	0	1	13	28	38	10	1	2	97

Notes: The figures represent Text IDs. Some of the texts are conflations of shorter texts. For the list of the texts, see Appendix A.

3.2.2 Northern Text Group

Table 3.2: Statistical Summary for Northern

	C10a	C13a	C13b	C14a
tokens	498	14	509	398
types	195	11	155	97
syncretism rate	NA	1	0.93	0.98
(spread) rate of s	0.36 (1.1)	0.91 (0)	0.85 (2.5)	0.8 (2.3)
(spread) rate of n	0.0051 (0.05)	0 (0)	0.019 (0.14)	0.01 (0.077)
(spread) rate of V	0.5 (1.7)	0 (0)	0.039 (0.14)	0.041 (0.17)
(spread) rate of $\emptyset$	0.12 (0.5)	0 (0)	0.065 (0.34)	0.1 (0.53)
(spread) rate of M	0.01 (0.33)	0.091 (1)	0.032 (0.63)	0.041 (0.5)

Notes: s, n, V, $\emptyset$, and M represent s-, n-, vowel-, $\emptyset$-, and minor plural types respectively. Figures in parentheses represent "spread rate" as distinct from simple "(type) rate." The syncretism rate appears as "NA" when there are no examples from dative environments. The spread rate appears as "NA" when there are no examples in text that historically took that plural type.

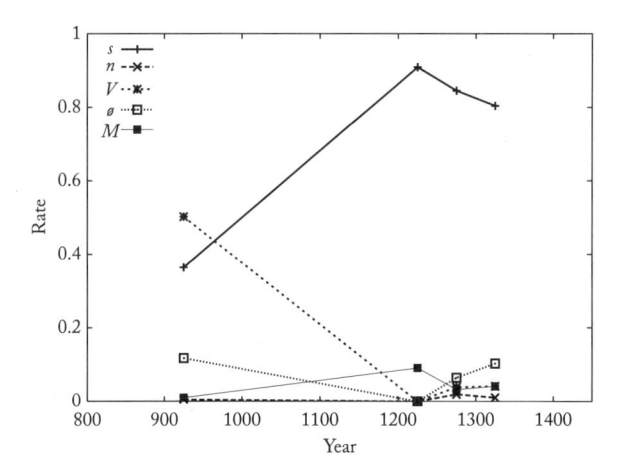

Figure 3.2: Rate for Northern

For Northern, three Early Middle English subperiods are compared. In addition I analysed a pre-Early Middle English northern plural system in the mid-tenth century Northumbrian gloss to *the Lindisfarne Gospel according to Saint Matthew* (ed. Skeat [Text ID #17000]) to make a slightly wider diachronic comparison between Late Old English and Early Middle English.

The most remarkable feature of the Late Old English Northumbrian dialect is the near-total absence of the n-plural. Most of the historical weak nouns either lost the final n or transferred to s-plurals. The plural system was thus made up of -*s* and -*V*. Toward Early Middle English the spread of -*s* accelerated while the *V*-plural became increasingly dysfunctional in distinguishing number.

The rate for -*s* was somewhat on the decrease in the course of Early Middle English, but the figures here may well be skewed due to scanty evidence from C13a. This aside, the data clearly point to the dominant status of the *s*-plural in this dialect. There still survived a few non-*s* plurals (e.g. plurals for Old English *hand*, *sunu*, *gēar*, *þing*, *fōt*, *mann*, and *bōc*), but we can safely say that the Northern dialect had nearly achieved the Modern English plural system by the Early Middle English period.

3.2.3 North-East Midland Text Group

Table 3.3: Statistical Summary for North-East Midland

	C12b	C13b	C14a
tokens	1828	5	1
types	192	4	1
syncretism rate	0.64	1	NA
(spread) rate of *s*	0.82 (2.5)	0.75 (3)	1 (1)
(spread) rate of *n*	0.021 (0.15)	0 (0)	0 (0)
(spread) rate of *V*	0.078 (0.3)	0 (0)	0 (0)
(spread) rate of *ø*	0.063 (0.28)	0 (0)	0 (0)
(spread) rate of *M*	0.021 (0.4)	0.25 (1)	0 (0)

Notes: *s*, *n*, *V*, *ø*, and *M* represent *s*-, *n*-, vowel-, *ø*-, and minor plural types respectively. Figures in parentheses represent "spread rate" as distinct from simple "(type) rate." The syncretism rate appears as "NA" when there are no examples from dative environments. The spread rate appears as "NA" when there are no examples in text that historically took that plural type.

The C12b North-East Midland data are sizeably represented by *The Ormulum* (ed. Holt [Text ID #29000]), but the other analysed periods do not produce many examples. The evidence from *The Ormulum* shows how far this dialect had advanced early on. By *ca.* 1200 the *s*-plural became the single dominant plural marker.

The small number of *V*- or *ø*-plurals surviving in *The Ormulum* include *shulldre*, *ahhte*, *cullfre*, *le(o)de*, *mile*, *þe(o)de*, *hande*; *lac*, *nowwt*, *deor* or *der*, *ȝer*, and *hunndredd*. The only surviving *n*-plurals in the text are *hewenn*, *wawenn*, and *eȝhne*.

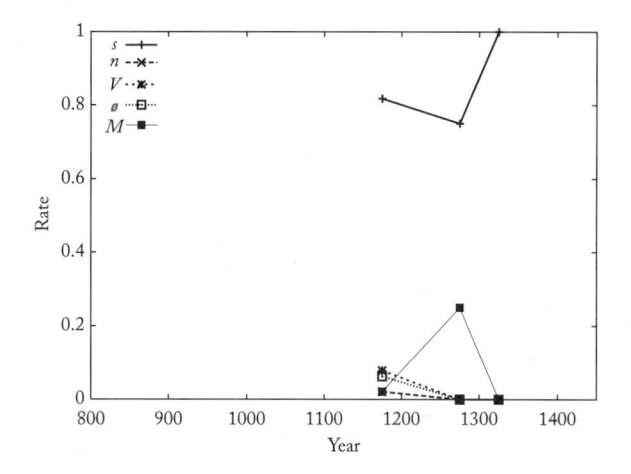

Figure 3.3: Rate for North-East Midland

3.2.4 South-East Midland Text Group

Table 3.4: Statistical Summary for South-East Midland

	C12a	C12b	C13a	C13b	C14a
tokens	146	1237	163	1323	102
types	75	287	63	315	43
syncretism rate	0	0.5	0.77	0.68	0.96
(spread) rate of s	0.6 (1.3)	0.59 (1.8)	0.75 (2)	0.74 (2.1)	0.77 (1.6)
(spread) rate of n	0.027 (0.25)	0.14 (0.76)	0.16 (3.3)	0.086 (0.47)	0.047 (0.5)
(spread) rate of V	0.2 (1.1)	0.19 (0.69)	0.048 (0.17)	0.089 (0.38)	0.047 (0.33)
(spread) rate of $ø$	0.13 (0.71)	0.066 (0.41)	0.016 (0.071)	0.063 (0.34)	0.07 (0.33)
(spread) rate of M	0.04 (0.75)	0.014 (0.31)	0.032 (0.5)	0.019 (0.38)	0.07 (1)

Notes: s, n, V, $ø$, and M represent s-, n-, vowel-, $ø$-, and minor plural types respectively. Figures in parentheses represent "spread rate" as distinct from simple "(type) rate." The syncretism rate appears as "NA" when there are no examples from dative environments. The spread rate appears as "NA" when there are no examples in text that historically took that plural type.

The C12a South-East Midland text group shows that the s-plural was growing steadily. The major source of innovative s-plurals was Neut-Ø, but some Fem-V nouns also contributed to the spread of -s. The other nouns of these two classes and the Neut-V nouns tended either to stay unchanged or to change over to -n or -V. The latter two endings were often interchangeable.

The C12a South-East Midland evidence may bring us to predict a further growth of -s for the following periods, but it is important to note that at this early stage plural formation transfer was multi-directional. In C12b -s kept

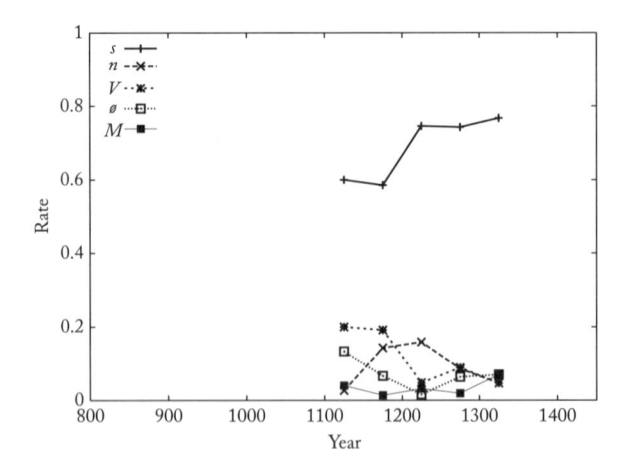

Figure 3.4: Rate for South-East Midland

spreading, attracting more Neut-V, Fem-V, and Neut-Ø nouns.

In C13a the spread of -s proceeded further. The dominance of -s was such that other plural formations such as -V and -ø were overshadowed. By C13b -s nearly finished its growth, with only a few nouns of the minor plural formation remaining. This state continued into C14a and thereafter.

The spread rates indicate that not only -s but also -n were spreading. We even find a number of Masc-S nouns that changed to -n or -V (e.g. *Wealan, calicen, gersuman; clerca, gærsuma, heðene, muneca, ræde, siþe*). Remember that the spread of -n was not known either to Northern or North-East Midland.

In C13a, -n revived slightly from the preceding period with a few innovative n-plurals, e.g. ȝaten (OE Neut-V *geat*), leme(n) (OE Masc-N *lēoma*), pine(n) (OE Fem-V *pīn*), senne(n) (OE Fem-V *synn*), ȝekynde(n) (OE Neut-Ø *cynd*), and wundren (OE Neut-Ø *wundor*).

The spread rate of -n may be a little exaggerated by the fact that the texts contain only a few weak nouns, but the revitalisation of -n was closely connected with the fall of -V and -ø. It is interesting that the n- and V-lines cross in C12b, which indicates that some of the V-plurals were taken over by -n.

After its short-lived revival in C13a, -n resumed its decline under pressure of the steadily growing -s, and finally bottomed out in C13b. As for the ø-plural, it was steadily diminishing through the Early Middle English period. Many historical ø-plurals were gradually taken over by -s, -n, or -V.

In sum, the South-East Midland development may be described as a series of processes—the ever increasing -s, the taking over of ø-plurals by -s, -n, or -V, the interchange between -n and -V, the short-term boom of -n, and the final decline of -n under pressure of -s. This chain of processes was repeated in other southern dialects.

3.2.5 North-West Midland Text Group

Table 3.5: Statistical Summary for North-West Midland

	C13a	C13b
tokens	535	52
types	167	41
syncretism rate	0.87	1
(spread) rate of s	0.8 (2.7)	0.95 (2)
(spread) rate of n	0.03 (0.19)	0 (0)
(spread) rate of V	0.084 (0.26)	0.024 (0.2)
(spread) rate of $ø$	0.06 (0.34)	0 (0)
(spread) rate of M	0.024 (0.5)	0.024 (1)

Notes: s, n, V, $ø$, and M represent s-, n-, vowel-, $ø$-, and minor plural types respectively. Figures in parentheses represent "spread rate" as distinct from simple "(type) rate." The syncretism rate appears as "NA" when there are no examples from dative environments. The spread rate appears as "NA" when there are no examples in text that historically took that plural type.

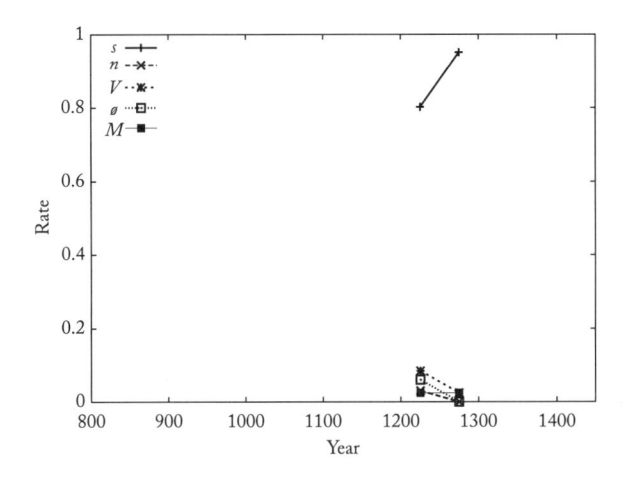

Figure 3.5: Rate for North-West Midland

Only two subperiods are represented in this dialect and those only poorly. Close diachronic analysis is therefore impossible; however, extrapolating from the neighbouring North-East Midland and South-West Midland configurations, it seems that the dominant status of -s had been well established by C13a. In this dialect the major changeover in plural formation seems to have finished some time before 1200.

3.2.6 South-West Midland Text Group

Table 3.6: Statistical Summary for South-West Midland

	C9a	C9b	C10a	C12b	C13a	C13b	C14a
tokens	183	48	484	1251	2550	1139	105
types	86	35	162	311	434	269	36
syncretism rate	0.15	0.038	NA	0.25	0.56	0.48	0.97
(spread) rate of s	0.3 (0.93)	0.34 (1)	0.32 (1.1)	0.38 (1.1)	0.53 (1.7)	0.59 (1.7)	0.78 (1.9)
(spread) rate of n	0.13 (1.2)	0.11 (0.8)	0.068 (0.42)	0.24 (1.5)	0.27 (1.5)	0.2 (1.4)	0.056 (0.5)
(spread) rate of V	0.28 (1)	0.37 (1.2)	0.36 (1.3)	0.23 (0.91)	0.13 (0.47)	0.11 (0.41)	0.083 (0.27)
(spread) rate of $ø$	0.22 (1)	0.11 (0.8)	0.22 (1)	0.11 (0.58)	0.053 (0.27)	0.086 (0.43)	0.028 (0.33)
(spread) rate of M	0.07 (0.86)	0.057 (1)	0.031 (0.63)	0.035 (0.85)	0.016 (0.47)	0.011 (0.23)	0.056 (0.67)

Notes: s, n, V, $ø$, and M represent s-, n-, vowel-, $ø$-, and minor plural types respectively. Figures in parentheses represent "spread rate" as distinct from simple "(type) rate." The syncretism rate appears as "NA" when there are no examples from dative environments. The spread rate appears as "NA" when there are no examples in text that historically took that plural type.

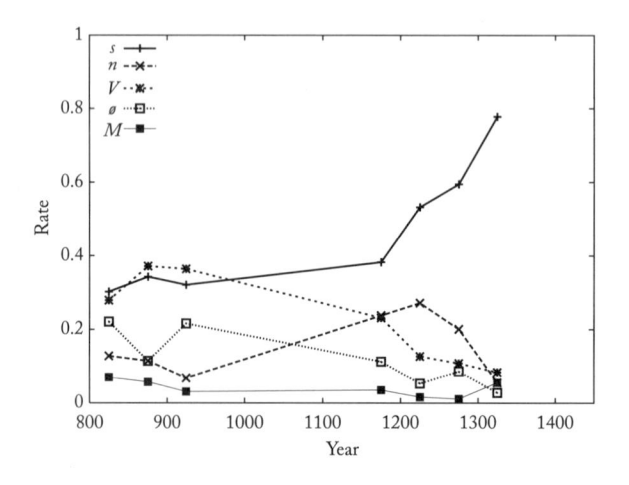

Figure 3.6: Rate for South-West Midland

The South-West Midland dialect is the richest in evidence, so there is good chance that diachronic analysis can reveal linguistic development in detail. In addition to texts from the core Early Middle English period, I analyse three texts from the Old English period for a longer-range diachronic comparison: the C9a *Vespasian Psalter Gloss* (ed. Sweet [Text ID #12000]), the C9b *Life of St Chad* (ed. Vleeskruyer [Text ID #13000]), and the Mercian part of the C10a2 *Rushworth Gloss to the Gospel according to Saint Matthew* (ed. Skeat [Text ID #11000]; hereafter cited as *Ru1*).[29]

The *Vespasian Psalter*, surviving in Cotton Vespasian A. I, is glossed in the West Mercian dialect of Old English in "a very fine hand, which cannot well be earlier or later than the first half of the ninth century" (Sweet 184). I collected examples from the first forty pages of Sweet's edition.

The nominal inflections in this text are hardly different from those in common West-Saxon texts. There are a few points to be made, however. First, there is an instance of *wines* for Latin *vini*. This Old English noun usually inflected as a strong neuter, the plural form being *wīn*. The *s*-form in the text was perhaps one of the earliest instances of transfer to -*s* in Old English Mercian, and came straight down to the later periods, seeing that the *s*-form is the only accepted plural in the *Ancrene Wisse/Riwle* as in "ouer alle wines."

The text shows no fluctuation in plural endings except for *strelas* ~ *strele*. In the part I analysed there are two instances of the former form and one of the latter. They all appear as accusative plurals in comparable contexts and serve as glosses for Latin *sagittas*. According to Vleeskruyer, this noun was originally a feminine (128). Assuming the feminine origin, we may say that the two instances of *strelas* attest the earliest spread of the *s*-plural in Old English Mercian. Another Old English Mercian text, the *Life of St Chad*, also gives *strelas*, while its textually associated Old English version of Bede's *History* gives *stræle* in the corresponding line. The use of the *s*-plural may thus be characteristic of the Old English Mercian dialect.

Now let us look more closely at the *Life of St Chad*. Agreeing with Napier, Vleeskruyer described the language of the *Life of St Chad* as "fundamentally Mercian, with some admixture of LOE. elements" (38). The text thus gives us two types of evidence, one for the Old English Mercian dialect in C9b and the other for the Late West Saxon dialect sporadically introduced by the scribe in C12a (the proposed date of the manuscript). Although the brevity of the text does not promise many examples, they will give hints for discerning the diachronic/dialectal gap between the C9 Mercian dialect and the C12a West-Saxon dialect.

Most of the nominative/accusative plurals follow the inflectional pattern that would be expected of the Late West-Saxon dialect. However, there are a few usages that seem peculiar to Old English Mercian. One such peculiarity is found in the inflections of *lufu*. The word occurs five times in the oblique case with *-n* apparently as a weak noun rather than as a strong noun. All the instances are singular, but we may suspect that the nominative/accusative plural would also take *-n*. In West-Saxon the noun was usually an $\bar{o}$-stem feminine, whereas in non-West-Saxon dialects it typically inflected weak (Vleeskruyer 133). As if to inherit this characteristic, all the Early Middle English texts from the South-West Midland dialect indeed show only *n*-plurals for the word.

Another possibly Old English Mercian usage in the text is represented by two instances of *lyftas* in lines 164 and 170. In West-Saxon, the noun normally occurred as a feminine.

On the other hand, there are some forms possibly attributed to the scribe's own C12a West-Saxon dialect. One of the examples that Vleeskruyer gives is one-off *lægetas* (as a *ja*-stem masc.) beside *legeto* (as a *ja*-stem neut.) occurring twice. Let us see how they occur in context (emphasis added).

- **lægetas** on eorðan. ꝫ lyftas þreadon. (lines 163–64)
- he gemonigfaldað **legeto**. (lines 169–70)
- he sceotað **legeto**. (line 171)

If we look at the corresponding lines of Bede's Old English *History*, the three instances occur as *legete*, *legetas*, and *legetas* respectively. There is a line from the *Vespasian Psalter* similar to the second quotation above: "legite gemonigfaldade." If we assume, as Vleeskruyer does, the *s*-form to be the scribe's own usage, the spread of the *s*-plural may have reached this particular noun sometime in the latest Old English period (127).

Another instance of possible scribal "slips" occurs in "heofones ꝫ eorðan beornendu*m*" (line 176). This is an absolute dative construction which corresponds to an absolute ablative construction in Bede's Latin *Historia*, which goes "caelis ac terris ardentibus." The literal translation of the first word should be *heofonum* instead of *heofones*. In fact the corresponding line of Bede's Old English *History* reads "heofonum ꝸ eorðan byrnen-dum." Vleeskruyer explained the form *heofones* in question as the scribe's own Middle English form, suggesting that case syncretism between the accusative and the dative was already going on (126).

A final example of possible scribal "slips" is *broðore* (line 70), which is used plurally beside *broðru* (lines 75 and 113) and *broðra* (line 122). Vleeskruyer explained the form *broðore* as a transitional spelling to the Early Middle English *brōðere* (134). It may be noted that one of the later texts of the dialect, the *Lambeth Homilies* (*ca.* 1200), shows an *re*-ending for the word frequently.

Finally for analysis of the Old English texts, I briefly comment on the nominal plurals in *Ru1*. The distribution of plural endings is not so greatly different from that in the common West-Saxon dialect, but there are two important features not found in it. The first is the tendency for the *n*-ending to be lacking in weak nouns. This tendency is especially remarkable in the masculine. Of seventeen unique weak masculines, only four retain *-n*. Taking account of all the genders together, more than two thirds of the historical weak nouns are *n*-less in the plural.

The second point is that the *s*-ending extends to historically unexpected classes of nouns. Examples are *burgas*, *cæstras*, *degles*, *feondas*, *fiondas*, *godspelles*, *huses*, *settlas*, *setulas*, *spearwas*, *stigas*, *sunas*, *weardas*, *wines*, and *wudehuniges*. The number of nouns that transferred to *-s* may not be very large, but these examples show that this was a preliminary stage to the spread of *-s* in Early Middle English.

Having said that, plural formation transfer was not limited to *-s*. There are several examples of transfer away from *-s*, e.g. *þeof* (beside *þeofes*), *lateuw* (beside *latewas*), *bocera*, and *riftra*.

Now that we have analysed the three Late Old English texts, let us move on to Early Middle English evidence. In the C12b text group, Neut-Ø nouns show multi-directional changeover. They either remained unchanged or changed to *-s*, *-V*, or *-n* in order of decreasing frequency. Most of the Fem-V nouns fluctuated between *-V* and *-n*, while a few of them changed over to *-s*. The same fluctuation is observed for historical *n*-plurals. Only a couple of historical

n-plurals are found to have changed to -s.

In C12b -s was surely spreading, but its spread rate was not particularly high. In contrast, -n was growing quite remarkably. The growth of -n was largely because many historical V- or $\emptyset$-plurals changed over to -n while only a few historical n-plurals transferred away.

The situation in C13a was a continuation of that in C12b. -s and -n were now dominant while -V and -$\emptyset$ were overshadowed. Fluctuation between -V and -n was still in evidence, but mostly -n took a stronger position. The largest source of new s-plurals was Neut-$\emptyset$ nouns, but an increasing number of Fem-V nouns also changed over to -s. All these changeovers were leading to a new plural system based on the two endings -s and -n.

The following C13b period was again a continuation of the preceding period with little change. It seems as if distribution in the plural system had hardly changed over the last half century. Such a standstill may be interpreted as the plural system having reached a "saturated" state in C13. I say saturated because in C13 the plural system was so stabilised on the two plural formations -s and n that no systemic optimisation was felt necessary. From a functional point of view, it was as perfect as the modern plural system where -s is the single dominant plural formation.

This peacefully "saturated" state might be a reason for the lack of significant change in the C13 South-West Midland plural system, but the changeless system may be more apparent than real. Although the South-West Midland plural system looks changeless through C13 as long as we judge from the figures based on written language, yet the corresponding system in speech was probably less "neat" and more variable depending on communities, individuals, social classes, and pragmatic situations. The plural systems which we recognise in the C13 South-West Midland written texts seem too "neat" to be real.

The "saturated" and "neat-looking" C13 system, however, was disturbed in C14a. The C14a text group shows that the rate of -n dropped dramatically. Now *feren* was the only instance of the n-plural, and the three other historical n-plurals occurred without -n (i.e. *felawes*, *tyme*, and *belle*).[30] In view of the systemic stability in C13b, the C14a drop of -n may be surprising. This dramatic fall of -n, however, is probably exaggerated in written language. It is likely either that the drop of -n in speech was more moderate than the figures (for written language) suggest, or that the "neat" C13 system simply masked the fact that the drop of -n was already going on in the C13 South-West Midland spoken variety, which is more directly represented in the C14 texts than in the C13 texts.

The sudden decline of -n as well as the steady decline of -V and -$\emptyset$ in C14 means that an s-dominant system was emerging. Soon afterwards -s finally won over all the lesser plural types, forming the basis for the Modern English plural system.

After all, -s was always far stronger than -n, but the fact that there was ever a period during which the spread of -s in this dialect levelled off is noteworthy in that no other dialect experienced comparable developments.

3.2.7 Southwestern Text Group

Table 3.7: Statistical Summary for Southwestern

	C12b	C13a	C13b	C14a	C14b	C15a
tokens	10	116	4	564	834	380
types	8	42	4	114	132	80
syncretism rate	0.67	0.73	0.5	0.83	0.94	0.87
(spread) rate of s	0.13 (0)	0.71 (1.9)	0.5 (2)	0.61 (1.5)	0.85 (2.2)	0.84 (2.2)
(spread) rate of n	0.38 (1.5)	0.095 (0.67)	0.25 (1)	0.21 (1.6)	0.045 (0.24)	0.063 (1)
(spread) rate of V	0.25 (0)	0.095 (0.36)	0 (0)	0.079 (0.38)	0.015 (0.065)	0.05 (0.18)
(spread) rate of $\emptyset$	0.25 (0.4)	0.071 (0.5)	0 (0)	0.079 (0.43)	0.061 (0.4)	0.025 (0.12)
(spread) rate of M	0 (0)	0.024 (0.33)	0.25 (1)	0.026 (0.38)	0.03 (0.67)	0.025 (0.4)

Notes: s, n, V, $\emptyset$, and M represent s-, n-, vowel-, $\emptyset$-, and minor plural types respectively. Figures in parentheses represent "spread rate" as distinct from simple "(type) rate." The syncretism rate appears as "NA" when there are no examples from dative environments. The spread rate appears as "NA" when there are no examples in text that historically took that plural type.

A diachronic summary of this dialect may not be entirely reliable because some subperiods are underrepresented. Some time before C13a there seems to have been a period when -s was spreading in an S-curve, but after this, the pace of change for this dialect slowed down.

A shortage of evidence from the C13b to C14b text groups makes it hard to see how the plural system developed in the intermediate period. One possible account for the plural system looking hardly changed is that there was actually little significant development taking place. Another possible account is that, after frequent but small-scaled multi-directional changeovers of plural types, the C15a configuration happens to look as if there had been little development

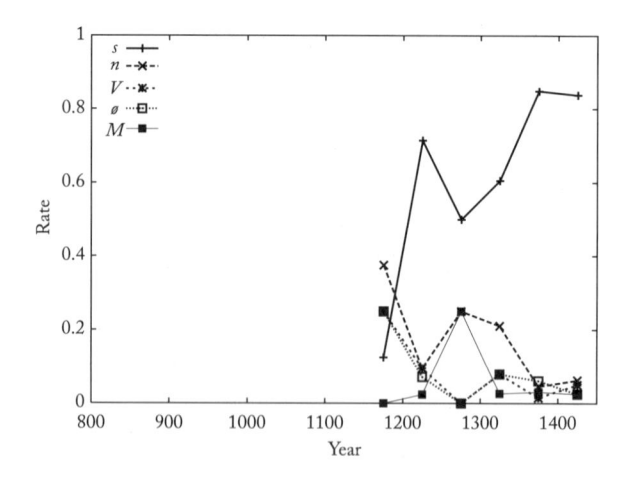

Figure 3.7: Rate for Southwestern

since C13a.

The latter interpretation is the more attractive, considering that the neighbouring South-West Midland dialect seems to have developed in a comparable way from C13a to C14a. Lack of evidence, however, must leave this interpretation open.

3.2.8 Southeastern Text Group

Table 3.8: Statistical Summary for Southeastern

	C13a	C14a	C15a
tokens	184	535	50
types	67	107	16
syncretism rate	0.76	0.9	0.46
(spread) rate of s	0.57 (1.7)	0.8 (2)	0.75 (2)
(spread) rate of n	0.21 (1.4)	0.1 (1.1)	0.13 (1)
(spread) rate of V	0.1 (0.3)	0.019 (0.087)	0.13 (0.5)
(spread) rate of $\emptyset$	0.1 (0.88)	0.056 (0.24)	0 (0)
(spread) rate of M	0.015 (0.33)	0.019 (0.4)	0 (0)

Notes: s, n, V, $\emptyset$, and M represent s-, n-, vowel-, $\emptyset$-, and minor plural types respectively. Figures in parentheses represent "spread rate" as distinct from simple "(type) rate." The syncretism rate appears as "NA" when there are no examples from dative environments. The spread rate appears as "NA" when there are no examples in text that historically took that plural type.

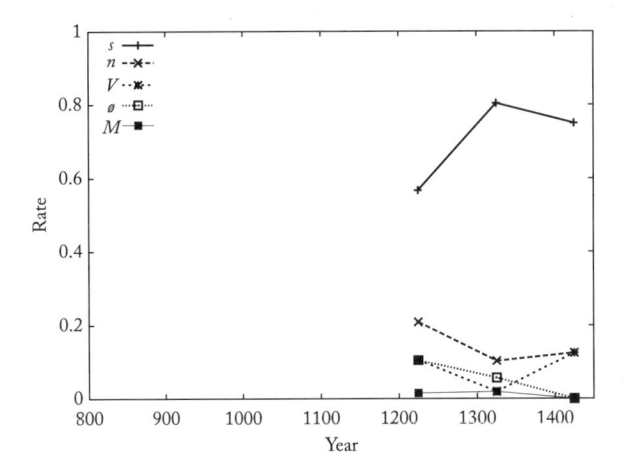

Figure 3.8: Rate for Southeastern

In the C13a Southeastern text group, we find innovative s-plurals from Masc-N, Fem-N, Neut-V, Fem-V, and Neut-Ø nouns. Some Fem-V nouns changed over to -n, increasing the rate for -n. Unlike the growing -s and -n, the V-plural was dramatically reduced. All in all, the situation was not very different from the contemporary South-East Midland and South-West Midland.

The C14a text group shows a continuing development from the preceding period as far as -s is concerned. It continued to grow by swallowing V- and ø-plurals. As for -n, there were a few additions from Fem-V and Neut-Ø, but they were offset by other changeovers.

The C15a situation represents a natural consequence of the developments in the preceding periods. Despite rather poor evidence in C15a, we can infer that -s was established as the dominant plural type.

Although the dialect is too underrepresented to give a detailed diachronic picture, it seems that this dialect experienced a major spread of -n before C13a but afterwards -n was in gradual decline, whereas the growth of -s continued unceasingly through the Early Middle English period.

Type rates for this dialect and the neighbouring Southwestern may be compared. In Southwestern -s was rising steadily and -n was declining gradually. Roughly the same was the case with the Southeastern group, but the ascending and descending curves were more gentle for Southeastern. We may say that Southeastern repeated a more gentle version of the South-East Midland development about a half century later.

3.2.9 Panchronic Summary of Plural Formation Transfer

In the preceding sections I showed diachronic developments of the plural types by period/dialect text group. It is time to make a "panchronic" summary out of the findings about each period/dialect.[31] I have constructed tables and graphs which show panchronically the type rates and spread rates for each of the five plural types. They are all available in Appendix C, but it will be useful here to print those for the spread rates of the two major endings -s and -n (see pages 71 and 72 respectively).

When we look at the spread rate graph for -s on page 71, most of the dialects follow curves roughly parallel to each other in the C12b to C13b range. If we leave North-West Midland and Southwestern out of account for the moment (because they are rather underrepresented), the highest scoring dialect in the range is North-East Midland, followed by South-East Midland, Southeastern and South-West Midland in that order. Dialects repeated the development of their immediate neighbours.

The spread rate graph for -n on page 72 is more difficult to read. This is because while -s was almost always growing in every dialect, -n was growing or declining depending on dialect and/or period. All the southern dialects experienced a short period when the spread rate for -n scored above 1.0. In contrast, the northern dialects always kept the spread rate for -n below 1.0, indicating that -n was in constant decline.

The spread rate graphs for -V, -$\emptyset$, and minor plural types (available on pages 224–26 in Appendix C) indicate that they hardly ever extended beyond their original share.

After all the observations it is possible to propose a pattern in which the plural system was reorganised from Old English to Early Middle English. Let me propose seven stages in the reorganisation process.

1. the ubiquitous spread of -s

2. the transfer of -$\emptyset$ to -s, -n, or -V

3. interchange between -n and -V

4. the disuse of -V

5. a short-term boom for -n

6. the decline of -n under pressure of -s

7. the establishment of -s as the dominant plural type

Not every stage of the development may be represented where data are meagre or where the reorganisation of the plural system took place within a fairly short period of time. North-West Midland and North-East Midland are the cases in point. In the northern dialects, the establishment of the s-dominant plural system took place so quickly that our analysis can only report the result of reorganisation instead of its progress. It may be that in the northern dialects, Stages 2 to 6 passed so quickly or were even skipped so completely before any amount of surviving evidence became available that we can only see

Table 3.9: Spread Rate for -s

	C9a	C9b	C10a	C10b	C11a	C11b	C12a	C12b	C13a	C13b	C14a	C14b	C15a
N	—	—	1.1	—	—	—	—	—	—	2.5	2.3	—	—
NEM	—	—	—	—	—	—	—	2.5	—	3	1	—	—
SEM	—	—	—	—	—	—	1.3	1.8	2	2.1	1.6	—	—
NWM	—	—	—	—	—	—	—	—	2.7	2	—	—	—
SWM	0.93	1	1.1	—	—	—	—	1.1	1.7	1.7	1.9	—	—
SW	—	—	—	—	—	—	—	—	1.8	2	1.5	2.2	2.2
SE	—	—	—	—	—	—	—	—	1.6	—	2	—	2

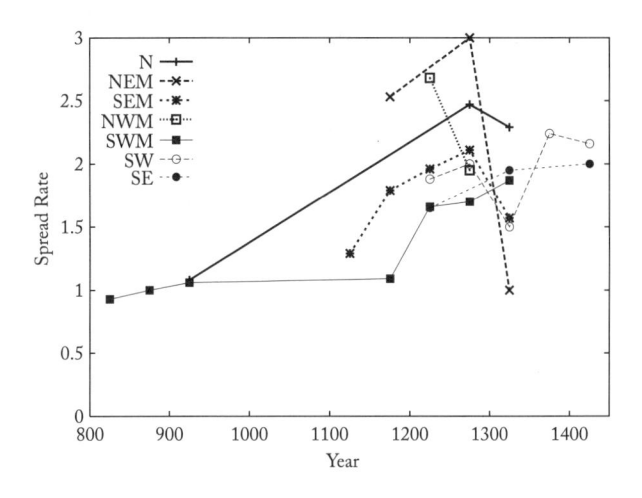

Figure 3.9: Spread Rate for -s

Table 3.10: Spread Rate for -n

	C9a	C9b	C10a	C10b	C11a	C11b	C12a	C12b	C13a	C13b	C14a	C14b	C15a
N	—	—	0.05	—	—	—	—	—	0	0.14	0.077	—	—
NEM	—	—	—	—	—	—	—	0.15	—	—	—	—	—
SEM	—	—	—	—	—	—	0.25	0.76	3.3	0.47	0.5	—	—
NWM	—	—	—	—	—	—	—	—	0.19	0	—	—	—
SWM	1.2	0.8	0.42	—	—	—	—	1.5	1.5	1.4	0.5	—	—
SW	—	—	—	—	—	—	—	1.5	0.67	1	1.6	0.24	1
SE	—	—	—	—	—	—	—	—	1.4	—	1.1	—	1

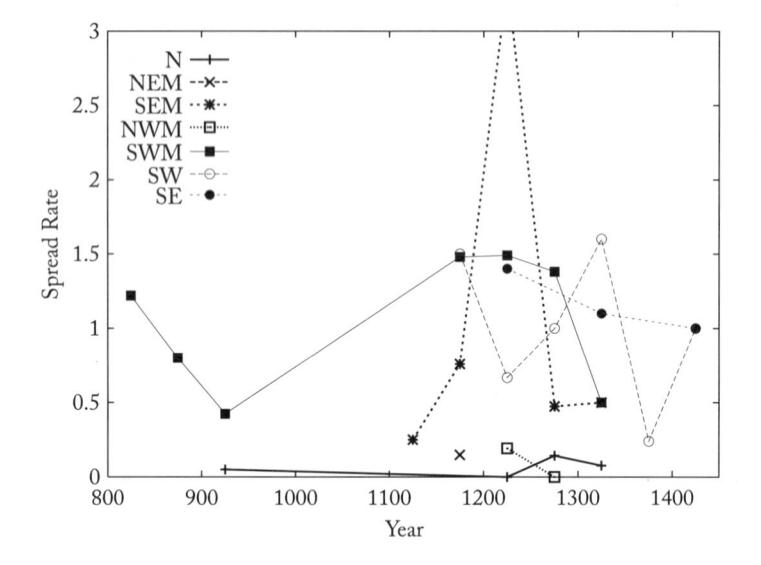

Figure 3.10: Spread Rate for -n

by the earliest Early Middle English evidence that Stages 6 and 7 are already underway. In contrast, in the South-West Midland dialect, all seven stages are fairly well represented. The dialect took such a long time before establishing the s-dominant plural system that individual stages can be easily recognised.

The seven stages are theoretical, and we should not assume that they passed exactly in the designated order or in every dialect. In light of the large evidence as panchronically sorted out, however, they should represent the most likely course of the development in many dialects.

3.3 Item-Based Study

We have so far seen the development of the plural system by period/dialect, but it can also be seen in terms of individual items since plural formation transfer varied according to individual item as well as according to period and dialect. I cannot investigate all items but must select a number of key items to focus on.

Key items should ideally fulfil two conditions. First, they should be common enough to appear in any text, period, and dialect. This is to ensure comparability across texts, periods, and dialects. Ideal key items should also show some degree of variation in plural formation not only based on text, period and dialect but also within the same group of texts. In reality, however, there are not many items that fulfil both conditions. Therefore, I set these conditions rather loosely in selecting key items.

I have thus selected sixty-six key items. They are listed below in order of the Old English reference class as introduced in Section 3.1.4: that is, Masc-S, Masc-N, Neut-N, Fem-N, Masc-V, Neut-V, Fem-V, Masc-Ø, Neut-Ø, Fem-Ø, Masc-M, Neut-M, and Fem-M. The Item Profiles for the key items are printed in Appendix E, and should be referred to as we go along the following sections.

1. blōstm (Masc-S)
2. dēofol (Masc-S)
3. sīþ (Masc-S)
4. fāh (Masc-N)
5. fēolaga (Masc-N)
6. fēra (Masc-N)
7. hālga (Masc-N)
8. hīwan (Masc-N)
9. nama (Masc-N)
10. steorra (Masc-N)
11. tīma (Masc-N)
12. wræcca (Masc-N)
13. ēage (Neut-N)
14. ēare (Neut-N)
15. cirice (Fem-N)
16. heorte (Fem-N)
17. hlæfdige (Fem-N)
18. mæsse (Fem-N)
19. nædre (Fem-N)
20. sunu (Masc-V)
21. bed (Neut-V)
22. bod (Neut-V)
23. geat (Neut-V)
24. lim (Neut-V)
25. mægden (Neut-V)
26. writ (Neut-V)
27. yfel (Neut-V)
28. -ung (Fem-V)
29. bēn (Fem-V)
30. bliss (Fem-V)
31. dǣd (Fem-V)
32. giefu (Fem-V)
33. hæs (Fem-V)
34. hand (Fem-V)
35. lagu (Fem-V)
36. lufu (Fem-V)
37. miht (Fem-V)
38. pīn (Fem-V)
39. sāwol (Fem-V)
40. synn (Fem-V)
41. wund (Fem-V)
42. brōþor (Masc-Ø)
43. bān (Neut-Ø)
44. bearn (Neut-Ø)
45. cynn (Neut-Ø)
46. dēor (Neut-Ø)
47. gēar (Neut-Ø)
48. gōd (Neut-Ø)
49. hors (Neut-Ø)
50. hundred (Neut-Ø)
51. land (Neut-Ø)
52. scēap (Neut-Ø)
53. trēow (Neut-Ø)
54. þing (Neut-Ø)
55. wǣpen (Neut-Ø)
56. wæter (Neut-Ø)
57. weorc (Neut-Ø)

58. wīf (Neut-Ø) 61. word (Neut-Ø) 64. frēond (Masc-M)
59. winter (Neut-Ø) 62. sweostor (Fem-Ø) 65. cild (Neut-M)
60. witt (Neut-Ø) 63. fēond (Masc-M) 66. niht (Fem-M)

3.3.1 Masc-S Nouns

The item *blōstm* is treated here as a Masc-S noun, but in Old English it alternatively took -*V* (as a Fem-V) or -*n* (as a Masc-N) in the plural.[32] Therefore it is not surprising at all to find variation in the plural formation in Early Middle English texts. -*s* appeared in Northern, South-East Midland and North-West Midland, but in South-East Midland -*V* and -*n* occurred beside -*s*. -*s* was not attested for this item in the analysed South-West Midland texts.

dēofol is another item which had varying plural forms from Old English to Early Middle English. In Old English this item took either -*s* or -*V*, but -*n* became widely used in the southern dialects in Early Middle English. It appears that in South-East Midland and North-West Midland -*s* was established earlier than in South-West Midland.

sīþ was frequently used in Old English in its dative case (e.g. *fēower sīþum*), therefore the *V*-ending derived from -*um* was common beside -*s* in Early Middle English . -*V* was only maintained vestigially early in the northern and eastern dialects, whereas in South-West Midland and Southeastern it survived into later Early Middle English.

3.3.2 Masc-N Nouns

fāh is among the few weak nouns that long resisted changeover to -*s*.[33] *N*-forms persisted in every text, period, and dialect. As Roedler pointed out (2: 429), the vowel-ending monosyllabics tended to preserve -*n* for a considerable time.

In items such as *fēra*, *hālga*, *nama*, *steorra*, and *tīma*, the innovative *s*-form developed early in the northern dialects, whereas the old *n*- or the reduced *V*-form persisted long in the southern dialects.

A few Masc-N nouns such as *fēolaga*[34] and *wræcca* transferred nearly completely to -*s* before the Early Middle English period.

3.3.3 Neut-N Nouns

In South-West Midland -V could be used for $\bar{e}age$ beside more common -n. This is an example to show that variation between -n and -V lingered in the southern dialects, whereas in the northern dialects it was rare.

$\bar{e}are$ was another Neut-N item of equally common nature. Although this item was conservative like $\bar{e}age$, a strong tendency toward -s is evidenced in the C13a North-West Midland dialect. This suggests that $\bar{e}are$ accepted -s much earlier than $\bar{e}age$.[35]

3.3.4 Fem-N Nouns

cirice shows a divide between South-East Midland and the more southern/western dialects. In South-East Midland the historical n-ending was replaced by -s as early as C12b, while in the more southern/western dialects it persisted much longer. *nǣdre* shows a similar distribution.

heorte and *mæsse* transferred to -s somewhat earlier both in the northern and the southern dialects, although for *mæsse* the C13b and C14a distributions show heavy fluctuation.

The item *hlǣfdige* never occurred with -n in Early Middle English texts. It is one of the earliest Fem-N items to transfer to -s.

3.3.5 Masc-V Nouns

The Masc-V *sunu* was one of the first nouns to change over to -s. Despite some n-plural instances across the country, -s was widely established as the norm.

3.3.6 Neut-V Nouns

In general, Neut-V nouns persisted in -V, changed to -s or -n, or even became -$\emptyset$.

bed and *bod* show heavy fluctuation in early South-East Midland or South-West Midland between -s, -n and -V. Although -s soon became dominant, the less common alternatives were slow to die.

geat is an interesting example with respect to the timing of transfer. This item occurred with -n in the earliest South-East Midland and South-West Midland dialects, but it was overtaken by -s before long. Surprisingly, transfer to -s took place earlier in South-West Midland than in South-East Midland. This is contrary to the common chronological order of the items that transferred to -*s*. Unlike *geat*, *lim* shows the expected distribution. The *V*-plural was first replaced by -*s* or -*n*, and afterwards -*s* became dominant.

maȝden was rarely attested in the texts analysed from before C13, so its earlier history is unknown. However, the item was certainly one of the first Neut-V nouns to transfer to -*s* throughout the country. Not very different from this was another Neut-V item *writ*. Transfer to -*s* was fairly early, and the *s*-plural was well established except for a few *V*-forms that continued later.

yfel was also among the earliest items to change to -*s*. The first appearance of the *s*-form is evidenced in the C12b South-West Midland dialect and more instances are found in the C13a South-East Midland and North-West Midland dialects. As was the case with *geat*, this is contrary to the expectation that South-East Midland or North-West Midland should show innovative -*s* earlier than South-West Midland. The unexpected distribution may be simply due to chance, but it may as well suggest that the South-West Midland development was independent of the South-East Midland or North-West Midland development and that transfer to -*s* affected different items first in different dialects.

All in all, this class was relatively early in transferring to -*s*.

3.3.7 Fem-V Nouns

Cross-dialectal comparison of the Fem-V nouns again underpins the divide between the northern and southern dialects. In North-East Midland, North-West Midland, and South-East Midland, the spread of -*s* was so quick and early that there was little time for *V*-plurals to change to -*n*, and therefore little chance for fluctuation. On the other hand, in South-West Midland, Southwestern, and Southeastern, the spread of -*s* was so slow and late that there was every chance for fluctuation. They remained unchanged or transferred to -*s* or -*n*.

-*ung* words seem to be among the earliest to change to -*s* in all dialects. They serve as a good example to show how South-West Midland and Southeastern followed in the footsteps of their neighbour South-East Midland. We can visualise an innovative wave running from South-East Midland to South-West Midland and Southeastern as *s*-forms were replacing old *V*-forms. What we see here is a parallel development, with a short time lag, between adjacent dialects. The time lag between the northern and the southern dialects can also be observed in less evidenced items such as *bēn, bliss,* and *giefu*. Like *-ung* words, *miht* was among the earliest to change to *-s*.

dǣd shows heavy fluctuation in C12b and C13a. In South-West Midland the innovative *n*-forms persisted long afterwards, whereas South-East Midland seems to have shifted to *-s* rather quickly. *hǣs* shows rich variation in the southern dialects. There is little northern evidence, making it impossible to compare cross-dialectally.

One of the Fem-V nouns that changed to *-s* very late is *hand*. In most dialects *-n* remained common for a long time, and even in the fairly well developed South-East Midland dialect, the innovative *-s* settled down slowly. It was certainly one of the *n*-plurals most resistant to *-s*. *lagu* is another example that resisted transfer to *-s*. In contrast to early transfer in the northern dialects, in the southern dialects *s*-pluralisation was slow.

lufu, pīn, sāwol, synn, and *wund* all represent the characteristic development of many Fem-V nouns in the southern dialects. First, fluctuation was the norm for them. Secondly, the first appearance of *-s* was later in the southern dialects than in the northern. Thirdly, the innovative *-s* settled only slowly.

On the whole Fem-V nouns were relatively late to transfer to *-s*. This is because many of the Fem-V items had *-n* (or even *-V*) as their first option.

3.3.8 Masc-Ø Nouns

brōþor developed its various plural forms in Early Middle English. The most common types throughout Early Middle English were *-n* and *-V*. *-s* is first recorded in the C13b South-East Midland dialect. This item was perhaps too basic to conform to "regular" transfer to *-s*.

3.3.9 Neut-Ø Nouns

Neut-Ø nouns were as versatile as Neut-V nouns in that some of them remained unchanged, while others changed over to *-s, -V,* or even *-n*. This was particularly the case with the southern dialects, where fluctuation was very common.

bān, bearn, cynn, dēor, and *gēar* developed the *s*-plural but long reserved the historical ø-ending. Similar in this respect were *þing, weorc, wīf,* and *word*. In contrast, *hors, hundred,* and *scēap* barely developed the *s*-plural, but remained uninflected. Yet another group of items including *land, wæter, weorc, wif,* and *witt* nearly always took -*s* in Early Middle English.

trēow fluctuated between -*s* and -*n* in South-East Midland while South-West Midland had -*n* established as the norm throughout the Early Middle English period. The *n*-plural was also developed for *wǣpen*, but it was used side by side with the historical -*V*. *winter* developed the *V*-plural beside the historical -ø.

It should be noted that *gōd* first appeared with -*s* in Southeastern in C13a, but not in the more northern/eastern dialects. This may be due to mere chance stemming from patchy evidence, but if it is something more than chance, this innovation may suggest an independent development in Southeastern.

3.3.10 Fem-Ø Nouns

We might associate the development of *sweostor* with that of *brōþor*, but there is an interesting difference. *brōþor* commonly took -*n* or -*V* and only accepted -*s* in the C13b South-East Midland dialect. In contrast, *sweostor* first accepted -*s* in the C12b South-East Midland and North-East Midland dialects. This is contrary to the expectation that masculines should normally accept innovative -*s* earlier than feminines. In the southern dialects no *s*-plural for *sweostor* is recorded.

3.3.11 Masc-M Nouns

fēond and *frēond* took the ø-plural in most cases, but *s*-forms occurred sporadically in the southern and northern dialects.[36] As *s*-forms were among the possible variants in Old English, we can say the Early Middle English distribution was simply a continuation from Old English.

3.3.12 Neut-M Nouns

cild alternated between -*n* and -*V* throughout the Early Middle English period.[37] In many nouns -*n* tended to overtake -*V*, but the more distinct infix -*r*- in the plural stem of this particular item served as a clear enough plural marker that there was hardly any functional motivation that would encourage transfer from -*V* to -*n*. The final victory of -*n* was also presumably by analogy with a large number nouns that transferred to -*n*.

3.3.13 Fem-M Nouns

niht fluctuated between *-ø* and *-s* in both the northern and southern dialects, but the first occurrences of *-s* were earlier in North-East Midland and South-East Midland than in South-West Midland. This agrees with many Fem-V nouns.

3.3.14 Summary of Item-Based Study

In the preceding sections I investigated individual items with an aim to reviewing the findings achieved so far for each period/dialect in terms of individual items. At the same time, I attempted to contextualise the developments of individual items against the general understanding achieved for each period/dialect. The bidirectional feedback between the macro-level overview of Early Middle English dialects and the micro-level scrutiny of individual key items is essential when we wish to draw a sensible conclusion out of an unmanageably large set of data.

In Section 3.2 I worked out a conspectus of the development of the Early Middle English plural system. I then pointed out a rough parallelism that existed among dialects. The parallelism was illustrated by parallel curves on the spread rate graph for *-s* on page 71. They strongly suggested that one dialect affected another through language contact.

Then Section 3.3 has focused on individual items. The analysis has largely confirmed the view that the northern developments were early and quick whereas the southern developments were late and slow. There are interesting counterexamples to the general tendency, however. As I noted earlier, items such as *geat*, *yfel*, and *gōd* accepted innovative *-s* earlier in some southern dialects than in some northern dialects.

One may argue that these counterexamples are in doubt because such a distribution may be merely due to chance of surviving evidence and, with more evidence at hand, the northern dialects might prove earlier. One may as well argue, however, that it represents a genuine distribution and serves as evidence to show that the order of items transferring to *-s* differed from dialect to dialect.

In the above I spoke first of the parallel development through cross-dialectal contact, and then suggested a possible independent development in each dialect. The two accounts may sound opposite, but are in fact complementary. Contact between dialects provided each dialect with a general model of plural formation transfer, or in other words, it introduced to each dialect a pattern of language change that encouraged linguistic homogeneity to be maintained among the neighbouring dialects. On the other hand, individual items showed a great dialect-by-dialect difference in the way and the order of their plural formation transfer.

In sum, the developments of individual items were motivated both by cross-dialectal contact and by factors peculiar to individual dialects. Likewise, the reorganisation of the plural system as a whole should be viewed both in terms of cross-dialectal contact and independent development in each dialect.

Chapter 4 Study of Selected Texts

In this chapter I closely examine Early Middle English texts surviving in more than one version or written in distinguishable languages.[38] The aim is twofold. First, I will contextualise the development outlined in the preceding chapter with actual examples from texts. Next, I will interpret these examples from text in light of the obtained outline. The following texts are analysed.

1. two distinct scribal texts of the *Lambeth Homilies*
2. three distinct scribal texts of *The Owl and the Nightingale*
3. four versions of the *Ancrene Wisse/Riwle*
4. seven versions of the *Poema Morale*
5. three scribal texts of *The Peterborough Chronicle*

In the following sections, numerical statements are first given for each comparative analysis. The PFPs of individual scribal texts are printed in Appendix D.

4.1 The *Lambeth Homilies*

Table 4.1: Statistical Summary for the *Lambeth Homilies*

	Lang 1	Lang 2	L
tokens	540	186	46
types	167	71	29
syncretism rate	0.27	0.43	0.27
(spread) rate of s	0.35 (1)	0.46 (1.4)	0.31 (1.3)
(spread) rate of n	0.25 (1.4)	0.17 (2.4)	0.069 (0.67)
(spread) rate of V	0.26 (1)	0.24 (0.81)	0.38 (1.1)
(spread) rate of $\emptyset$	0.084 (0.47)	0.099 (0.41)	0.21 (0.86)
(spread) rate of M	0.054 (1)	0.028 (0.5)	0.034 (0.5)

Notes: s, n, V, $\emptyset$, and M represent s-, n-, vowel-, $\emptyset$-, and minor plural types respectively. Figures in parentheses represent "spread rate" as distinct from simple "(type) rate." The syncretism rate appears as "NA" when there are no examples from dative environments. The spread rate appears as "NA" when there are no examples in text that historically took that plural type.

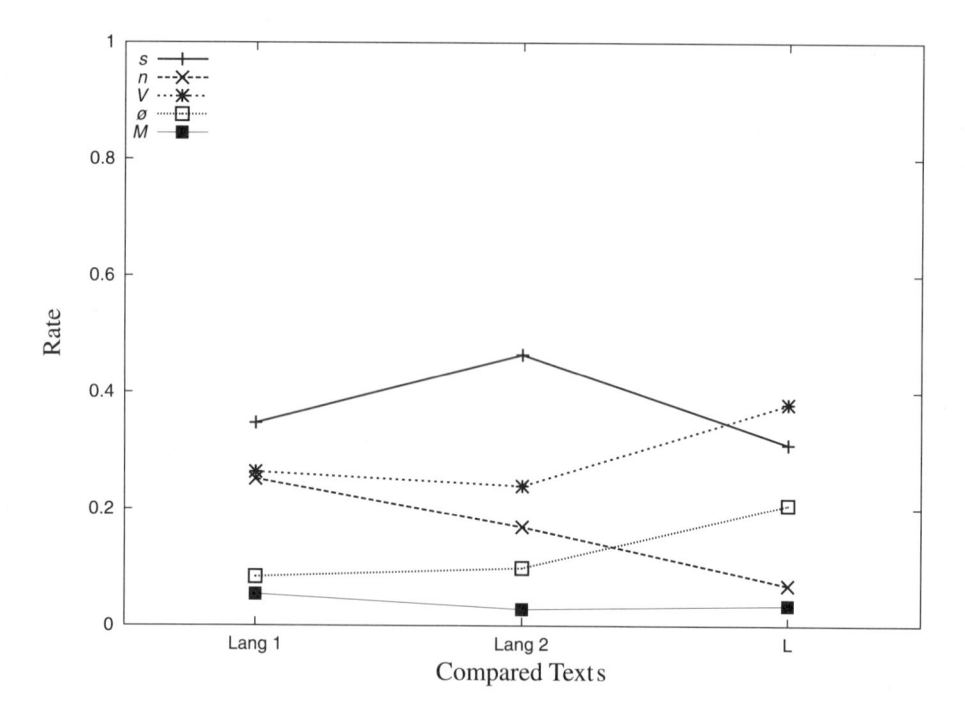

Figure 4.1: Rate for the *Lambeth Homilies*

As has been established since Sisam's study, the *Lambeth Homilies* in Lambeth Palace Library 487 are divided into two groups by their spelling systems. The first group is made up of Sermons I to V and IX to XIII (see PFP 2000 in Appendix D.1.1), while the second group consists of Sermons IV to VIII and XIV to XVII (see PFP 2001 in Appendix D.1.2). Hereafter the languages represented in the two groups are cited as Lang 1 and Lang 2 respectively.

Lang 2 appears also in a version of the *Poema Morale* (designated L), which immediately follows the series of sermons in the manuscript. The *Poema Morale* is compared separately from the rest of the Lang 2 part because of its literary distinction from the preceding series of sermons and its involving rhyming (see PFP 5 in Appendix D.4.1).[39] In the manuscript the *Poema Morale* is in turn followed by an unfinished version of *Wel swuþe god Ureison of God Almihti*. The latter is written in a later hand, and left outside the scope of the present analysis.

Langs 1 and 2 show distinct spelling systems, but both parts were written by the same hand. This means that the scribe was a mechanical copyist rather than a translator. The sermons in the Lambeth MS are said to be "an important source of English at the transitional period *c.* 1200" (Sisam 105). Since the language of the transitional period tolerated the coexistence of old and new variant forms, examining the distribution of variants in the Lambeth sermons will throw light on the kind of linguistic change that was going on in the C12b South-West Midland dialect.

Many of the sermons in Lang 1 belong to the old tradition in the sense that their textual histories go back to Late Old English.[40] In contrast, the Lang 2 part belongs to the new tradition, as Sisam's orthographic study showed. Lang 2 should therefore be expected to be morphologically more advanced than Lang 1.

Let us not forget that summaries given in the PFPs should be interpreted as rough profiles of the two languages because each part has its own complicated history, text length, vocabulary used, etc. For example, the Lang 1 part is much longer than the Lang 2 part, the former providing three times the number of plural examples. The *Poema Morale* part is even smaller. All this makes comparison among the three parts rather tricky.

The analysis of the text by Morris's edition (*Homilies*, 1st ser., Part 1) shows that Lang 1 is relatively conservative, as expected. The plural distribution has not changed dramatically since Old English. There is, however, some plural formation transfer recognised. Especially remarkable is the extension of the n-plurals. PFP 2000 shows that there are various sources of the new n-plurals.

Interestingly, a good number of nouns that take the n-plural also take the V-plural. This indicates that there was some kind of alternation or interchange between the n- and V-plural. The status of the word final $-n$ was so unstable that the n-less and n-forms were interchanged.

As for the extension of $-s$, many neuter nouns have changed over, but in general the spread rate is not so impressive.

Lang 2 represents a more advanced stage than Lang 1. The spread of $-s$ is more remarkable, and the extension of $-n$ is more dramatic. The apparent dramatic spread of $-n$, however, may be somewhat exaggerated due to the small number of relevant examples. As was the case with Lang 1, there is interchange going on between n- and V-plurals.

The difference between Lang 1 and Lang 2 is in quantity rather than in quality. Both languages point to the same direction of development. Both languages show an increase in the rates of the s- and n-plural and a decrease in the rates of the other plural types. This situation represents a preliminary stage to the s/n-dichotomic system found in later AB language texts.

Let us look at the *Poema Morale* part in comparison with the Lang 1 and Lang 2 parts. In terms of the spelling system, the *Poema Morale* belongs with the Lang 2 sermons, but the plural distribution of the *Poema Morale* looks almost the same as that expected for common West-Saxon. This is perhaps because verse text tends to be more conservative than prose text for metrical exigencies and for its general archaising nature. In addition, the number of collected plural forms from the *Poema Morale* is small, which is partly why the distribution apparently deviates from expectation.

The *Poema Morale* thus fails to fit in the average C12b South-West Midland condition as obtained in Section 3.2.6, in which both $-s$ and $-n$ were growing. Conversely, Langs 1 and 2 fit well with the average picture for C12b South-West Midland. In terms of the spread rates for $-s$ and $-n$, Lang 1 scores slightly below the average and Lang 2 scores above the average. This is in accordance with the proposed view that Lang 1 and 2 reflect the old and new traditions respectively.

Let me briefly mention the context-induced choice of variants. Choice of variants is a function of different parameters including dialect, period, scribal habits, and history of textual transmission. To these may be added a contextual (therefore perhaps nonce) factor. For example, when several nouns are enumerated in succession, they may repeat a plural ending throughout as if by inertia. This is exemplified in the following two contexts from Sermon V (emphasis added).

- þer wunieð in-ne faȝe **neddren**. *and* beoreð atter u*n*der heore tunge. Blake **tadden** *and* habbeð atter uppon heore heorte. ȝeluwe **froggen**. *ande* **crabben**. (Morris, *Homilies*, 1st ser.: 51)
- ȝe ne beo noht þe foaȝe **neddre**. ne þe blake **tadde**. ne þe ȝolewe **frogge**. (Morris, *Homilies*, 1st ser.: 53)

In the first quotation the enumerated animal names take -*n* throughout, while in the second the *n*-less forms are used for all. Inertial choice of this kind is commonplace in Early Middle English texts, but we have to understand that it provides a weak explanation for the system-wide spread of a certain ending because contexts are usually one-off. If we assume, as we should, that language change refers to systematic change rather than casual usage variation, the contribution of contextual inertia to language change will be small (see Section 6.7 for a related discussion).

4.2 The Owl and the Nightingale

Table 4.2: Statistical Summary for *The Owl and the Nightingale*

	J	C1	C2
tokens	155	117	41
types	71	57	25
syncretism rate	0.22	0.3	0.067
(spread) rate of s	0.66 (1.2)	0.63 (1.1)	0.72 (1.8)
(spread) rate of n	0.056 (0.57)	0.088 (0.83)	0.04 (0.5)
(spread) rate of V	0.17 (1.7)	0.16 (2.3)	0.08 (0.67)
(spread) rate of $ø$	0.099 (0.54)	0.11 (0.67)	0.12 (0.33)
(spread) rate of M	0.014 (0.17)	0.018 (0.2)	0.04 (1)

Notes: s, n, V, $ø$, and M represent s-, n-, vowel-, $ø$-, and minor plural types respectively. Figures in parentheses represent "spread rate" as distinct from simple "(type)" rate. The syncretism rate appears as "NA" when there are no examples from dative environments. The spread rate appears as "NA" when there are no examples in text that historically took that plural type.

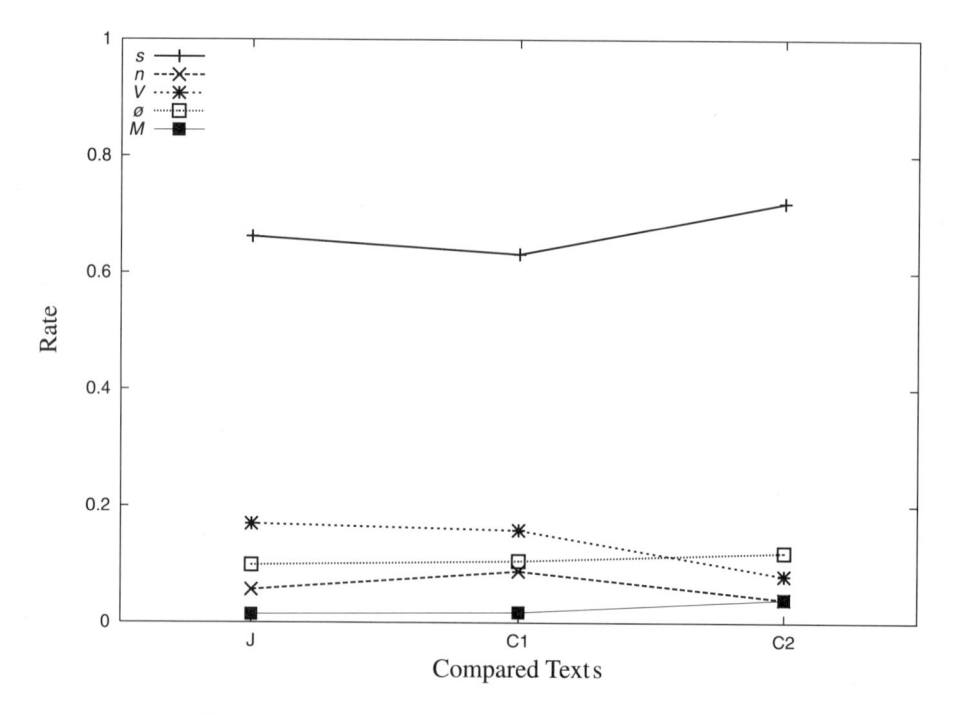

Figure 4.2: Rate for *The Owl and the Nightingale*

In this section I analyse the two extant versions of *The Owl and the Nightingale* (hereafter *O&N*) to see how the text languages tally with the overview of the C13b South-West Midland dialect we saw in Section 3.2.6.

O&N has been studied from various angles, and some similarities to other Early Middle English texts have been pointed out. For example, Atkins remarks that the first of the two orthographic systems in the C version is "found to coincide in almost all its essential details (cf. the treatment of O.E. $\bar{æ}$, *eo*, *hw*, medial *g*) with the spellings characteristic of works written about 1200, e.g. *O.E. Homilies*, *S. Juliana*, *Sawles Ward*, and *Ancrene Riwle* (Titus MS.)" (xxx).

The similarity Atkins pointed out is not morphological but orthographic or phonological, and there is much left to be studied on the morphology of *O&N*. Even Roedler mentioned no more than the form *nyhtes* in the text as an example of innovative *s*-plurals (1: 66).

To describe the text in brief, *O&N* survives in two manuscripts: BL Cotton Caligula A ix (hereafter C) and Oxford, Jesus College 29 (hereafter J). C and J are considered to be derived from a common text which is not the original itself. It is well known that the C scribe was a mechanical copyist who reproduced the two orthographic systems, as they were alternately used in the exemplar, whereas the J scribe more freely handled the exemplar, letting his spontaneous features show in the copied text frequently (Atkins xxvi-xxxiv).

The two orthographic systems in C in turn represent two different languages, which I call C1 and C2. C1 is responsible for lines 1–901 and 961–1183 (1124 lines in total); and C2 for lines 902–60 and 1184–1794 (670 lines in total). C2 represents the more traditional spelling system, and Atkins believes that it keeps the original spellings better than C1.

The three distinct languages of J, C1, and C2 are all assigned to South-West Midland, not far away from one another, and all dated in the last quarter of the thirteenth century (see PFPs 1, 2, and 3 in Appendices D.2.1, D.2.2, and D.2.3 respectively). From rhyming usage it has been suggested that the original text was written around the opening decade of the thirteenth century in the Surrey dialect (Stanley, *Owl* 18). Cartlidge, however, has recently observed that the original text may have been composed not long before the extant copies and almost anywhere in Wessex, the Home Counties, or the South-West Midlands (xiv).

The PFPs for J, C1, and C2 show general similarity in the distribution of the plurals. This should not surprise us because they were not only (presumably) copied out of a common exemplar but also localised and dated closely. But how does this similarity fit the proposed contrast between the J scribe's innovative orthography and the C scribe's conservative one? Did the scribes have different orthographic sets but share a morphology? This is likely the case since orthography and morphology are two separate levels of language and can be independent of each other.

Innovative plurals are not numerous in *O&N*, but where they occur, the Neut-Ø class is the largest source of the *s*-innovation. Variations within and across the three texts are not numerous either, but the following are some interesting examples, quoted in context in pair from Grattan and Sykes' edition (emphasis added).

- An lutle **children** in þe cradele. (C1: line 631)
- & lutle **childre** in þe cradele. (J: line 631)

- Vor **children** gromeſ heme & hine. (C1: line 1115)
- Vor **children**. gromes. heme. & hine. (J: line 1115)

- Ich pot ʒef treon ſchule blope. / Ich þat ʒef **cornes** ſchule grope. (C2: lines 1201–02)
- Ic wot if tren ſchulle blowe. / Ic wot if **corn** ſchulle growe. (J: lines 1201–02)

To look at the variants for "children," line 631 gives *children* for C and *childre* for J, while line 1115 gives *children* for both. It is possible that the J scribe translated *children*, presumably as found in the exemplar, into his spontaneous alternative form *childre* in line 631, but in line 1115 he was constrained by the form *children* as in the exemplar, which he perpetuated. For lack of further evidence it is hardly possible to know for sure whether *childre* was more familiar to him than *children*. It is certain, however, that both forms were *available* to him.

The quotations for "corns" come in a two-line context to show that the usages in C and J are controlled by the number of syllables. Assuming that *cornes* was the form in the exemplar as in C, it was translated into *corn* by the J scribe, who in doing so created an octosyllabic line that would go metrically well with the preceding line. The disyllabic pair *treon / cornes* in C corresponds to the monosyllabic *tren / corn* in J. J's usage as compared to C's seems to underpin what is described as "[t]he editorial activity of the scribe of J" (Grattan and Sykes xvi).

The analysis of the plurals shows that the J and C scribes both retained the author's original plural morphology by copying the exemplar mostly mechanically. This is consistent with the accepted view that the C scribe was a mechanical copyist, but how can it square with the accepted view that the J scribe was rather a translator? To this question I would reply that the J scribe used his own distinct *orthography* but on a *morphological* level he essentially perpetuated exemplar forms as long as they were within his dialectal horizon. Only on a few occasions did he let his spontaneous distinct morphology show.

His constrained behaviour on a morphological level is understandable because in a verse text like *O&N*, translation of forms may involve a potential risk of spoiling metrical arrangements. As we saw above, a small change from *corn* to *cornes* would be significant enough to affect the metrical structure of a line.

Now let us see if the *O&N* evidence fits in with the overview picture for the C13b South-West Midland situation. As seen in Section 3.2.6, the average spread rates of *-s* and *-n* for the C13b South-West Midland dialect were much above 1.0. This indicates that the plural system was then reorganised into the *s/n*-dominant system at the expense of the other plural formations. However, all rates for the three scribal texts of *O&N* are far below the average. How can this discrepancy be explained?

First of all, as I argued above, C and J are likely to retain some of the authorial language, perhaps the C13a Surrey dialect. As a result, the scribes' own languages were more or less constrained by the exemplar.

This is not to say, however, that the surviving texts fail to show the scribes' dialect altogether. It is possible especially with J that the scribe copied exemplar forms not because he was a mechanical copyist but because they were within his variational horizon if not within his active repertoire. It is likely that the J scribe chose to perpetuate a good number of forms from the exemplar because he was so familiar with, and tolerant of, them that he felt no need to replace them with his spontaneous variants. If this view is accepted, a good number of plural forms in J were within the J scribe's horizon to start with. Given that the distributional difference is not too great between J and C, the language of C may also represent a variety of the C13b South-West Midland language, perhaps not very different from a variety of his own.

Now let us return to the discrepancy between the O&N profile and the average C13b South-West Midland profile. Judging from independent evidence from other texts, there is no doubt that the s/n-dichotomic system was developing in the C13 South-West Midland dialect. At the same time, as I showed above, the O&N language can be considered to represent another linguistic variety current in the C13b South-West Midland dialect—perhaps a more written variety.

The developing s/n-dichotomic system is confirmed by such a large amount of the C13b South-West Midland evidence that we might believe that it was the "standard" plural system prevalent in South-West Midland in C13b. It seems to me, however, that the s/n-dichotomic system looks too "neat" to be real. Spoken language would be less neat-looking and more varied.

There is dispute about the view of the AB language being "standard" in South-West Midland. On this issue Smith argues that "AB language appears to be a dialectal 'layer' in a number of other contemporary texts" and "in the various usages of the South-West Midlands, we are dealing not with a 'standard' surrounded by deviant usages, but rather with various local attempts to reorganise the traditional spelling of the area" ("Standard" 129–30). In the second quotation from Smith, would it not possible to replace "spelling" with "the plural system"? I suspect that the s/n-dichotomic system was one of the various systems available in South-West Midland, presumably one that represents a more spoken variety, while the plural system represented in O&N was another system, perhaps of a more written variety.

If this interpretation is accepted, the discrepancy between O&N and its contemporary South-West Midland texts is none other than a reflection of the linguistic varieties present in South-West Midland in C13b. They all represent linguistic realities of South-West Midland in C13b, only that some systems happen to resemble more closely the local spoken (as opposed to conservative written) system than others.

4.3 The *Ancrene Wisse/Riwle*

Table 4.3: Statistical Summary for the *Ancrene Wisse/Riwle*

	A	C	N	T
tokens	335	620	252	437
types	115	168	90	136
syncretism rate	0.68	0.65	0.75	0.86
(spread) rate of s	0.67 (1.6)	0.62 (1.8)	0.64 (1.7)	0.79 (2.8)
(spread) rate of n	0.25 (1.9)	0.28 (1.7)	0.29 (2.2)	0.029 (0.2)
(spread) rate of V	0.017 (0.071)	0.054 (0.21)	0.011 (0.045)	0.1 (0.3)
(spread) rate of $\emptyset$	0.043 (0.24)	0.03 (0.15)	0.033 (0.17)	0.044 (0.26)
(spread) rate of M	0.017 (0.5)	0.018 (0.6)	0.022 (0.67)	0.029 (0.57)

Notes: s, n, V, $\emptyset$, and M represent s-, n-, vowel-, $\emptyset$-, and minor plural types respectively. Figures in parentheses represent "spread rate" as distinct from simple "(type) rate." The syncretism rate appears as "NA" when there are no examples from dative environments. The spread rate appears as "NA" when there are no examples in text that historically took that plural type.

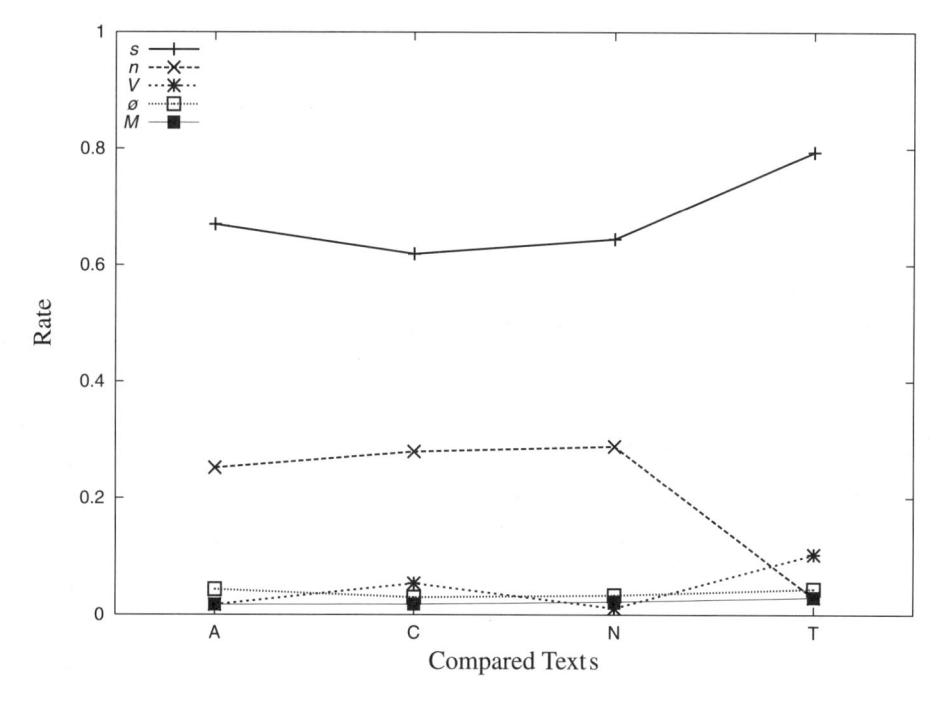

Figure 4.3: Rate for the *Ancrene Wisse/Riwle*

The four versions of the *Ancrene Wisse/Riwle* analysed are:

A: Cambridge, Corpus Christi College 402 (ed. Tolkien). PFP 272 in Appendix D.3.1.

C: BL Cotton Cleopatra C vi (ed. Dobson, *Ancrene*). PFP 273 in Appendix D.3.2.

N: BL Cotton Nero A xiv (ed. Day). PFP 245 in Appendix D.3.3.

T: BL Cotton Titus D xviii (ed. Mack). PFP 118 in Appendix D.3.4.

To compare A, C, and N, I also consulted Kubouchi and Ikegami's parallel edition.

I examined Parts 6 and 7 of the editions for A, C, and N, and the fols. 14r-40ra part for T from the *LAEME* text database.[41] The first three are commonly localised to South-West Midland, so they are first put to comparative analysis. Then I briefly compare them with the Titus text of North-West Midland.

The statistical figures for the three South-West Midland versions indicate that the distribution of the plurals does not differ very much among them. All three versions represent the s/n-dichotomic system, where nearly ninety percent of the plurals take either -s or -n. This similarity is attributable to the fact that they were all copied within relatively short intervals in roughly the same localisation.

More than a third of the nouns in the texts follow conservative plural formations: -s for most strong masculines, -n for many weak nouns, -$\emptyset$ for some strong neuters, and -V for a few strong feminines. There are certainly many innovations, however. For example, Shepherd remarked that in A -s was chiefly found in the strong masculines and neuters, whereas -n was chiefly found in the feminines and the weak nouns (xvii). Moreover, in his close analysis of N, Roedler (1: 63) pointed out that -s tended to be suffixed to the long-syllabic strong neuters as well as some long-syllabic strong feminines ending in -*ung* and -*nis*, whereas -n was a typical plural suffix to most strong feminines and weak nouns. He made another important point that fluctuation between -s and -n was common for short-syllabic strong neuter nouns.

Shepherd's and Roedler's observations are not rules but tendencies that permit a number of exceptions. d'Ardenne tried to find alternative accounts for some such exceptions in the AB language (207). First, she suggested that -*s* was favoured by "nouns denoting persons or classes of persons irrespective of the form of the nom. singular," whereas -*n* was favoured by "nouns (denoting inanimate things) ending in a vowel in the nom. singular, irrespective of the Old English plural or gender." This could account for *feolahes* and perhaps *wrecches* and *ancres* (in A and C), all of which were historically weak. This account, however, fails to explain *sustren* and even *wrecche* and *ancren*.

She also suggested the semantic association of synonyms. For example, -*s* in *licomes* (a historical weak noun) was, according to her suggestion, perhaps due to its semantic association with its common synonym *bodies*, which itself was an earlier innovation from a historical strong neuter.

Various attempts have thus been made to summarise the distribution of the plurals, but they did not account for all cases. Trying to establish firm rules would fail because variation is so commonplace in language. The following are some examples of variation found in each of the texts (frequency in parentheses). Some sets of variation are shared.

A: *wrecches* (2) ∼ *wrecche* (1); *ancres* (1) ∼ *ancren* (1); *ʒeres* (1) ∼ *ʒer* (1); *þinges* (11) ∼ *þing* (4); *wordes* (2) ∼ *word* (1)

C: *wrecches* (1) ∼ *wreche* (2); *ʒeres* (1) ∼ *ʒer* (1); *þinges* (13) ∼ *þing* (5); *wordes* (2) ∼ *word* (1)

N: *drunches* (2) ∼ *drincken* (1); *wrecches* (1) ∼ *wrecche* (2); *ʒeres* (1) ∼ *ʒer* (1); *þinges* (18) ∼ *þing* (3)

More interesting is the variation found across the three texts. I give some examples in Table 4.4 on page 94. The fourth column gives references to Parts 5–8 of Kubouchi and Ikegami's parallel edition (page and folio/line in A).

In the list there are several examples that point to affinity between A and C, and a few others that point to affinity between C and N. From this evidence we may recognise the following typological relationship between the versions: A is related closely to C, which is in turn related to some degree to N. This typological relationship has been suggested by Smith in his series of articles.[42] He compared items in the three versions (plus the other two contemporary

Table 4.4: Plural Forms Comparison for the *Ancrene Wisse/Riwle*: 1

A	C	N	reference
þus lo rih/te ancres	Þus Lo richte / ancres	þus loke rihte / ancren	97 (A 95v22–23)
þes twa word	beos / twa word	beos two wordes	100 (A 96r15)
biuore paraise ȝeten	bifor parayse ȝeten	biuoren þe / ȝeten of parais	101 (A 96v01)
in heouene ȝeten	in heouene ȝetes	ine heouene ȝetes	129 (A 101v03)
we wrecche sunfule	we wreche sunefule	we wreche sunfule	107 (A 97r24)
we wrecches sunfule	we wreche sunefule	we wrec/che sunfu_le	111 (A 98r03)
to se lahe wrecch/ces	to se lachȝe wrecches	to so louwe wrecches	147 (A 105r07)
we his limen alle	we his / limen alle	we alle his limes	109 (A 97v16)
twa þwongede scheos	twa þongede scheon	two þongede scheon	111 (A 98r06)
clowes de gilofre	clou de gilofre (sg.)	clou de gilofre (sg.)	122 (A 100r18)
an hundret wei/es	an hundred / weies	an hundred weien	125 (A 100v16)
flesches pinsunges	flesches pinunges	flesches pinunge	125 (A 100v18)
Alle go/des heastes	alle godes hestes	alle godes hesten	146 (A 104v18–19)
on alle cunne wise	on alle cune wisen	on alle kunne wisen	146–47 (A 104v26)
schawde hire his mihte (sg?)	Schaude hire his / michte (sg?)	scheawede hire his / mihten	149–50 (A 105v02–03)

texts) from a phonological point of view, as shown in Table 4.5 ("Standard" 132). Smith remarks:

> It will be observed that the texts as presented form a typological sequence in which the Nero manuscript stands at one end of the cline and the Corpus manuscript at the other. This pattern, generally (though not entirely precisely), coincides with the provisional localisations for each of these texts . . . . ("Standard" 134)

Table 4.5: Smith's Phonological Comparison for the *Ancrene Wisse/Riwle*

	A	C	N
EACH	euche	euche	ech(e)
ANY	eani	ani	eni
WAS	wes	wes	was
THEY	ha	heo, ha	heo
SELF	seolf	seolf	sulf
THEIR	hare	hare	hore
THEM	ham, heom	ham, heom	ham

The concern of the present analysis is morphological rather than phonological, but Smith's argument and mine are in agreement on the typological sequence of the three versions. Now let us see the typological sequence in morphological terms (see Table 4.6 on page 96).

There are, however, a few cases where the suggested typological relation fails. For example, A is sometimes closer to N than to C, as shown in Table 4.7 on page 96.

These few examples, however, will not be strong counterargument against the proposed typology.

It is interesting to ask how this intricate network of morphological typology was produced. First, rather obviously, a diatopic parameter must be at work. The three versions are all closely localised in South-West Midland, but South-West Midland is not an entirely homogeneous area, admitting of a considerable degree of variation within it.

Secondly, difference in the plural distribution may be of diachronic relevance. A and C are dated about 1225/30, and N about 1240.[43] The interval may not

Table 4.6: Plural Forms Comparison for the *Ancrene Wisse/Riwle*: 2

	A	C	N
ANCHORESSES	ancres, ancren	ancres, ancren	ancren
COMMANDMENTS	heastes	hestes	hesten
LIMBS	limen	limen	limes
MORTIFICATIONS	pinsunges	pinunges	pinunge
WAYS	weies	weies	weien
WORDS	word, wordes	word, wordes	wordes
GATES	ʒeten	ʒeten, ʒetes	ʒeten, ʒetes
SHOES	scheos	scheon	scheon
MANNERS	wise	wisen	wisen

Table 4.7: Plural Forms Comparison for the *Ancrene Wisse/Riwle*: 3

A	C	N	reference
of drunches	of˜drunh (sg.)	'of' drunches	121 (A 100r01)
of þes twa bitter/nesses	of þeos twa bitternesse	of 'þeos' two bitternesses	126 (A 100v26)
aʒeines fondunges	aʒeines fondun/ge (sg?)	aʒean / uondunges	127 (A 101r14)

be very long, but there is a sign that the scribal attitudes changed more than the scribe's language itself around this time in C13a.

Smith reasoned that the linguistic innovation in C and especially N was motivated by the increased social demand for copies in a hurry and the consequent change of scribal and manuscript-producing customs ("Tradition" 64). If this view is accepted, the proposed typological continuum for the three versions reflects variation in scribal attitudes rather than linguistic variation.

A third parameter responsible for the typological sequence is the scribal history of each version. Smith suggested that the main hand of C showed constrained behaviour from time to time, so that some forms would be judged rather as his passive repertoire than as his spontaneous usages ("Tradition" 60). This view not only tallies with the proposed linguistic affinity between C and A, but also hints that C scribe's spontaneous language would have been a little more advanced or perhaps even somewhat closer to N's language.

Finally I mention in brief the distribution of the plurals in the Titus version of the *Ancrene Riwle*, localised to the North-West Midlands. Comparison with the South-West Midland versions makes it clear how distinct T's distribution is. The spread rate of *-s* is dramatic while that of *-n* is notably low. To show the dominance of *-s*, T alone has the following items pluralise in *-s*: *hertes* (OE Fem-N *heorte*), *beodes* (OE Neut-V *bed*), *blisses* (OE Fem-V *bliss*), *gledes* (OE Fem-V *glēd*), *hondes* (OE Fem-V *hand*), *mihtes* (OE Fem-V *miht*), *pines* (OE Fem-V *pīn*), *wundes* (OE Fem-V *wund*), *cneos* (OE Neut-Ø *cnēow*), and *wepnes* (OE Neut-Ø *wǣpen*).

This is an impressive situation considering that T is dated closely to the three South-West Midland versions. This clearly indicates that there was a great linguistic divide between South-West Midland and North-West Midland.

4.4 The *Poema Morale*

Table 4.8: Statistical Summary for the *Poema Morale*

	L	e	E	J	M	T	D
tokens	46	64	64	69	54	72	70
types	29	37	38	39	29	39	39
syncretism rate	0.27	0.5	0.56	0.47	0.67	0.58	0.54
(spread) rate of s	0.31 (1.3)	0.38 (1.3)	0.47 (1.4)	0.44 (1.5)	0.59 (1.7)	0.44 (1.4)	0.33 (1.2)
(spread) rate of n	0.069 (0.67)	0.081 (0.38)	0.18 (0.88)	0.26 (1.7)	0.034 (0.5)	0.18 (1)	0.31 (2)
(spread) rate of V	0.38 (1.1)	0.35 (1.4)	0.16 (0.75)	0.077 (0.33)	0.21 (0.86)	0.18 (0.78)	0.15 (0.43)
(spread) rate of $ø$	0.21 (0.86)	0.16 (1)	0.16 (1)	0.21 (0.89)	0.14 (0.57)	0.18 (0.88)	0.18 (1.4)
(spread) rate of M	0.034 (0.5)	0.027 (0.33)	0.026 (0.33)	0.026 (0.25)	0.034 (0.33)	0.026 (0.33)	0.026 (0.33)

Notes: s, n, V, $ø$, and M represent s-, n-, vowel-, $ø$-, and minor plural types respectively. Figures in parentheses represent "spread rate" as distinct from simple "(type) rate." The syncretism rate appears as "NA" when there are no examples from dative environments. The spread rate appears as "NA" when there are no examples in text that historically took that plural type.

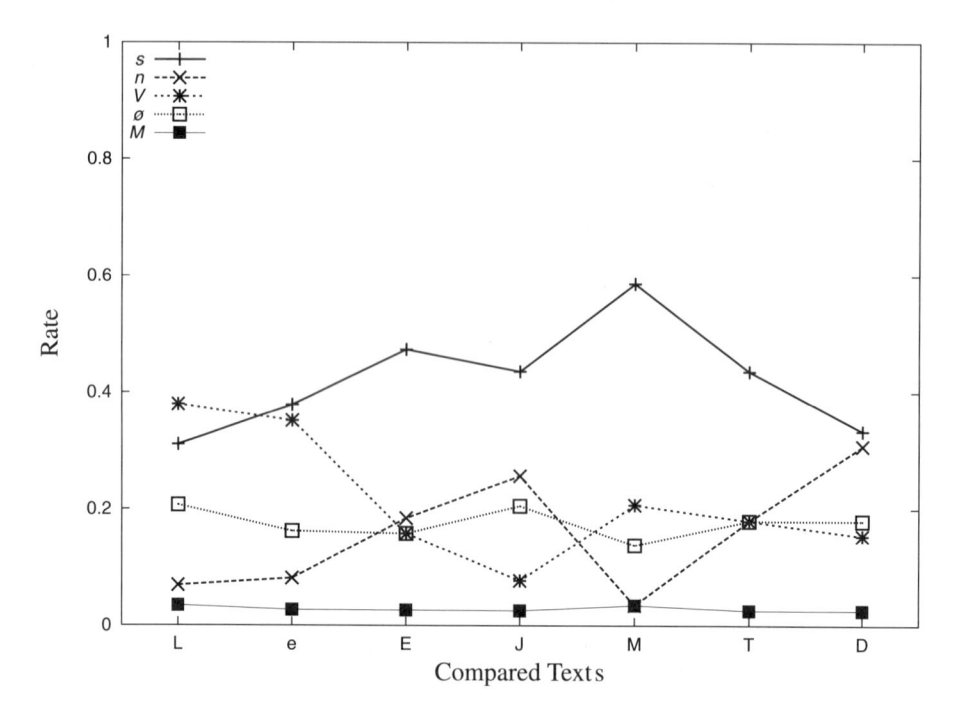

Figure 4.4: Rate for the *Poema Morale*

4 Study of Selected Texts   99

Surviving in as many as seven different versions, the *Poema Morale* (hereafter *PMor*) offers a rare opportunity for looking into the diachronic and diatopic variation of the period. Diachronically the seven texts span over a century; diatopically they are variously localised in the more southern parts of England.

In this section, I compare the different versions of *PMor* to bring into relief the plural system in each version. Then the findings are checked against the average profile obtained in Section 3.2.

To start with, I describe seven versions of *PMor*.

L: London, Lambeth Palace Library 487, fols. 59v–65r. 267 long lines written in prose, ending imperfectly. Edited by Morris (*Homilies*, 1st ser.: 159–75 [odd pages]) and reproduced by Hall (*Selections* 1: 30–46 [even pages]). C12b2 (*ca.* 1200). "MLS [Michael Louis Samuels] places the language on the border of N Herefords and Salop" (Laing, *Catalogue* 111). PFP 5 in Appendix D.4.1.

e: London, British Library, Egerton 613, fols. 64r–70v. 367 long lines, ending imperfectly. Edited by Zupitza and Schipper. C13a1 (*ca.* 1225). Assigned to the South West by most scholars (Hill, "*Conduct*" 109). PFP 6 in Appendix D.4.2.

E: London, British Library, Egerton 613, fols. 7r–12v. 398 long lines in a different hand from e. Edited by Morris (*Homilies*, 1st ser.: 288–95 followed by 175–83 [odd pages]). C13a2 (*ca.* 1250). Assigned to the South West by most scholars (Hill, "*Conduct*" 109). PFP 7 in Appendix D.4.3.

J: Oxford, Jesus College 29, Part II, fols. 169r–174v. 388 long lines. Edited by Morris (*Miscellany* 58–71). C13b2. "The language is placed in *LALME* as LP 8440 in Southeastern Herefords. It would fit equally well in NW Gloucs" (Laing, *Catalogue* 147). PFP 9 in Appendix D.4.4.

M: Cambridge, Fitzwilliam Museum 123, fols. 115r–120r. 335 long lines, wanting 70 lines found in T. Edited by Paues (227–37). C13b2 (*ca.* 1300). "M is Kentish with a strong intermixture of more westerly forms" and "the immediate original of our text . . . was taken down from memory" (Paues 219, 225). Alternatively, Samuels believes that the language is that of Essex with some western admixture (Hill, "*Conduct*" 110). Laing suspected that it belonged somewhere in the Central South Midlands ("Linguistic" 573), but has recently localised it to the South-West Midlands. PFP 10 in Appendix D.4.5.

T: Cambridge, Trinity College B.14.52, fols. 2r–9v. 298 long lines. Edited by Hall (*Selections* 1: 31–53 [odd pages]). C12b2. Hill cites Michael Samuels as believing the language to have a London provenance but of a type "influenced by immigration, perhaps from East Anglia" ("*Conduct*" 107). PFP 4 in Appendix D.4.6.

D: Oxford, Bodleian Library, Digby 4, fols. 97r–110v. 764 half lines arranged in quatrains. Edited by Zupitza. C13a. "It displays Kentish features which may possibly be mixed with an ingredient from the London area. The language may, however, represent a linguistically homogeneous dialect from somewhere in between, such as NW Kent or NE Surrey" (Laing, *Catalogue* 127). On the other hand, Hill says, "Professor Samuels concluded that the language of D showed either two layers of copying (Kent + London *or* London + Kent), or possibly a single scribe writing in the dialect of an area of Kent or Surrey bordering on London, i.e. North-West Kent or North-East Surrey" ("*Conduct*" 110). PFP 8 in Appendix D.4.7.

The diachronic and diatopic assignment of the seven versions are schematised in Table 4.9.

Table 4.9: Diachronic and Diatopic Assignment of the Seven *Poema Morale* Texts

	South-West Midland	South-East Midland	Southeastern
C12b	L (*ca.* 1200)	T (C12b2)	
C13a	e (*ca.* 1225), E (*ca.* 1250)		D (C13a)
C13b	J (C13b2), M (*ca.* 1300)		

With its seven comparable texts, *PMor* is extremely important to Early Middle English dialectologists, but there are some methodological difficulties we must confront. Laing mentions two problems particularly.

The first problem concerns diachronic versus diatopic variation. This may be best described in Laing's words: "one should not attempt to distinguish too sharply between diachronic and diatopic variation" ("Linguistic" 576–77). The presence of plural endings generally deemed "old" such as V-plurals may mean either a diachronically early usage or a conservative dialectal usage or both.

The second problem concerns language mixture. In language mixture, it is unclear whether linguistic similarities and differences between the versions mirror those of scribe's dialects or those of exemplars. To address this problem, we need to understand first the scribal custom in Early Middle English.

It is known that the scribal custom in Early Middle English was more to copy exemplars *literatim* than to "translate" them.[44] This practise was particularly common in verse texts, since metrical exigencies should require copyists to perpetuate exemplar forms carefully. Accordingly we may safely expect to encounter more archaisms than innovations in such a verse text as *PMor*.

Despite the general mechanical copying habit in Early Middle English, there is evidence that scribes sometimes let their spontaneous forms show in their texts as they copied. This is most clearly seen where scribes spoilt rhymes by introducing innovative forms, although in-line examples are not unknown. There are three ways in which scribes let their spontaneous usages show.

The first is via the scribe's habitual dependence on "mind ear" in copying texts. As Sisam pointed out, "There was no reason why a scribe copying a vernacular text should not memorise phrases or sentences from his pattern manuscript and write them down in the forms he was accustomed to" (112).

The second is via possible correction by preachers rather than by scribes. It is likely that preachers translated archaic forms into those of current use so that they could be understood by a local congregation to whom the text was read aloud (Sisam 112).

Thirdly, *PMor* was probably transmitted by oral as well as written means. We may note that Paues suspected that the M version might have been written down from memory (225). If this is true, the reciter must have shown his own usages where memory failed.

As should be clear by now, it is very important to be able to tell which forms represent the scribes' dialect and which forms represent the exemplar. We could only make sensible judgement after considering the following issues:

textual history between versions, internal linguistic consistency, comparison with other texts copied by the same scribe, and comparison between different versions.

The following is my working strategy to distinguish the scribe's usage from the exemplar's. If a particular form appears in the majority of the seven versions, it is likely to be an authorial form or at least one close to it. To put it the other way round, if a form in a version differs from its equivalents in many of the other versions, it is likely to be an innovative form introduced by the scribe or one of his predecessors. In this case the form in question may represent his spontaneous usage.

Let me take forms for the plural noun "works," for example The plural noun occurs with -s in all seven versions. There are sporadic occurrences of the s-less form beside the s-form in some versions, but the universal occurrence of the s-form suggests that it was most likely contained in earlier exemplars, perhaps even in the authorial text.

Another example on similar lines is *wununges* and its other variants with an s-ending. The s-plural occurs in e, J, M, and T, while D gives *woniinge* (L and E lack the corresponding line). If we assume that the appearance of the s-plural in four versions implies its probable presence also in earlier copies, we may interpret that the Fem-V noun transferred to the s-plural fairly early in dialects in which the ancestors of the four manuscripts were composed.

In the following, I analyse the plural system of each of the seven texts. Then I try to plot the findings in the diachronic and diatopic network obtained in Section 3.2.

Let us start with the L text. This is the earliest of the five South-West Midland versions (L, e, E, J, and M). The plural system of L is considerably conservative. The archaic nature of L's language is recognised by the limited spread of the s- and n-plurals. Much of this conservatism, however, is perhaps not representative of the scribe's language but due to his mechanical copying of the exemplar which contained old forms. The scribe's spontaneous repertoire might have shown some more innovative forms either with -s or -n.

L's highly conservative language is also represented in other texts in the same manuscript. In the *Lambeth Homilies* and *Wel swuþe god Ureison of God Almihti*, however, we find innovative plural forms such as *wifes*, *weordes*, *laȝen*, *saulen*, and *sunnen* beside historically expected forms, whereas the L version of *PMor* gives historically expected forms only such as *wif*, *word*, *laȝe*, *saule*, and *sunne*.

The e and E versions are considered to have been contained in the same manuscript but written in different hands. They are textually closely related and copied from the same exemplar. The e and E texts are dated around 1225 and 1250 respectively and localised close to each other in South-West Midland. Both texts look linguistically archaic for the date, e being the more archaic.

Let me analyse the e text first. The spread of *-s* is occasionally found but no innovation in *-n* is in evidence. In addition there are no more than two weak nouns with *-n*: *eȝen* and *swikene*.[45] The loss of *n* may be the scribe's own, but the general archaic nature of the text suggests that the scribe was so heavily constrained by the exemplar that he perpetuated some *n*-less plurals contained in it.

This observation is in accordance with the proposed view about e's archaism. Laing comments that e was possibly copied with a strong intention of orthographic archaising by a scribe aware of the archaic nature of the subject ("Linguistic" 576).

Smith's following view is also relevant: "Early Middle English scribes were aware that traditional English spellings existed and, wishing to uphold tradition, wrote on purpose what may well have seemed to them archaic forms" ("Tradition" 54–55).

It seems reasonable to conclude that most evidence from e represents forms that felt archaic even to the scribe himself. The scribe's spontaneous usages would have contained more innovative plurals than the text shows.

Turning to E, we find more innovations and fluctuations than in e. The following contrastive pairs from e and E prove E's less archaic nature in the distribution of *-s* and especially of *-n* (rhymes are given where relevant): *laȝhe* (e: 170) / *laȝes* (E: 172); *dede* (e: 10) / *deden* (E: 10); *mis dede* (e: 271) [:*læde* (e: 272)] / *mis-deden* (E: 271); *euete* (e: 273) / *eueten* (E: 273). Since e and E are assumed to be descendants of a common exemplar, innovations observed only in E are likely to be the scribe's own.

An interesting question to ask is why such difference exists between e and E if they were copied out of the same exemplar. One answer will be the supposed time gap of about a quarter of a century. Alternatively, e and E may simply represent a more conservative and a more innovative copying habit on the part of the scribes.

It is worth noting what Smith said about the changing attitudes of scribes in the period concerned. Studying the spelling forms in different versions of the *Ancrene Riwle*, he pointed out that the scribe of MS Cleopatra (dated in 1225/30), with a traditional attitude toward copying, appeared to be heavily constrained by the exemplar written probably in the AB language, whereas the scribe of MS Nero (dated about 1240) showed his own language in the text much more frequently through a process of dialectal translation ("Tradition" 61). If, as he argued, this change of copying attitudes implies contemporary intellectual developments, differences in the copying attitudes between e and E may be explained likewise.

All in all, neither e nor E ties in with the average C13a South-West Midland profile. Both texts score far below the average in the spread rates of -s and -n. This is likely due to the general archaic nature of *PMor*, but there are certainly some innovative s- and n-plurals. Evidence of E shows in particular that the spread of -s and -n was surely in process in the language. The scribe's spontaneous usages were thus largely overshadowed by the archaic nature of the verse, but his spontaneous language might have squared better with the average C13a South-West Midland profile where -s and -n were constantly on the rise.

Next let us analyse the J version. Thanks to a great deal of study made on the C and J versions of *The Owl and the Nightingale*, it is now established that the J scribe was more a translator than a mechanical copyist. Though he preserved much of the archaic flavour from the exemplar, many forms in the J text represent the scribe's repertoire, whether active or passive.

In J we find a good number of innovations with -s and -n, and the spread rates for these two plural types are higher than for the three South-West Midland versions we have just analysed.

The rhyming pair of *wyhtes* and *sihtes* in lines 279 and 280 is particularly interesting in that J is the only text that shows this rhyme with -*es*. We may note that beside *wyhtes* the form *wyhte* occurs as an in-line form in line 78. The s-less form was perhaps more natural to the scribe than the s-form, but given the high spread rate in J, it would be unsurprising if the s-form were as common.

In inverse proportion to -*s* and -*n* is the *V*-plural. With a decreasing number of *V*-plurals, J's system approaches the characteristic *s*/*n*-dichotomic system, as in other C13 South-West Midland texts like the AB group. In fact, J's rates are very close to the C13b South-West Midland average. J is clearly one of the most typical C13b South-West Midland texts.

M is another South-West Midland text dated not long after J, so it is worth comparing the two texts.[46]

Both texts show some extension of -*s*, but the distributions of the *n*-plural differ. In J the *n*-plural spreads to a certain extent, whereas M totally lacks the *n*-plural. We may see the following contrastive pairs from J and M: *soulen* (J: 280) / *saule* (M: 260); *deden* (J: 10) / *dede* (M: 12); *reuen* (J: 252) [:*ileuen* (J: 251)] / *reue* (M: 242) [:*yleue* (M: 241)].

The virtual lack of the *n*-plural is a striking feature of M.[47] In M we find a great number of *V*-plurals instead of *n*-plurals. It is worth noting that there are no dative plurals with -*n* either in this text.

The absence of the *n*-plural in M is striking since just about a quarter of a century before, J not only kept historical forms in -*n* but also recorded additional innovative *n*-plurals. It is difficult to believe that there was a change that reorganised the plural system so dramatically within such a short period of time. Rather, considering the unusual thoroughness with which M lacks -*n*, I suspect that the M scribe consciously eliminated it as he copied the text.

In my opinion M's lack of -*n* is an exaggerated representation of one linguistic process around 1300 in South-West Midland. As the overview of the C14a South-West Midland situation suggests, the *n*-plural finished its spread by the turn of the century and began to decrease due to the loss of -*n* in inflectional endings. The M scribe must have been well aware of this process and consciously extended this tendency to all plural forms—a case of hyperadaptation. The loss of *n* was certainly occurring but cannot have been so dramatic as the text language actually shows.

Unlike the distribution of -*n*, the extension of -*s* is a shared feature of J and M. Interestingly, innovation in -*s* reaches different items in J and M. The following are innovations of -*s* in J: *hestes, wonynges, yeftes, þinges,* and *werkes.* On the other hand, M shows these innovations: *woniegges, sennes, workes*, *wiues*, *wintres*, and *wordes*.

There seem to be some reasons for this difference. First, it may simply be due to different textual histories (let us remember that M was supposedly handed down partly through memory rather than the written word). Moreover, according to Zupitza's stemma, J and M are distantly related "genetically." Furthermore, M's uncertain localisation would warn us against assuming that comparison of J and M should be meaningful at all.

Now that I have analysed the five South-West Midland texts, let me summarise the diachronic development of the plural system in South-West Midland. L (C12b) generally keeps the Old English plural system well but shows signs that -*s* and -*n* were starting to spread. Soon after L's period development of the *s*/*n*-dichotomic system was underway, as can partly be seen in e and E. The development continued until the period represented by J (C13b), where the *s*/*n*-dichotomic system was almost fully established. Not long after, the spread of -*s* sped up while the *n*-plural was dramatically reduced. This stage is represented, as it seems to me, with not a little exaggeration in M's language.

Now let us move on to the T version localised to South-East Midland. It is a C12b text, so comparison with L will highlight contemporary dialectal differences between South-East Midland and South-West Midland. Since the T scribe is known to have been a mechanical copyist rather than a translator, much of his output should represent the exemplar's dialect of Essex rather than his own usage. This means that many of the innovative plurals appearing in T probably have their origin at least one scribal generation back.

As we may expect, the South-East Midland text provides more examples to show the spread of -*s* than the South-West Midland text. Two of the recorded *s*-innovations even abort rhymes: *fiendes* (223) [:*friende* (224)] and *wihten* (285) [:*sihte* (286)].

T also keeps *n*-plurals more consistently than L. Some *n*-plurals abort rhymes, as in *iferen* (102, 233, 297) [:*here* (101, 234, 298)]. These rhyme-spoiling forms may perhaps mirror the scribe's spontaneous language. The retention of -*n* in T is further exemplified in the following contrastive pairs from T and L: *deflen* (T: 97) / *doule* (L: 97); *tiden* (T: 139) [:*abiden* (T: 140)] / *tide* (L: 137) [:*abiden* (L: 138)]; *iferen* (T: 102) [:*here* (T: 101)] / *ifere* (L: 102) [:*here* (L: 101)]; *iferen* (L: 233) [:*here* (L: 234)] / *iuere* (L: 229) [:*here* (L: 230)];

wallen (T: 41) (after a preposition) / *walle* (L: 41) (after a preposition); *dichen* (T: 41) (after a preposition) / *diche* (L: 41) (after a preposition).

T is thus distinguished from L by more innovation of the *s*-plural and more retention of the *n*-plural. Although vowel endings are still fairly alive, it is safe to say that T is closer to the characteristic *s*/*n*-dichotomic system than L. This agrees with the observation that the *s*/*n*-dichotomic system of South-East Midland was developing toward C13a.

If we recall that L represents only an initial stage of the development toward the *s*/*n*-dichotomic system, the diatopic relationship between L and T may be mapped onto a diachronic one. Both text languages were developing in the same direction, only T was ahead.

Finally, I analyse the D version localised to Southeastern and dated C13a. The D scribe seems to have been greatly constrained by the exemplar, but on occasion he revealed his own usage in the text. Without more information about the D scribe's copying practise, it is hard to be certain how much the text represents his own usage, but the general homogeneity of the text language suggests that the language is mostly his own.

D's plural system shows innovations both in -*s* and -*n*, approaching the *s*/*n*-dichotomic system. Fluctuation between *sennes* and *sennen* is a good example to show the spread of both -*s* and -*n*. One striking feature about D's language is that the scribe did not mind breaking rhymes very much. In spoiling rhymes he let some of his spontaneous forms appear in the text. Examples are: *diches* (20a; after a preposition) [:*heueriche* (20b)], *iueren* (47b, 112a) [:*hiere* (47a, 112b)], *wrenchen* (123a; after a preposition) [:*penche* (123b)] and *fruden* (132a) [:*prude* (132b)].[48]

diches in the first example is unique in that the other versions give either *diche* (L, e, E, J, M) or *dichen* (T) in the corresponding line.

fruden in the last example agrees with J in breaking the rhyme, and this may be best explained as a result of an item enumeration environment in the context "Þer bieð naddren and snaken, eueten and ec fruden." Repeating the same inflectional endings in such an item enumeration environment is fairly common in Early Middle English texts (see Section 6.7 for a related discussion).

As the examples above show, the scribal addition of -*n* is common in D. Besides, -*n* is rarely lost in historical weak nouns, e.g. *eueten* (132a), *ireuen*

(125b) [:*ileuen* (125a)], *snaken* (132a), and *sterren* (36b). The rich presence of -*n* is thus another notable feature of D.

According to the C13a Southeastern profile, both -*s* and -*n* were steadily growing in the direction of the *s/n*-dichotomic system. D's situation therefore mostly agrees with the average picture of the C13a Southeastern situation.

I have closely analysed the seven versions of *PMor* with a view to placing the plural system of each language in a diachronic and diatopic network of Early Middle English. The texts of *PMor* are admittedly difficult to compare due to the many philological and textual complications involved; however, further study of L, J, and T in particular will help to disentangle the complexities. Fortunately they have a number of scribally related texts within and outside the manuscripts.

The J, M, T, and D texts provided a number of forms reasonably considered the scribe's own usage or the exemplar's dialect. To this extent they can serve as "anchors" for localisations of other Early Middle English texts, as Laing insists ("Anchor"). In contrast, the L, E, and e texts were mostly mechanically copied, so that much of the scribes' own usage is kept hidden. If carefully interpreted and supported by other independent evidence, however, examples from L, E, and e could contribute to a reconstruction of the plural systems in the southern dialects of Early Middle English. Future study along this line will be fruitful.

4.5 The Peterborough Chronicle

Table 4.10: Statistical Summary for *The Peterborough Chronicle*

	CA	1C	FC
tokens	459	146	109
types	156	75	44
syncretism rate	0.008	0	0
(spread) rate of s	0.4 (1.2)	0.6 (1.3)	0.82 (2.1)
(spread) rate of n	0.2 (1.7)	0.027 (0.25)	0.068 (0.33)
(spread) rate of V	0.26 (0.98)	0.2 (1.1)	0 (0)
(spread) rate of $\emptyset$	0.13 (0.54)	0.13 (0.71)	0.068 (0.5)
(spread) rate of M	0.013 (0.25)	0.04 (0.75)	0.045 (0.67)

Notes: s, n, V, $\emptyset$, and M represent s-, n-, vowel-, $\emptyset$-, and minor plural types respectively. Figures in parentheses represent "spread rate" as distinct from simple "(type) rate." The syncretism rate appears as "NA" when there are no examples from dative environments. The spread rate appears as "NA" when there are no examples in text that historically took that plural type.

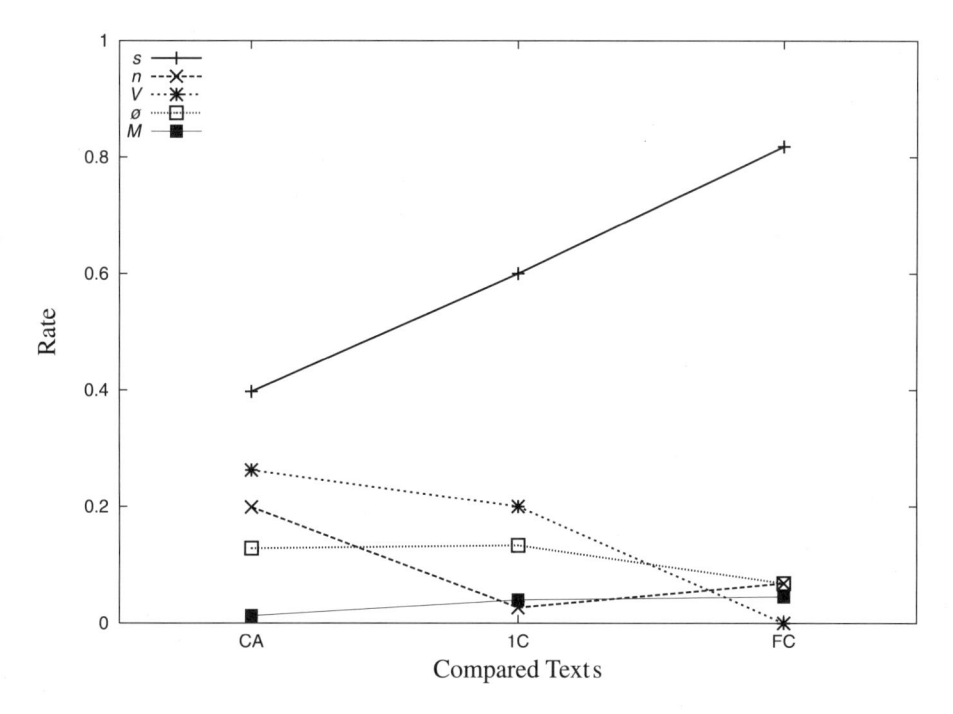

Figure 4.5: Rate for *The Peterborough Chronicle*

The text of the *Peterborough Chronicle*, Bodleian, Laud Misc. 636, consists of three parts, each of which has distinct linguistic features. The first part is known as the Copied Annals (hereafter CA, covering the entries up to 1121, written in one hand soon after the last entry (see PFP 15000 in Appendix D.5.1). The language is close to standard Late West-Saxon but with a tint of Southern peculiarities.

The second part is known as the First Continuation (hereafter 1C), covering entries 1122 to 1131 (see PFP 16000 in Appendix D.5.2). It is written in six blocks in the same hand as the Copied Annals. The composition was soon after the last entry. There are additional interpolations throughout the Copied Annals, and they are concurrently made by the same hand, so it is common to deal with them and the First Continuation together for linguistic analysis.

The third part is known as the Final Continuation (hereafter FC) from 1132 to 1154, written by another scribe all at one time immediately after the last entry (see PFP 149 in Appendix D.5.3). Both Continuations represent a local dialect of Peterborough, South-East Midland.

For the present study I fully analyse 1C (with the Interpolations) and FC from Earle and Plummer's edition. As for CA, I only cover entries 1070 to 1121 following Clark's edition.

Since the language of CA is Late West-Saxon rather than South-East Midland, comparison between CA on the one hand and 1C and FC on the other will not make a meaningful diachronic study, but just highlight contrasts between Late West-Saxon and the Early Middle English Peterborough dialect. On the other hand, comparison of 1C and FC will make a good diachronic study of the Peterborough dialect.

That the language of CA is not entirely in accordance with what we would expect for standard Late West-Saxon is indicated by the high rate of $-s$ and $-n$. Especially remarkable is the spread of the n-plural, which extends to nouns of the V-ending class, the Masc-S class and the Neut-$\emptyset$ class. There is also a sharp decrease in the $\emptyset$-plurals, which show common transfers to $-s$, $-n$ or $-V$. Furthermore, there is frequent interchange between the n- and V-ending plurals.

Deviation of CA's language from standard Late West-Saxon may only be a function of time or due to mixture of some Southern peculiarities. We might argue that at least some of the innovative features in CA are due to the Early Middle English copyist carrying over his spontaneous usages to the text. This possibility, however, cannot be accepted. When we compare CA and 1C, there are not many innovative plurals shared by the two texts. Innovations in CA are apparently independent of those in 1C (for example, compare in the PFPs of CA and 1C forms for *gærsum, sunu, abbodrīce, biscoprīce, lagu, mynster*, and *bōc*). Most of the innovations in CA should therefore be understood as due to diachronic development of language, not as the copyist's carry-overs from his exemplar.

Let us move on to the language of 1C. The text is not a copy but the scribe's own composition; most scholars agree, however, that the language is a heavy mixture of the scribe's spontaneous usages and his West-Saxon influenced usages. He was often "wrongly" influenced by the West-Saxon *Schriftsprache*, producing what Clark called "false archaism" (lxi).

In 1C the growth of the *s*-plural and the fall of the *n*-plural seem mostly genuine, but some of the apparently innovative *V*-plurals may in fact be false archaisms rather than genuine developments. It may be noted that no fewer than four Masc-S nouns have changed over to -*V* (i.e. *gærsum, hæþen, munuc,* and *rǣd*).

Some of these new *V*-plurals might be the scribe's own innovations, but I would rather accept the explanation of false archaism on the grounds that at the time when word-final -*n* or -*V* in inflectional endings became increasingly reduced, there was little functional motivation for any noun to transfer to the *V*-plural.

The growth of -*V* put aside, 1C's language represents a typical stage at which -*s* was establishing its dominance over the other plural types. Due to the scribe's false archaism, 1C's language looks more archaic than the scribe's spontaneous repertoire would have been. In other words, the scribe's own Peterborough dialect would have been slightly more "advanced" in terms of the spread rate for -*s* than 1C's language makes us believe.

The next stage of the development is represented by FC's language, where -*s* almost dominates the plural system. The *s*-plural shows constant growth, whereas the *n*-plural is remarkably reduced. As for the *V*-plural, the FC part of the text records no examples. Given a fairly short interval, the morphological difference between 1C and FC is striking. It is as if the reorganisation had proceeded with dramatic speed. A likely explanation for the great difference is that, as I mentioned earlier, 1C's language was so deliberately archaised that the scribe's own usage was overshadowed. Dramatic development between 1C and FC must therefore be more apparent than real.

It is worth mentioning that in terms of the rates FC is far above the average among the contemporary South-East Midland texts. This is presumably because FC is localised in the far north of South-East Midland. The profile of the South-East Midland diachronic development places the average type rate for -*s* about 0.6 in C12. If, however, we consider only 1C and FC, the rate approaches 0.8, and therefore they are more comparable to contemporary North-East Midland texts (scoring 0.82 for C12b) than other South-East Midland texts.

Let us now have a close look at the variation in plural forms within and across the three parts of the text. All but a few of the Masc-S class nouns remain unchanged and take -*s*. Among the few exceptions are *muneca* and *clerca* from the entry for the year 963 (hereafter, reference is made to the year of the entry). This *a*-plural for Masc-S nouns is a unique innovation, as these forms occur in a particular sentence with another *a*-plural *nunna*.

- ⁊ draf út þa **clerca** of þe biscoprice, forþan þ hi noldon nan regul healden, ⁊ sætta þær **muneca**. He macode þær twa abbotrice. an of **muneca** oðer of **nunna** (Interpolation 963; emphasis added)

The three *a*-plurals appear only in this particular part of the 1C text, and elsewhere we have *clerekes* and, even in the same year, *munecas*. As for "nuns" there are no other occurrences of this form in the text. Meyer explains this peculiar *a*-ending as due to analogy on the *u*-stem plurals such as *suna* (qtd. in Roedler, 1: 28). Seeing that all these forms occur in succession only in this particular part of the Interpolations and are all semantically related, they are likely to be the scribe's nonce coinages to achieve an archaic air.[49] Otherwise, he may have intended the effect of vowel assonance to make masculine *muneca* and feminine *nunna* resonate semantically as well as for rhyme.

Other Masc-S nouns that have changed over to other plural types include *ræde*, *að*, and *horn*. All of these occur in 1C, as follows (emphasis added): "God ælmihtig adylege iuele **ræde**" (1130); "he wæs an hæfod ða **að** to swerene"

(1127); "þa muncccs herdon ða **horn** blawen" (1127). Reading them as plurals is supported by the context as well as on the final vowel of the adjective *iuele* and of the determiner *ða*. The singular reading, however, is not impossible.

As for the Masc-N nouns, many of them keep *-n* but some have transferred to *-s*. The plural form *heretogas* appears beside three *s*-plurals in successive prepositional phrases, as follows (emphasis added): "mid þas kyningas ꝛ mid eorles ꝛ mid **heorotogas** ꝛ mid þægnas" (Interpolation 656). In environments where items are enumerated one after another, such a plural formation transfer is common in Early Middle English texts (see Section 6.7 for a related discussion).

The word for "outlaws" shows heavy fluctuation. The three plural endings *-s*, *-n* and *-V* all appear in the entries 1070 and 1071. The two variants *utlages* and *utlaga* indeed appear only two lines away from each other. The *V*-form can be explained as loss of the *n*-ending which might have existed. The loss of *-n* also explains *untime* (OE Masc-N *tīma*) in 1124.

huntes resonates with *hundes*, serving to connect the two phrases rhythmically (emphasis added): "Þa **huntes** wæron swarte ꝛ micele ꝛ ladlice. ꝛ here **hundes** ealle swarte ꝛ bradegede ꝛ ladlice" (1127). *snakes* stands between two *s*-plurals of the historically Fem-N nouns (emphasis added): "þar nadres ꝛ **snakes** ꝛ pades wæron inne" (1137).

Turning to the Fem-N nouns, *mæssahakeles* appears with innovative *-s* in an enumeration environment (emphasis added): "þet wæron C*ristes* bec ꝛ **mæssahakeles** ꝛ cantelcapas ꝛ reafes ꝛ swilce litles hwat" (1070). Another example of *-s* is in "foruton feawe bec. ꝛ .iii. **messehakeles**" (1122).

Not so many of the Fem-V nouns have transferred to *-s*. *laces* stands in a context where topographical nouns with *-s* occur in succession (emphasis added): "þurh ælle þa meres ꝛ feonnes þa liggen toward Huntendune porte. ꝛ þas meres ꝛ **laces**" (Interpolation 656).

treothes appears (emphasis added) in "hi nan treuthe ne heolden. alle he waron forsworen ꝛ here **treothes** forloren" (1137). Here *treothes* effectively marks its plurality by means of its clear *s*-ending in contrast with the singular *treuthe* earlier in the sentence. Let me note that the year 1093 gives the old *V*-plural (or possibly singular?) *getrywða* in "[he] swilce **getrywða** dyde" (emphasis added).

The Neut-V and Neut-Ø nouns heavily fluctuate between historically expected endings and -s. Examples are *land* ~ *landes*, *write* ~ *writes*, *mynstra* ~ *mynstres*, *gyld* ~ *gildes*, and *limu* ~ *limes*.

Some of the Neut-Ø nouns transfer to -V or -n, as in the quotations below (emphasis added).

- Ic . . . geate ealle þas **worde** (Interpolation 963)
- he ne mihte ðolen þa micele **unrihte** ꝫ þa micele unsibbe (1127)
- he . . . na*m* swilce **gerihta** swa se cyng him geuðe (1074)
- hwilce **gerihtæ** he ahte to habbanne (1085)
- heo . . . mid hire prestan to cyrcean eode. ꝫ hire **gerihtan** underfeng (1093)
- se cyng Henri . . . þær þa **biscopricen** ꝫ **abbodric*en*** geaf (1107)

Various kinds of transfer by the Neut-Ø nouns are considered functionally motivated. In Old English the Neut-Ø nouns did not distinguish grammatical number morphologically (e.g. *hūs* for both singular and plural). During the transitional period, it became increasingly necessary for nouns to mark plurality on their own rather than by indirect means such as the inflections of the governing determiners or adjectives, because the latter themselves became rapidly dysfunctional as a result of the levelling and loss of sounds in unaccented inflectional syllables. Now, if nominal plurality was to be marked explicitly, distinct singular and plural forms needed to be developed. It was likely, under these circumstances, that the ø-ending nouns were ready to transfer away.

Transfer of the Neut-Ø nouns to -*n* and -*V* was common both in CA and 1C. Such transfer was arguably independently taking place in two linguistic varieties associated with the two distinct texts.

In the above I compared the three distinct texts of *The Peterborough Chronicle*. By way of conclusion I make two points. First, it is likely that innovation in CA is independent of that in 1C and FC, and the deviant features in CA from the standard Late West-Saxon are attributed simply to diachronic development rather than to the Early Middle English copyist's carry-overs. Therefore, if innovations in CA are shared by 1C or FC, it is likely mere chance, and independent parallel development should be assumed.

Secondly, the 1C scribe's spontaneous language would have been closer to FC's text language than 1C's text language is, considering that 1C's text language seems heavily affected by the scribe's false archaism. Accordingly, in interpreting diachronic development from 1C to FC, we have to be aware of the possibility that linguistic difference between them may be overemphasised to such an extent that false archaism is involved in 1C.

Chapter 5   HOW: Lexical Diffusion

5.1   Introduction to Lexical Diffusion

In Chapter 3, I analysed texts, presented facts about the distribution of various nominal plural types, and arranged them according to keys such as dialect, period, and item. In Chapter 4, I analysed five sets of comparable texts to place the findings in context. I am now ready to sort out these individual findings theoretically to achieve a general understanding of "how" the plural system developed in Early Middle English.

A recent development in theories of language change is Lexical Diffusion. It was first proposed by Wang in his "Competing Changes as a Cause of Residue" as a model for sound change, and ever since the theory has been developed to address linguistic change in general.[50]

Lexical Diffusion was first proposed to explain the implementation of sound change as an argument against the widely acknowledged Neogrammarian hypothesis of the regularity of sound change. Neogrammarians thought that sound change was phonetically gradual and lexically abrupt, explaining away exceptions to their rule as either due to analogy or dialectal borrowing.

In some cases, analogy may indeed be the only reasonable explanation, but since analogy is primarily a morphological process, for languages without a complicated morphology such as Chinese, the Neogrammarian argument for analogy must fail (Chen and Wang 256). Dialectal borrowing may be an alternative account for exceptions, but again the Neogrammarian argument for dialectal borrowing was often ad hoc, not exploring far enough into the dynamism of diatopic interaction.

One of the major differences between the Neogrammarians and the diffusionists lies in the way of viewing the implementation of sound change. There are four logical patterns in which sound change can be implemented:

1. phonetically abrupt and lexically abrupt
2. phonetically abrupt and lexically gradual
3. phonetically gradual and lexically abrupt
4. phonetically gradual and lexically gradual

The Neogrammarians assumed Type 3 whereas diffusionists find Type 2 more likely.[51] In the diffusionist view, sound change implements itself not abruptly but gradually through the lexicon, perhaps by a few words at a time. The basic pattern of implementation can be described as follows.

The diffusion starts slowly, affecting only a handful of words. Some time later, there comes a moment when the diffusion gathers momentum and quickens through the majority of the lexicon. This quick diffusion continues until it affects most of the lexicon, and then tapers off toward the end, leaving a handful of words unaffected by change. The pattern is often compared to a snowball bounding down a hill. Charted in a graph, the pattern shows a characteristic S-curve (see Figure 5.1 on page 119).[52]

Examined closely, the S-curve of diffusion itself consists of a series of smaller S-curves (Aitchison, *Language* 92–93). This is to say that diffusion spreads through the lexicon by groups of a few words at a time. Each of the groupings may depend on linguistic factors that are phonetic, morphological, syntactic, or semantic.

Lexical Diffusion should in principle be understood as a theory of implementation as distinct from actuation of language change, as Wang and Lien clearly distinguished the two. This clear separation of actuation and implementation of language change is theoretically important, but in fact they are indivisible. The problem of actuation and implementation may be addressed in two related questions: "what factors determine which lexical items will be affected first by change" and "what determines the momentum of a diffusing change" (McMahon 56).

Seeing that Lexical Diffusion typically proceeds by groups of a few items and each group is typically characterised in terms of linguistic categories or environments, the first question may be rephrased as "what are the linguistic environments or categories of the group of items that are first affected by diffusion?" It is doubtful that there is a general rule that determines the starters

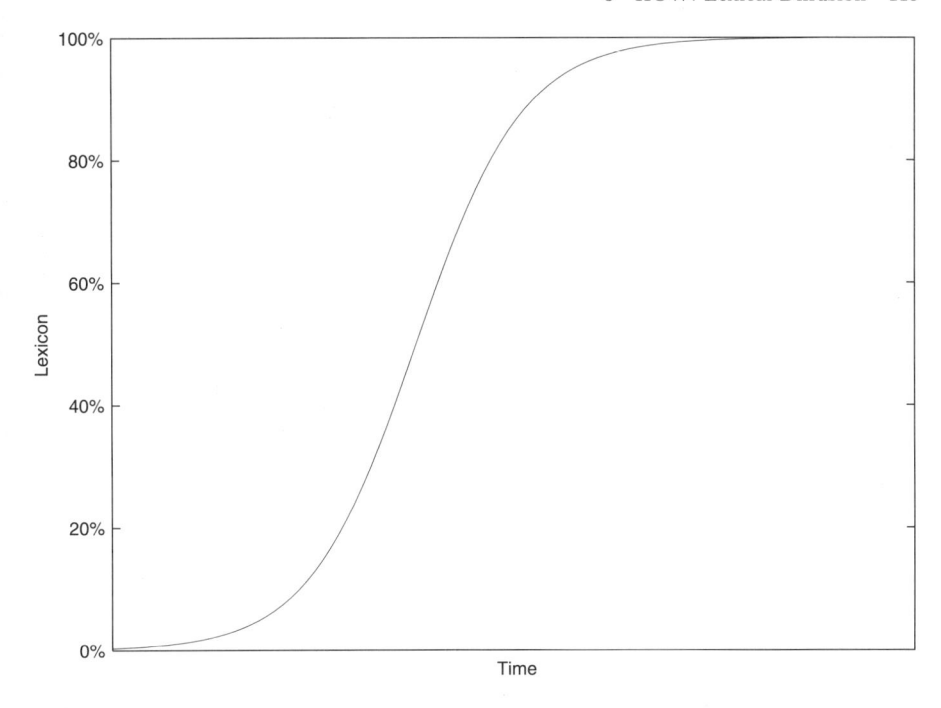

Figure 5.1: Characteristic S-Curve of Lexical Diffusion

of change; some patterns are, however, repeatedly observed in many linguistic changes, so we may speak of tendencies if not universals. For example, in their study of reduction of word-final consonants in languages such as Chinese, Chen and Wang concluded that sound change must be partly actuated by "the inherent constraints of the physiological and perceptual apparatus of the language user" (255). Linguists have also noted that frequency affects the timing that particular items start changing.[53]

As for the second question of "what determines the momentum of a diffusing change," Aitchison proposes the schedule of "a conspiracy followed by a snowball," which

> fleshes out the S-curve model by explaining how it happens: the slow, early part of the S are the smallish, fairly piecemeal changes which then combine into a conspiracy, which sets off the steep part of the curve, the snowball. The snowball itself fleshes out the notion of analogy: there

comes a point at which further generalisation is inevitable, and swift. ("Missing" 25)

This "mechanical" explanation may work well for the ideal case of diffusion, that is, where no interfering force, either language-internal or -external, is involved in the process. In many actual cases, however, various forces are involved so that a less typical diffusing S-curve tends to result. Conditioning factors that determine the schedule of diffusion may be language-internal ones like phonological environments and grammatical categories or language-external ones like language contact.

I have so far assumed that Lexical Diffusion is a diffusion of linguistic innovation through the lexicon, that is, innovative features spread through the lexicon of a speaker or a site. There is, however, another level of diffusion, i.e. diffusion through the population, as linguistic innovations diffuse from speaker to speaker through the population just as well as from word to word through the lexicon. Ogura and Wang's recent studies have demonstrated that the speaker-to-speaker diffusion also draws a characteristic S-curve ("Snowball" and "Evolution").

Ogura and Wang call these two different levels of diffusion W-diffusion and S-diffusion. W-diffusion proceeds from word to word of a single speaker or at a single site, while S-diffusion proceeds from speaker to speaker, or from site to site of a single word. Students of language change have sometimes spoken of this "double diffusion," which may be compared to diffusion of infectious diseases:

> These diffusion processes are comparable to epidemics of infectious diseases, and the standard model of an epidemic produces an S-curve (called logistic) describing the increase of frequency of the trait. There are potentially two epidemics, or more exactly two dimensions in which the epidemic can proceed. One dimension is represented by W-diffusion and the other dimension by S-diffusion. (Ogura and Wang, "Evolution" 322)[54]

Besides W-diffusion and S-diffusion, we may conceive of another dimension of diffusion from dialect to dialect, which is a macro-level representation of diffusion from speaker to speaker or from site to site.[55] Chambers and Trudgill mention yet other levels of diffusion: sociolinguistic diffusion from one social group to another, linguistic diffusion from one linguistic environment to another, and spatial diffusion from place to place (160). In sociolinguistic diffusion, we might even conceive of pragmatic, stylistic and register-related sublevels.

Lexical Diffusion is thus a multi-level theory that addresses language change from various points of view. Although it is still a developing model of language change, its theoretical advantages have been recognised, as will be discussed in the next section.

5.2 Advantages of Lexical Diffusion

This section discusses why the Lexical Diffusion model can contribute to a better understanding of language change. The first advantage of the model is its capability of handling "residues" of language change. Residues are items which failed to be affected by change where they could be subject to it. If the Neogrammarian view of sound change being regular were assumed, how could residues be accounted for if not (often dubiously) due to analogy or dialectal borrowing? If we assume gradual language change as Lexical Diffusion does, various explanations are possible.

For the first thing, the change may simply have not affected certain items yet, so it may reach them some time in the future. Alternatively, the change may have ceased for ever, leaving certain items unaffected by change. Another possibility is that the change may have reversed its direction before it could affect certain items. Finally, the change may have been prevented by another change which interfered with it. Whichever the case, as long as gradual diffusion is assumed, residues that are produced in the process of diffusion can be accounted for.

Another advantage of Lexical Diffusion is its capability of handling linguistic variation. As McMahon rightly comments: "The theory of lexical diffusion is attractive to dialectologists as well as linguists, since it gives some theoretical status to the variation which emerges from dialect surveys, especially in transition areas between dialects" (51). Lexical Diffusion is fully capable of linguistic variation or coexistence of variants, because it assumes, to begin with, that language change is implemented gradually through the lexicon or the population, and therefore that there is necessarily a period of coexistence of old and new variants.

Moreover, Lexical Diffusion can address the competition between variants as a sublevel diffusion. As we saw in the study of individual items in Section 3.3, the relative ratio of innovative forms to historical forms increases over time, again typically following an S-curve.

When a new variant displaces an old one in the course of linguistic change, it does so not abruptly but gradually through several intermediate stages. The following might be a hypothetical scenario. At an early stage of the change, the innovative variant may occur, say, at ten percent frequency while the old variant scores ninety percent. Some time later, perhaps when the rate slowly approaches somewhere around twenty percent, diffusion gathers momentum and "takes off." The innovative variant continues to increase with speed under its own impetus, and then slackens again perhaps around eighty percent and tapers off toward the end of the displacement process. This increasing ratio of the new variant to the old would square perfectly with common S-curves in W-diffusion. This level of diffusion may be called "item-internal diffusion."

Yet another theoretical strength of Lexical Diffusion is its applicability to language change at different levels such as morphology, syntax, and even semantics.[56] This is not to say, however, that the principle originally developed for sound change can apply to morphology, syntax, or semantics without modification. This issue is taken up in the next section.

Finally, it should be counted as another strength of Lexical Diffusion that the basic mechanism of implementation it proposes applies to contact-induced change as well as to system-internally motivated change. Hashimoto remarks: "Lexical diffusion can explain not only the internal development of languages, but also developments caused by language contact" (190).

Lexical Diffusion should provide a useful framework for the present study of the development of the Early Middle English plural system, but before applying the theory to it, let us consider to what extent the theory originally proposed for sound change can hold for morphological change.

5.3 Applicability of Lexical Diffusion to Morphological Change

Even before Lexical Diffusion was explicitly proposed as a rival sound change theory against the Neogrammarian view, the notion of gradual diffusion was long understood by linguists. Far from being a novel notion, gradual diffusion was taken as a matter of course for morphological changes. Most morphological change involves analogy, and analogy diffuses gradually by nature.

There are certainly differences in the implementation of phonological and morphological changes. In order to apply the theory to the present subject, it is necessary to understand in what respects morphological change is similar to, and different from, phonological change. Let us review two of the case studies of morphological change, one by Aitchison and the other by Ogura and Wang.

In her "Missing Link," Aitchison investigated the nominal plural marking in Tok Pisin, a language spoken in Papua New Guinea. In Tok Pisin, there are three plural markers: prenominal *ol*, suffix -*s*, and suffix -*pela*. The distribution of the three markers can be summarised as follows. The suffix -*pela* is now non-productive and used in a number of pronouns and numerals. The prenominal *ol* is the commonest plural marker, preferentially used with human nouns, together with *sampela* "several," with adjectives and with *s*-plurals not preceded by numerals. It can also occur with inanimate nouns. The suffix -*s*, derived from the English equivalent, occurs with words designating time, English foods, and people. It tends to occur together with *ol* or a numeral.

Aitchison is of the opinion that *ol* spread from one lexical group to another: it started probably from the names of people and extended to human nouns in general, while occurrence with *sampela* produced a new pattern in which *ol* came to occur with any adjective. The English derived suffix -*s* also seems to have spread but less remarkably so. The distribution of each marker remains mostly complementary at the moment, but Aitchison predicts that *ol* will replace -*s* in the near future (23).

If Aitchison's proposed development is correct, the morphological change of the plural marking in Tok Pisin is a strikingly typical case of Lexical Diffusion-based language change. Diffusion of *ol* implements itself by "rule generalisations," that is, environments affected by change extend from people's names to human nouns in general and from post-*sampela* positions to post-adjectival positions in general. These rule generalisations are governed by semantic and morphosyntactic factors.

Aitchison observes that the Tok Pisin case has every feature of Lexical Diffusion-based language change:

> . . . in brief, we find the change involving variation, with words with and without a plural marker coexisting; vocabulary items, even within the same linguistic environment are not equally affected; some types of words prefer *ol* or -*s*, others do not; various factors seem to play a role in deciding which lexical items get affected early; the change is proceeding through the language by a process of lexical diffusion, progressing through various linguistic environments; the change appears to have begun slowly, then accelerated, showing the development of a typical S-curve pattern; the progress of either one of the plural markers discussed is not inevitable, and could be halted. (23–24)

The other case study of Lexical Diffusion in morphology is Ogura and Wang's "Snowball Effect in Lexical Diffusion," which investigated the development of -*s* in the third person singular present indicative in Early Modern English. They collected examples of *s*- and *th*-forms from the Early Modern English part of the Helsinki corpus.

They found that against common expectation, high frequency verbs such as *have*, *do*, and *say* started first, not last, to change over to -*s*. They also found that these first changes took a long time to complete. In contrast, low frequency verbs changed over relatively quickly although they started to change later.

In addition they discovered that verbs ending in a sibilant were less willing to accept *s*-forms than verbs ending in a non-sibilant. All these observations led them to conclude that it was "the interplay between word frequency and the phonological environments" that determined the schedule of the change (131).

Both case studies ensure that Lexical Diffusion is just as applicable to morphological change as to phonological change. Then what differences are there at all between phonology and morphology in terms of Lexical Diffusion? One difference is in the speed of change. Morphological change is likely to diffuse more slowly than phonological change. This is because there are more morphemes than phonemes and there are more morphological environments to work through than phonological ones (Aitchison, "Missing" 25).

Another difference is that morphological change usually shows a higher degree of irregularity than phonological change because slower changes are more likely to be involved in unexpected interferences as they proceed. The irregularity of morphological change is due also to the complexities of morphological categories. To take the Early Middle English nouns for example, there are intertwined categories such as case, number, gender, and declension type. The complex interdependence of these categories makes it difficult for any morphological change to proceed regularly.

Furthermore, morphemes are associated with meanings while phonemes are normally not (phonaesthesia aside, of course). It is no wonder, therefore, that morphology is more subject to semantic association than phonology.

One final point is that since morphology is more closely related to syntax than phonology, it is more likely to be conditioned by syntactic contexts as well. On this matter Ogura and Wang cite Stein as considering that the major factors that determine the schedule of change from *-s* to *-th* in verbs include the sentence type as well as phonotactics and verb types ("Snowball" 124).

In summary, Lexical Diffusion is applicable in principle to morphological change in much the same way as it is to phonological change. Morphological change proceeds from word to word in an S-curve; it proceeds by groups of a few words at a time; it proceeds from speaker to speaker and from site to site; and it proceeds with variations, sometimes leaving some items unaffected. The following point, however, must be kept in mind. Compared to phonological change, morphological change is likely to proceed slowly and irregularly, because it is more subject to interference of the complex interweave of various morphological categories, semantic associations, and syntactic environments.

5.4 Lexical Diffusion and the Early Middle English Plural System

In this section, I will try to apply Lexical Diffusion to the development of the Early Middle English plural system. As I mentioned in Section 5.1, there are two levels of diffusion: W-diffusion and S-diffusion. Let us first focus on W-diffusion. W-diffusion is a process where language innovation proceeds through the vocabulary of a speaker or at a site. A possible scenario of the W-diffusion of the *s*-plural is as follows: a particular speaker or site first accepted the innovative *s*-plural for a few nouns; some time later they applied the innovation to more nouns; and finally most of their vocabulary was affected by the spread of -*s*.

Let us look at the graph of the rate for -*s* in Figure 5.2 on page 127 (for the other related graphs, see Appendix C). To start with, the *s*-plurals were relatively numerous in every dialect. Then they spread over to noun classes other than the *a*-stem masculines. The spread started slowly but sped up over time. When the rate reached somewhere between seventy and ninety percent of the vocabulary, the diffusion slowed down, tapering off. Although the slope of the curve varied according to dialect, the described pattern applies roughly to every dialect.

Then let us turn to the graph of the rate for -*n* in Figure 5.3 on page 127. In contrast to the spread of the *s*-plural, the *n*-plural became less frequent in many of the dialects. As we saw earlier, the southern dialects had a period when the *n*-plural underwent a temporary revival. Therefore, we may speak of the *n*-plural diffusion beside the *s*-plural diffusion although it was limited in distribution and scale.

As the graph illustrates, the only dialect to show any remarkable spread of -*n* is South-West Midland. The curve is not a typical S-curve, however, as Lexical Diffusion would predict. This is primarily because the diffusion of its rival *s*-plural worked as an offset. Not surprisingly, while -*n* was resurgent, the spread of -*s* was slackening. This is why the South-West Midland dialect shows strange shaped curves for both -*s* and -*n*.

The graphs clearly show W-diffusion at work, but they also illustrate the

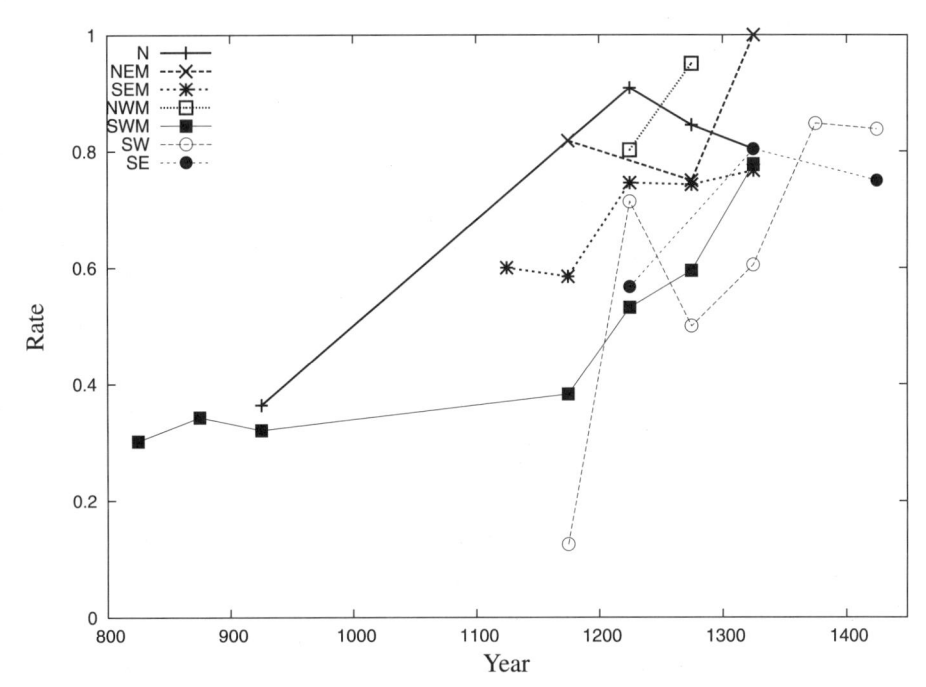

Figure 5.2: Rate for -s

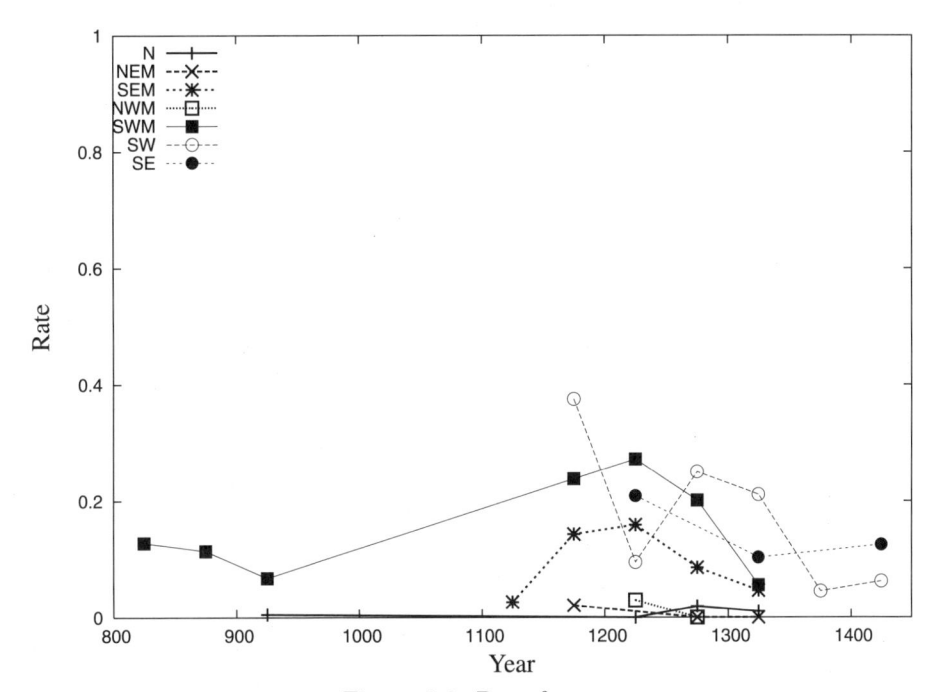

Figure 5.3: Rate for -n

working of S-diffusion, which proceeds through the population. At a micro-level it occurs from speaker to speaker; at a macro-level it occurs from site to site or from dialect to dialect. Since the curves for different dialects are roughly, if not exactly, parallel, they imply that diffusion was proceeding from one dialect to another.

The paucity of texts as well as the unevenness of data distribution prevents close investigation of cross-dialectal diffusion, but the diachronic/diatopic distribution of various plural types clearly shows that the spread of -*s* was early in Northern, North-East Midland, and South-East Midland while it was late in South-West Midland. On the other hand, the *n*-plural was more frequent in South-West Midland than in the northern dialects. We may be able to visualise from the graphs a wave of innovation for -*s* moving from the northeast to the southwest.

Beside W-diffusion and S-diffusion, there is yet another level of diffusion to be considered, i.e. item-internal diffusion (as mentioned on page 122). Let us take the word *synn* for example. The plural of the word had a few variants in some Early Middle English dialects, but as time went on, the relative rate for the *s*-variant increased over the *n*- and *V*-variants (see the Item Profile for the noun on page 250 in Appendix E). Here we are looking at an item-internal competition. The *s*-variant did not suddenly overtake the other variants but gradually increased in its relative rate.

Already in C12b the *s*-plural for this item was well established but other options such as -*n* and -*V* were still available. Toward C13a, the *V*-plural fell into disuse as far as our data go, while -*s* and -*n* continued, the former outnumbering the latter. The following C13b shows only *s*-plurals.

In South-West Midland the *n*-plural for *synn* developed from C12b to C13a, which illustrates the revitalisation of the *n*-plural peculiar to the dialect. The following C13b, however, scores a high frequency of the *s*-form as if to displace the old *n*-variant. A similar competition took place with *dǣd* (see the Item Profile on page 248) in South-West Midland, which suggests that the two Fem-V items were developing perhaps hand in hand.

The Southeastern shows a yet different picture of the item-internal diffusion. The *s*-plural for *synn* is attested in C13a texts but only infrequently. Data from C13b are missing, but seeing that the C14a data show a high frequency of -s for the item, we may extrapolate that this intermediate period was the middle of the S-curve of the item-internal diffusion.

Another well-evidenced item that represents item-internal diffusion is *þing* (see the Item Profile on page 254). It occurred with -s fairly early in every dialect but its item-internal diffusion was so slow that it did not completely displace the historical ø-plural during Middle English. A similar development is observed for another neuter noun *gēar* (see the Item Profile on page 252).

Neuter nouns such as *weorc* and *word* show a different item-internal S-curve (see the Item Profiles on pages 255 and 256 respectively). They first occurred with -s as early as *þing* and *gēar*, and the *s*-variants were certainly applying pressure on the *n*-variants, which diminished toward Late Middle English. The difference in the speed and schedule between *þing* and *gēar* on the one hand and *weorc* and *word* on the other may be due to the first group being more frequently used along with numerals or other quantifiers than the second group, thus not requiring an explicit plural marker as strongly as the second group.

The course and schedule of item-internal change differs from item to item. The difference may be due to phonological configurations, word frequency, assignment to classes, syntactic context, and so on. These factors combine in a complicated way to determine finally the schedule and speed of item-internal diffusion.

Here is an interesting question to ask: does the speed and schedule of item-internal diffusion determined this way for a single speaker or a single site repeat itself for another speaker or site? It is difficult to answer definitively, but it is likely that if a speaker uses, say, *sinnes* more often than *sinnen*, another speaker affected by the first speaker will come to use *sinnes* more often than *sinnen* before long. Some time later, a third speaker in close relation to the first two may also learn to use *sinnes* more often than *sinnen*. Diffusion from speaker to speaker may continue this way, and theoretically taken further, it may become diffusion from site to site or from dialect to dialect.

If S-diffusion proceeds as described above, the speed and schedule of item-internal diffusion will be repeated from speaker to speaker, from site to site, or from dialect to dialect. However, can this theoretical course of diffusion be possible in the real world? The answer is not necessarily so, as we saw from the case of *synn* that the speed and schedule of item-internal diffusion varied with dialects.

In addition, there is evidence that the chronological order of affected items differed from dialect to dialect. For example, as I pointed out in Section 3.3.6, *geat* (see the Item Profile on page 246) accepted the *s*-plural earlier in South-West Midland and Southwestern than in South-East Midland. This runs against the expectation that South-East Midland should be more "advanced." In this case we have to allow for the possibility of independent development in the western dialects. *yfel* and *gōd* were similar examples (see the Item Profiles on pages 247 and 252).

In the arguments above, I suggested that W-diffusion and S-diffusion proceeded hand in hand since curves of W-diffusion were more or less parallel. On the other hand, I pointed out that item-internal diffusion and S-diffusion did not necessarily go hand in hand. How were these different levels of diffusion related to each other?

My view is that although S-curves of W-diffusion were more or less parallel between dialects, the internal details of the S-curves differed. By the internal details I mean the speed and schedule of item-internal diffusion for individual items as well as the order of affected items or item-groups.

General parallelism of W-diffusion between speakers, sites, or dialects reflects the shared recognition, perhaps unconscious, in a linguistic community that an innovation is taking place through the vocabulary. This shared awareness creates a "drift" which helps to propagate the innovation throughout the vocabulary. We might note that the "drift" concerns the general direction of linguistic innovation, not the behaviour of individual linguistic items.

In spite of the shared "drift," individual speakers, sites, or dialects may react differently to the usage of individual items. Speakers may be either conservative or innovative with certain items according to their sociolinguistic preference (perhaps affected by stylistic consideration, fashion, or prestige). As diffusion goes on, personal factors of this kind will accumulate to such an extent that a difference in usage may result among individual speakers, sites, or dialects although they as a community still share the "drift."

From the above, the development of the plural types in Early Middle English can be described as a composite function of more or less cross-dialectally shared W-diffusion, S-diffusion, and item-internal diffusions; and of some irregular behaviours of individual speakers, sites, and dialects.

Chapter 6 WHY: Language-Internal Motivation

In the preceding chapter I addressed the "how" of change from a Lexical Diffusion viewpoint, but the question "why" remains to be answered. Causes of language change can be considered from various points of view, but they fall broadly into language-internal and -external causes.

Language-internal causes of change are associated with linguistic processes such as systemic regulation and analogy, whereas language-external causes concern language contact and other social/geographical backgrounds in which change takes place.

Whatever the first motivation for change, once change starts, it usually has a systemic effect, affecting more than one level of language. For example, the levelling of weak vowels and the loss of n in inflectional endings started as genuine sound changes, but before long they had a great morphological impact. These sound changes also had an effect on syntax, particularly the way syntactic agreement was made between nouns and other parts of speech such as determiners, adjectives, and verbs. Thus the different levels of language closely interact with one another. It will be inappropriate, therefore, to discuss language change as if it were confined to a particular level of language.

With the above in mind, in what follows I will seek intralinguistic motives for which the Early Middle English plural system developed the way it did.

6.1 Mobility across Classes

We have seen a dramatic change in the plural system from Late Old English to Early Middle English, but we cannot ignore that there were some cases of plural formation transfer already in Old English.

Some Old English nouns belonged to more than one gender or declension type and took variable inflectional endings. It is likely that this double assignment of some nouns provided an analogical base for plural formation transfer of other nouns from one class to another. In fact, it is often uncertain whether a given case should be considered a double assignment (a synchronic viewpoint) or an ongoing transfer from one class to another (a diachronic viewpoint).

I mentioned in Section 3.1.4 that in Old English most plural formation transfer took place either within a gender or between the strong masculine and the strong neuter. The motive for transfer within a gender was the centripetal force of the major declension type of that gender. In the masculine the major a-stem declension attracted the wa-stem, ja-stem, the i-stem, and u-stem items. Likewise in the neuter, the wa-stem and ja-stem nouns were assimilated into the major a-stem. In the feminine the major $\bar{o}$-stem declension attracted the $w\bar{o}$-stem, $j\bar{o}$-stem, and i-stem items by Late Old English.

This centripetal force of the major a-stem and $\bar{o}$-stem declensions originated in their high frequency. Since inflectional difference between various declension types was fairly little to begin with, the merger was a natural course of development.

The motive for transfer between the strong masculines and the strong neuters in particular was in their inflectional similarity. The only differences were in the nominative/accusative plural, where the masculines took -as while the neuters took either -$\emptyset$ or -u.

Variations due to ambiguous gender, ambiguous class assignment, or inflectional similarities continued to be an important driving force behind plural formation transfer after Late Old English. They provided analogical grounds on which further plural formation transfer was made possible. In this sense they were "underlying" motives for transfer. They were not strong enough to shake the plural system immediately, but they had a lasting effect on the change.

6.2 Levelling of Inflectional Endings

In Early Middle English nominal morphology, the most important phonological changes were the levelling of weak vowels and the deletion of n in unaccented inflectional syllables that started from Late Old English on. These vowels and n could often be plural markers themselves, so the destructive phonological processes had a direct impact on the plural system.

On the one hand, vowel alternation in inflectional endings often functioned as number markers. For example, in Old English $\bar{o}$-stem nouns like *giefu* and *u*-stem nouns like *sunu* both had *-u* in the nominative singular and *-a* in the nominative plural. The levelling of weak vowels in inflectional endings to a vowel written <e>, probably pronounced schwa, could therefore be a significant factor that caused the restructuring of the plural system from Late Old English to Early Middle English.

On the other hand, the reduction of final n was more destructive than the levelling of vowels because it affected all weak nouns. It also obscured the number distinction in the dative, making the dative plural *en*-ending (derived from *-um*) indistinguishable from the dative singular as in *-e* (e.g. *stāne* either for the dative singular or for the dative plural).

There is considerable uncertainty about the chronology of these phonological changes. According to Moore, "the completion of levelling [of vowels] was contemporary with the earlier stages of the loss of final n" ("Earliest" 247). They are commonly believed to have occurred in Late Old English, particularly in the eleventh century, but Kitson gives evidence to show that the front and back vowels were distinguished in unaccented inflectional syllables even in the late twelfth century at least in the South-West Midland and Southeastern dialects ("When").

The absolute chronology thus varied across dialects, but it is certain, as I will discuss in the next section, that in each dialect the phonological levelling or loss in unaccented inflectional syllables combined with the subsequent morphological adjustment to form the basis for restructuring of the plural system.

6.3 Systemic Reorganisation of the Nominal Morphology

While sound reduction was gradually proceeding, plural forms with and without final vowels or n were coexistent. In this transitional period, there were two opposite processes going on. On the one hand, sounds in inflectional syllables were *phonologically* weakened. On the one hand, the same weakening sounds were sometimes *morphologically* restored.

The levelling of weak vowels into schwa and the occasional loss or restoration of this schwa resulted in the merger of several declension types into the major types. As was previously stated, the *i*-stem declension already showed a tendency to be assimilated into the *a*-stem in Old English, but these sound changes in Early Middle English acted as a catalyst for this tendency.

As a consequence of unstressed vowels levelling into schwa, there were no more than four distinct nominative/accusative endings, apart from the few exceptional nouns such as athematic nouns pluralising with *i*-mutation: -*s*, -*n*, -*V*, and -*ø*. These endings were distributed across genders and declension types, as shown in Table 6.1.

Table 6.1: Distribution of Plural Types by Gender and Declension

EME Plural Type	OE Gender	OE Declension
-*s*	Masc.	*a*-stems, most *i*-stems, most *u*-stems
-*n*	Masc.	*n*-stems
	Neut.	*n*-stems
	Fem.	*n*-stems
-*V*	Masc.	some *i*-stems, some *u*-stems
	Neut.	light-syllabic *a*-stems, some *i*-stems
	Fem.	*ō*-stems, *i*-stems, *u*-stems
-*ø*	Neut.	heavy-syllabic *a*-stems, some *i*-stems

This distribution, however, was soon subject to a shakeup as the functional validity of final -*V* and -*n* came into question. They were functionally so unstable that they were often interchanged with each other and, in some cases, with -*ø* through the loss of the final vowel.

In fact, as sound reduction was going on, many of the *V*-plural nouns were associated with the *n*-plural nouns. Thus, most feminines and some neuters became so closely associated with *n*-plurals that in the southern dialects they readily transferred to the *n*-plural.

The question might arise as to why the transfer went from -*V* to -*n* rather than the other way around if -*V* and -*n* could interchange with each other. The clue to this question is the fact that the mechanically initiated sound reduction in unstressed inflectional syllables soon transformed into a morphological or analogical process. Moore observed that the loss of *n* in inflectional endings started mechanically but was soon restored "by the operation of analogical processes" ("Earliest" 244). What was happening then was that during the period of apparent interchangeability in the loss or recovery of final vowels and *n*, systemic regulation kicked in to keep number distinction alive. In consequence, a new subsystem gradually emerged in which -*V* marked the singular whereas -*n* marked the plural.

This systemic reorganisation was a gradual process, but in the end, except for a few surviving *V*-plurals, the *V*-plural class was almost fully assimilated into the *n*-plural class, so that there were now no more than three distinct plural endings available: -*s*, -*n*, and -*ø*.

In the southern dialects, transfer from -*V* to -*n* was characteristic of the strong feminines and the light-syllabic strong neuters. In contrast, most of the masculines of the *V*-plural class did not transfer to -*n*, but merged into the major *a*-stem declension, pluralising with -*s*.

As for the neuters of the *ø*-plural class, some were associated with the *V*-plural class by suffixing "inorganic -*e*." Then they changed over to the *n*-plural along with other nouns of the *V*-plural class. Other *ø*-plural neuters remained endingless, and yet others changed over to the *s*-plural.

6.4 Loss of Gender

The category of grammatical gender diminished from Late Old English to Early Middle English, but it lingered on until Late Middle English particularly in the southern dialects and had some effect on the restructuring of the plural system.

As we saw in the preceding section, in the southern dialects the strong feminines were so closely associated with the weak nouns that they often pluralised with -*n*. On the other hand, the *s*-plural was closely associated with the masculine. Distinction between the masculine and the feminine was thus felt in terms of these endings (we may note that the neuters could be associated with either -*n* or -*s*).

Once the association between particular genders and particular plural endings was established, it became more difficult for nouns to change plural formation across the boundary. This is why few feminines changed over to -s although it was certainly the dominant ending in the plural system in Early Middle English.

The lingering gender barrier was thus partly responsible for the delay in the spread of -s in the southern dialects. In time, however, the weakening of grammatical gender dissociated the connections between particular genders and particular plural endings, allowing more free plural formation transfer.

Since the s-plural was effectively the single dominant plural ending by Late Middle English and word final n was always subject to potential reduction, it was just a matter of time before n-plurals would change over to s-plurals.

6.5 Phonetic and Phonological Conditions

In this section I discuss how phonetic/phonological environments may have affected the development of plural formation transfer. There is some evidence that the syllable weight of a noun was relevant to the choice of -s or -n.[57] Let us take a-stem neuters, for example. They are divided into two types by syllable weight: heavy-syllabics (e.g. *word*) and light-syllabics (e.g. *scip*).

In West-Saxon, *word* had an unchanged plural form whereas *scip* pluralised with a u-ending. In Early Middle English this distinction contributed somewhat to plural formation.

Let us look at the statistics from my data.[58] Table 6.2 on page 139 illustrates that both the heavy- and light-syllabic a-stem neuters show a strong inclination to transfer to the s-plural; but otherwise they were quite different in their way of transfer. While a quarter of the heavy-syllabics stayed unchanged and a moderate number transferred either to -n or -V, light-syllabics favoured transfer to -n or remained -V.

Part of the reason why more light-syllabics changed over to -n than heavy-syllabics seems to be that the former accepted inorganic -e in the nominative singular more frequently than the latter. To take *scip* for example, it accepted an inorganic -e in Early Middle English, thus giving *scipe* as the singular form. It soon became associated with weak nouns, which also had -e in the nominative singular. The word was therefore strongly tied with weak nouns, pluralising with -n or occasionally without -n just like historical weak nouns.

Syllable weight as determiner of the transfer type is suggested, though less

Table 6.2: Transfer Rates of Heavy- and Light-Syllabic *a*-Stem Neuters

	Heavy-syllabics	Light-syllabics
s	0.49	0.45
n	0.10	0.21
V	0.14	0.27
ø	0.26	0.055
M	0.0060	0.014

clearly, by feminine forms as well. The strong feminines (the $\bar{o}$-stem, the *i*-stem, and the *u*-stem) were either heavy- or light-syllabics (e.g. *synn* and *lagu* respectively). Table 6.3 shows that heavy-syllabics had a little stronger inclination to transfer to -*s* and a little weaker inclination to transfer to -*n* and -*V*.[59]

Table 6.3: Transfer Rates of Heavy- and Light-Syllabic Strong Feminines

	Heavy-syllabics	Light-syllabics
s	0.43	0.35
n	0.23	0.25
V	0.31	0.40
ø	0.027	0.00
M	0.0050	0.00

The figures might not be a significant indicator statistically of the role of the syllable weight, but it is plausible that light-syllabics like *lagu*, with their vowel endings both in the nominative singular and nominative plural, were more strongly associated with weak nouns than heavy-syllabics, which historically lacked -*e* in the nominative singular.

Roedler (2: 497) remarks that inorganic -*e* was only inconsistently added to the heavy-syllabic strong feminines.[60] This means that some heavy-syllabics remained endingless in the nominative singular, and therefore were less closely associated with the weak nouns. In this case, they may have been more readily associated with the *a*-stem nouns.

Another relevance of syllabic structure for plural formation is that monosyllabic nouns show a stronger inclination to transfer to the n-plural than polysyllabic ones. The open monosyllabics have particularly favoured the n-plural. The following n-plurals have been attested in the history of English: *ashen, been, een, fān, fleen, keen, keien, kneen, shon, ton, treon,* and *weien*. Many of these have survived even to this day in regional varieties. We might note that these nouns are all everyday vocabulary.[61]

Thirdly, let me draw attention to a euphony called nunnation. Morris describes this phonetic process as follows:

> A tendency to add a euphonic n to the final e of the genitive singular of feminine nouns of the complex order, of the dative singular of complex nouns, of the plural of nouns (complex order) and of adverbs and prepositions. This *nunnation*, as it has been called, is very common in Laʒamon, who probably carried this novelty to its utmost limits. . . .
> (*Homilies*, 1st ser.: xviii)

Nunnation was particularly common in the southern and western dialects. For example, Stanley mentioned nunnation as "a widespread dialectal peculiarity of Worcestershire well into the fourteenth century" ("Laʒamon's" 23).

Although nunnation can refer to various kinds of additional n, I will focus on the nunnation of nominal plural forms which functioned as euphony at a word boundary.[62] There are a number of instances of nunnation between vowels at a word boundary in my collected Early Middle English data. It is usually difficult, however, to tell whether a given instance is a genuine case of nunnation because n-forms might have occurred anyway without the effect of nunnation. Examples include (emphasis added): "oure **sunnes** forto lete" and "For þe opre **sunnen of** þisse porlde bere" (Cotton Caligula A ix, the *Doomsday*, on pages 35 and 40 in Brown, *13th*); "hire **sennen i**beten," "vorþuhte ham here **sennen and**," and "here **sennes** beten" (Bodley Digby 4, the *Poema Morale*, lines 16b, 131a and 131b in Zupitza); "ðos **faten of** watere" and "þo **faten of** watere" (Laud Misc 471, the *Kentish Sermons*, 29.19 and 29.23 in Morris, *Miscellany*; no other Early Middle English texts I studied records an n-form for this particular word).

To judge whether nunnation is in effect is difficult in the following pairs of quotations, where *n*-marked and *n*-less forms seem to be free variants (emphasis added): "þe wrecche **saulen a-honge**" but "feole **saule a-honge**" (the *Lambeth Homilies*, Lang 1, 41.22 and 41.28 in Morris, *Homilies*, 1st ser.); "þa ermi*ng* **saulen** habbeð" but "þa ermi*ng* **saule habbeð**" (the *Lambeth Homilies*, Lang 1, 41.13 and 47.5 in Morris, *Homilies*, 1st ser.).

Nunnation as euphony would be peripheral to the general development of the *n*-plural, but it surely provided nouns with an option of taking an *n*-ending where phonetic context encouraged it. To this extent, nunnation contributed at least to the generation of linguistic variation, a prerequisite to any systemic language change.

As another case of phonetic/phonological relevance to the plural forms, I will make a short note about French loanwords ending in sibilants. As Mossé commented, they tended to refuse an additional *s*-suffix to avoid successive sibilants for euphony, e.g. *the seven scÿence, tweyne of his prentis, many caas,* and *tēn vers* (52). Some of the examples from Early Middle English include *amendes, burgeys, cerges, erites, herbe[r]gers, primices,* and *serges,* all in their plurals. There are exceptions, however, such as *charmeresses* and *richesses.*

Finally I suggest a phonetic reason why -*s* won over -*n* finally. To put it simply, [s] was phonetically more distinctive and resistant to natural reduction than [n]. In fact, in the history of the Germanic languages, the *s*-ending of unaccented inflections survived longer than any other consonant ending. The *s*-ending, though rhotacised in some later Germanic languages, was phonetically much stronger than the *n*-ending, which was far more often subject to loss in weakly accented syllables.

6.6 Syntactic Agreement

The grammatical concept of number extends beyond morphology. It is also reflected in syntax, as in determiner-noun agreement, quantifier-noun agreement, subject-verb agreement, and pronominal reference to nouns. In this section we look at how number was marked syntactically and consider how syntactic number markings interacted with morphological number marking.

Determiner-noun agreement is commonly found in Indo-European languages.

In Modern French, for example, nominal plurality is primarily marked by inflection of the definite articles rather than of nouns themselves. There are indeed the *s*- and *x*-endings for nouns to mark plurality, but it is only spelt, not normally pronounced (unless followed by a word beginning with a vowel). Instead, the articles serve as effective plural markers, as in *le mot* (singular) / *les mots* (plural) or *un arbre* (singular) / *des arbres* (plural).

When we look at Modern German, there are various forms of the definite article indicating case, number, and gender. All genders have the nominative plural form *die*, while the nominative singular has *der*, *die*, or *das* for the masculine, the feminine, and the neuter respectively. We might note that the feminine alone makes no formal distinction between the nominative singular and nominative plural.[63]

Let us return to English. Although Present-Day English shows no inflections for the definite article, early English had a variety of inflected forms. In Old English, the definite article (or the determiner, or whatever we may call the precursor of Present-Day English "the") inflected differently depending on case, number, and gender.

From Late Old English to Early Middle English, inflectional variation for the definite article was dramatically reduced due to the same sound changes as affected the nominal inflections. Since, however, it was not that the historical variants were suddenly integrated into a common *the*, the few variants surviving in Early Middle English could have served as auxiliary number markers at least for some time. Let us consider whether there was a correlation between the functionality of the plural inflections of nouns and that of the definite article.

To take Lang 1 of the *Lambeth Homilies*, there are five variants of the definite article in the nominative/accusative case: *þe*, *þa*, *þeo*, *þo*, and *þi*. Of them *þo* appears only twice, and *þi* nearly always occurs in the phrase *for-þi*, so in most cases the other three variants are used.

The three variants can precede either singular or plural nouns apparently interchangeably. However, *þa* shows a particularly strong tendency to govern plural nouns while *þe* tends to govern singular nouns. As for *þeo*, in spite of its fairly low frequency, there is a strong tendency to govern feminine nouns. All these tendencies point to the surviving sense of historical number and gender.

A functionalistic analysis would be that if the definite article was able to mark the grammatical number of the governed noun inflectionally, the noun itself did not need to make a number distinction, as is the case with modern French. This analysis, however, is difficult to test in actual text.

þa could be an auxiliary plural marker, but all nouns preceded by þa in the text already have the n-ending. This makes it impossible to judge whether there is any relationship between the functionality of the definite article and the motivation for nouns to take a distinct plural marker. In general, however, in texts with the definite article well-inflected, nouns cannot distinguish number well through their own inflections, whereas in texts with the definite article uninflected, nouns can do so.

My view is that although the function of þa as a plural marker was not completely dead in some Early Middle English texts (particularly in those copied archaistically), it was destined to be lost in time. As Millar argues, ambiguity in form between several vowel-ending variants of the definite article brought about functional mergers in gender (e.g. nom. sg. masc. þe and nom. sg. fem. þeo), case (e.g. nom. sg. fem. þeo and acc. sg. fem. þa), and number (e.g. nom. sg. masc. þe and gender-free nom. pl. þa) (205–12). Considering that such a large-scale reorganisation was underway, the function of þa as a plural marker, if any, must have been insignificant.

Like the definite article, quantifying adjectives could be auxiliary means to mark the number of a governed noun. Typical quantifying adjectives include numerals as well as "some", "many," and "all."

That these quantifiers served as effective plural markers can be observed in numerous examples of ø-plurals preceded by them. Mustanoja has the following to say on this point:

> The unchanged plural after an expression of number or quantity is in fact a linguistic phenomenon of universal occurrence. It has primarily a psychological background if the idea of plurality is obvious from the attributive numeral or adjective, no plural ending or other sign is needed to indicate the number of the governing noun. (58)

Besides the historical strong neuters, nouns denoting countable units and hunting animals tended to take the ø-plural in history (e.g. "couple," "score," "hundred," "thousand," "year," "winter," "month," "night," "sith," "foot," "fathom," "mile," "pound," "stone," "mark," "eel," "fish," "fowl," and "goat"). We may note, however, that many of these nouns had alternative plural forms in Middle English, normally either in -s or -n.

I find it too functionalistic a view to assume that these nouns continued to form unmarked plurals only because the preceding quantifiers were adequate plural markers. I say too functionalistic because even if there is no positive functional need to introduce innovative plural forms, language can still introduce innovation for non-functional motives. We should rather understand that functional motivation underlies language change as a long-standing weak systemic pressure which other causation can readily take advantage of.

Subject-verb agreement was another syntactic device to mark number. For example, in the clause "Ðær wurdon þa forewearda full worhte" (*The Peterborough Chronicle*, 1109), the most reliable plural marker of the subject noun *forewearda* is effectively the verb form *wurdon*. Neither the *a*-ending of the noun nor the article *þa* is a reliable plural marker here.

Cases like this are rarely found, however. Like the inflections of nouns and articles, those of verbs went through phonetic reduction in unstressed final syllables. In addition, if verbal agreement served as an auxiliary device to mark number, such functionality was only available to subject nouns. It was anything but a general nominal plural marker.

Finally I will mention pronominal reference to nouns. This syntactic device played only a mior role in the development of the nominal plural inflections. Pronouns indeed took either singular or plural forms according to their referent, so they could indirectly mark the number of that referent noun. This is clearly a poor device for number marking, however. It could only apply to nouns which happened to be referred to by pronouns. Besides, the pronominal reference to nouns was not always logical. Sometimes a plural referent was referred to by "it," sometimes a generic singular was referred to by "they."

6.7 Semantic and Lexical Considerations

This section discusses semantic/lexical factors which may have conditioned the development of the nominal plural system. Below I make five points, some of which I have mentioned before in the present study.

First, many of the ø-plurals in Middle English fall semantically into either nouns for countable units or nouns for hunting animals. These nouns shared not only a common semantic component but also syntactic contexts in which they commonly occurred; for example, they were often preceded by quantifiers.

Secondly, semantically associated nouns may undergo the same inflection by analogy. d'Ardenne speaks of "the attraction of commoner synonyms," indicating that the *s*-ending of *licomes* in the AB language was affected by its synonym *bodies* (207).

The plural formation of kinship nouns may be another case in point. In the southern dialects of Early Middle English, kinship nouns took unhistorical *n*-plurals such as *bretheren, sustren, modren,* and *douʒtren*. Wyld notes that this is a case of the *n*-plural extension within a particular semantic field (*Modern* 246). The extension presumably started with *sustren* since it was the most stable *n*-plural in the group.

Thirdly, a noun in an item enumeration context often took the same plural ending as other nouns around it. This is related to the second point above in the sense that enumerated items tended to be semantically related to each other. I reproduce a couple of examples given previously (emphasis added).

- mid þas kyningas ⁊ mid eorles ⁊ mid **heorotogas** ⁊ mid þægnas. (*The Peterborough Chronicle*, Interpolation 656)

- þet wæron C*ris*tes bec ⁊ **mæssahakeles** ⁊ cantelcapas ⁊ reafes ⁊ swilce litles hwat (*The Peterborough Chronicle*, 1070)

In these quotations, the historical weak *heretoga* and *mæssehacele* pluralise with *s*-endings, apparently because they are surrounded by other *s*-plurals. In the following quotations, items are not exactly enumerated side by side, but are arranged for a stylistic or syntactic effect (emphasis added).

- ⁊ draf út þa **clerca** of þe biscoprice, forþan þ̄ hi noldon nan regul healden, ⁊ sætta þær **muneca**. He macode þær twa abbotrice. an of **muneca** oðer of **nunna** (*The Peterborough Chronicle*, Interpolation 963)

- þer wunieð in-ne faʒe **neddren**. *and* beoreð atter u*n*der heore tunge. Blake **tadden** *and* habbeð atter uppon heore heorte. ʒeluwe froggen. *ande* **crabben**. (the *Lambeth Homilies*, Sermon V, page 51 in Morris, *Homilies*, 1st ser.)

- ȝe ne beo noht þe foaȝe **neddre**. ne þe blake **tadde**. ne þe ȝolewe **frogge**. (the *Lambeth Homilies*, Sermon V, page 53 in Morris, *Homilies*, 1st ser.)

These quotations show that plural forms appear to be affected by the surrounding context. Contexts, however, are usually one-off and cannot induce general motivation for systemic change. Therefore, context-motivated plural variants cannot be directly irrelevant to the systemic development of plural forms.

Having said that, since the presence of variants is prerequisite to any systemic change, even one-off plural variants may be considered relevant to some extent from a theoretical point of view. Even if they end their life as literally one-off variants, they are always potential sources for systemic change.

Fourthly, the animacy/inanimacy distinction may have been responsible for some choices between *-s* and *-n*, as we saw in *feolahes*, *wrecches*, and *ancres* from the *Ancrene Wisse/Riwle* (d'Ardenne 207; see also page 93). Let me mention that a comparable development was going on in Early High German. By the Early New High German period the *n*-plural was closely associated with feminine nouns, especially with those unaffected by *i*-mutation, so many historical weak masculines transferred away from the *n*-ending. Since, on the other hand, the *n*-ending was associated with animate nouns, weak masculines denoting animate beings tended to remain *n*-plurals instead of transferring away (see page 28).

Finally, some phrases were so common that their component noun often took an uncommon (perhaps archaic) plural form. For example, "hands and feet" is a phrase frequently occurring in Early Middle English. It appears as "honde & fēt," "handen (and) fiet," "þine fet and þine honde," and so on. In *Sir Ferumbras* (ed. Herrtage), most of the plural forms for "hand" are *s*-ending, but *honde* occurs in the phrase *honde & fēt*. Another example is the Early Middle English phrase for "over all (other) things." The ø-form for "things" frequently occurs in this phrase even in texts where the *s*-form is normally used for the word "things."

6.8 Case Syncretism and the Spread of -s

The development of case syncretism varied diatopically as much as that of the plural formation.[64] The graph in Figure 6.1 below shows how case syncretism proceeded in individual dialects. The curves may be compared with those for the rate of -s in the range of dialects under study as reproduced in Figure 6.2 on page 148. In both processes, the northern dialects were more advanced than the southern at most points in time.

It is likely that many other linguistic changes underway in Early Middle English would show a similar pattern (e.g. the loss of gender and the inflectional levelling of the definite article). It is possible that these different processes were all correlated and, taken together, pushed forward the global systemic change of the language in the Early Middle English period.

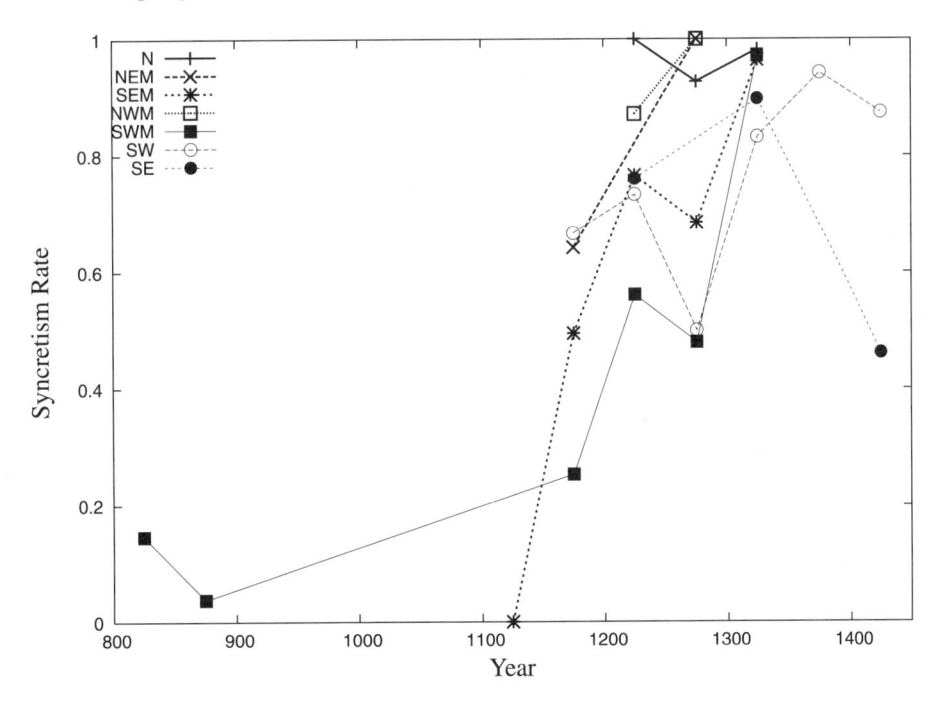

Figure 6.1: Rate of Case Syncretism

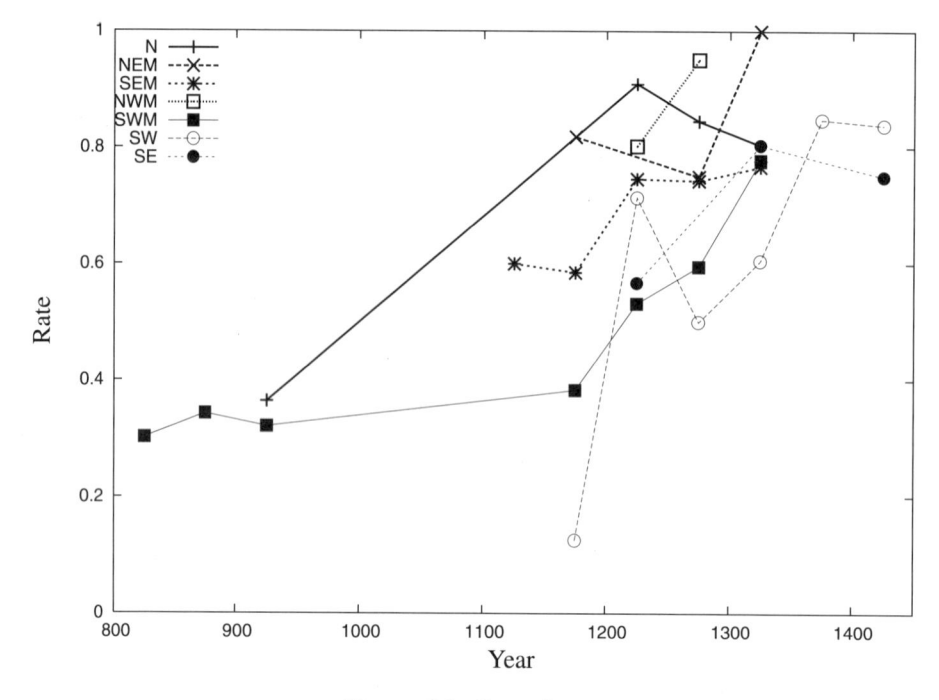

Figure 6.2: Rate for -*s*

6.9 Summary of Language-Internal Motivation

Let me list the language-internal causes I have mentioned above.

1. Nouns of ambiguous gender- or class-assignment were ready to transfer from one plural formation to another.

2. Nouns of one gender sometimes transferred from one plural formation to another that was available to that gender.

3. Nouns of similar inflections sometimes transferred from one plural formation to another.

4. The centripetal force of the major declension types reduced the variation of plural formation.

5. The V-plural was assimilated into the n-plural due to morphological reanalysis.

6. The loss of gender lowered the barrier between the feminine-associated *n*-plurals and the masculine-associated *s*-plurals, enabling more free transfer across genders.
7. The syllable weight of nouns played a role in directing plural formation transfer.
8. Nunnation possibly had a minor effect on the development of the *n*-plural.
9. French loanwords with a sibilant-ending favoured unchanged plurals.
10. The phonetic strength of [s] was part of the reason for the final victory of the *s*-plural over the other plural types.
11. Quantifier-noun agreement likely encouraged some plural types (typically the ø-plural).
12. Article-noun agreement may have functioned as an auxiliary device to mark plurality, but only to a limited extent if at all.
13. Many of the ø-plurals were associated with special semantic fields such as countable units and hunting animals.
14. Some semantically associated nouns, typically synonyms, took the same plural ending.
15. Item enumeration contexts often influenced the choice of plural forms
16. Nouns denoting animacy or inanimacy tended to have distinct plural forms.
17. Fixed phrases preferred uncommon (usually archaic) plural forms.
18. Many linguistic processes in Early Middle English (case syncretism, the loss of gender, etc.) were arguably correlated, so the development of the plural system should be seen in this broader context of language change.

All the factors—phonetic, morphological, syntactic, and semantic—contributed interactively to the overall development of the nominal plural system. Some motives had a more systemic effect on the development, while others did little more than to offer minor linguistic variants possibly of a one-off nature.

Language-internal motivations are relatively weak. They prepare a workspace, as it were, where further language change can take place. Language-internal motivation does not positively determine the direction of the development but just underlies the development.

One "conspiracy" seems to underlie all the language-internal motivation as to the development of plural formation: persistence in number distinction. English has always persisted in distinguishing between the singular and the plural formally and functionally. When one number marking system became dysfunctional, the system settled in on another.

Persistence in number distinction is not peculiar to English but commonly found in Indo-European languages. From a worldwide point of view, however, it is not uncommon to find languages without clear number distinction. In Japanese, number distinction is not only secondary but there are hardly any obligatory morphological means of marking nominal plurality. In the language, it is possible to mark number explicitly by lexical means if need be, but number distinction is simply unnecessary on most occasions. From this point of view, persistence in number distinction in English might look even obsessive.

Having said that, it is not useless here to propose some reasons for English to have protected the number category from decaying in history. First, the category of number is a logical one and more directly related to extralinguistic matters than the categories of gender and case, which are more language-specific concepts. The category of number, therefore, should die relatively hard.

In addition, the category of number is not only associated with nouns but entwined with other parts of speech such as determiners, adjectives, verbs, and pronouns through syntactic agreement. Even if number were morphologically dissociated from nouns, it would live on as long as its syntactic agreement with other parts of speech is functional.

Language-internal motivation was surely at work, but I doubt that it alone can give a convincing enough account for the North-South divide in the development of the plural system. In the northern dialects, -s started to grow early in Late Old English and then developed dramatically toward Early Middle English, whereas in the southern dialects the spread of -s had not really started even when the s-dominant *Ormulum* was written around 1200 in North-East Midland. In short, the North-South divide seems simply far greater than would be expected from normal dialectal divergence. To understand how and why the North-South divide came into being, we need to investigate relevant factors from a language-external point of view.

Chapter 7 WHY: Language-External Motivation

7.1 Language Contact

Language contact induces linguistic change. This is a fact no one doubts. Linguists differ, however, in their attitude toward language contact in discussing language change. In what follows I propose that language contact was responsible for the development of the Early Middle English plural system.

As we saw in the preceding chapter, language-internal factors played a significant role in the development of the plural system. It is inappropriate, however, to ignore a language-external point of view. Such ignorance is unacceptable even if language-internal factors alone seem to provide convincing enough accounts for a case of language change. Multiple causation should be assumed in considering language change.[65] The following quotations are from Thomason:

> It clearly is not justified, for instance, to assume that you can only argue successfully for a contact origin if you fail to find any plausible internal motivation for a particular change. One reason is that the goal is always to find the best historical explanation for a change, and a good solid contact explanation is preferable to a weak internal one; another reason is that the possibility of multiple causation should always be considered and, as we saw above, it often happens that an internal motivation combines with an external motivation to produce a change. (91)

> Yet another unjustified assumption is that contact-induced change should not be proposed as an explanation if a similar or identical change happened elsewhere too, without any contact or at least without the same contact situation. (92)

When I speak of language-external motives of language change, I have various types of language contact in mind, e.g. contact between languages, between dialects, and between social classes. To estimate which contacts are relevant to a particular language change, it is necessary to consider socio-geographical conditions and find out historical correspondence between linguistic and social factors.

One of the most obvious sociolinguistic facts of Early Middle English is the Old Norse presence in the North and East of England. Their invasion, settlement, and subsequent amalgamation with the English was a fairly long process from Late Old English to Late Middle English, but the linguistic impact of Old Norse was strongest in the Late Old English period, though showing up in written sources in Early Middle English.

Another linguistic contact we should consider is cross-dialectal contact. In Early Middle English, most of the linguistic innovations diffused from the North and East to the South and West. In Section 7.6 I will briefly discuss the sociolinguistic scenario for the southwestward wave of linguistic innovation in Early Middle English.

I should mention that I will not take up the previously proposed view that contact with Old French may have motivated the establishment of the *s*-dominant plural system. It has now been almost totally ruled out.[66]

7.2 Contact with Old Norse

As introduced in Section 2.2, the view that the spread of -*s* was facilitated by Old Norse contact was first proposed by Classen. His argument was based on the assumption that the distributional differences between the North and the South would be too great to be accounted for by common dialectal differences:

> There must have been some force operating in the North, then, which hindered the normal development, as seen in the South. . . . One is naturally tempted to look to Old Norse for such a force in any phenomenon affecting the Northern dialect. ("Plurals" 95)

Classen's Old Norse contact hypothesis is thus grounded on the widely accepted view of intimate contact between the two languages. Many studies have documented the presence of Old Norse loanwords in Middle English (see

Björkman in particular). The number of attested Old Norse loanwords surviving in standard Present-Day English is estimated at about 900, and as many more words are probably of Scandinavian origin according to Baugh and Cable (102). If we take regional varieties into consideration, the number of recorded Old Norse loanwords increases greatly. It is also known that more than 1400 Scandinavian place names have been attested in England (Baugh and Cable 96).

In addition to the number of loanwords, we have to take account of their quality. Most of the Old Norse loanwords were part of everyday vocabulary in contrast with French and Latin loanwords of a more aristocratic nature. More than a few Old Norse loanwords even replaced common native Old English words (e.g. *egg* for *ey*, *sister* for *sweostor*, *weak* for *wāc*, and *take* for *niman*). There were also some cases of semantic borrowing. The modern meanings of *bloom*, *gift*, and *plow*, for example, are attributed to the Old Norse meanings.

The Old Norse linguistic impact on English was not limited to the lexicon, but other linguistic levels such as phonology, morphology, and syntax were also deeply affected. Let us take an overview of what features in English were supposedly affected by Old Norse contact.

The northern dialects show many phonological features reasonably attributable to Old Norse.[67] For example, /g/ as in *garth* and *garn* should be of Old Norse origin since it would have softened to /j/ if it had developed natively in English (standard Present-Day English has *yard* and *yarn*).

Another example is /k/ as in *kist* and *kirn* and /sk/ as in *skift*, *skelf*, *skrike*, and *scrood*. Moreover, the later loss of the sound spelt *gh* in *night* and *daughter* may have been due to influence from the Old Norse equivalents *nat* and *datter*.

As for morphology, the following features in early English have been attributed to Old Norse contact. Some of them have been well established while others should perhaps be understood as arguable cases of Old Norse impact.

1. functional words such as *they*, *till*, *fro*, *though*, *both*, *are*, and *same*
2. the third person singular present ending -*s* of the verb in the North[68]
3. the present participle ending -*and* of the verb in the North[69]
4. the ending -*t* as in *scant*, *want*, and *athwart*, which are attributed to the Old Norse neuter ending of the adjective[70]

5. the genitive ending -*er*, as in *on nighter tale* and *bi nighter tale*[71]
6. the reflexive ending -*sk*, as in *busk* and *bask*[72]
7. *are* in the North in contrast with *be* in the South[73]
8. the loss of the prefix *ge-* for the past participle of the verb[74]
9. the preterit plural and the preterit subjunctive forms of certain verbs belonging to the strong classes IV and V[75]

Finally, it is asserted that some syntactic features are attributable to Old Norse, though most of them are uncertain.

1. the tendency to omit the relative pronoun *þat* in Middle English in contrast with the Old English tendency to retain it[76]
2. the Modern English differentiated usage of the auxiliaries *will* and *shall*, which is comparable to the Scandinavian usage[77]
3. the Modern English usage of sentence-final prepositions, as in "He has someone to rely on," which is comparable to the Scandinavian usage[78]
4. the position of an auxiliary in the subjunctive pluperfect construction, and its pattern of omission[79]
5. the Middle English tendency to put a genitive noun before the noun it modified[80]

Morphological or syntactic impact of Old Norse has been explored less than Old Norse loanwords, but there is reason. Morphology and syntax are more abstract, more deeply embedded in language, than the lexicon, so if change takes place at these deep levels, the causation of change is often difficult to pinpoint. Arguments often result in something like "perhaps it started language-internally, perhaps it was induced by language contact."

Despite this difficulty, English historical linguists have always been interested in the linguistic consequences of Norse-English contact. They usually point out the socio-historical significance of Old Norse contact and conclude that the morphosyntactic simplification of English from Late Old English to Early Middle English was accelerated because of the contact.

7.3 Theoretical Assumptions

Before examining the Old Norse contact hypothesis, I must discuss several theoretical issues concerning the Norse-English contact. Below I take up 1) the chronological/geographical relevance, 2) the nature of the contact, 3) the relevant dialects of Old English and Old Norse, and 4) evidential issues.

In the first place, we need to consider whether Old Norse contact was relevant to the development of the plural system in Early Middle English in terms of time and space. This is because if an innovative feature occurred chronologically too early or geographically too remote from the Norse-settled area, we will have to rule out the Old Norse contact explanation at the outset.

Let us examine the traditional view that the phonological and morphological simplification of English was stimulated by Old Norse contact. This view is based on the assumption that while Old English and Old Norse speakers were in contact, they levelled inflectional endings since these were the major difference between the two languages. The point here is that although the simplification may have been started before Old Norse contact was relevant, the contact situation *encouraged* the process already underway.

According to Thomason and Kaufman, the main period of Old Norse influence in the North and East of England was from 875 to 1045 (275). They are against the view that Old Norse stimulated the simplification, since it had already started in the Old English period before Old Norse contact became relevant (301). In my view, however, the arrival of Old Norse was not necessarily too late to *encourage*, not to say *trigger*, the internally started process.

The mid-tenth century Northumbrian *Lindisfarne Gospels* already show a high degree of simplification at a morphological level. Old Norse involvement is chronologically possible if we accept the core period of the impact from 875 to 1045. The relatively small number of Old Norse loanwords in the text, however, should make us doubt that Old Norse involvement was too strong. I do not believe, therefore, that Old Norse contact *triggered* the simplification. It is still possible, however, to argue that it *encouraged* the process already underway.

The situation in the other Norse-settled areas such as East Anglia and East

Mercia is blurred for lack of Old English evidence surviving from these areas. The earliest surviving evidence is the mid-eleventh century *Peterborough Chronicle*. As we saw in Section 4.5, the First and Final Continuations of the text show that the simplification had been in process for some time at the time of composition. It is unclear, however, exactly when the simplification started in the East of England. Accordingly it is an open question whether Old Norse pushed the ongoing process in the East of England as well as in the North of England.

Then let us see how the arguments above can apply to the spread of the *s*-plural. The *Lindisfarne Gospels* already show some spread of -*s*, and although the start of the spread can hardly be attributed to Old Norse contact, it is still possible to argue that Old Norse may have stimulated the spread of -*s* that had also started language-internally.

Likewise, the Continuations of *The Peterborough Chronicle* indicate an increasing rate of the *s*-plural in C12. Considering the language of the First Continuation is heavily mixed with the old West-Saxon *Schriftsprache*, it is likely that the actual rate of -*s* in speech was higher than the text shows. If this view is accurate, the East of England had mostly completed the spread of -*s* by C12a. Despite a lack of earlier surviving evidence, it seems reasonable to infer that Old Norse contact was involved if only partly in the spread of -*s*.

Hereafter I assume that Old Norse contact was chronologically as well as geographically relevant to the reorganisation of the plural system in the North and East of England.

In the second place, let us examine the nature of language contact between Old Norse and Old English. Old Norse contact is often said to be more intimate and profound than any other foreign contact that the English language has had in history. This view is supported by the everyday nature of Old Norse loanwords in contrast to those from French and Latin and by the deep-level repercussions of contact on functional words, morphology, and syntax.

In my view this special status of the Norse-English contact has been somewhat overemphasised. Remarkable as it was, the kind of effect that Old Norse had on English was not really unique but rather a common kind of language contact. As Thomason and Kaufman note, "the extent of Norse influence on English between 900 and 1100, though remarkable, was not extreme given the preexisting typological and genetic closeness of the two languages" (264).

Thomason and Kaufman classify language contact into two types: borrowing and shift-induced interference (3–4). In borrowing, interference features are introduced into the receiving language by fluent bilinguals, whereas in shift-induced interference they are introduced by imperfect learners. Borrowing usually starts at a lexical level and effects little structural change, while shift-induced interference usually starts at a phonological or syntactic level and effects structural change.

Borrowing and shift-induced interference are two end points on a cline, so there are countless intermediate levels in between. The precise nature and depth of language contact depends on various sociolinguistic or linguistic parameters.[81] Thomason and Kaufman see the Norse-English contact as a case of intense borrowing—"borrowing" because the relatively small population of perfect learners were responsible for the contact-induced language change, and "intense" because interference was not limited to the lexicon but reached morphology and syntax as well.

The most important linguistic parameter for the nature and depth of the Norse-English contact is the typological similarity between the two languages. As Thomason says, "even features that are highly marked or highly integrated into an interlocking structure are readily exchanged between typologically similar systems" (77).

If Old Norse contact was relevant to the spread of *-s*, the effect of contact would be morphological rather than lexical. Such a morphological effect may be regarded as "deeper" than mere lexical borrowing, but it may not be extremely profound because no innovative features were added to the English system after all (*-s* was available to the language to start with). What happened was not a systemic replacement but merely a systemic reorganisation with resources already available.

Thirdly, one problem with the study of Norse-English contact is that our knowledge of Old Norse dialects is rather limited. As Old Norse is only known to us either in runic inscriptions or in literature that comes from much later periods, we do not have rich information about the particular dialect spoken by the Norse who had the greatest effect on English in the Danelaw.

On the Old English side, we are particularly interested in the northern and eastern varieties spoken during the Late Old English to Early Middle English period. On the Old Norse side, we are particularly interested in the Danish varieties spoken in the Danelaw during the Late Old English to Early Middle English period.[82] Ideally, therefore, the study of Norse-English contact should be based on these particular varieties of Old Norse and Old English; however, when I compare inflectional paradigms of the two languages in the next section, I use those of West-Saxon and Old Icelandic because they are best known and they represent the dialects of Late Old English and Old Norse reasonably enough for the present purposes.[83]

Fourthly, let us consider the availability of evidence. For one thing, we have no surviving texts localised to the North and East of England dated from the Late Old English to the Early Middle English period, with the exception of the mid-tenth century *Lindisfarne Gospels*, *Rushworth Gospels*, *Durham Ritual*, a few northern charters (see Stevenson), and the three late Old English Northumbrian documents (printed in *Herrigs Archiv* 111: 275ff). Thereafter there is no sizable vernacular text surviving except a few inscriptions[84] until the mid-twelfth century *Peterborough Chronicle*. The shortage of evidence must leave any conclusion to be reached provisional.

Another kind of evidential problem arises out of the typological similarity of the two languages. Björkman points to the difficulty in testing Old Norse loanwords in that many of them were anglicised and could be easily mistaken for native English words.

For example, it is likely that Old English speakers in the Danelaw understood Old Norse well and identified Scandinavian *-sk* with Old English *-sc*. When they came across Old Norse forms with *-sk*, they may have pronounced *-sk* in these words as *-sc* after their own pattern. In this case, we cannot decide whether a particular word was borrowed at all because it looks just like its native English counterparts. In many cases minor differences that originally existed between the languages were thus levelled in the process of Anglicisation.

Anglicisation occurred, according to Björkman, through the "etymological identity" between Old English and Old Norse words (10). It was through this etymological identity that the Old English speakers identified Old Norse and Old English forms such as *-sk* and *-sc*. Likewise, the Old English plural ending *-s* could have been identified with the Old Norse plural ending *-r* because the two endings were "etymologically identical." I will explore this matter in the next section.

7.4 Old Norse Contact Hypothesis

Classen's argument for the Old Norse contact hypothesis depended on "a very close resemblance between the Old Norse weak inflexions and the Old English strong inflexions in the singular" ("Plurals" 96). The close resemblance, he concluded, caused Old Norse weak nouns to decline in the same way as Old English strong nouns both in the singular and the plural, and as a result more and more English weak nouns followed the strong declension, hence the general increase of the *s*-plural.

His argument, however, is unclear in two respects. The first point is whether he was right when he said "the -*n* plurals represent the normal development of the Old English system" (94), whereas the -*s* plurals are due to some force which "hindered the normal development" (95).

Classen's view of the *n*-plurals representing the normal development was based on the assumption that weak nouns were more numerous than nouns of any single strong declension in Old English. Unfortunately, the assumption seems simply wrong. Table 7.1 summarises Quirk and Wrenn's figures (20).

Table 7.1: Distribution of Old English Declensions

a-stem masc.	0.36
ō-stem fem.	0.25
a-stem neut.	0.25
n-stem masc. and minor declension masc.	0.09
n-stem fem. and minor declension fem.	0.05
n-stem neut.	insignificant

It is unclear how Quirk and Wrenn arrived at the rates, but if we accept them, *a*-stem masculines were by far the most numerous in Old English. Weak nouns occurred at a rate of not more than 0.14 of all the genders combined. This figure is less than the rate for the strong declension of any single gender.

Although Classen's assumption seems wrong, there are still reasons for believing that the growth of the weak noun should represent the more natural development. For the sake of argument, let us assume that the survival and growth of the n-plural represented the natural course of development. Under this assumption, we do not need to question the southern growth of -n, but we do need to ask why the northern dialects took the opposite course of development. Then we must consider language-external motives, and this is exactly what I am trying to do in this chapter.

On the other hand, if we assume that the spread of -s represented the natural course of development, then how can the "unnatural" development of -n in the southern dialects be explained? It is difficult to find any decisive reason why -n survived and even somewhat grew in the southern dialects.

Another reason for believing the growth of the n-plural to represent the natural development is that the weak inflections were homogeneous across the genders except in the nominative/accusative singular. Although weak nouns were smaller in number than strong nouns, their gender-free nature must have been a favourable factor to retaining and even growing in share among the nominal inflections (Roedler 1: 495).

Moreover, the weak declension of adjectives must have encouraged the survival and growth of the n-plural. As Behm points out, "a superiority to the weak declension . . . was no doubt largely owing to the prevalence of the weak declension of adjectives" (41).

The following quotation from Stein summarises the argument above:

> Generally the North exhibits a much more advanced state of inflectional reduction, also with respect to n-loss. The impression is that the South exhibits a kind of 'normal' pattern of phonologically induced and phonetically determined reduction, which can be observed in the North as well, such as the phonotactically motivated preferences pointed out by e.g. Blakeley (1949/1950), but that the North displays distinct additional features or a particular 'style' of evolution that cannot be explained by intrinsic Anglo-Saxon drift alone. Given that the phonological cause and structural starting point was the same for both the North and the South, the question must be asked what caused the distinct divergence of devel-

opment in the two regions. The most plausible answer seems to lie in the specific sociocultural conditions in the North, i.e. the Scandinavian influence. ("OE" 647)

The second of the unclear points in Classen's argument is what exactly he meant by "close resemblance" in declensions between Old Norse and Old English. As this inflectional resemblance is part and parcel of the Old Norse contact hypothesis, I must clarify this point.

Classen refers to a resemblance between the Old Norse *weak* declension and the Old English *strong* declension. I present the paradigms of the two declensions in Table 7.2 on page 164.[85]

Classen maintains that "there is clearly a very close resemblance" between the two declensions. I wonder whether the resemblance is so clearly close. If he means by "resemblance" that the majority of the inflectional endings in both declensions are vowels, I agree. Difference in the vowel value was perhaps insignificant because toward the end of Old English most word final vowels were reduced to schwa at least on the English side.

Another common feature would be that both declensions lack the *n*-ending except for the *(e)na*-ending for the genitive plural. In Germanic languages the weak declension was normally associated with the *n*-ending, but the Old Norse weak declension normally lacked -*n*. This means that Old Norse made less of a distinction between strong and weak declensions than other Germanic languages including Old English.

In the singular inflections, vowel endings are dominant in both declensions. Aside from a few ø-endings, the major difference lies in the masculine/neuter genitive, for which Old English has -*s* and Old Norse has a vowel. In the plural, both declensions have comparable endings for the genitive and the dative, though this is true of most of the nominal declension types in the two languages. As for the nominative/accusative, the neuter inflections in both declensions are alike in that they could take a *u*-ending.

As for the masculine and feminine, the two declensions show a striking difference in the nominative/accusative plural. In Old Norse the nominative/accusative plurals take endings such as -*ar*, -*ur*, and -*a*, while in Old English they take -*as*, -*a*, and -*e*.

Table 7.2: Old Norse Weak and Old English Strong Declensions

	Old Norse weak declension			Old English strong declension					
	an-stem masc.	*an*-stem neut.	*on*-stem fem.	*a*-stem masc.	*a*-stem neut.	*ō*-stem fem.	*i*-stem masc.	*u*-stem masc./fem.
nom. sg.	-i, -e	-a	-a	-ø	-ø	-u, -ø	-e, -ø	-u, -ø
acc. sg.	-a	-a	-u	-ø	-ø	-e	-e, -ø	-u, -ø
gen. sg.	-a	-a	-u	-es	-es	-e	-es	-a
dat. sg.	-a	-a	-u	-e	-e	-e	-e	-a
nom. pl.	-ar	-u, -o	-ur	-as	-ø, -u	-a, -e	-e, -as	-a
acc. pl.	-a	-u, -o	-ur	-as	-ø, -u	-a, -e	-e, -as	-a
gen. pl.	-a	-na	-na	-a	-a	-a, -ena	-a	-a
dat. pl.	-um	-um	-um	-um	-um	-um	-um	-um

Classen argues that since the two declensions were generally similar, language contact helped to level the few differences that did exist. Despite some inaccuracy involved in his initial assumption, I can nevertheless accept Classen's argumentation on the whole.

Classen only compared the paradigms of the Old Norse *weak* declension and the Old English *strong* declensions. Interestingly enough, I have recognised another significant comparison that strengthens the hypothesis. There is inflectional correspondence, if not inflectional similarity, between the Old Norse *strong* declension and the Old English *strong* declension. Table 7.3 on page 166 shows the paradigm of the Old Norse strong declension, as adapted from Noreen (*Altisländische* 246–75).

I will highlight a few differences between the Old Norse and Old English strong declensions. First, the Old Norse strong singular is largely dominated by *V*- or ø-endings, but in the nominative singular, Old Norse often has a distinctive *r*-ending, for which Old English has no equivalent. This is one of the major differences in the two declensions.

Secondly, the Old Norse genitive singular has consonantal endings such as -*s* and -*ar* (even for the feminine!), which correspond to the Old English genitive singular *es*-ending (which is limited to the masculine and the neuter). Remember that the Old Norse *weak* genitive singular does not take consonant endings. In this respect, the Old Norse strong declension is a step closer to the Old English strong declension than to the Old Norse weak declension (although this may not be surprising since we are comparing the same strong declensions of two closely related languages after all).

Thirdly, for the plural inflections, the Old Norse and Old English strong declensions share the genitive plural -*a* and dative plural -*um*. In addition they share the neuter nominative/accusative plural -ø. The masculine/feminine inflections, however, differ greatly in the Old Norse and Old English strong declensions. For the masculine Old Norse takes -*ar* in the nominative and -*a* in the accusative, whereas Old English takes -*as* in both the nominative and the accusative. For the feminine, Old Norse takes -*ar* in the nominative/accusative, whereas Old English takes -*a*. Note that in Old Norse the feminine as well as the masculine takes the consonantal endings for the nominative/accusative plural, and that the consonantal endings in the feminine are unfamiliar to Old

Table 7.3: Old Norse Strong Declensions

	a-stem masc.	*a*-stem neut.	*ō*-stem fem.	*i*-stem masc.	*i*-stem fem.	*u*-stem masc.
nom. sg.	-r	-∅	-∅	-r	-r	-r
acc. sg.	-∅	-∅	-∅, -u, -o	-∅	-∅	-∅
gen. sg.	-s	-s	-ar	-s, -ar	-ar	-ar
dat. sg.	-i, -e	-i, -e	-∅, -u, -o	-∅	-∅	-i, -e, -∅
nom. pl.	-ar	-∅	-ar	-ir, -er	-ir, -er	-ir, -er
acc. pl.	-a	-∅	-ar	-i, -e	-ir, -er	-u, -o, -i, -e
gen. pl.	-a	-a	-a	-a	-a	-a
dat. pl.	-um, -om	-um, -om	-um, -om	-um, -om	-um, -om	-um, -om

English. All this means that Old Norse shows less inflectional contrast between the masculine and the feminine than Old English does.

I have just pointed out that Old Norse shows less formal contrast than Old English between the masculine and the feminine. On the other hand, I have also said that Old Norse shows less formal contrast than Old English between the weak and strong declensions. These two facts should bring us to conclude that in the nominal paradigm the Old Norse inflections are more homogeneous than the Old English counterparts. Indeed, the Old Norse *r*-ending occurs in a larger number of slots of the inflectional paradigm than the Old English *s*-ending: it occurs regardless of the masculine/feminine, the nominative/accusative, or the strong/weak inflections.

The consequence of all this is that Old Norse nouns, strong or weak, are inflectionally close to Old English strong masculine nouns, one proviso being that the Old English -*s* corresponds to the Old Norse -*r*, not -*s*. In fact, this proviso should not be serious because the Old English -*s* and the Old Norse -*r* largely overlapped in function as well as in distribution. There is adequate reason for believing that Old Norse and Old English speakers treated the two endings identically.

First, in Old Norse, -*s* and -*ar* could be alternative genitive singular endings. For example, *i*-stem masculines took either ending in the genitive singular, e.g. *bekks/bekkiar* "bench's." There are many instances of *a*-stem nouns alternatively taking -*s* or -*ar* in the genitive singular, e.g. *apald(r)s/apaldar* "apple tree's," *auþs/auþar* "riches'," *bastarþs/bastarþar* "bastard's," *eiþs/eiþar* "oath's," *heiþs/heiþar* "honour's," *krapts/kraptar* "might's," *lāvarþs/lāvarþar* "lord's," *lunds/lundar* "grove's," *meiþs/meiþar* "longitudinal beam's," and *meldrs/meldrar* "flour's" (Noreen, *Altisländische* 249–50). This alternation likely contributed to the functional identification of the Old Norse -*r* with the Old English -*s* even outside the genitive singular.

Secondly, the correspondence between the Old Norse -*r* and the Old English -*s* can also be found in the verbal conjugations of the two languages. In Old Norse the present indicative second and third person singular ending of a verb was -*ar* while in Old English the second person singular ending was -*es(t)*. Knowles gives examples that show a similar correspondence between Modern Danish -*r* and Present-Day English -*s*. Modern Danish *har*, *går*, *er*, and *var* correspond respectively to Present-Day English *has*, *goes*, *is*, and *was* (34, 42).

Thirdly, historically speaking, this correspondence is not surprising since the Old Norse *-r* represents a sound developed from [z] through a series of phonetic changes. The Old Norse consonant written *r* may in fact have been phonetically close to [z]. If *-r* was pronounced close to [z], the sense of correspondence between the Old Norse *-r* and the Old English *-s* was strengthened phonetically as well. The exact value of the Old Norse *-r* is uncertain, however. According to Gordon, the Germanic /z/ developed first to *r*-coloured [z] written *R* in the pre-literary period of Old Norse, then to palatalised [r], and later to trilled [r] (268). On the other hand, Haugen remarks that *R* had been merged with *r* by 1100 (*Scandinavian* 155). Another account on this issue is found in Ralf, who considers it probable that "palatal *r*" was phonetically a fricative [ʒ] or [r] (715). All things considered, it might be that *r*-coloured [z] was still heard in Old Norse in the late Old English period, but I will leave the question about the phonetic value of the Old Norse *-r* open.

Now, what happened to speakers and their languages in the Danelaw when they recognised the functional correspondence between Old Norse *-r* and Old English *-s*? Intense language contact must have led them to use interchangeably one ending where the other ending would be historically expected. Then, through everyday communication with the Norse, the English learnt to extend the use of their own *-s* wherever Norse speakers would use *-r*, and vice versa.

Through bidirectional interaction, the two peoples were gradually developing a simplified plural system. Although the Old Norse *-r* itself proved to be a lesser variant, it indirectly contributed to the increasing frequency of the corresponding Old English *-s*. Because the Old Norse strong feminines and weak nouns pluralised with *-r*, more and more of their Old English equivalents transferred to the *s*-plural. Figure 7.1 on page 169 schematises this process.

Let us remember that the key to understanding how Old Norse contact contributed to the spread of the *s*-plural is that Old Norse nouns as a whole, strong or weak, were inflectionally close to Old English strong masculine nouns. It is via this inflectional closeness, via etymological/lexical identification between cognates, and via the functional correspondence of *-r* and *-s* that many Old English non-*s* plurals were made to change over to *s*-plurals.[86]

```
┌─────────────────┐   correspondence between
│  OE str. masc.  │◄─────────────────────────
└─────────────────┘         OE -s and ON -r
         ▲                                    ┌──────────────────────┐
         │                                    │  ON str. fem. & wk.  │
   s-pluralisation                            └──────────────────────┘
         │                                          ▲
┌──────────────────┐                               ╱
│ OE str. fem. & wk.│──────────────────────────────
└──────────────────┘  etymological/lexical identification
```

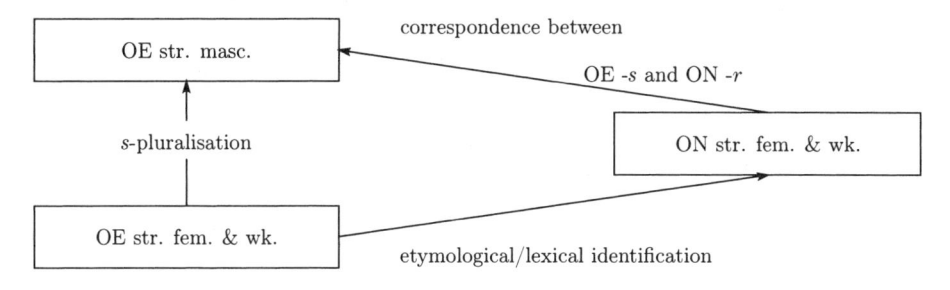

Figure 7.1: Illustration of Old Norse Contact Hypothesis

7.5 Illustration of Forms

This section will flesh out the Old Norse contact hypothesis by listing plural forms that might possibly have been affected by the contact. Forms are taken from four texts localised to the North and East of England and dated from the Late Old English to the Early Middle English period: the *Lindisfarne Gospels* (ed. Skeat), *The Peterborough Chronicle* (ed. Earle and Plummer; and Clark), and *The Ormulum* (ed. Holt).

In order to argue for possible Old Norse involvement, we must make sure that *s*-plurals in question fulfil the following three conditions. First, it is necessary that their historically expected plural forms be non-*s* since I wish to show evidence of transfers from non-*s*-plurals to *s*-plurals.

Secondly, we must identify the Old Norse plural form corresponding to the Old English noun in question. If it is not identified, Old Norse influence cannot be assessed. For this reason I leave out *s*-plurals that have no Old Norse equivalents. Thirdly, it is necessary that the Old Norse equivalent plural have an *r*-ending.

Each example from the three texts is given as a set of five forms. The first form is an Old English West-Saxon form in its nominative singular with its gender, declension type, and meaning in Present-Day English given. The second form is the expected Old English West-Saxon nominative/accusative plural form. The third is a form attested in the text. The fourth and fifth are the Old Norse equivalent forms in their nominative plural and nominative singular with its gender and declension type information given.

For example, the first line below reads like this: we speak of the possible Old Norse effect on the plural form of *burg* "borough" of the feminine athematic stem (the first form); its historically expected plural form is *byrʒ* (the second form), but the plural actually occurs in the text as *burgas* (the third form); this *s*-ending may be affected by the *r*-ending of the Old Norse plural *borgir* (the fourth form); its dictionary entry, or its nominative singular form, is *borg* (the fifth form), classified in Old Norse as a feminine *i*-stem noun.

For inflections, I mainly referred to Noreen (*Altisländische*), Bosworth and Toller, Zoëga, and *The Oxford English Dictionary*. The Old Norse nominal declensions are included in Appendix F.

The *Lindisfarne Gospels*

burg (Fem. athematic stem) "borough" — byrʒ — burgas — borgir — borg (Fem. *i*-stem)
cild (Neut. *es/os*-stem) "child" — cild/cildru — cildas — kindir/kindr — kind (Fem. *i*-stem or Fem. athematic stem)
fēond (Masc. *nd*-stem) "fiend" — fīend — fiondas/fiondes — fjāndr — fjāndi (Masc. *nd*-stem)
frēond (Masc. *nd*-stem) "friend" — frīend — freondas — frændr — frændi (Masc. *nd*-stem)
fȳr (Neut. *a*-stem) "fire" — fȳr — fyres — fūrar — fūrr (Masc. *a*-stem)
hol (Neut. *a*-stem) "hole" — holu — holas — holor/hol — hola (Fem. *n*-stem)/hol (Neut. *a*-stem)
spearwa (Masc. *n*-stem) "sparrow" — spearwan — hronsparuas — spörar — spörr (Masc. *a*-stem)
swica (Masc. *n*-stem) "deceiver" — swican — gesuicas — drōttin-svikar — drōttin-sviki (Masc. *n*-stem)
wītega (Masc. *n*-stem) "wise man" — wītegan — witgas — vitkar — vitki (Masc. *n*-stem)

The *Peterborough Chronicle*

bera (Masc. *n*-stem) "bear" — beran — baras — birnir — björn (Masc. *u*-stem)
brycg (Fem. *ō*-stem) "bridge" — brycga — brigges — bryggjur — bryggja (Fem. *n*-stem)
bōc (Fem. athematic stem) "book" — bēc — bokes — boekr — bōk (Fem. athematic stem)
dǣd (Fem. *i*-stem) "deed" — dǣda — dǣdes — dāðar — dāð (Fem. *ō*-stem)
fetor (Fem. *ō*-stem) "fetter" — fetora — feteres — fjötrar — fjöturr (Masc. *a*-stem)
foreweard (Fem. *ō*-stem) "condition" — forewearda — foruuardes — forverðir — forvörðr (Masc. *u*-stem)

heretoga (Masc. *n*-stem) "commander" — heretogan — heorotogas — hertogar — hertogi (Masc. *n*-stem)

lagu (Fem. *ō*-stem) "law" — laga — laʒhess — lagar/lög — sg. form unknown (Fem. *ō*-stem or Neut. *a*-stem)

lim (Neut. *a*-stem) "limb" — leomu – limes — limir — limr (Masc. *u*-stem)

mæssehacele (Fem. *n*-stem) "mass-vestment" — mæssehacelan — mæssahakeles/messehakeles — höklar — hökull (Masc. *a*-stem)

mōt (Neut. *a*-stem) "society" — mōt — motes — mūtur — mūta (Fem. *n*-stem)

nǣdre (Fem. *n*-stem) "adder" — nǣdran — nadres — naðrar/naðrur — naðr (Masc. *a*-stem)/naðra (Fem. *n*-stem)

nefa (Masc. *n*-stem) "nephew" — nefan — neues — nefar — nefi (Masc. *n*-stem)

padde (Fem. *n*-stem) "toad" — paddan — pades — paddur — padda (Fem. *n*-stem)

riht (Neut. *a*-stem) "right" — riht — rihtes — rīttir — rēttr (Masc. *u*-stem)

snaca (Masc. *n*-stem) "snake" — snacan — snakes — snākar — snākr (Masc. *a*-stem)

steorra (Masc. *n*-stem) "star" — steorran — sterres — stjörnur — stjarna (Fem. *n*-stem)

sunu (Masc. *u*-stem) "son" — suna — sunes — synir/sønir — sonr/sunr (Masc. *u*-stem)

swica (Masc. *n*-stem) "deceiver" — swican — swikes/suikes — drōttin-svikar — drōttin-sviki (Masc. *n*-stem)

synn (Fem. *ō*-stem) "sin" — synna — sinnes — syndir — synd (Fem. *i*-stem)

trēowþ (Fem. *ō*-stem) "truth" — trēowþa — treothes/treuthes — tryggðir — sg. form unknown (Fem. *i*-stem)

þūma (Masc. *n*-stem) "thumb" — þūman — þumbes — þumlungar/þumal-fingr — þumlungr (Masc. *a*-stem)/þumal-fingr (Masc. *a*-stem)

ūtlaga (Masc. *n*-stem) "outlaw" — ūtlagan — utlagas/utlages — ūtlagar — ūtlagi (Masc. *n*-stem)

wudu (Masc. *u*-stem) "wood" — wuda — wudas — viðir — viðr (Masc. *u*-stem)

The Ormulum

arc (Fem. *ō*-stem) "ark" — arca — arrkess — arkir — örk (Fem. *i*-stem)

asce (Fem. *n*-stem) "ash" — ascan — asskess — öskur — aska (Fem. *n*-stem)

benc (Fem. *ō*-stem) "bench" — benca — bannkess/bennkess — bakkar — bakki (Masc. *n*-stem)

bucca (Masc. *n*-stem) "buck" — buccan — buckess/bukkess — bokkar — bokki (Masc. *n*-stem)

burg (Fem. athematic stem) "borough" — byrʒ — burrʒhess — borgir — borg (Fem. *i*-stem)

bēn (Fem. *i*-stem) "prayer" — bēna — beness/boness — boenir — boen (Fem. *i*-stem)

bōc (Fem. athematic stem) "book" — bēc — Goddspellbokess/bokess/laʒhebokess — boekr — bōk (Fem. athematic stem)

clawu (Fem. *ō*-stem) "claw" — clawa — clawwess — kloer — klō (Fem. athematic stem)

cynd (Neut. *a*-stem) "kind" — cynd — kindess — kindir/kindr — kind (Fem. *i*-stem or Fem. athematic stem)

dǣd (Fem. *i*-stem) "deed" — dǣda — dedess — dāðar — dāð (Fem. *ō*-stem)

dælu (Neut. *a*-stem) "dale" — dælu — daless — dalar/dalir — dalr (Masc. *a*-stem or Masc. *i*-stem)

genga (Masc. *n*-stem) "fellow-traveller" — gengan — gengess — göngar — gangr (Masc. *a*-stem)
giefu (Fem. *ō*-stem) "gift" — giefa — ȝifess — gjafar/gjafir — gjöf (Fem. *ō*-stem or Fem. *i*-stem)
glēd (Fem. *i*-stem) "coal" — glēda — gledess — gloeðr — glōð (Fem. athematic stem)
græf (Neut. *a*-stem) "cave" — græfu — græfess — grafir/grafar — gröf (Fem. *i*-stem or Fem. *ō*-stem)
hand (Fem. *u*-stem) "hand" — handa — hanndess — hendr — hönd (Fem. athematic stem)
lagu (Fem. *ō*-stem) "law" — laga — laȝhess — lagar/lög — (sg. form unknown) (Fem. *ō*-stem or Neut. *a*-stem)
lār (Fem. *ō*-stem) "learning" — lāra — laress — læringar — læring (Fem. *ō*-stem)
lendenu (pl.) (Neut. *a*-stem) "loins" — lendenu — lendess — lendir/lendar — lend (Fem. *i*-stem or Fem. *ō*-stem)
lim (Neut. *a*-stem) "limb" — leomu – limess — limir — limr (Masc. *u*-stem)
lot (Neut. *a*-stem) "fraud" — lotu — lotess — hlutir — hlutr (Masc. *i*-stem)
mæsse (Fem. *n*-stem) "mass" — mæssan — messess — messur — messa (Fem. *n*-stem)
miht (Fem. *i*-stem) "might" — mihta — mahhtess — māttar — māttr (Masc. *a*-stem)
nædre (Fem. *n*-stem) "adder" — nædran — neddress — naðrar/naðrur — naðr (Masc. *a*-stem)/naðra (Fem. *n*-stem)
niht (Fem. athematic stem) "night" — nihta — nahhtess/nihhtess — nætr — nātt (Fem. athematic stem)
rest (Fem. *ō*-stem) "rest" — resta — resstess — rastir — röst (Fem. *i*-stem)
sacu (Fem. *ō*-stem) "conflict" — saca — sakess — sakar/sakir — sök (Fem. *ō*-stem or Fem. *i*-stem)
sǣlþ (Fem. *ō*-stem) "fortune" — sǣlþa — seollþess — sælur — sæla (Fem. *n*-stem)
sand (Neut. *a*-stem) "sand" — sand — sandess — söndar — sandr (Masc. *a*-stem)
sāwol (Fem. *ō*-stem) "soul" — sāwla — sawless — sālur — sāla (Fem. *n*-stem)
scanca (Masc. *n*-stem) "shank" — scancan — shannkess — skakkar — skakkr (Masc. *a*-stem)
stæl (Neut. *a*-stem) "place" — stælu — stalless — stallar — stallr (Masc. *a*-stem)
steorra (Masc. *n*-stem) "star" — steorran — steorrness/sterness/sterrness — stjörnur — stjarna (Fem. *n*-stem)
sticca (Masc. *n*-stem) "stick" — sticcan — stikkess — stikur — stika (Fem. *n*-stem)
stīg (Fem. *ō*-stem) "narrow path" — stīga — stiȝhess — stigar/stīgir — stigr (Masc. *a*-stem)/stīgr (Masc. *u*-stem)
stoc (Neut. *a*-stem) "place" — stocu — stokess — stokkar — stokkr (Masc. *a*-stem)
sunu (Masc. *u*-stem) "son" — suna — sunes — synir/sønir — sonr/sunr (Masc. *u*-stem)
synn (Fem. *ō*-stem) "sin" — synna — siness/sinnes/sinness — syndir — synd (Fem. *i*-stem)
talu (Fem. *ō*-stem) "tale" — tala — taless — talur — tala (Fem. *n*-stem)
tīma (Masc. *n*-stem) "time" — tīman — timess — tīmar — tīmi (Masc. *n*-stem)
wæcce (Fem. *n*-stem) "watch" — wæccan — wecchess — vakur — vaka (Fem. *n*-stem)
wītega (Masc. *n*-stem) "wise man" — wītegan — Uþwitess/witess/wittess — vitkar — vitki (Masc. *n*-stem)
wiþþe (Fem. *n*-stem) "cord" — wiþþan — wiþþess — viðjar/viðjur — við (Fem. *ō*-stem)/viðja (Fem. *n*-stem)
wrǣcca (Masc. *n*-stem) "wretch" — wrǣccan — wrecchess — rekingar — rekingr (Masc. *a*-stem)
wucu (Fem. *ō*-stem) "week" — wuce — wukess — vikur — vika (Fem. *n*-stem)
wund (Fem. *ō*-stem) "wound" — wunda — wundess — undir — und (Fem. *i*-stem)

It is notable how many innovative *s*-plurals could possibly have been affected by Old Norse contact. However, there are more than a few examples which could not be attributed to Old Norse contact. For example, there are new *s*-plurals whose Old Norse equivalents have no *r*-ending. They are mostly strong neuters, which pluralised with -*u* or -*ø* both in Old Norse and in Old English.[87]

Outside the strong neuters there are a few examples for which Old Norse contact could not be relevant: *herrtess* (a weak feminine corresponding to the Old Norse weak neuter *hjörtu*), *dohhtress* (a feminine kinship noun to the Old Norse *doetr*), *susstress* (a feminine kinship noun to the Old Norse *systr*), *godnessess* (a strong feminine to the Old Norse *ia*-stem neuter *gōðrrœði*), *namess* (a weak masculine to the Old Norse strong neuter *nöfn*), and *wittness* (a strong feminine to the Old Norse strong neuter *vitni*), all from *The Ormulum*.

These new *s*-plurals could not be relevant to Old Norse contact, but they do not necessarily constitute counterexamples to the hypothesis. By listing examples of possible and impossible Old Norse influence, I did not mean to identify which items were *actually* affected by contact and which were not; rather I meant that some of the new *s*-plurals could *possibly* have been affected by contact. As I have repeated so far, the spread of -*s* started before Old Norse contact became fully relevant, so the Old Norse contact hypothesis must be accepted as an additional plausible extralinguistic account for the spread of -*s*.

In the above I have discussed the validity of the Old Norse contact hypothesis in the theoretical framework of contact linguistics, the reassessment of Classen's proposal, and the listing of possibly affected items.

Various evidential problems must prevent anything more than speculation, but if the speculation is theoretically reasonable in light of sociolinguistic contexts of the time, there is no reason why we should rule out the hypothesis.

Language change should be motivated by a combination of language-internal and -external factors. If language-internal factors provide a reasonable explanation, this does not mean that language-external factors should be dismissed. It is always desirable to seek additional possible motivation for language change.

7.6 Contact between Dialects

Language contact takes place not only between languages but also between dialects. One of the justifications for advancing the Old Norse contact hypothesis was the great divide that existed in the growth of the *s*-plural between the northern and the southern dialects. The gap, however, was gradually filled toward the Late Middle English period as the southern dialects were trying to catch up with the northern development.

As the growth of *-s* in the northern dialects had to be explained by both language-internal and -external motives, so the catching-up process of the southern dialects has to be explained from both points of view. For the first thing, although the delayed growth of the *s*-plural in the southern dialects may be explained intralinguistically, this may not be the only explanation. We should go on to ask if language-external motivation was also relevant since language change is multi-factorial.

Moreover, as we saw in the graph in Figure 3.9 on page 71, the spread rates of *-s* show roughly parallel S-curves among different dialects, indicating a wavy movement from the Northeast to the Southwest. Each S-curve has a distinct slope, but the general parallelism is so clear that we must assume contact between dialects.

Furthermore, we know other Early Middle English innovative features which diffused from the Northeast to the Southwest. For example, according to Ogura and Wang, the third person present indicative verval ending *-th* first emerged as *-s* in C10 in Old Northumbrian texts ("Snowball" 130). The new ending did not reach the northern East Midlands until the beginning of C13, but afterwards it gradually displaced the old ending in Lincolnshire, Norfolk, and finally London.

Most innovations due to Norse-English contact diffused from the Northeast to the Southwest. Rynell illustrated this by the passage of Old Norse loanwords (360). Most of them took a long while before they were accepted in the South and West. We also know that the use of the pronoun "she" originated in East Midland and spread south later.

It is true that linguists have long taken for granted the Northeast to the Southwest waves of language change in Middle English: innovation normally took place first in the North and East and then spread to the South and West; however, they hardly ever highlighted it explicitly. We may pay more explicit attention to the role that dialect contact played in the history of English.

The question naturally arises as to why the waves proceeded from the Northeast to the Southwest rather than the other way round. Is there an adequate sociolinguistic explanation why? On this matter, Thomason and Kaufman note:

> Until about 1225 innovations starting in the South were spreading northward (e.g., /aː/ > /oə/, ɣ > w/y), after 1250 practically all innovations in English were starting in the North and spreading southward (e.g. lengthening of short stressed vowel in open syllable, dropping of final unstressed schwa, degemination, spread of third person singular present tense -es at the expense of -eth). No explanation (except that York, England's second city, is located in Deira) can as yet be offered for why the North should have been so influential on the Midlands and South from 1250 to 1400, since it was much poorer than the rest of England, and was constantly being raided by the Scots, with whom the Northerners (ruefully, one supposes) shared a dialect. (274)

The social importance of York may be part of an explanation, but it remains uncertain how much linguistic influence the northern city may have exerted on the southern areas.[88] I cannot offer a strong alternative, but it is possible that as carriers of Norsified English in the North and East passed innovative linguistic features to neighbouring areas through person-to-person communication, the receiving areas willingly picked up the Norsified features as "faddish." For the time being, however, I would like to leave this question open.

Chapter 8 Conclusion

The period from Late Old English through Early Middle English to Late Middle English was one of dynamic linguistic change. Morphologically speaking, it was arguably the most dynamic period in the history of English as the inflectional system as a whole was vulnerable to phonological levelling and loss in weak syllables. Nominal plural formations were affected by this destructive process, and the systemic reorganisation was a natural course of development.

With the wisdom of hindsight, the English plural system eventually found its way to reach the modern system in which the *s*-plural is effectively the single dominant formation. When, however, the reorganisation was in process in Early Middle English, the way it proceeded varied greatly from dialect to dialect, as we saw in Section 3.2.

Different dialects had different schedules of plural formation transfer. The spread of -*s* started first in Northern, which was then followed by North-East Midland, North-West Midland, South-East Midland, Southeastern, South-West Midland and Southwestern roughly in that order. The relatively slow and late spread of -*s* in the southern dialects was largely due to the longer survival of its rival -*n*. The South-West Midland profile in particular showed that the growth of -*s* was in inverse proportion to the survival or revival of -*n*.

The lexical subsets that underwent plural formation transfer also differed from dialect to dialect. The item-by-item investigation in Section 3.3 made us see that certain items underwent plural formation transfer in one dialect, but not in another. In addition, even when two dialects showed the same transfers, their timings were often different.

These differences between dialects should not surprise us. After all, each dialect was an individual unit with its own linguistic characteristics. I would rather be surprised at the general similarity across dialects in the way plural formation transfer was implemented.

The graph of the spread rate for -*s* in Figure 3.9 on page 71 showed that the spread of -*s* followed a characteristic S-curve for each dialect—a common pattern of language change that Lexical Diffusion would predict. Even though the exact shape of the S-curve differs from dialect to dialect, rough parallelism between the S-curves strongly suggests that the innovation diffused from one dialect to another. Since the geographical adjacency of dialects matches the chronological order in which the spread of -*s* proceeded, it is most likely that the innovation diffused like a wave from the Northeast to the Southwest.

Different dialects showed different developments on an item-by-item basis, but globally seen, they bore a striking similarity in plural formation transfer. In other words, each of the dialects was unique on a micro-level, but they were after all varieties of one language on a macro-level.

After I described the "how" of development, the question of "why" was addressed from two perspectives. First, I took a language-internal approach to finding out possible systemic motivation for the development. I proposed different levels of language-internal motivation, including phonetic, morphological, syntactic, and semantic.

To recapitulate the main language-internal motives, sound reduction in weak inflectional syllables was arguably the most responsible for triggering the spread of -*s*; the reduction and merger of various declension types was another strong factor in accelerating the process of the inflectional reorganisation; the collapse of morphological categories such as case and gender was yet another contributing factor; the decreased functionality of syntactic agreement between nouns on the one hand and the articles and quantifiers on the other was probably of some relevance to the development of the nominal plural system; and semantic associations occasionally provided a motive for plural formation transfer. Some of these motives were more directly relevant to the development than others, but taken together, all of them contributed to the overall reorganisation of the nominal plural system.

The language-internal motivation thus provided a reasonable functionalistic account for the development, but it was not strong enough to account for why development in the northern dialects was so different from that in the southern dialects. Explaining it away as due to mere dialectal difference was not enough; rather, we needed to take account of the other approach, that is, the language-external one.

Given the situation where the northern dialects were far more advanced in the spread of -*s*, we were naturally led to suspect that Old Norse was involved in the development. Developing the Old Norse contact hypothesis on the spread of -*s*, I argued that it was a sufficiently plausible hypothesis on theoretical grounds. Contact across dialects was also seen as part of the language-external explanation of the development.

The present study primarily aimed to describe "how" and explain "why" the plural formation transfer started and proceeded in Early Middle English, but I also stressed that to achieve the goals I would take advantage of the latest methodologies and techniques developed in (English) historical linguistics.

First, I made use of the *LAEME* text database, on a trial basis, for about half of the Early Middle English texts that were analysed (134 scribal texts out of the 247). Designed for the computer-age, it ensures speed, accuracy, and consistent comparability across texts. Although it was not tagged for all the information I needed for the present study (for example, the Old English declension type was not encoded), it was relatively easy to take out relevant examples from a massive collection of texts. Many of the examples thus collected of course had to be carefully processed with philological considerations, but the advantage of using the digital corpus was clear.

Secondly, I took advantage of the localisation of Early Middle English texts provisionally proposed in the *LAEME* project. Most analysed texts were accordingly assigned to a certain period/dialect group. Various figures were calculated on each period/dialect group of texts, and they were then compared from one group to another. Although textual representativeness varied from dialect to dialect and from period to period, the bundling of texts made it possible for me to obtain an average picture for each period/dialect.

Thirdly, I found that the development of the *s*-plural proceeded roughly in a manner that the recently developing lexical diffusion model would predict. Comparing S-curves for different dialects made us note that a similar pattern repeatedly occurred from one dialect to another. Now that Lexical Diffusion is capable of addressing various levels of language change, it may be time for the model to be tested for other related subjects in English historical linguistics.

I hope that the findings and the methodology of the present study will contribute to the development of English historical linguistics as an increasingly interesting area.

Appendix A   Text List by ID

The list below gives the scribal texts I analysed for this study in full or in part. The numbering of IDs is not systematic but are provided for referential convenience. Each entry usually consists of manuscript reference, text reference, dialect (grid reference where available), date, conflation status, and consulted edition(s)/corpus; but there are a number of entries that lack some of the information because of uncertainty. IDs with asterisks signify that the texts were analysed from the *LAEME* text database (before publication) rather than from printed editions. The texts that were analysed only in part are marked with parentheses around their IDs. Each of the IDs from #1100 to #2002 refers to a conflated set of scribal texts assumed to be linguistically homogeneous, while each of the IDs from #100000 to #390000 refers to a bundled set of texts that are assigned to a period/dialect. The information is largely based on Laing's *Catalogue* and on her updated list of text localisations, the latter of which was made available to me in 2003.

#1 Oxford, Jesus College 29, fols. 156r–168v: The Owl and the Nightingale (cited as J). SWM (372, 244) C13b2. Conflated as #1100. Ed. Grattan and Sykes, Wells, and Atkins.

#2 London, British Library, Cotton Caligula A ix, fols. 233r–239v l13, 240r l6–241v l15: The Owl and the Nightingale, language 1 (cited as C1). SWM (390, 262) C13b2. Ed. Grattan and Sykes, Wells, and Atkins.

#3 London, British Library, Cotton Caligula A ix, fols. 239v l14–240r l5, 241v l16–246r: The Owl and the Nightingale, language 2 (cited as C2). SWM (379, 267) C13b2. Ed. Grattan and Sykes, Wells, and Atkins.

#4 Cambridge, Trinity College B. 14. 52, fols. 2r–9v: Poema Morale (cited as T). SEM (557, 222) C12b. Ed. Hall (*Selections*, Text VIII).

#5 London, Lambeth Palace Library 487, fols. 59v–65r: Poema Morale (cited as L). SWM (372, 262) C12b2. Ed. Hall (*Selections*, Text VIII) and Morris (*Homilies*, 1st ser., Part 1: 159–83).

#6 London, British Library, Egerton 613, fols. 64r–70v: Poema Morale (cited as e). SWM (385, 239) C13a. Ed. Zupitza and Schipper.

#7 London, British Library, Egerton 613, fols. 7r–12v: Poema Morale (cited as E). SWM (378, 246) C13a. Ed. Morris (*Homilies*, 1st ser., Part 1: 288–95, 175–83).

#8 Oxford, Bodley Digby 4, fols. 97r–110v: Poema Morale (cited as D). SE (568, 157) C13a. Ed. Zupitza.

#9 Oxford, Jesus College 29, fols. 169r–174v: Poema Morale (cited as J). SWM (372, 244) C13b2. Conflated as #1100. Ed. Morris (*Miscellany* 58–71).

#10 Cambridge, Fitzwilliam Museum, McClean 123, fols. 115r–120r: Poema Morale (cited as M). SWM (394, 213) C13b2. Ed. Paues.

#11 London, PRO, Patent Rolls 43 Henry III, m. 15. 40: Proclamation of Henry III Huntingtonshire. SEM (529, 179) C13b1. Ed. Dickins and Wilson (Text III).

#13 Durham, D and C Library A III 12, fol. 49r: Candet Nudatum Pectus. SEM C13a2. Ed. Brown (*14th*, Verse 1A) and Thomson.

#14 Oxford, Bodley Digby 45, fol. 25r: Candet Nudatum Pectus. Ed. Laing (*Catalogue* 128).

#15 Oxford, Bodley Digby 55, fol. 49r: Candet Nudatum Pectus, etc. NEM (550, 365) C13b1. Ed. Thomson.

*#16 Oxford, Bodley Rawlinson C 317, fol. 89v: Candet Nudatum Pectus. NWM (344, 452) C13a1. Ed. *LAEME* text database.

(#17) Cambridge, St John's College A. 15, fols. 120v, 72r: Candet, etc. SE C13a2. Analysed for fol. 72r only. Ed. Brown (*13th*, Verse 35A) and Brown (*14th*, Verse 2B).

#18 Oxford, Bodley 42, fol. 250r: Candet Nudatum Pectus, etc. C13b2. Ed. Brown (*14th*, Verses 1B and 2A).

(#19) London, British Library Additional 11579, fols. 35v–36v, 72v–73r: Candet Nudatum, etc. Analysed for fol. 35v only. C13b1. Ed. Brown (*14th* 241).

#20 Oxford, Bodleian Library, Bodley 34, fols. 72–80v: Sawles Warde. SWM (352, 275) C13a1. Ed. Bennett and Smithers (Text XIX) and Morris (*Homilies*, 1st ser., Part 1: 245–67 [odd pages]).

*#21 Cambridge, Trinity College B. 14. 52: Trinity Homilies I, hand A. SEM (552, 238) C12b2. Conflated as #1200. Ed. *LAEME* text database and Morris (*Homilies*, 2nd ser., Text I).

*#22 Cambridge, Trinity College B. 14. 52: Trinity Homilies II, hand A. SEM (552, 238) C12b2. Conflated as #1200. Ed. *LAEME* text database and Morris (*Homilies*, 2nd ser., Text II).

*#23 Cambridge, Trinity College B. 14. 52: Trinity Homilies III, hand A. SEM (552, 238) C12b2. Conflated as #1200. Ed. *LAEME* text database and Morris (*Homilies*, 2nd ser., Text III).

*#24 Cambridge, Trinity College B. 14. 52: Trinity Homilies IV, hand A. SEM (552, 238) C12b2. Conflated as #1200. Ed. *LAEME* text database and Morris (*Homilies*, 2nd ser., Text IV).

*#25 Cambridge, Trinity College B. 14. 52: Trinity Homilies V, hand A. SEM (552, 238) C12b2. Conflated as #1200. Ed. *LAEME* text database and Morris (*Homilies*, 2nd ser., Text V).

*#26 Cambridge, Trinity College B. 14. 52: Trinity Homilies VI, hand A. SEM (552, 238) C12b2. Conflated as #1200. Ed. *LAEME* text database and Morris (*Homilies*, 2nd ser., Text VI).

*#27 Cambridge, Trinity College B. 14. 52: Trinity Homilies VI, hand B. SEM (571, 267) C12b2. Conflated as #1300. Ed. *LAEME* text database and Morris (*Homilies*, 2nd ser., Text VI).

*#28 Cambridge, Trinity College B. 14. 52: Trinity Homilies VII, hand B. SEM (571, 267) C12b2. Conflated as #1300. Ed. *LAEME* text database and Morris (*Homilies*, 2nd ser., Text VII).

*#29 Cambridge, Trinity College B. 14. 52: Trinity Homilies VIII, hand B. SEM (571, 267) C12b2. Conflated as #1300. Ed. *LAEME* text database and Morris (*Homilies*, 2nd ser., Text VIII).

*#30 Cambridge, Trinity College B. 14. 52: Trinity Homilies IX, hand B. SEM (571, 267) C12b2. Conflated as #1300. Ed. *LAEME* text database and Morris (*Homilies*, 2nd ser., Text IX).

*#31 Cambridge, Trinity College B. 14. 52: Trinity Homilies X, hand B. SEM (571, 267) C12b2. Conflated as #1300. Ed. *LAEME* text database and Morris (*Homilies*, 2nd ser., Text X).

*#32 Cambridge, Trinity College B. 14. 52: Trinity Homilies XI, hand B. SEM (571, 267) C12b2. Conflated as #1300. Ed. *LAEME* text database and Morris (*Homilies*, 2nd ser., Text XI).

*#33 Cambridge, Trinity College B. 14. 52: Trinity Homilies XII, hand B. SEM (571, 267) C12b2. Conflated as #1300. Ed. *LAEME* text database and Morris (*Homilies*, 2nd ser., Text XII).

*#34 Cambridge, Trinity College B. 14. 52: Trinity Homilies XII, hand A. SEM (552, 238) C12b2. Conflated as #1200. Ed. *LAEME* text database and Morris (*Homilies*, 2nd ser., Text XII).

Appendix A   183

*#35 Cambridge, Trinity College B. 14. 52: Trinity Homilies XIII, hand B. SEM (571, 267) C12b2. Conflated as #1300. Ed. *LAEME* text database and Morris (*Homilies*, 2nd ser., Text XIII).

*#36 Cambridge, Trinity College B. 14. 52: Trinity Homilies XIII, hand A. SEM (552, 238) C12b2. Conflated as #1200. Ed. *LAEME* text database and Morris (*Homilies*, 2nd ser., Text XIII).

*#37 Cambridge, Trinity College B. 14. 52: Trinity Homilies XIV, hand B. SEM (571, 267) C12b2. Conflated as #1300. Ed. *LAEME* text database and Morris (*Homilies*, 2nd ser., Text XIV).

*#38 Cambridge, Trinity College B. 14. 52: Trinity Homilies XV, hand B. SEM (571, 267) C12b2. Conflated as #1300. Ed. *LAEME* text database and Morris (*Homilies*, 2nd ser., Text XV).

*#39 Cambridge, Trinity College B. 14. 52: Trinity Homilies XVI, hand B. SEM (571, 267) C12b2. Conflated as #1300. Ed. *LAEME* text database and Morris (*Homilies*, 2nd ser., Text XVI).

*#40 Cambridge, Trinity College B. 14. 52: Trinity Homilies XVII, hand B. SEM (571, 267) C12b2. Conflated as #1300. Ed. *LAEME* text database and Morris (*Homilies*, 2nd ser., Text XVII).

*#41 Cambridge, Trinity College B. 14. 52: Trinity Homilies XVIII, hand B. SEM (571, 267) C12b2. Conflated as #1300. Ed. *LAEME* text database and Morris (*Homilies*, 2nd ser., Text XVIII).

*#42 Cambridge, Trinity College B. 14. 52: Trinity Homilies XIX, hand B. SEM (571, 267) C12b2. Conflated as #1300. Ed. *LAEME* text database and Morris (*Homilies*, 2nd ser., Text XIX).

*#43 Cambridge, Trinity College B. 14. 52: Trinity Homilies XX, hand B. SEM (571, 267) C12b2. Conflated as #1300. Ed. *LAEME* text database and Morris (*Homilies*, 2nd ser., Text XX).

*#44 Cambridge, Trinity College B. 14. 52: Trinity Homilies XXI, hand B. SEM (571, 267) C12b2. Conflated as #1300. Ed. *LAEME* text database and Morris (*Homilies*, 2nd ser., Text XXI).

*#45 Cambridge, Trinity College B. 14. 52: Trinity Homilies XXII, hand B. SEM (571, 267) C12b2. Conflated as #1300. Ed. *LAEME* text database and Morris (*Homilies*, 2nd ser., Text XXII).

*#46 Cambridge, Trinity College B. 14. 52: Trinity Homilies XXIII, hand B. SEM (571, 267) C12b2. Conflated as #1300. Ed. *LAEME* text database and Morris (*Homilies*, 2nd ser., Text XXIII).

*#47 Cambridge, Trinity College B. 14. 52: Trinity Homilies XXIV, hand B. SEM (571, 267) C12b2. Conflated as #1300. Ed. *LAEME* text database and Morris (*Homilies*, 2nd ser., Text XXIV).

*#48 Cambridge, Trinity College B. 14. 52: Trinity Homilies XXV, hand B. SEM (571, 267) C12b2. Conflated as #1300. Ed. *LAEME* text database and Morris (*Homilies*, 2nd ser., Text XXV).

*#49 Cambridge, Trinity College B. 14. 52: Trinity Homilies XXVI, hand B. SEM (571, 267) C12b2. Conflated as #1300. Ed. *LAEME* text database and Morris (*Homilies*, 2nd ser., Text XXVI).

*#50 Cambridge, Trinity College B. 14. 52: Trinity Homilies XXVII, hand B. SEM (571, 267) C12b2. Conflated as #1300. Ed. *LAEME* text database and Morris (*Homilies*, 2nd ser., Text XXVII).

*#51 Cambridge, Trinity College B. 14. 52: Trinity Homilies XXVII, hand A. SEM (552, 238) C12b2. Conflated as #1200. Ed. *LAEME* text database and Morris (*Homilies*, 2nd ser., Text XXVII).

*#52 Cambridge, Trinity College B. 14. 52: Trinity Homilies XXVIII, hand B. SEM (571, 267) C12b2. Conflated as #1300. Ed. *LAEME* text database and Morris (*Homilies*, 2nd ser., Text XXVIII).

*#53 Cambridge, Trinity College B. 14. 52: Trinity Homilies XXVIII, hand A. SEM (552, 238) C12b2. Conflated as #1200. Ed. *LAEME* text database and Morris (*Homilies*, 2nd ser., Text XXVIII).

*#54 Cambridge, Trinity College B. 14. 52: Trinity Homilies XXIX, hand B. SEM (571, 267) C12b2. Conflated as #1300. Ed. *LAEME* text database and Morris (*Homilies*, 2nd ser., Text XXIX).

*#55 Cambridge, Trinity College B. 14. 52: Trinity Homilies XXIX, hand A. SEM (552, 238) C12b2. Conflated as #1200. Ed. *LAEME* text database and Morris (*Homilies*, 2nd ser., Text XXIX).

*#56 Cambridge, Trinity College B. 14. 52: Trinity Homilies XXX, hand A. SEM (552, 238) C12b2. Conflated as #1200. Ed. *LAEME* text database and Morris (*Homilies*, 2nd ser., Text XXX).

*#57 Cambridge, Trinity College B. 14. 52: Trinity Homilies XXX, hand B. SEM (571, 267) C12b2. Conflated as #1300. Ed. *LAEME* text database and Morris (*Homilies*, 2nd ser., Text XXX).

*#58 Cambridge, Trinity College B. 14. 52: Trinity Homilies XXXI, hand A. SEM (552, 238) C12b2. Conflated as #1200. Ed. *LAEME* text database and Morris (*Homilies*, 2nd ser., Text XXXI).

*#59 Cambridge, Trinity College B. 14. 52: Trinity Homilies XXXI, hand B. SEM (571, 267) C12b2. Conflated as #1300. Ed. *LAEME* text database and Morris (*Homilies*, 2nd ser., Text XXXI).

*#60 Cambridge, Trinity College B. 14. 52: Trinity Homilies XXXII, hand B. SEM (571, 267) C12b2. Conflated as #1300. Ed. *LAEME* text database and Morris (*Homilies*, 2nd ser., Text XXXII).

*#61 Cambridge, Trinity College B. 14. 52: Trinity Homilies XXXIII, hand B. SEM (571, 267) C12b2. Conflated as #1300. Ed. *LAEME* text database and Morris (*Homilies*, 2nd ser., Text XXXIII).

*#62 Cambridge, Trinity College B. 14. 52: Trinity Homilies XXXIII, hand A. SEM (552, 238) C12b2. Conflated as #1200. Ed. *LAEME* text database and Morris (*Homilies*, 2nd ser., Text XXXIII).

*#63 Cambridge, Trinity College B. 14. 52: Trinity Homilies XXXIV, hand C. SW (427, 185) C12b2. Ed. *LAEME* text database and Morris (*Homilies*, 2nd ser., Text XXXIV).

(#64) London, British Library, Stowe 34: Vices and Virtues, hand A. SEM (547, 207) C13a1. Analysed to page 40 from Holthausen's edition. Ed. Holthausen (Part 2).

#67 Maidstone Museum A. 13: Death's Wither-Clench (or Long Life), main hand of English. SE (549, 136) C13a. Ed. Brown (*13th*, Verse 10A).

*#69 Cambridge University Library Ff. II. 33, fol. 20r: Sawyer 507. SEM (560, 308) C13b2. Conflated as #1400. Ed. *LAEME* text database.

*#70 Cambridge University Library Ff. II. 33, fol. 20v: Sawyer 980. SEM (560, 308) C13b2. Conflated as #1400. Ed. *LAEME* text database.

*#71 Cambridge University Library Ff. II. 33, fol. 22r: Sawyer 1045. SEM (560, 308) C13b2. Conflated as #1400. Ed. *LAEME* text database.

*#72 Cambridge University Library Ff. II. 33, fol. 22r: Sawyer 1069. SEM (560, 308) C13b2. Conflated as #1400. Ed. *LAEME* text database.

*#73 Cambridge University Library Ff. II. 33, fol. 22r–v: Sawyer 1078. SEM (560, 308) C13b2. Conflated as #1400. Ed. *LAEME* text database.

*#74 Cambridge University Library Ff. II. 33, fol. 22v: Sawyer 1084. SEM (560, 308) C13b2. Conflated as #1400. Ed. *LAEME* text database.

*#75 Cambridge University Library Ff. II. 33, fol. 22v: Sawyer 1072. SEM (560, 308) C13b2. Conflated as #1400. Ed. *LAEME* text database.

*#76 Cambridge University Library Ff. II. 33, fol. 22v: Sawyer 1079. SEM (560, 308) C13b2. Conflated as #1400. Ed. *LAEME* text database.

*#77 Cambridge University Library Ff. II. 33, fol. 22v: Sawyer 1071. SEM (560, 308) C13b2. Conflated as #1400. Ed. *LAEME* text database.

*#78 Cambridge University Library Ff. II. 33, fol. 22v: Sawyer 1068. SEM (560, 308) C13b2. Conflated as #1400. Ed. *LAEME* text database.

*#79 Cambridge University Library Ff. II. 33, fol. 22v: Sawyer 1083. SEM (560, 308) C13b2. Conflated as #1400. Ed. *LAEME* text database.

*#80 Cambridge University Library Ff. II. 33, fols. 22v–23r: Sawyer 1082. SEM (560, 308) C13b2. Conflated as #1400. Ed. *LAEME* text database.

*#81 Cambridge University Library Ff. II. 33, fol. 23r: Sawyer 1077. SEM (560, 308) C13b2. Conflated as #1400. Ed. *LAEME* text database.

*#82 Cambridge University Library Ff. II. 33, fol. 23r: Sawyer 1073. SEM (560, 308) C13b2. Conflated as #1400. Ed. *LAEME* text database.

*#83 Cambridge University Library Ff. II. 33, fol. 23r: Sawyer 1085. SEM (560, 308) C13b2. Conflated as #1400. Ed. *LAEME* text database.

*#84 Cambridge University Library Ff. II. 33, fol. 23r: Sawyer 1075. SEM (560, 308) C13b2. Conflated as #1400. Ed. *LAEME* text database.

*#85 Cambridge University Library Ff. II. 33, fol. 23r: Sawyer 1046. SEM (560, 308) C13b2. Conflated as #1400. Ed. *LAEME* text database.

*#86 Cambridge University Library Ff. II. 33, fol. 23r: Sawyer 1081. SEM (560, 308) C13b2. Conflated as #1400. Ed. *LAEME* text database.

*#87 Cambridge University Library Ff. II. 33, fol. 23r: Sawyer 1080. SEM (560, 308) C13b2. Conflated as #1400. Ed. *LAEME* text database.

*#88 Cambridge University Library Ff. II. 33, fol. 23r–v: Sawyer 1074. SEM (560, 308) C13b2. Conflated as #1400. Ed. *LAEME* text database.

*#89 Cambridge University Library Ff. II. 33, fol. 23v: Sawyer 1076. SEM (560, 308) C13b2. Conflated as #1400. Ed. *LAEME* text database.

*#90 Cambridge University Library Ff. II. 33, fol. 24r: Pelteret 19. SEM (560, 308) C13b2. Conflated as #1400. Ed. *LAEME* text database.

*#91 Cambridge University Library Ff. II. 33, fols. 27v–28r: Pelteret 5. SEM (560, 308) C13b2. Conflated as #1400. Ed. *LAEME* text database.

*#92 Cambridge University Library Ff. II. 33, fol. 28r: Pelteret 18. SEM (560, 308) C13b2. Conflated as #1400. Ed. *LAEME* text database.

*#93 Cambridge University Library Ff. II. 33, fol. 28r: Pelteret 20. SEM (560, 308) C13b2. Conflated as #1400. Ed. *LAEME* text database.

*#94 Cambridge University Library Ff. II. 33, fol. 45r: Will of Alfrich Modercope, or Sawyer 1490. SEM (560, 308) C13b2. Conflated as #1400. Ed. *LAEME* text database.

*#95 Cambridge University Library Ff. II. 33, fol. 45r: Will of Thurketel, or Sawyer 1528. SEM (560, 308) C13b2. Conflated as #1400. Ed. *LAEME* text database.

*#96 Cambridge University Library Ff. II. 33, fol. 45r: Will of Leofgifu, or Sawyer 1521. SEM (560, 308) C13b2. Conflated as #1400. Ed. *LAEME* text database.

*#97 Cambridge University Library Ff. II. 33, fol. 45r–v: Will of Edwin, or Sawyer 1516. SEM (560, 308) C13b2. Conflated as #1400. Ed. *LAEME* text database.

*#98 Cambridge University Library Ff. II. 33, fols. 45v–46r: Will of Ketel, or Sawyer 1519. SEM (560, 308) C13b2. Conflated as #1400. Ed. *LAEME* text database.

*#99 Cambridge University Library Ff. II. 33, fol. 46r: Will of Aelfgar, or Sawyer 1483. SEM (560, 308) C13b2. Conflated as #1400. Ed. *LAEME* text database.

*#100 Cambridge University Library Ff. II. 33, fol. 46v: Sawyer 703. SEM (560, 308) C13b2. Conflated as #1400. Ed. *LAEME* text database.

*#101 Cambridge University Library Ff. II. 33, fols. 46v–47r: Will of Aethelfled, or Sawyer 1494. SEM (560, 308) C13b2. Conflated as #1400. Ed. *LAEME* text database.

*#102 Cambridge University Library Ff. II. 33, fol. 47r: Will of Aelfflaed, or Sawyer 1486. SEM (560, 308) C13b2. Conflated as #1400. Ed. *LAEME* text database.

*#103 Cambridge University Library Ff. II. 33, fol. 48r: Will of Theodred, or Sawyer 1526. SEM (560, 308) C13b2. Conflated as #1400. Ed. *LAEME* text database.

*#104 Cambridge University Library Ff. II. 33, fol. 48r–v: Will of Bishop Aelfric, or Sawyer 1489. SEM (560, 308) C13b2. Conflated as #1400. Ed. *LAEME* text database.

*#105 Cambridge University Library Ff. II. 33, fol. 48v: Will of Thurketel, or Sawyer 1527. SEM (560, 308) C13b2. Conflated as #1400. Ed. *LAEME* text database.

*#106 Cambridge University Library Ff. II. 33, fol. 49r: Bequest of Aethelmaer, or Sawyer 1499. SEM (560, 308) C13b2. Conflated as #1400. Ed. *LAEME* text database.

*#107 Cambridge University Library Ff. II. 33, fol. 49r: Sawyer 1468. SEM (560, 308) C13b2. Conflated as #1400. Ed. *LAEME* text database.

*#108 Cambridge University Library Ff. II. 33, fol. 49r–v: Will of Thurstan, or Sawyer 1531. SEM (560, 308) C13b2. Conflated as #1400. Ed. *LAEME* text database.

*#109 Cambridge University Library Ff. II. 33, fol. 49v: Sawyer 1470. SEM (560, 308) C13b2. Conflated as #1400. Ed. *LAEME* text database.

*#110 Cambridge University Library Ff. II. 33, fol. 49v: Sawyer 1219. SEM (560, 308) C13b2. Conflated as #1400. Ed. *LAEME* text database.

*#111 Cambridge University Library Ff. II. 33, fols. 49v–50r: Wills of Siflaed, or Sawyer 1525. SEM (560, 308) C13b2. Conflated as #1400. Ed. *LAEME* text database.

*#112 Cambridge University Library Ff. II. 33, fol. 50r: Will of Wulfsige, or Sawyer 1537. SEM (560, 308) C13b2. Conflated as #1400. Ed. *LAEME* text database.

*#113 Cambridge University Library Ff. II. 33, fol. 50r: Sawyer 1224. SEM (560, 308) C13b2. Conflated as #1400. Ed. *LAEME* text database.

*#114 Cambridge University Library Ff. II. 33, fol. 50r: Sawyer 1225. SEM (560, 308) C13b2. Conflated as #1400. Ed. *LAEME* text database.

*#115 Cambridge University Library Ff. II. 33, fol. 50r: Sawyer 1529. SEM (560, 308) C13b2. Conflated as #1400. Ed. *LAEME* text database.

*#116 Cambridge University Library Ff. II. 33, fol. 50r: Will of Aethelric, or Sawyer 1501. SEM (560, 308) C13b2. Conflated as #1400. Ed. *LAEME* text database.

(*#118) London, British Library, Cotton Titus D xviii, fols. 14r–105r (except T2 sections): Ancrene Riwle, language T1 (cited as T). NWM (370, 349) C13a1. Analysed for the tagged part only (fols. 14r–40ra1). Ed. *LAEME* text database and Mack.

#122 London, British Library, Cotton Titus D xviii, fols. 127r–133r: Wohunge of ure Lauerd. NWM (391, 389) C13a1. Ed. Thompson, and Morris (*Homilies*, 1st ser., Part 1: 268–87).

*#123 London, British Library, Cotton Titus D xviii, fols. 133v–147v: Saint Katherine. C13a2. Ed. *LAEME* text database.

#124 Oxford, Bodleian Library, Tanner 169*, p. 175: Stabat iuxta crucem Christi. NWM (341, 366) C13a2. Ed. Brown (*13th*, Verse 4).

*#125 Herefordshire Record Office AL 19/2, Registrum Ricardi de Swinfield, fol. 152r: Bromfield Writ. SWM (351, 239) C14a1. Ed. *LAEME* text database.

*#126 Stratford-upon-Avon, Shakespeare Birthplace Library, DR 10/1408, Gregory Leger-Book, pp. 23–24: Coventry Writ. SWM (435, 280) C13b2. Ed. *LAEME* text database.

#128 London, Lincoln's Inn Hale 135, fol. 137v: Nou sprinkes the sprai. NEM (507, 395) C13b2. Ed. Brown (*13th*, Verse 62).

#129 Cambridge University Library, Ff. VI. 15, fol. 21r: Ten Commandments. NEM (537, 388) C14a1. Ed. Morris (*Miscellany* 200).

#130 Oxford, Bodleian Library, Rawlinson C 510, fol. 3r: Fragment of lyric. NEM (512, 369). Ed. Laing (*Catalogue* 139).

*#136 London, Lambeth Palace Library 499, fols. 64r–69r, 125v: alliterative lyrics. NWM (344, 377) C13b2. Ed. *LAEME* text database.

#137 London, British Library, Arundel 248, fols. 154r–155r: four lyrics. SEM (557, 263) C13b2. Ed. Brown (*13th*, Verses 44–47).

#138 London, Corporation of London RO, Liber de antiquis Legibus, fols. 160v–161v: Prisoner's Prayer. SEM (538, 182) C13a2. Ed. Brown (*13th*, Verse 5).

(#140) Cambridge, Emmanuel College 27, fols. 111v, 162r–163r: Lyrics. SW (413, 130) C14a1. fols. 111v and 163r unanalysed. Ed. Person (Verses 29–37 for fol. 162r–v) and Brown (*13th*, Verse 70B for fol. 162r).

#141 Oxford, Bodleian Library, Laud Misc 471, fol. 65r: Death's Wither-Clench (or Long Life). C13b2. Ed. Brown (*13th*, Verse 10B), and Dobson and Harrison (122–30).

#142 Oxford, Bodleian Library, Laud Misc 471, fols. 128v–133v: Kentish Sermons. SE (583, 153) C13a. Ed. Morris (*Miscellany* 26–36).

Appendix A   187

#144 London, British Library, Harley 978, fol. 11v: Svmer is icumen in. SW (472, 172) C13a. Ed. Brown (*13th*, Verse 6).

#145 Oxford, Jesus College 29, fols. 187r–188v: A Luue Ron. SWM (372, 244) C13b2. Conflated as #1100. Ed. Dobson and Harrison, and Brown (*13th*, Verse 43).

*#146 Oxford, Bodleian Library, Hatton 26, fol. 211r: 10 Commandments and 7 Gifts. SWM (392, 298) C13a2. Ed. *LAEME* text database.

*#147 London, British Library, Cotton Roll ii 11 lang A: 3 documents from Crediton. SW (283, 100). Ed. *LAEME* text database.

*#148 London, British Library, Cotton Roll ii 11 lang B: document from Crediton. SW (283, 100). Ed. *LAEME* text database.

#149 Oxford, Bodleian Library, Laud Misc 636, fols. 88v–91v: Peterborough Chronicle final continuation (cited as FC). SEM (519, 298) C12b1. Ed. Earle and Plummer, and Clark.

#150 London, British Library, Arundel 292, fol. 4r–10v: The Bestiary. SEM (579, 307) C13b2. Ed. Morris (*Miscellany* 1–25), Dickins and Wilson (Text XI), and Bennett and Smithers (Text XII).

#155 Cambridge, Corpus Christi College 444, fols. 1r–81r.: Genesis and Exodus. SEM (582, 312) C13b2. Ed. Arngart, and Buehler.

*#156 Wells Cathedral Library, Liber Albus I, language 1, fol. 14r: 4 documents. SW (355, 146) C13a2. Ed. *LAEME* text database.

*#157 Wells Cathedral Library, Liber Albus I, language 2, language 2, fols. 17v–18r: 5 documents. SW (355, 146) C13a2. Ed. *LAEME* text database.

#158 Oxford, Bodleian Library, Bodley 652, fols. 1r–10v: Iacob and Iosep. SWM (418, 235) C13b1. Ed. Dickins and Wilson (Text XXI).

#159 London, British Library, Additional 23986, verso of roll: Interludium de Clerico et Puella. NEM (482, 402) C13b2. Ed. McKnight (21–23), Bennett and Smithers (Text XV), and Dickins and Wilson (Text XXXVIII).

*#163 Aberdeen University Library 154, fol. 368v: couplet and 3 quatrains. SW (378, 159) C13b. Ed. *LAEME* text database.

#164 London, British Library, Cotton Nero A xiv, fols. 120v–123v: On God Ureison of ure Lefdi. SWM (378, 253) C13a2. Conflated as #1800. Ed. Brown (*13th*, Verse 3) and Morris (*Homilies*, 1st ser., Part 1: 191–99).

#165 London, British Library, Cotton Nero A xiv, fols. 123v–126v: Ureison of God Almihti. SWM (378, 253) C13a2. Conflated as #1800. Ed. Thompson (5–9) and Morris (*Homilies*, 1st ser., Part 1: 200–07).

#166 London, British Library, Cotton Nero A xiv, fols. 126v–128r: On lofsong of ure lefdi. SWM (378, 253) C13a2. Conflated as #1800. Ed. Thompson (16–18) and Morris (*Homilies*, 1st ser., Part 1: 204–07).

#167 London, British Library, Cotton Nero A xiv, fols. 128r–131r: Lofsong of ure Louerde. SWM (378, 253) C13a2. Conflated as #1800. Ed. Thompson (10–15) and Morris (*Homilies*, 1st ser., Part 1: 209–17).

#168 London, British Library, Cotton Nero A xiv, fols. 131r–v: Lesse crede. SWM (378, 253) C13a2. Conflated as #1800. Ed. Morris (*Homilies*, 1st ser., Part 1: 217).

*#170 Worcester Cathedral, Dean and Chapter Library Q 29, fols. 130v–131r: SWM (384, 254) C12b2. Ed. *LAEME* text database and Morris (*Homilies*, 2nd ser.: 217–19).

*#171 Oxford, Bodleian Library, Junius 121, fol. Vi (flyleaf), tremulous hand: Nicene Creed. SWM (384, 254) C13a2. Conflated as #1900. Ed. *LAEME* text database.

*#172 Worcester Cathedral, Dean and Chapter Library F 174, fols. 63r–66v: Worcester fragments. SWM (384, 254) C13a. Conflated as #1900. Ed. *LAEME* text database.

*#173 Worcester Cathedral, Dean and Chapter Library F 174, fols. 1r–63r: Ælfric's Grammar and Glossary. SWM (384, 254) C13a. Conflated as #1900. Ed. *LAEME* text database.

#175 Oxford, Bodleian Library, Ashmole 360, fol. 145v, hand B: lyric. SEM (565, 313) C13b2. Ed. Brown (*13th*, Verse 37).

*#187 Worcester, Herefordshire and Worcestershire Record Office, BA 3814, fol. 38v: Copy of a writ of King Edward. SWM (384, 254) C13b2. Ed. *LAEME* text database.

#189 Lambeth Palace Library 487, fols. 65v–67r, hand B: On Ureison of Ure Loverde. SWM (342, 269) C12b2. Ed. Thompson (1–4) and Morris (*Homilies*, 1st ser., Part 1: 183–89).

#190 Lambeth Palace Library 487, fols. 1r–3r, hand A, lang 1: Lambeth Homily I. SWM (372, 262) C12b2. Conflated as #2000. Ed. Morris (*Homilies*, 1st ser., Part 1, Text I).

#191 Lambeth Palace Library 487, fols. 3r–9r, hand A, lang 1: Lambeth Homily II. SWM (372, 262) C12b2. Conflated as #2000. Morris (*Homilies*, 1st ser., Part 2, Text II).

#192 Lambeth Palace Library 487, fols. 9r–15v, hand A, lang 1: Lambeth Homily III. SWM (372, 262) C12b2. Conflated as #2000. Morris (*Homilies*, 1st ser., Part 2, Text III).

#193 Lambeth Palace Library 487, fols. 15v–18v, hand A, lang 1: Lambeth Homily IV. SWM (372, 262) C12b2. Conflated as #2000. Ed. Morris (*Homilies*, 1st ser., Part 1, Text IV).

#194 Lambeth Palace Library 487, fols. 18v–21v, hand A, lang 1: Lambeth Homily V. SWM (372, 262) C12b2. Conflated as #2000. Ed. Morris (*Homilies*, 1st ser., Part 1, Text V).

#195 Lambeth Palace Library 487, fols. 21v–25r, hand A, lang 2: Lambeth Homily VI. SWM (372, 262) C12b2. Conflated as #2001. Ed. Morris (*Homilies*, 1st ser., Part 1, Text VI).

#196 Lambeth Palace Library 487, fols. 25r–27v, hand A, lang 2: Lambeth Homily VII. SWM (372, 262) C12b2. Conflated as #2001. Ed. Morris (*Homilies*, 1st ser., Part 1, Text VII).

#197 Lambeth Palace Library 487, fols. 27v–30v, hand A, lang 2: Lambeth Homily VIII. SWM (372, 262) C12b2. Conflated as #2001. Ed. Morris (*Homilies*, 1st ser., Part 1, Text VIII).

#198 Lambeth Palace Library 487, fols. 30v–37v, hand A, lang 1: Lambeth Homily IX. SWM (372, 262) C12b2. Conflated as #2000. Ed. Morris (*Homilies*, 1st ser., Part 1, Text IX).

#199 Lambeth Palace Library 487, fols. 37v–45r, hand A, lang 1: Lambeth Homily X. SWM (372, 262) C12b2. Conflated as #2000. Ed. Morris (*Homilies*, 1st ser., Part 1, Text X).

#200 Lambeth Palace Library 487, fols. 45r–47r, hand A, lang 1: Lambeth Homily XI. SWM (372, 262) C12b2. Conflated as #2000. Ed. Morris (*Homilies*, 1st ser., Part 1, Text XI).

#201 Lambeth Palace Library 487, fols. 47r–49r, hand A, lang 1: Lambeth Homily XII. SWM (372, 262) C12b2. Conflated as #2000. Ed. Morris (*Homilies*, 1st ser., Part 1, Text XII).

#202 Lambeth Palace Library 487, fols. 49r–51v, hand A, lang 1: Lambeth Homily XIII. SWM (372, 262) C12b2. Conflated as #2000. Ed. Morris (*Homilies*, 1st ser., Part 1, Text XIII).

#203 Lambeth Palace Library 487, fols. 51v–54r, hand A, lang 2: Lambeth Homily XIV. SWM (372, 262) C12b2. Conflated as #2001. Ed. Morris (*Homilies*, 1st ser., Part 1, Text XIV).

#204 Lambeth Palace Library 487, fols. 54r–56r, hand A, lang 2: Lambeth Homily XV. SWM (372, 262) C12b2. Conflated as #2001. Ed. Morris (*Homilies*, 1st ser., Part 1, Text XV).

#205 Lambeth Palace Library 487, fols. 56r–57v, hand A, lang 2: Lambeth Homily XVI. SWM (372, 262) C12b2. Conflated as #2001. Ed. Morris (*Homilies*, 1st ser., Part 1, Text XVI).

#206 Lambeth Palace Library 487, fols. 57v–59v, hand A, lang 2: Lambeth Homily XVII. SWM (372, 262) C12b2. Conflated as #2001. Ed. Morris (*Homilies*, 1st ser., Part 1, Text XVII).

*#207 Oxford, Bodleian Library, Digby 86, fols. 119r–120v: Harrowing of Hell. SWM (375, 232) C13b2. Conflated as #2002. Ed. *LAEME* text database.

*#208 Oxford, Bodleian Library, Digby 86, fols. 120v–122v: 15 Signs before Doomsday. SWM (375, 232) C13b2. Conflated as #2002. Ed. *LAEME* text database.

*#209 Oxford, Bodleian Library, Digby 86, fols. 122v–125v: Life of St Eustace. SWM (375, 232) C13b2. Conflated as #2002. Ed. *LAEME* text database.

*#210 Oxford, Bodleian Library, Digby 86, fols. 125v–127r: Sayings of St Bernard. SWM (375, 232) C13b2. Conflated as #2002. Ed. *LAEME* text database.

#211 Oxford, Bodleian Library, Digby 86, fol. 127r–v: Stond wel moder. SWM (375, 232) C13b2. Conflated as #2002. Ed. Brown (*13th*, Verse 49A).

*#212 Oxford, Bodleian Library, Digby 86, fols. 127v–130r: Sayings of Bede. SWM (375, 232) C13b2. Conflated as #2002. Ed. *LAEME* text database.

*#213 Oxford, Bodleian Library, Digby 86, fols. 130r–132r: Our Lady's Psalter. SWM (375, 232) C13b2. Conflated as #2002. Ed. *LAEME* text database.

*#214 Oxford, Bodleian Library, Digby 86, fols. 132r–134v: The XI Pains of Hell and Sweet Ihesu. SWM (575, 232) C13b2. Ed. *LAEME* text database.

#215 Oxford, Bodleian Library, Digby 86, fols. 134r–136v: Le Regret de Maximian. SWM (375, 232) C13b2. Conflated as #2002. Ed. Brown (*13th*, Verse 51).

#216 Oxford, Bodleian Library, Digby 86, fols. 136v–138r: The Thrush and the Nightingale. SWM (375, 232) C13b2. Conflated as #2002. Ed. Dickins and Wilson (Text XIII), and Brown (*13th*, Verse 52).

*#217 Oxford, Bodleian Library, Digby 86, fols. 138r–140r: The Fox and the Wolf. SWM (375, 232) C13b2. Conflated as #2002. Ed. Bennett and Smithers (Text V), Dickins and Wilson (Text XII), and McKnight.

*#218 Oxford, Bodleian Library, Digby 86, fols. 140v–143r: The Proverbs of Hending. SWM (375, 232) C13b2. Ed. *LAEME* text database.

*#219 Oxford, Bodleian Library, Digby 86, fols. 163v–164r: lyric on the vanity of the world. SWM (375, 232) C13b2. Conflated as #2002. Ed. *LAEME* text database.

#220 Oxford, Bodleian Library, Digby 86, fols. 165r–168r: Dame Sirith. SWM (375, 232) C13b2. Ed. Bennett and Smithers (Text VI), and McKnight.

*#221 Oxford, Bodleian Library, Digby 86, fol. 168r–v: names of the hare. SWM (375, 232) C13b2. Conflated as #2002. Ed. *LAEME* text database.

*#222 Oxford, Bodleian Library, Digby 86, fols. 195v–197v: Debate between Body and Soul. SWM (375, 232) C13b2. Ed. *LAEME* text database.

*#223 Oxford, Bodleian Library, Digby 86, fols. 197v–198r: Doomsday. SWM (375, 232) C13b2. Conflated as #2002. Ed. *LAEME* text database.

*#224 Oxford, Bodleian Library, Digby 86, fols. 198r–200r: The Latemest Day. SWM (375, 232) C13b2. Conflated as #2002. Ed. *LAEME* text database.

#225 Oxford, Bodleian Library, Digby 86, fol. 200r: lyric beg. loue is sofft. SWM (375, 232) C13b2. Conflated as #2002. Ed. Brown (*13th*, Verse 53).

*#226 Oxford, Bodleian Library, Digby 86, fol. 206r: In Manus Tuas. SWM (375, 232) C13b2. Conflated as #2002. Ed. *LAEME* text database.

#229 Oxford, Corpus Christi College, MS 59, fols. 66r–v, 113v, 116v: verses on God and the BVM. SWM (384, 219) C13b2. Ed. Brown (*13th*, Verses 59–61) and Morris (*Homilies*, 2nd ser.: 255–59).

*#231 London, British Library, Cotton Cleopatra B vi, fol. 204v: Pater Noster, etc. N (389, 461) C13a2. Ed. *LAEME* text database.

#232 London, British Library, Additional 27909, fol. 2r: Penitence for Wasted Life. SWM (433, 228). Ed. Brown (*13th*, Verse 2).

#234 London, British Library, Egerton 613, fol. 1v: Somer is comen. SWM (390, 232). Ed. Brown (*13th*, Verse 54).

#238 London, British Library, Cotton Caligula A ix, fol. 246r–v: Death's Wither Clench (or Long Life). SWM (372, 244) C13b2. Morris (*Miscellany* 156–58 [even pages]).

#239 London, British Library, Cotton Caligula A ix, fol. 246v: Orison to Our Lady. C13b2. Ed. Brown (*13th*, Verse 32B) and Morris (*Miscellany* 158–62 [even pages]).

#240 London, British Library, Cotton Caligula A ix, fol. 246v: Will and Wit. C13b2. Ed. Brown (*13th*, Verse 39) and Morris (*Miscellany* 192).

#241 London, British Library, Cotton Caligula A ix, fols. 246v–247r: Doomsday. C13b2. Ed. Brown (*13th*, Verse 28B) and Morris (*Miscellany* 162–68 [even pages]).

#242 London, British Library, Cotton Caligula A ix, fols. 247r–248v: The Latemest Day. C13b2. Ed. Brown (*13th*, Verse 29B) and Morris (*Miscellany* 168–84 [even pages]).

#243 London, British Library, Cotton Caligula A ix, fol. 248v: Ten Abuses. C13b2. Ed. Morris (*Miscellany* 184).

#244 London, British Library, Cotton Caligula A ix, fols. 248v–249r: Lutel Soth Sermun. C13b2. Ed. Morris (*Miscellany* 186–90 [even pages]).

(#245) London, British Library, Cotton Nero A xiv, fols. 1r–120v, hand A: Ancrene Riwle (cited as N). SWM (378, 253) C13a2. Analysed for Parts 6 and 7 only. Ed. Day.

(#246) Cambridge, Trinity College B. 14. 39 (323), fols. 19r, 25v, 27r col 2, 28r–29v, 32r–33v, 36r–46r, 47r–v, 83v–84r, hand A: verses. SWM (366, 255) C13b. Analysed only for parts designated in the following. Ed. Brown (*13th*: Verse 14 for fol. 19r; Verse 19 for fol. 25v; Verse 20 for fol. 27r col. 2; Verse 21 for fol. 28r; Verse 22 for fols. 28v–29r; Verse 23 for fol. 29r; Verse 24 for fols. 32v–33r; passages in notes to Verse 26 for fols. 39v–40r, 36r, 36v, 37v–38r, 41v–42r; Verse 27 for fol. 42v; Verse 28A for fol. 43r–v; Verse 29A for fol. 43v–45v; Verse 30; a passage in its notes for fol. 47v; Verses 33 and 34 for fol. 83v; and Verse 38 for fol. 84r).

(#247) Cambridge, Trinity College B. 14. 39 (323), fols. 20r–25r, 26r–27r col 1, 27v, 34r, 35r–v, hand B: verses. SWM (371, 237) C13b. Analysed only for parts designated in the following. Ed. Brown (*13th*: Verse 15 for fol. 24r; Verses 16 and 17 for fol. 24v; Verse 18 for fol. 25r; Verse 25 for fol. 34r; Verse 26 for fol. 35r–v).

#248 Cambridge, Trinity College B.14.39 (323), fols. 30r–31v, 81v, hand C: verses. SWM (360, 240) C13b. Ed. Brown (*13th*, Verse 31 for fol. 81v).

#249 Cambridge, Trinity College B.14.39 (323), fols. 81v–82r, 85r–87v, hand D: verses. SWM (365, 232) C13b. Ed. Brown (*13th*, Verse 32 for fol. 81v–82r).

#250 Oxford, Jesus College 29, fols. 179v–180v: Death's Wither Clench, or Long Life. SWM (372, 244) C13b2. Conflated as #1100. Ed. Morris (*Miscellany* 157–59 [odd pages]).

#251 Oxford, Jesus College 29, fols. 180v: Orison to Our Lady. SWM (372, 244) C13b2. Conflated as #1100. Ed. Morris (*Miscellany* 159–63 [odd pages]).

#252 Oxford, Jesus College 29, fol. 182r–v: Doomsday. SWM (372, 244) C13b2. Conflated as #1100. Ed. Morris (*Miscellany* 163–69 [odd pages]).

#253 Oxford, Jesus College 29, fols. 182v–184v: The Latemest Day. SWM (372, 244) C13b2. Conflated as #1100. Ed. Morris (*Miscellany* 169–85 [odd pages]).

#254 Oxford, Jesus College 29, fol. 184v: Ten Abuses. SWM (372, 244) C13b2. Conflated as #1100. Ed. Morris (*Miscellany* 185).

#255 Oxford, Jesus College 29, fol. 185r–v: Lutel Soth Sermun. SWM (372, 244) C13b2. Conflated as #1100. Ed. Morris (*Miscellany* 187–91 [odd pages]).

*#258 Salisbury Cathedral Library 82, fol. 271v: Pater Noster. SW (413, 130) C14a1. Ed. *LAEME* text database.

(*#260) London, British Library, Royal 17. A. xxvii, fols. 1r–8v, 11r–45v, hand A: Sawles Warde, St Katherine and part of St Margaret. SWM (367, 276) C13a1. Analysed for the tagged part only (fols. 1r–37r). Ed. *LAEME* text database and Wilson.

*#261 London, British Library, Royal 17. A. xxvii, fols. 9r–10v, 58v–70v, hand B: end of Sawles Warde, most of St Juliana, Oreisun of Seinte Marie. SWM (367, 276) C13a1. Ed. *LAEME* text database and Wilson.

*#262 London, British Library, Royal 17. A. xxvii, fols. 45v–58r, hand C: part of St Margaret, beginning of St Juliana. SWM (367, 276) C13a1. Ed. *LAEME* text database.

#263 London, British Library, Royal 2. F. viii, fol. 1v: 2 lyrics. SW (392, 153) C13b2. Ed. Brown (*13th*, Verses 32C and 63).

#264 Cambridge, Corpus Christi College 8, p. 547: Worldes blisce haue god day. SWM (419, 226) C13b2. Ed. Brown (*13th*, Verse 58).

#269 London, British Library, Royal 12. E. i, fols. 193r–194v, hand A: Stond wel moder. SEM (562, 321) C13b2. Ed. Brown (*13th*, Verse 49B).

#270 London, British Library, Royal 12. E. i, fols. 193r–194v, hand B: versions of My Leman on the Rood, and Thenk man. SEM (562, 321) C13b2. Ed. Brown (*13th*, Verse 35B; and its notes).

*#271 London, British Library, Cotton Vitellius D. iii, fols. 6r–8v: fragments of Floris and Blauncheflur. SWM (399, 233) C13b. Ed. *LAEME* text database.

(#272) Cambridge, Corpus Christi College 402, fols. 1r–117v: Ancrene Wisse (cited as A). SWM (352, 275) C13a2. Analysed for Parts 6 and 7 only. Ed. Tolkien, and Bennett and Smithers (Text XVIII).

(#273) London, British Library, Cotton Cleopatra C.vi, fols. 4r–194r, hand A: Ancrene Riwle (cited as C). SWM (349, 258) C13a2. Analysed for Parts 6 and 7 only. Ed. Dobson (*Ancrene*).

(#278) London, British Library, Cotton Caligula A.ix, fols. 3r–17rb (foot); 17va lines 1–4; 18vb line 7–25vb (foot); 27ra line 6 (tat)–87vb (foot), 89rb line 4–194v (end), hand B: Layamon A. SWM (381, 271) C13b2. Analysed only for bits from fols. 164vb–168v2. Ed. Bennett and Smithers (Text X).

#285 Oxford, Bodleian Library, Laud Misc 108, hand C, fols. 219v–228r: Havelok. SEM (554, 300) C13b2. Ed. Skeat and Sisam, and Smithers.

*#286 Cambridge, Corpus Christi College 145, hand A, fols. 1r–210v: The South English Legendary (fols. 63r–77r l8, 82r line 11–02v l18, 122r l35–133r l8 for Inventio Crucis, SS Quiriac, Brendan; Barnabas, Theophilus, Alban, John the Baptist; James the Great, Christopher, Martha, Oswald the king). SW (429, 195) C14a1. Ed. *LAEME* text database.

(#291) London, British Library, Arundel 57, fols. 2r–4r, 13r–96v: Ayenbite of Inwyt. SE (615, 158) C14a2. Analysed to page 39 line 35 from Gradon's edition. Ed. Gradon.

*#296 Edinburgh, Royal College of Physicians, MS of Cursor Mundi, hand C, fols. 37r–50v: Extracts from Cursor Mundi. N (400, 450) C13b2. Ed. *LAEME* text database.

*#297 Edinburgh, Royal College of Physicians, MS of Cursor Mundi, hand A, fols. 1r–15v: Extracts from Cursor Mundi. N C13b2. Ed. *LAEME* text database.

*#298 Edinburgh, Royal College of Physicians, MS of Cursor Mundi, hand B, fols. 16r–36v: Extracts from the Northern Homily Collection. N C14a. Ed. *LAEME* text database.

#1100 Oxford, Jesus College 29: Jesus College 29 texts. SWM (372, 244) C13b2. Conflating ##1, 9, 145, 250, 251, 252, 253, 254, 255.

#1200 Cambridge, Trinity College B. 14. 52: Trinity Homilies I, hand A. SEM (552, 238) C12b2. Conflating ##21, 22, 23, 24, 25, 26, 34, 36, 51, 53, 55, 56, 58, 62.

#1300 Cambridge, Trinity College B. 14. 52: Trinity Homilies VI, hand B. SEM (571, 267) C12b2. Conflating ##27, 28, 29, 30, 31, 32, 33, 35, 37, 38, 39, 40, 41, 42, 43, 44, 45, 46, 47, 48, 49, 50, 52, 54, 57, 59, 60, 61.

#1400 Cambridge University Library Ff. II. 33: Bury documents. SEM (560, 308) C13b2. Conflating ##69, 70, 71, 72, 73, 74, 75, 76, 77, 78, 79, 80, 81, 82, 83, 84, 85, 86, 87, 88, 89, 90, 91, 92, 93, 94, 95, 96, 97, 98, 99, 100, 101, 102, 103, 104, 105, 106, 107, 108, 109, 110, 111, 112, 113, 114, 115, 116.

#1800 London, British Library, Cotton Nero A xiv: Cotton Nero texts. SWM (378, 253) C13a2. Conflating ##164, 165, 166, 167.

#1900 Oxford, Bodleian Library, Junius 121, fol. Vi (flyleaf); Worcester Cathedral, Dean and Chapter Library F 174, fols. 63r–66v and fols. 1r–63r: The Worcester Tremulous hand. SWM (384, 254) C13a. Conflating ##171, 172, 173.

#2000 Lambeth Palace Library 487: Lambeth Homilies, hand A, lang 1 (cited as Lang 1). SWM (372, 262) C12b2. Conflating ##190, 191, 192, 193, 194, 198, 199, 200, 201, 202.

#2001 Lambeth Palace Library 487: Lambeth Homilies, hand A, lang 2 (cited as Lang 2). SWM (372, 262) C12b2. Conflating ##195, 196, 197, 203, 204, 205, 206.

#2002 Oxford, Bodleian Library, Digby 86, fols. 119r–143r, 163v–164r, 165r–168v, 195v–200r, 206r: verse texts excluding, XI Pains of Hell, Proverbs of Hending, Dame Sirith and Debate between the Body and Soul. SWM (375, 232) C13b3. Conflating ##207, 208, 209, 210, 211, 212, 213, 215, 216, 217, 219, 221, 223, 224, 225, 226.

#10000 London, British Library, Cotton Vespasian A xxii, fols. 54r–59b: Vespasian Homilies. SWM C12b2. Ed. Morris (*Homilies*, 1st ser., Part 1: 217–45).

(#11000) Rushworth Gloss to the Gospel according to Saint Matthew. SWM C10a2. Analysed only for nom./acc.pl. Ed. Skeat.

(#12000) Cotton Vespasian A. I: Vespasian Psalter Gloss. SWM C9a. Analysed from the first 40 pages of Sweet's edition. Ed. Sweet (188–401).

#13000 Oxford, Bodleian Library, Hatton 116: The Life of St. Chad. SWM C9b. Ed. Vleeskruyer.

#14000 Oxford, Bodley 343: Bodley 343 Homilies. SWM C12b. Ed. Irvine (*Homilies*).

#15000 Oxford, Bodleian Library, Laud Misc 636, fols. 58v–81r: Peterborough Chronicle, Copied Annals (1070–1121) (cited as CA). Ed. Earle and Plummer, and Clark.

#16000 Oxford, Bodleian Library, Laud Misc 636, fols. 81r–91v: Peterborough Chronicle, First Continuation (1122–1131) with later interpolations (cited as 1C). SEM (519, 298) C12a2. Ed. Earle and Plummer, and Clark.

(#17000) Lindisfarne Gloss to the Gospel according to Saint Matthew. N C10a2. Analysed only for nom./acc.pl. Ed. Skeat.

#20000 Oxford, Bodleian Library, Top. Kent d.3 (Cartulary of St Laurence's Hospital). Davis, no. 210. fols. 11r–13v: Ordinances of St Laurence's Hospital, Canterbury. SE (615, 158) C15a. Ed. Horobin and Smith.

#21000 Oxford, Merton College 248, hand of fols. 66v, 139v, 141v, 148v: Bishop Sheppey's Collection. SE (574, 169) C14a. Ed. Brown (*14th*, Verses 35–38 for fols. 66v, 139v, 141v and 148v).

(*#22000) London, Lambeth Palace Library 216, fol. 111r–v: Bidding Prayer. SE (567, 144). Analysed to 111r.b40. Ed. *LAEME* text database.

#23000 London, British Library, Cotton Faustina B III: Saint Editha. SW C15a1. Ed. Horstmann (*Editha*).

(#24000) Oxford, Bodleian Library, Ashmole 33: Sir Ferumbras. SW (298, 097) C14b2. Analysed for the first half to line 3136. Ed. Herrtage.

#25000 Edinburgh, National Library of Scotland, Advocates' 19.2.1 (the Auchinleck MS), hand A (main hand): Sir Orfeo. SEM (532, 190) C14a2. Ed. Bliss.

#26000 Cambridge University Library Gg. IV. 27 (2), fols. 6r–13r: King Horn. SW (437, 181) C13a2. Ed. Lumby, and Hall (*King*).

#27000 London, British Library, Harley 2253: King Horn. SWM C14a2. Ed. Lumby, and Hall (*King*).

#28000 Oxford, Bodley, Laud. Misc. 108: King Horn. C13a2. Ed. Lumby, and Hall (*King*).

#29000 Oxford, Bodley, Junius 1: Ormulum. NEM C12b2. Ed. Holt.

#100000 N C10a texts bundled. #17000.

#110000 N C13a texts bundled. #231.

#120000 N C13b texts bundled. ##296, 297.

#130000 N C14a texts bundled. #298.

#140000 NEM C12b texts bundled. #29000.

#150000 NEM C13b texts bundled. ##15, 128, 159.

#160000 NEM C14a texts bundled. #129.

#170000 SEM C12a texts bundled. #16000.

#180000 SEM C12b texts bundled. ##4, 149, 1200, 1300.

#190000 SEM C13a texts bundled. ##13, 64, 138.

#200000 SEM C13b texts bundled. ##11, 137, 150, 155, 175, 269, 270, 285, 1400.

#210000 SEM C14a texts bundled. #25000.

#220000 NWM C13a texts bundled. ##16, 118, 122, 124.

#230000 NWM C13b texts bundled. #136.

#240000 SWM C9a texts bundled. #12000.

#250000 SWM C9b texts bundled. #13000.

#260000 SWM C10a texts bundled. #11000.

#270000 SWM C12b texts bundled. ##5, 170, 189, 2000, 2001, 10000, 14000.

#280000 SWM C13a texts bundled. ##6, 7, 20, 146, 245, 260, 261, 262, 272, 273, 1800, 1900.

#290000 SWM C13b texts bundled. ##2, 3, 10, 126, 158, 187, 214, 218, 220, 222, 229, 238, 246, 247, 248, 249, 264, 271, 278, 1100, 2002.

#300000 SWM C14a texts bundled. ##125, 27000.

#310000 SW C12b texts bundled. #63.

#320000 SW C13a texts bundled. ##144, 156, 157, 26000.

#330000 SW C13b texts bundled. ##163, 263.
#340000 SW C14a texts bundled. ##140, 258, 286.
#350000 SW C14b texts bundled. #24000.
#360000 SW C15a texts bundled. #23000.
#370000 SE C13a texts bundled. ##8, 17, 67, 142.
#380000 SE C14a texts bundled. ##291, 21000.
#390000 SE C15a texts bundled. #20000.

Appendix B   PFPs of Period/Dialect Text Groups

The PFPs presented in the following pages are those for the texts bundled according to period/dialect group as discussed in Section 3.2.

Each PFP is assigned an ID number (see Appendix A). In the TOKENS section, several token-based numerical statements are given. "Syncretised Dative/Prepositional Plurals" gives the number of plural forms that occur in positions that would syntactically require their dative forms in standard Old English West-Saxon but that actually take effectively the same forms as their nominative/accusative forms because they are case-syncretised. This and "Unsyncretised Dative/Prepositional Plurals" provide the base for calculating "Syncretism Rate," for discussion of which see Section 3.1.3. The syncretism rate appears as "NA" when there are no examples from dative environments. Figures without parentheses designate frequencies in non-rhyming positions, whereas those in parentheses count for rhyming positions.

In the TYPES AND RATES section, the type-based figures are given for the different plural types. For how to calculate the spread rate, see Section 3.1.5. The spread rate appears as "NA" when there are no examples in text that historically took that plural type. Figures with parentheses take account of Middle English innovative forms that lack Old English equivalents.

After the numerical overview, all recorded plural forms are listed in their Old English reference form, arranged according to the Old English reference class (see Section 3.1.4). Each Old English reference form is followed by the token frequency for each of the plural types it takes. Plural types considered to have undergone plural formation transfer are in square brackets, whereas those considered to have been possible alternatives in Old English are in parentheses.

For example, "**Fem-V** synn [s]117 [n]12 V11" reads: the plural of the historical strong feminine word *synn* is attested in the text, 117 times with -*s*, 12 times with -*n* (both in parentheses because they take these endings as a

Appendix B   195

result of plural formation transfer from Old English), and 11 times with -V (not parenthesised because vowel endings are historically expected).

B.1 PFPs of Northern Text Group

B.1.1 PFP 100000 (C10a Northern)

TEXT INFO TEXT: #17000
TOKENS Nominative/Accusative Plurals 498 (0), Syncretised Dative/Prepositional Plurals 0 (0), Unsyncretised Dative/Prepositional Plurals 0 (0), Syncretism Rate NA (NA), Genitive Plurals 0 (0), Total of Plurals 498 (0)
TYPES AND RATES

	s	n	V	$\emptyset$	M	TOTAL
TYPES	71 (72)	1 (1)	98 (98)	23 (23)	2 (2)	195 (196)
RATE	0.36 (0.37)	0.0051 (0.0051)	0.5 (0.5)	0.12 (0.12)	0.01 (0.01)	1 (1)
SPREAD RATE	1.1 (1.1)	0.05 (0.05)	1.7 (1.7)	0.5 (0.5)	0.33 (0.33)	—

Masc-S -ere s17, -ling s2, āþ s1, bēam s1, būend [V]1 [$\emptyset$]2, castel s1, cawl s3, cniht s2 [$\emptyset$]1, cræft s3 [$\emptyset$]4, cwealm [V]1, cyning s1, cyrtel s1, dæg s3, dēofol s12, disc s1, discipul s1, dōgor ($\emptyset$)1, ēar [V]1, earn s1, engel s9, eorþcrypel s1, fearh s1, fisc s3, fiscþrūt s1, fox s1, fugel s1, gāst s2, healm s1, heofon s3, here s3, hierde [V]1, hlāf s8 [V]1, hrycg s1, hwelp s1, lārēow s3, lāttēow s3, lyge [V]1, māþum s1, pening s2, prēost s1, sācerd s2, sǣ s1, scilling s2, scōh [V]2, slege [V]1, stær s1, stān s2, strēam s2, þegn s55, þēof s2, þēow s2, þorn s1, þrēat s9 [V]1, þwang (V)1, wæg s1, wæstm s3 (V)3 [$\emptyset$]4, wer s2, wind s3, wulf s1

Masc-N cempa [V]1, cræftiga [V]2, flēogenda [V]2, fruma [V]1, hūsa [V]1, sceaþa [V]1, spearwa [s]1, stapela [s]1, steorra [V]1, swica [s]1 [V]1, wā [s]1, wita n1 [V]12, wītega [V]10

Neut-N ēage [V]8, ēare [V]2

Fem-N āte [V]2, cwene [V]2, nǣdre [V]2

Masc-V sifeþa V2, sunu V17

Neut-V bod V2, bred V1, fæt V5, foþor [$\emptyset$]1, geat [$\emptyset$]1, grot [s]1 V1, hēafod V1, hol [s]1, met [$\emptyset$]1, rīce [s]1, scip V1 [$\emptyset$]4, timbre V1, twig V1, writ V3, yfel V4

Fem-V -ing V1, -ness V7, -ung V5 [$\emptyset$]1, -waru [s]2, ādl V1, ǣht V1, byrgen V3, byrþen V1, bysen V1, bytt V1, cǣg [s]1, ceaster V2 [$\emptyset$]1, cnēorisn V3, culfer V2, duru V1, ēa V1, feorm V2, hǣlu V1, hand V1, lāf V1, lār V1, mand V1, meord V1, miht V5 [$\emptyset$]1, rest V1, scyld V1, stīg V1, stōw V1, synn V7, þēofend V1, þēostru V1, wēn V1, witnes V2, wlōh [$\emptyset$]1, yfelsung [s]2

Masc-Ø brōþor [V]8 $\emptyset$1

Neut-Ø bēacen [V]2, brȳdhlōp [V]1, cicen [V]1, cynn [V]4, dīegol [V]1, feoht [V]1, fracoþ [V]1, fȳr [s]1, gēar $\emptyset$1, gōd [V]1, hǣr [V]1, hām [s]1, hrægl [V]2, hunig $\emptyset$1, hūs [V]1, land [V]1, mægen [V]2, morþor $\emptyset$1, nēat [V]3, nest [s]1 [V]1, riht [V]1, rīp [s]1, seld [V]1, setl [s]1 [V]1, spell $\emptyset$1, strēon [V]2, tācen [V]1, ticcen [V]1, tungol (V)1, wēod [V]3, weorc [s]1 [V]3 $\emptyset$2, wīf [V]2 $\emptyset$1, wīn [s]1, winter $\emptyset$1, word [V]6 $\emptyset$3, wundor [V]1

Fem-Ø sweostor [V]1 $\emptyset$1

Masc-M fēond (s)3, fōt M2, frēond (s)1, mann M27

Masc-M cild [s]1

Fem-M burg [s]3

B.1.2 PFP 110000 (C13a Northern)

TEXT INFO TEXT: #231

TOKENS Nominative/Accusative Plurals 2 (0), Syncretised Dative/Prepositional Plurals 12 (0), Unsyncretised Dative/Prepositional Plurals 0 (0), Syncretism Rate 1 (NA), Genitive Plurals 0 (0), Total of Plurals 14 (0)

TYPES AND RATES

	s	n	V	ø	M	TOTAL
TYPES	10 (10)	0 (0)	0 (0)	0 (0)	1 (1)	11 (11)
RATE	0.91 (0.91)	0 (0)	0 (0)	0 (0)	0.091 (0.091)	1 (1)
SPREAD RATE	NA (NA)	0 (0)	0 (0)	0 (0)	1 (1)	—

Masc-N hālga [s]1, pāpa [s]1, winna [s]1
Fem-N flēoge [s]1
Neut-V set [s]1
Fem-V dǣd [s]1, synn [s]2, wund [s]2
Neut-Ø gift [s]1, þing [s]1
Masc-M mann $M2$

B.1.3 PFP 120000 (C13b Northern)

TEXT INFO TEXT: ##296, 297

TOKENS Nominative/Accusative Plurals 369 (46), Syncretised Dative/Prepositional Plurals 140 (53), Unsyncretised Dative/Prepositional Plurals 11 (4), Syncretism Rate 0.93 (0.93), Genitive Plurals 14 (0), Total of Plurals 534 (103)

TYPES AND RATES

	s	n	V	ø	M	TOTAL
TYPES	131 (177)	3 (3)	6 (6)	10 (12)	5 (5)	155 (203)
RATE	0.84 (0.87)	0.019 (0.015)	0.039 (0.03)	0.065 (0.059)	0.032 (0.025)	1 (1)
SPREAD RATE	2.5 (3.3)	0.14 (0.14)	0.14 (0.14)	0.34 (0.41)	0.63 (0.63)	—

Masc-S -ere s3, -ing s2, -ling s1, -scipe s1, apostol s13, biscop s2, blōstm s1, cāsere s1, castel s1, cleric s1, clūd s2, cræft s2, crīsten [ø]2, crypel s1, cyning s3, dæg s13, dēofol s2, dīacon s2, discipul s4, dynt s3, engel s9, eorl s1, fisc s1 [V]2, flyht s1, god s5, heofon s1, hierde s1, list s1, magister s8, martyr s1, munuc s1, nægl s2, pening s1, pliht s1, posl s7, pott s1, prēost s3, rǣd s1, rāp s1, sanct s10, sang s1, sīþ s1 [V]1, smiþ s1, storm s1, tēar s2, tūr s1, þorn s1, þrēa s1, wæg s4, wind s1, wyrm s2
Masc-N burna [s]1, draca [s]1, fēolaga [s]1, fēra [s]1, ieldra [s]1, lēo [s]1, nama [s]1, sceaþa [s]1, stēda [s]1, steorra [s]1, wǣrloga [s]2, wana [s]1, wrǣcca [s]6
Neut-N ēage n3, ēare n1
Fem-N cirice [s]1, heorte [s]6, hlǣfdige [s]1, nǣdre [s]2, nunne [s]1, wuduwe [s]1
Masc-V ielde [s]1, Saracene [s]2, sculdor [s]1, sunu [s]1
Neut-V bod [s]4, hēafod [s]1, lim [s]4 [ø]1, rīce [s]3, sceap V1, scip [s]2, set [s]1, yfel [s]1
Fem-V bend (s)3, bliss [ø]1, caru [s]2, dǣd [s]4, fȳlþ [s]1, hand [s]3 $V6$ [M]3, help (s)2, heord [s]2, lǣst [s]1, lagu [s]3, lēode [s]1, miht [s]3, myrgþ [s]3, nīed [s]1, pīn [s]4, sāwol [s]2, sceaft (s)1, sprǣc [s]1 $V1$, strengþ [s]3, stund [s]1, synn [s]5 [ø]1, þrāg [s]1, wamb [s]2, wiht [s]1, witnes [s]3, woruld [s]1, wund [s]1
Masc-Ø mōnaþ ø1

Neut-Ø bæc [s]1, bealu [s]1, bearn [s]1, brēost (s)1, cnēow [s]1, dor [s]2, folc [s]1 ø1, gēar ø7, gift [s]9, hord (s)1, inn [s]1, land [s]2, lēoht [s]1, spell [s]1, tācen [s]7, trēow [s]4, þing [s]4 ø7, wæter [s]2, weorc [s]5, wīl [s]1, winter [s]1 ø3, witt [s]2, word [s]5, wrang [s]1

Fem-Ø mægþ [n]1

Masc-M fōt M4, frēond (s)5, mann [V]2 [ø]1 M63, tōþ M1

Masc-M cild M4

Fem-M bōc [s]1

B.1.4   PFP 130000 (C14a Northern)

TEXT INFO TEXT: #298

TOKENS Nominative/Accusative Plurals 286 (50), Syncretised Dative/Prepositional Plurals 112 (52), Unsyncretised Dative/Prepositional Plurals 2 (8), Syncretism Rate 0.98 (0.87), Genitive Plurals 14 (0), Total of Plurals 414 (110)

TYPES AND RATES

	s	n	V	ø	M	TOTAL
TYPES	78 (115)	1 (1)	4 (4)	10 (10)	4 (4)	97 (134)
RATE	0.8 (0.86)	0.01 (0.0075)	0.041 (0.03)	0.1 (0.075)	0.041 (0.03)	1 (1)
SPREAD RATE	2.3 (3.4)	0.077 (0.077)	0.17 (0.17)	0.53 (0.53)	0.5 (0.5)	—

Masc-S -ere s1, bēam s1, biscop s1, bridd s1, cleric s6, clūt s3, cniht s2, cost s2, cræft s2, cyning s14, dæg s6, discipul s6, dynt s1, earm s1, engel s1, eorl s1, fætels s2, fisc s2, fugel s6, hræw s1, magister s1, munuc s1, pening s1, prēost s3, pytt s1, tēar s2, tūn s2, tūr s1, þēof s1, þōht s1, þwang s1, wæg s1, wang s1, wyrm s15

Masc-N fāh [s]2, fēolaga [s]9, hīwan n1 [V]1, ieldra [s]1, nama [s]2, snaca [s]1, steorra [s]2, turtla [s]2

Fem-N cuppe [s]1, nædre [s]1, tāde [V]1, wīse [ø]1

Masc-V sunu [s]1 [ø]1

Neut-V bed V1, geat [s]4, græf [s]1, græs [ø]1, lim [s]1, mægden [s]1

Fem-V -ing [s]1, āþexe [s]1, bend (s)2, bisen [s]1, dǣd [s]14, duru [s]1, hand [s]1 [ø]1 [M]1, nīed [s]4, pīn [s]2, sāwol [s]1 [ø]1, sagu [s]1, synn [s]7

Masc-Ø fæder [s]1

Neut-Ø bān [s]5, berǣrn [s]2, gēar ø1, gift [s]4, hūs [s]1, inn [s]1, lēaf [s]2, spell [s]3, swīn ø1, tācen [s]1, trēow [s]1, þing [s]4 [V]1 ø5, weorc [s]2, winter ø1, word [s]11

Fem-Ø dohtor [s]3

Masc-M fēond (s)3, fōt [ø]1 M4, frēond (s)3, mann M95

Masc-M cild M1

Fem-M bōc [s]1, burg [s]3

B.2   PFPs of North-East Midland Text Group

B.2.1   PFP 140000 (C12b North-East Midland)

TEXT INFO TEXT: #29000

TOKENS Nominative/Accusative Plurals 1715 (0), Syncretised Dative/Prepositional Plurals 113 (0), Unsyncretised Dative/Prepositional Plurals 63 (0), Syncretism Rate 0.64 (NA), Genitive Plurals 66 (0), Total of Plurals 1957 (0)

TYPES AND RATES

	s	n	V	ø	M	TOTAL
TYPES	157 (172)	4 (4)	15 (15)	12 (12)	4 (4)	192 (207)
RATE	0.82 (0.83)	0.021 (0.019)	0.078 (0.072)	0.063 (0.058)	0.021 (0.019)	1 (1)
SPREAD RATE	2.5 (2.8)	0.15 (0.15)	0.3 (0.3)	0.28 (0.28)	0.4 (0.4)	—

Masc-S -dōm s11, -ing s5, apostol s39, āþ s1, biscop s6, bōg s7, bridd s4, byrele s4, clāþ s10, clūd s2, clūt s2, cniht s68, cost s1, cræft s3, cyning s47, cyrtel s3, dǣl s24, dæg s32, dēaþ s1, dēofol s6, dīacon s4, dōm s1, drinc s4, earm s2, engel s36, eorl s1, fǣtels s19, fisc s1, flocc s2, flōd s1, gāst s8, Grēcas s1, gylt s7, heofon s8, hīred s19, hlāf s3, hund s2, lǣce s1, lārēow s1, lust s14, magister s1, māþum s6, mete s4, munt s5, prēost s43, ræcc s1, scēaf s1, sīþ s7, stæf s10, stān s21, steall s1, stenc s2, tēar s2, tūn s3, þeaw s43, þōht s9, þorn s2, wǣg s8, wǣstm s1, weall s1, wer s8, wine s1

Masc-N bucca [s]6, cruma [s]1, fēra [s]2, gærshoppa [V]1, genga [s]2, grǣfa [s]1, hīwan n2, nama [s]3 [V]3, scanca [s]1, steorra [s]6, sticca [s]1, tīma [s]2, turtla [s]4, þēowa [s]52, wā n2, wita [s]19, wrǣcca [s]1, wyrhta [s]7

Neut-N ēage n1

Fem-N asce [s]5, belle [s]5, cuppe [s]1, heorte [s]9, mǣsse [s]1, nǣdre [s]4, wiþþe [s]4

Masc-V hād [s]7, sculdor V1, sunu [s]14

Neut-V bed [s]11, græs [s]2, lendenu [s]2, lim [s]4, lot [s]2, sæt [s]1, stoc [s]2, writ [s]6

Fem-V -ing [s]1, -ness [s]9, ǣht V4, ælmesse [s]1, bēn [s]7, benc [s]1, bend (s)9, bisen [s]1, brēr [s]2, clawu [s]1, culfer [s]7 V2, dǣd [s]55, ēst (s)2, earc [s]1, giefu [s]7, glēd [s]3, hand [s]1 V3, lagu [s]45, lār [s]2, lēode V4, miht [s]23, mīl V1, rest [s]1, sacu [s]2, sǣlþ [s]2, sāwol [s]25, sceaft (s)8 V20, sprǣc [s]3, stīg (s)2, synn [s]126, talu [s]1, þēod V13, wǣcc [s]4, witnes [s]1, wucu [s]1, wund [s]2

Masc-Ø brōþor [V]12, mōnaþ ø5

Neut-Ø bān [s]2, bearn [s]2 ø1, bord [s]6, brēost (s)2, cnēow [s]5, cynd [s]1, dēor [s]1 ø8, gēar [s]10 ø7, gield [s]1, hors ø1, hundred ø4, hwēol [s]7, lāc [s]25 ø2, land [s]2, lēaf [s]1, līf [s]5, mǣl [M]2, mynster [s]1, nēat ø5, sand [s]1, scēap ø10, spell [s]16, swīn ø1, swinc [s]2, tācen [s]28, trēow [s]6, þēoh [s]1, þing [s]19 [V]1, wǣpen [n]2, wæter [s]2, weorc [s]14, wīf [s]5, word [s]49, wundor [V]1

Fem-Ø dohtor [s]6, sweostor [s]4

Masc-M fōt M1, frēond [ø]4, mann M244

Masc-M cild [V]24, lamb [V]1

Fem-M bōc [s]14, burg [s]1, gāt M1, niht [s]5 [ø]1

B.2.2   PFP 150000 (C13b North-East Midland)

TEXT INFO TEXT: ##15, 128, 159

TOKENS Nominative/Accusative Plurals 3 (0), Syncretised Dative/Prepositional Plurals 2 (0), Unsyncretised Dative/Prepositional Plurals 0 (0), Syncretism Rate 1 (NA), Genitive Plurals 0 (0), Total of Plurals 5 (0)

TYPES AND RATES

	s	n	V	ø	M	TOTAL
TYPES	3 (3)	0 (0)	0 (0)	0 (0)	1 (1)	4 (4)
RATE	0.75 (0.75)	0 (0)	0 (0)	0 (0)	0.25 (0.25)	1 (1)
SPREAD RATE	3 (3)	NA (NA)	0 (0)	0 (0)	1 (1)	—

Appendix B   199

Masc-S earm $s1$
Fem-V synn $[s]2$
Neut-Ø word $[s]1$
Masc-M fōt $M1$

B.2.3   PFP 160000 (C14a North-East Midland)

TEXT INFO TEXT: #129
TOKENS Nominative/Accusative Plurals 1 (0), Syncretised Dative/Prepositional Plurals 0 (0), Unsyncretised Dative/Prepositional Plurals 0 (0), Syncretism Rate NA (NA), Genitive Plurals 1 (0), Total of Plurals 2 (0)
TYPES AND RATES

	s	n	V	ø	M	TOTAL
TYPES	1 (1)	0 (0)	0 (0)	0 (0)	0 (0)	1 (1)
RATE	1 (1)	0 (0)	0 (0)	0 (0)	0 (0)	1 (1)
SPREAD RATE	1 (1)	NA (NA)	NA (NA)	NA (NA)	NA (NA)	—

Masc-S dæg $s1$

B.3   PFPs of South-East Midland Text Group

B.3.1   PFP 170000 (C12a South-East Midland)

TEXT INFO TEXT: #16000
TOKENS Nominative/Accusative Plurals 146 (0), Syncretised Dative/Prepositional Plurals 0 (0), Unsyncretised Dative/Prepositional Plurals 5 (0), Syncretism Rate 0 (NA), Genitive Plurals 9 (0), Total of Plurals 160 (0)
TYPES AND RATES

	s	n	V	ø	M	TOTAL
TYPES	45 (45)	2 (2)	15 (15)	10 (10)	3 (3)	75 (75)
RATE	0.6 (0.6)	0.027 (0.027)	0.2 (0.2)	0.13 (0.13)	0.04 (0.04)	1 (1)
SPREAD RATE	1.3 (1.3)	0.25 (0.25)	1.1 (1.1)	0.71 (0.71)	0.75 (0.75)	—

Masc-S -ere $s1$ $[V]1$, abbod $s4$, æcer $s1$, āþ $s1$ $[ø]1$, biscop $s14$, būc $s1$, canon $s1$, castel $s4$, cell $s1$, cniht $s2$, cræft $s1$, dæg $s5$, dīacon $s1$, earm $s1$, eorl $s3$, fugel $s1$, gærsum $s2$ $[V]1$, hǣþen $[V]1$, horn $[ø]2$, hund $s1$, munt $s1$, munuc $s11$, pening $s1$, plōg $s1$, prior $s1$, rǣd $[V]1$, scilling $s3$, stān $s2$, tūn $s1$, þegn $s5$, þēof $s1$, wrenc $s1$
Masc-N hunta $[s]2$, pāpa $[s]1$, tīma $[V]1$, winna $[s]1$
Fem-N āte $n1$, belle $[V]1$, bēo $n1$, hacele $[s]1$
Masc-V wudu $[s]1$
Neut-V abbodrīce $[s]2$, hēafod $[ø]1$, rīce $[s]1$, writ $V1$
Fem-V ǣht $V2$, bend $(s)1$, brycg $[s]1$, drān $V2$, giefu $V2$, hand $V1$, lagu $[s]1$, mīl $V1$, sibb $V1$
Neut-Ø -lac $[s]1$, dwild $ø1$, gēar $ø1$, gield $[s]1$, hors $ø1$, hundred $ø2$, mōt $[s]1$, riht $[s]1$ $[V]1$, swīn $ø1$, tācen $[V]1$, þing $ø2$, wīf $[s]3$, wīl $[s]1$
Masc-M fēond $[ø]1$, frēond $M2$, mann $M17$
Fem-M bōc $M1$

B.3.2 PFP 180000 (C12b South-East Midland)

TEXT INFO TEXT: ##4, 149, 1200, 1300
TOKENS Nominative/Accusative Plurals 964 (14), Syncretised Dative/Prepositional Plurals 273 (2), Unsyncretised Dative/Prepositional Plurals 278 (8), Syncretism Rate 0.5 (0.2), Genitive Plurals 89 (3), Total of Plurals 1604 (27)
TYPES AND RATES

	s	n	V	ø	M	TOTAL
TYPES	168 (183)	41 (41)	55 (59)	19 (20)	4 (4)	287 (307)
RATE	0.58 (0.6)	0.14 (0.13)	0.19 (0.19)	0.066 (0.065)	0.014 (0.013)	1 (1)
SPREAD RATE	1.8 (1.9)	0.76 (0.76)	0.69 (0.74)	0.41 (0.43)	0.31 (0.31)	—

Masc-S -ere s4, -ing s3, -ling s7, ǣt s2, apostol s15, āþ s3, biscop s6, blōstm s4 [n]1 (V)2, bōg s3, borg s1, bremel s1, bridd s3, castel s9, cierr [ø]1, claþ s13, cleric s1, cnoll s1, cræft s2, curs s1, cyme s2, cyning s3, dæg s13 [V]1, dēaþ s1, dēofol s6 [n]7, discipul s4, drinc s2, dynt s4, earm s1, engel s14 [n]1, eorl s3, fisc s3, fugel s5, gāst s9, giest s1, gīsl s1, gylt s15, gyrn s1 [n]1 [V]1, hafoc s1, harm s1, heofon (V)1, heorr (V)1, hlǣw s2, hund s1, lǣce s1, lārēow s8, leahtor s10, lust s18, martyr s2, mete s5, mūþ s1, munuc s8, nægl s1, oferǣt s1, olfend s1, pæþ s4, palm s2, prēost s5 [V]1, rāp s1, regn s1, sand s1, sang s9, scūr s1, sealm s2, sice s1, sīþ s7, stān s1, stede s1, stōpel s1, storm s4, strēam s1, streng s1, stride s2, tēar s16, tūn s2, þanc s1, þēaw s5, þēof s2, þorn s3, þrǣl s2, þrēa s1 [V]1, wǣg s4, wine s1, wrenc s5, wulf s1, wyrm s3

Masc-N ǣrendraca [s]1 [V]1, assa n1, bīleofa [s]1, boda [s]1, bucca [s]2, efeta n1, fāh n2, hālga n3, hīwan n1, ieldra n1 [V]3, līchama [s]1, lippa [V]1, nama [s]2, nefa [s]1, pāpa [s]1, plega [V]1, scanca [s]1, snaca [s]1 n1, steorra [s]5, swica [s]2 n1, tilia n2 [V]1, tīma [s]1 [V]1, turtla [s]1, þūma [s]1, wā [V]1, wītega [s]1 [V]1, wrǣcca [s]5, wuna [V]1

Neut-N ēage n11, ēare n2 [V]1

Fem-N asce n1, bīeme [s]1 [V]1, cirice [s]1, heorte [s]3 [V]4, hōre [s]1, more n2, nǣdre [s]1 n1, padde [s]1, tunge [V]1, wicce n1, wīce n2 [V]3, wīse [V]1

Masc-V hād [s]2, sculdor [s]1, sunu [s]2

Neut-V bed [s]3 [n]1 V5, clif [s]1, dæl [s]1, geat [n]5, hol V1, lim [s]6 [n]3, nīeten [n]1, wigle [s]1, writ [s]1, yfel [ø]1

Fem-V -ing [s]2 V3, -ness [s]1, -ung [s]4 V1, æht V3, bēn V1, bend (s)8 [ø]1, bīwist (s)1, bisen V1, brū [s]1, candel [s]1, dǣd [s]7 [n]6 V14, fetor [s]1, foreweard [s]1, fyrhto V1, hǣrn [s]1, hǣs V3, hǣtu [n]1, hand [n]5 V1 [ø]1, heord [s]11, lǣst [s]7, lagu [s]1 V1, lufu [s]1, mēd [s]1 V1, miht [s]5 [n]1 V1, nīed V1, pīn [n]1 V3, racen-tēah [s]1, rōd [s]1 [n]1, sāwol [s]1 V4, sceaft V1, sprǣc [s]2 V1, stund V1, synn [s]117 [n]12 V11, tīd [n]1, trēowþ [s]2, wǣcc V1, wǣd [s]8 [n]3 V1, wucu V1, wund [s]3 [n]3, wynn [n]1 V2, ȳþ [s]1 V1

Masc-Ø brōþor [n]2, fæder [s]2

Neut-Ø bearn [s]2, cynn [s]1 [V]6, dēor ø10, fers (s)1, folc [s]1, gēar [s]7 ø2, geoc [s]1, gield [s]2, gift [s]1, hǣr [V]1, hors ø1, hrīþer [n]1, lāc [s]2 ø2, land [s]7, lēaf [s]1, limp [s]1, riht [s]2, scēap ø7, spell [s]1, swīn ø4, swinc ø1, trēow [s]4 [n]1, þing [s]6 [V]1 ø50, þūsend [n]1, ungelimp (s)1, wǣpen [s]5 [V]3, wǣter [s]3, wēod [s]1, weorc [s]13 ø1, winter (V)9 ø1, word [s]17 ø31, wundor ø2

Fem-Ø dohtor [s]2, sweostor [s]1

Masc-M fēond [ø]2, fōt M11, frēond [ø]9, mann [n]2 [ø]2 M191, Scieppend [s]1, tōþ M2, tȳdriend [V]1

Masc-M cild [n]6 [V]2

Fem-M burg [s]3, gāt M3

B.3.3   PFP 190000 (C13a South-East Midland)

TEXT INFO TEXT: ##13, 64, 138

TOKENS Nominative/Accusative Plurals 78 (1), Syncretised Dative/Prepositional Plurals 85 (0), Unsyncretised Dative/Prepositional Plurals 26 (0), Syncretism Rate 0.77 (NA), Genitive Plurals 2 (0), Total of Plurals 191 (1)

TYPES AND RATES

	s	n	V	ø	M	TOTAL
TYPES	47 (54)	10 (10)	3 (3)	1 (1)	2 (2)	63 (70)
RATE	0.75 (0.77)	0.16 (0.14)	0.048 (0.043)	0.016 (0.014)	0.032 (0.029)	1 (1)
SPREAD RATE	2 (2.3)	3.3 (3.3)	0.17 (0.17)	0.071 (0.071)	0.5 (0.5)	—

Masc-S -ere s2, āncor s1, apostol s1, bēam s1, canonic s1, clāþ s1, dæg s2, dēofol s1, earm s1, engel s3, gāst s3, lust s2, martyr s1, munuc s1, pistol s1, sīþ s1, stede s1, strēam s1, tēar s1, þēaw s3, þōht s7, þrǣd s1, wine s1, wyrm s1

Masc-N fera n1, hālga n1, winna n1

Masc-V hād [s]1

Neut-V bod V2, geat [n]2, lim [n]1, writ [s]1, yfel [s]1

Fem-V -ing [s]4, cēast [s]1, dǣd [s]2, lufu [s]1, miht [s]4, pīn [s]1 [n]2, sāwol [s]2, sprǣc [s]2, synn [s]15 [n]2, wrǣþþo [s]1

Masc-Ø fæder [s]1

Neut-Ø cynd [n]1, cynn [s]1, gōd [V]1, hāt [s]1, þing [s]1 ø7, ungelimp (s)1, wǣt [s]1, weorc [s]14, winter (V)1, witt [s]5, word [s]13, wundor [n]1

Masc-M fōt M1, mann M14

Masc-M cild [n]1

Fem-M niht [s]1

B.3.4   PFP 200000 (C13b South-East Midland)

TEXT INFO TEXT: ##11, 137, 150, 155, 175, 269, 270, 285, 1400

TOKENS Nominative/Accusative Plurals 1084 (147), Syncretised Dative/Prepositional Plurals 239 (77), Unsyncretised Dative/Prepositional Plurals 110 (17), Syncretism Rate 0.69 (0.82), Genitive Plurals 59 (1), Total of Plurals 1492 (242)

TYPES AND RATES

	s	n	V	ø	M	TOTAL
TYPES	234 (301)	27 (28)	28 (29)	20 (20)	6 (7)	315 (385)
RATE	0.74 (0.78)	0.086 (0.073)	0.089 (0.075)	0.064 (0.052)	0.019 (0.018)	1 (1)
SPREAD RATE	2.1 (2.7)	0.47 (0.49)	0.38 (0.4)	0.34 (0.34)	0.38 (0.44)	—

Masc-S -ere s4, -gengel s1, -ing s2, æcer s13 [V]8, ǣl s1 [V]1, æppel s1, alter s1, āþ s5, bār s1, bēag s2 [n]1 [V]1, beard s1, beorg s1, biscop s5, bōg s1, borg s1, brǣd s1, bridd s1, bydel s1, camel s1, canon s1, castel s7, ceafl s1, ceorl s2, clāþ s3, cleric s3, clūt s1, cniht s26, cost s3, cran s1, cyning s5, dæg s24, dǣl s4, dīc s2, disc s1, drēam s7, dreng s2, drinc s1, dynt s3, earm s6, ellen (V)3, elpend s1, engel s11, eorl s9, eoten s1, finn s1, fisc s5, flocc s1, fugel s8, gang [ø]2, giest [V]1, gimm s1, god s5, hege s2, helm s1, heorot s1, hierde s2, hīred s1, hring s5, hund s1, lēap s1, magister s2, mancus s2, mete s3, munuc s9, mūþ s1, nægl s1, pǣl s1, pening s2, prēon s1, prēost s7, rāp s1, sacc s4, sǣcc s1, saltere s1, sanct s1, sand s6, scield s2 [V]1, sēam s2, sīþ s6 [V]2, spring s1, stān s4, stede s1, stīweard s1, storm s1, swan s1, tēar s7, titt [n]1, toft s1, tūn s4, turtur s1, þēaw s2, þegn s22, þēof s2, þōht s1, þorn s1, þrǣl s1, þunor s1, wæg s2, wægn s1, wang s1, weall s1, wiell s1, wine [n]1, wulf s1, wyrm s2

Masc-N assa [s]1, bera [s]1, boga [s]1, bula [s]1, cnapa [s]1, docga [s]6, fāh n4, fēolaga [s]1, fera [s]3 n2, franca n1, gærshoppa [s]2, gealga [s]3, hālga n1, hosa n2, hūsbonda [s]1, ieldra n6 [V]2, lēo [s]1, nama [s]2, nefa [V]1, offerenda [s]2, rēfa [s]1 n1, scanca [s]1, spura [s]1, stēda [s]2, stēora [s]2, steorra [s]1, sticca [s]2, swica [s]2, targa n1, tīma [s]2, þēowa n1, ūtlaga [s]1, wicca [s]4, wræcca [s]2, wuna n2

Neut-N ēage n3

Fem-N asce [s]1, belle [s]3, berie [s]2, cirice [s]3, cuppe [s]1 n2, flēoge [s]2, grȳpe [s]1, hacele n1, heorte [s]1, hlǣfdige [s]1, nǣdre [s]1, nunne [s]1, pylece [s]1, sīde [s]1, tā [s]2, wicce [s]1, wuduwe [s]1

Masc-V feld [s]2, sculdor [s]2, sunu [s]24 [n]1, wudu [s]5

Neut-V bed [s]2, bod [s]2, cræt [s]1 V1, fæt [s]1, geat [s]1, hēafod [s]2, hlid [s]1, lim [s]5, mægden [s]10, mǣre V1, rǣde V1, rib [s]1, scip [s]4, spere [n]2 V1, writ [s]3 V8, wriþ [s]1

Fem-V -ing V1, -ness [s]2, -ung [s]1, ār [s]1, ǣht [s]1, bēan [s]1, bēn [s]2, bend (s)4, bledu [n]1, bliss [s]1, bysen [s]1, cǣg [s]1, dǣd [s]2, dūn [s]5, fetor [s]3, feþer [s]1, fierd [s]1, hand [s]13 [n]1 [M]1, help (s)1, henn [s]1, hīd V8, lagu [s]2, mearc [n]1 [ø]2, mēd [s]2, mund [s]1, rād V1, risc [s]1, sāwol [s]1, scēarra [s]1, sceaft (s)1 V1, seono V2, sōcn V1, sorg [s]1 [n]2, sprǣc [s]3, stefn [s]1, strengþ [s]1, synn [s]5, wǣd [n]1, wamb [s]1, witnes V1, wucu [s]1, wund [s]9, ysl [s]1

Masc-Ø brōþor [s]1 [n]1 [V]17, mōnaþ ø5

Neut-Ø bæc [s]1, bān [s]6, bearn ø4, cnēow [s]5, cynd [s]3, cynrēd [s]1, dāl [s]1, dēor [s]1 ø2, ēar [s]1, fōdor [s]1, fȳr [s]1, gēar [s]1 [V]1 ø41, gift [s]3, hors ø6, hrīþer [n]1, hūs [s]1, hundred ø8, land [s]6 [V]4 ø6, lēaf [s]1, līc [s]2, marc [s]6 ø7, nēat [s]1 ø1, pund ø17, scēap [s]1 ø7, sweord [s]5 [V]2, tācen [s]6, teld [s]1, trēow [s]1 [n]2, þing [s]1 [V]9 ø2, þūsend [s]1 ø9, wǣpen ø1, wæter [s]6, weorc [s]1, wīf [s]15, wīl [s]1, winter [s]1 ø19, word [s]6 ø1

Fem-Ø dohtor [s]12, sweostor [s]6

Masc-M fēond (s)4, fōt M10, frēond [ø]6, mann [V]2 M206, tōþ M2

Masc-M cild [n]16 [V]20 M1

Fem-M bōc [s]1, burg [s]14, gōs M1, hnutu [s]1, niht [s]4 [ø]6, turf [s]1

B.3.5 PFP 210000 (C14a South-East Midland)

TEXT INFO TEXT: #25000
TOKENS Nominative/Accusative Plurals 75 (13), Syncretised Dative/Prepositional Plurals 27 (14), Unsyncretised Dative/Prepositional Plurals 1 (3), Syncretism Rate 0.96 (0.82), Genitive Plurals 0 (0), Total of Plurals 103 (30)
TYPES AND RATES

	s	n	V	ø	M	TOTAL
TYPES	33 (53)	2 (2)	2 (2)	3 (4)	3 (3)	43 (64)
RATE	0.77 (0.83)	0.047 (0.031)	0.047 (0.031)	0.07 (0.063)	0.07 (0.047)	1 (1)
SPREAD RATE	1.6 (2.5)	0.5 (0.5)	0.33 (0.33)	0.33 (0.44)	1 (1)	—

Masc-S -ere s2, -ing s2, castel s2, claþ s3, cleric s1, cniht s6, cyning s1, earm s2, eorl s2, finger s1, fugel s3, god s1, hlāford s1, holt s1, hund s1, nægl s1, stān s1, tēar s1, tūr s1, wulf s1, wyrm s1

Masc-N lēo [s]1, stēda [s]1
Neut-N ēage n1
Fem-N hlǣfdige [s]8
Neut-V græs [s]1, lim [s]1, mægden [s]3
Fem-V -ung [s]1, hand [n]1, mīl V1
Neut-Ø gēar [V]2 ø1, hors ø2, land [s]1, lēaf [s]1, þing [s]2 ø3, wīf [s]1, word [s]1
Masc-M fōt M1, mann M2, tōþ M1

B.4 PFPs of North-West Midland Text Group

B.4.1 PFP 220000 (C13a North-West Midland)

TEXT INFO TEXT: ##16, 118, 122, 124
TOKENS Nominative/Accusative Plurals 333 (1), Syncretised Dative/Prepositional Plurals 202 (1), Unsyncretised Dative/Prepositional Plurals 30 (0), Syncretism Rate 0.87 (1), Genitive Plurals 20 (0), Total of Plurals 585 (2)
TYPES AND RATES

	s	n	V	ø	M	TOTAL
TYPES	134 (184)	5 (5)	14 (14)	10 (11)	4 (4)	167 (218)
RATE	0.8 (0.84)	0.03 (0.023)	0.084 (0.064)	0.06 (0.051)	0.024 (0.018)	1 (1)
SPREAD RATE	2.7 (3.7)	0.19 (0.19)	0.26 (0.26)	0.34 (0.38)	0.5 (0.5)	—

Masc-S -ere s5, -scipe s1, bōg s1, bridd s21, cleric s1, clūt s1, coss s1, crūc s2, cyning s1, cyrnel s1, dæg s1, dēofol s1, discipul s2, dōm s1, drinc [ø]1, dynt s5, earm s2, engel s2, fox s6, fugel s1, glǣm s1, gylt s1, hamm s1, hlāford s1, hund s2, lust s6, magister s1, martyr s1, mūþ s3, nægl s3, pening s1, sceacel s1, sealm s1, sīþ [V]1, stān s3, stede s2, stice s1, storm s1, strēam s2, sweng s1, tēar s3, þēaw s5, þēof s2, þōht s3, þorn s2, þrǣl s1, wǣg s1, wāg s1, wulf s2, wyrm s1
Masc-N docga [s]1, dropa [s]1, fāh n4, fēra [s]1, hālga [s]2, līchama [s]1, lippa [s]1, līra [s]1, prica [s]1, ūtlaga [s]1, wā [s]1, wrǣcca [s]1
Neut-N ēage n10, ēare [s]13 n1 [V]1, wange [s]1
Fem-N āncre [s]17 [V]1 [ø]1, arwe [s]3, cēace [s]3, heorte [s]1, molde [s]1, nǣdre [s]1, tunge [s]1
Masc-V sculdor [s]2, sunu [s]1
Neut-V bed [s]1, dæl [s]1, geat [s]2, hol [s]3 [n]1, lim [s]5, lot [s]1, mægden [s]1, spere [s]1, þyrel [s]4, yfel [s]1
Fem-V -ung [s]12, andswaru [s]1, bliss [s]4, bōt [s]1, clūs [s]1, dǣd [s]1 V1, feþer [s]2, fȳlþ [s]2, fȳst [s]1, giefu [s]1, glēd [s]1, grīn [s]1, hand [s]3 [n]1 V4, healf [ø]1, henn [s]1, heord [s]2 V1, hulu [s]1, lǣs [s]1, miht [s]1, myrgþ [s]1, pīn [s]5, rūn [s]1, sāwol [s]1, scamu [s]1, sceaft (s)2, siht [s]1, sorg [s]1, sprǣc [s]3, swipu [s]2, synn [s]11, talu [s]1, tīd [s]2, trēowþ [s]1, wæcc V1, wucu [s]1, wund [s]4, ȳþ [s]1
Masc-Ø brōþor [V]3
Neut-Ø bān [s]1, bealu [s]1, bearn [s]2, cnēow [s]1, cynn [s]2, dēor [V]1, flǣsc [s]1, gēar ø1, hǣr [s]1, hocor [s]1, lēaf [s]1, mǣl ø1, nest [s]4, riht ø1, sǣd [s]1, spell [s]1, ticcen [s]5, þing [s]16 [V]1 ø2, wǣpen [s]1, weorc [s]6, witt [s]14, word [s]22 ø1, wundor [s]4
Fem-Ø dohtor [V]1, sweostor [V]5
Masc-M fēond [ø]1, fōt M5, frēond [ø]5, mann M29
Masc-M ǣg [V]1, cild [V]4
Fem-M gāt M6, gōs M1

B.4.2 PFP 230000 (C13b North-West Midland)

TEXT INFO TEXT: #136

TOKENS Nominative/Accusative Plurals 48 (1), Syncretised Dative/Prepositional Plurals 4 (3), Unsyncretised Dative/Prepositional Plurals 0 (0), Syncretism Rate 1 (1), Genitive Plurals 3 (0), Total of Plurals 55 (4)

TYPES AND RATES

	s	n	V	ø	M	TOTAL
TYPES	39 (44)	0 (0)	1 (1)	0 (0)	1 (1)	41 (46)
RATE	0.95 (0.96)	0 (0)	0.024 (0.022)	0 (0)	0.024 (0.022)	1 (1)
SPREAD RATE	2 (2.2)	0 (0)	0.2 (0.2)	0 (0)	1 (1)	—

Masc-S bār s2, beard s2, beorn s3, blōstm s2, bōg s1, bridd s1, brocc s1, cost s1, finc s1, fisc s1, flōd s1, flyht s1, fox s1, sanct s1, storm s1, strēam s1, þēof s1, wæg s1, wind s1, wyrm s1

Masc-N fēra [s]1

Fem-N sīde [s]1

Masc-V ford [s]1, wudu [s]1

Fem-V bicce [s]1, bōt [s]1, byrd [s]1

Neut-Ø bān [s]1, bold [V]1, brēost (s)1, būr [s]1, fām [s]1, fearn [s]1, fell [s]1, fenn (s)1, þing [s]1, wæter [s]2, weder [s]1, wolcen [s]1, word [s]1

Masc-M mann M1

B.5 PFPs of South-West Midland Text Group

B.5.1 PFP 240000 (C9a South-West Midland)

TEXT INFO TEXT: #12000

TOKENS Nominative/Accusative Plurals 168 (0), Syncretised Dative/Prepositional Plurals 15 (0), Unsyncretised Dative/Prepositional Plurals 88 (0), Syncretism Rate 0.15 (NA), Genitive Plurals 66 (0), Total of Plurals 337 (0)

TYPES AND RATES

	s	n	V	ø	M	TOTAL
TYPES	26 (26)	11 (11)	24 (24)	19 (19)	6 (6)	86 (86)
RATE	0.3 (0.3)	0.13 (0.13)	0.28 (0.28)	0.22 (0.22)	0.07 (0.07)	1 (1)
SPREAD RATE	0.93 (0.93)	1.2 (1.2)	1 (1)	1 (1)	0.86 (0.86)	—

Masc-S bēam s2, brǣw s1, cyning s1, dæg s1, dōm s4, ealdor s1, earm s1, ele s1, ende s1, ēþel s1, fearr s1, fisc s1, flōd s1, fugel s1, gang s2, heofon s5, heorot s1, hund s1, lust s1, rāp s1, sǣ s1, staþol s2, strǣl s2 (V)1, þrēa [V]1, wæg s7, weler (V)1, wiell (n)1

Masc-N burna n1, oxa n1, steorra n1, þearfa n1, willa n1, wita n1, wiþerbreca n1

Neut-N ēage n9

Fem-N cēace n1

Neut-V col V2, fæt V1, geat V4, līget V1, lof V1, mǣre V2, nīeten V1, yfel [ø]4

Fem-V -ness V10, -ung V1, ǣdr V2, bēn V1, ceaster V1, grīn [n]1, hand V4, sāwol V1, sprǣc V2, stefn V1, stīg V2, swaþu V2, synn V2, þēod V7, þēostru V2

Masc-Ø fæder [s]1

Neut-Ø bān ø5, bearn ø8, flǣsc ø1, folc ø1, gēar ø1, gōd ø3, hāt ø1, hrægl ø1, mægen ø1, sār ø1, scēap ø1, wæter ø2, weorc ø6, wīc ø1, wīn [s]1, wolcen ø1, word ø5, wundor ø3
Masc-M fēond [ø]7 M4, fōt M6, mann M2, tōþ M1
Masc-M cealf M1
Fem-M niht M1

B.5.2 PFP 250000 (C9b South-West Midland)

TEXT INFO TEXT: #13000
TOKENS Nominative/Accusative Plurals 46 (0), Syncretised Dative/Prepositional Plurals 2 (0), Unsyncretised Dative/Prepositional Plurals 51 (0), Syncretism Rate 0.038 (NA), Genitive Plurals 33 (0), Total of Plurals 132 (0)
TYPES AND RATES

	s	n	V	ø	M	TOTAL
TYPES	12 (12)	4 (4)	13 (13)	4 (4)	2 (2)	35 (35)
RATE	0.34 (0.34)	0.11 (0.11)	0.37 (0.37)	0.11 (0.11)	0.057 (0.057)	1 (1)
SPREAD RATE	1 (1)	0.8 (0.8)	1.2 (1.2)	0.8 (0.8)	1 (1)	—

Masc-S -scipe s1, biscop s1, dīacon s1, gāst [ø]1, heofon s1, hierde s1, lyft s2, prēost s1, stān s1, strǣl s1, þēaw s1, wind s1
Masc-N genga n1 [V]1, geongra n1, intinga n1
Fem-N heorte n1
Neut-V līget (s)1 V2
Fem-V -ness V1, bisen V1, hǣlu V1, hand V2, segen V1, swaþu V1, þēod V1, þunorrād V1, ȳst V1
Masc-Ø brōþor [V]4
Neut-Ø land ø1, mōd ø1, þing ø2, wundor [V]1
Masc-M mann M5
Fem-M bōc M3

B.5.3 PFP 260000 (C10a South-West Midland)

TEXT INFO TEXT: #11000
TOKENS Nominative/Accusative Plurals 484(0), Syncretised Dative/Prepositional Plurals 0(0), Unsyncretised Dative/Prepositional Plurals 0(0), Syncretism Rate NA(NA), Genitive Plurals 1(0), Total of Plurals 485(0)
TYPES AND RATES

	s	n	V	ø	M	TOTAL
TYPES	52 (53)	11 (11)	59 (60)	35 (35)	5 (5)	162 (164)
RATE	0.321 (0.323)	0.0679 (0.0671)	0.364 (0.366)	0.216 (0.213)	0.0309 (0.0305)	1 (1)
SPREAD RATE	1.061 (1.082)	0.4231 (0.4231)	1.311 (1.333)	1.029 (1.029)	0.625 (0.625)	—

Masc-S -ere s78 [V]2, -ling [n]1, æcer s1, āþ s1, belg s3, cniht s4, cyning s1, dæg s6, dēofol [ø]6, discipul s5, dōm [V]1, ealdor s2, earn s1, engel s9, esne s11, fearr s1, fisc s5, fox s1, fugel s5, gāst s2, heofon s1, here s2, hierde s1, hlāf s10, hwelp s1, lārēow s1, lāttēow s2 [ø]1, locc s1, riftre [V]1, sācerd s10, Sadduceas s3, scilling s2, scōh s2, stān s2, telgor [n]1, þegn s1, þēof s2 [ø]1, þōht s3, þorn s2, þwang (V)1, wǣg s2, wæstm s4 [ø]2, wer s1, wind s2, wulf s1

Masc-N begenga [V]2, cempa [V]2, cræftiga [V]1, fēra n1, fruma [V]1, gærshoppa [V]1, hīwan n1, hlīsa [V]1, myrþra [V]1, nama [V]1, nȳdnima [V]1, spearwa [s]2, steorra n1, þēowa [V]1, wita [V]2, wītega n1 [V]6, wyrhta [V]2

Neut-N ēage n6 [V]2, ēare n3 [V]1

Fem-N fǣmne n3, nǣdre [V]1, tunece [V]1, þæcele [V]1

Masc-V sunu [s]2 V2

Neut-V bod V1 [ø]1, fæt V7, hēafod [ø]1, hol V1, lendenu V1, met [ø]1, rīce V1, selegesceot V2, stæl V1, swic V1, timbre V1, writ V3, yfel V1 [ø]2

Fem-V -ness V9, -ung V3, ǣ V2, ǣht V2, byrgen V3, cǣg [n]1, ceaster [s]1 V2, culfer (n)1 V1, duru V1, firen V1, hand V2, lār V1, mand V2, mynd V1, scyld V2, stīg (s)1, stōw V1, synn V7, talu V1, tīd V1, þēod V3, þēostru V1, weard (s)1, witnes V1, yfelsung V1

Masc-Ø brōþor [V]4 ø6

Neut-Ø bēacen ø1, bearn ø15, cicen ø1, cynn ø2, dīegol [s]1, feoht ø1, gōd ø5, hord ø3, hrægl ø4, hūs [s]1, hunig [s]1, land ø1, mǣgen [V]1 ø6, morþor ø1, nett ø3, sǣd ø1, scēap ø5, setl [s]2 ø1, spell [s]2 ø1, tācen ø2, ticcen ø1, wēod ø5, weorc ø3, wīf ø2, wīn [s]1, winter ø1, word ø9, wundor ø1

Fem-Ø sweostor ø2

Masc-M fēond (s)3, fōt M3, mann M13, timbrend M1

Masc-M cild [ø]2

Fem-M bōc M1, burg [s]1, niht M2

B.5.4 PFP 270000 (C12b South-West Midland)

TEXT INFO TEXT: ##5, 170, 189, 2000, 2001, 10000, 14000

TOKENS Nominative/Accusative Plurals 1092 (21), Syncretised Dative/Prepositional Plurals 159 (2), Unsyncretised Dative/Prepositional Plurals 469 (15), Syncretism Rate 0.25 (0.12), Genitive Plurals 177 (2), Total of Plurals 1897 (40)

TYPES AND RATES

	s	n	V	ø	M	TOTAL
TYPES	119 (129)	74 (77)	72 (72)	35 (36)	11 (11)	311 (325)
RATE	0.38 (0.4)	0.24 (0.24)	0.23 (0.22)	0.11 (0.11)	0.035 (0.034)	1 (1)
SPREAD RATE	1.1 (1.2)	1.5 (1.5)	0.91 (0.91)	0.58 (0.6)	0.85 (0.85)	—

Masc-S -ere s24, -ing s2, -ling s3, -scipe s1 [n]1 [V]1, apostol s30 [M]2, biscop s3, blōstm [n]1 (V)1, borg s1, brand s2, brēmel s1, bydel s2, cāsere s2, castel s1, cierr s1, clāþ s11, cniht s17, cost s1, cyning s6, dæg s19, dēofol s2 [n]3 (V)1, discipul s2, dōm s3, drēam s1, drinc [n]2, dynt s1, earm s7, engel s30 [ø]1, ent s1, fæþm [V]3, finger [M]1, fisc s4, fugel s4, gāst s7, giest s1, gimm s1, god s2, gylt s8, hafoc s1, hēap s2, heofon s2, hlāf s3, hlāford s2, hring s1, hund s1, lārēow s1, leahtor s3, līeg s2, lust s9, mǣg s4, mānāþ s1, manslieht s1, martyr s1, māþum s1, mete s1 (V)1, munt s1, mūþ s1, munuc s1, nægl s2, nēahgebūr s2, nīþ s1, pening s2, pic s1, posl s1, prēost s2, rāp s7, repel s1, sang s2, scōh s1, scūr s1, scyttel s1, sealm s1, sēam s1, sele s1, sīþ s1, slege [n]1, sott s1, spring s1, stæpe s1, stān s5 [M]1, strēam s1, tēar s16, torr s1, tūn s1, þanc s1, þēaw s13, þegn s4, þēof s7, þōht s2, þorn s2, þrǣl s2, wǣg s6, wæstm s2 (V)1, wer s1 [M]1, wiell (n)1, wielm s1, wind s1, wine s2, wyrm s3

Masc-N ǣrendraca [s]4 n1, boda n2, cempa n1, crabba n1, draca n1, fāh n4 [ø]4, fēra n3, frogga n1 [V]1, gelēafa n1, hālga n9 [V]1, ieldra [V]1, līchama [V]4, loca n1, mǣcca n1, nama n2, rīca [V]1, slaga [V]1, spura n1, steorra n6, swica n1, wā [V]1, wela n4, wītega n2 [V]2, wrǣcca [s]1 n3 [V]2, wyrhta n1

Appendix B   207

Neut-N ēage n17, ēare n3
Fem-N ampre [s]1, blēme n1, cirice n1, heorte n5 [V]1, mæsse n1, nǣdre n2 [V]2, sīde [V]1, tāde n2 [V]1, tunge n2 [V]1, þēote n1, wīce n1, wuduwe n1
Masc-V hād [ø]1, sunu [s]4 [n]1
Neut-V bed [n]2 V3, bod [s]1 [n]4 V17, clif [s]1, fæt V1, geat [n]2 V4, lim [n]6, mægden V1, nīeten V3, ofermēde V1, oferslege [M]1, rīce [n]1 V1, twig V1, writ [n]1, yfel [s]2 [ø]2
Fem-V -ing V2, -ness [n]1 V2, -rǣden [ø]1, -ung V3, -waru V2, ǣ V1, ǣht [n]2 V2, ælmesse [n]4, bend (s)2, bisen V1, bliss [n]1 V1, bōt V1, cyþþ [n]1, dǣd [n]1 V12, dūn [n]1 V2, duru [n]1, ēst [n]1, gesǣlþ V1, giefu V3, glēd [n]1, gleng V1, hǣs [n]3 V9, hand [n]4, heord [n]1, lagu [n]4 V14, miht [n]2 V3, mōdor [s]2, myrgþ V1, nīed V1, pīn [n]1 V2, renc [s]1, rōd [n]1, sand [n]2, sāwol [n]8 V10, sceaft V10, sprǣc [n]3, stīg (s)2, stund V1, swaþu V1, synn [n]34 V40, tīd V1, wund [n]5 V1, ȳþ V1
Masc-Ø brōþor [n]2 [V]10, fæder [s]5, mōnaþ ø1
Neut-Ø bān ø5, bearn ø13, brēost (s)1, cynn [s]1 ø2, dēor ø5, edlēan ø1, fers ø1, gēar [V]2 ø1, gōd ø2, hām [s]1, hors ø1, hūs [s]1, lāc ø1, lāst [s]1, lēaf ø1, lēoht ø1, līf ø2, mægen [V]1, mǣl [s]1, mynster [V]1, rēaf ø1, sār ø1, scēap ø1, setl [s]2, swīn ø1, swinc ø1, tācen [V]6, trēow [n]1, tungol [n]1 (V)1, þing [s]3 [V]2 ø52, wǣpen [n]1 [V]6, wæter [s]1, webb ø1, weder [s]2, weorc [s]13 ø3, werod ø4, wīf [s]2 ø1 [M]1, winter (V)5, witt [s]1, word [s]13 [V]2 ø15, wundor [V]16 ø1
Fem-Ø dohtor [n]1, sweostor [n]1 [V]3
Masc-M fēond (s)1 [ø]8, fōt M12, frēond [ø]12, mann [V]6 [ø]2 M192
Masc-M cild [n]4 [V]2
Fem-M bōc M3, mūs M1, niht [ø]2 M1

B.5.5   PFP 280000 (C13a South-West Midland)

TEXT INFO TEXT: ##6, 7, 20, 146, 245, 260, 261, 262, 272, 273, 1800, 1900
TOKENS Nominative/Accusative Plurals 1858 (36), Syncretised Dative/Prepositional Plurals 692 (5), Unsyncretised Dative/Prepositional Plurals 541 (27), Syncretism Rate 0.56 (0.16), Genitive Plurals 221 (4), Total of Plurals 3312 (72)
TYPES AND RATES

	s	n	V	ø	M	TOTAL
TYPES	231 (310)	118 (123)	55 (57)	23 (25)	7 (8)	434 (523)
RATE	0.53 (0.59)	0.27 (0.23)	0.13 (0.11)	0.053 (0.048)	0.016 (0.015)	1 (1)
SPREAD RATE	1.7 (2.2)	1.5 (1.6)	0.47 (0.49)	0.27 (0.3)	0.47 (0.53)	—

Masc-S -dōm s5, -ere s13, -ing s6, -ling s3, -scipe s16, æcer s1, æl s2, apostol s5, āþ s1, awel [ø]1, bēag s2, bearm s1, belg s2, biscop s1, blōstm [n]2, bōg s1, brand s3, brēmel s2, bridd s1, bryce [n]3, bydel s1, cāsere s5, castel s3, clāþ s15, cleric s5, clūt s1, cnīf s1, cniht s12, coss s2, cradol s1, cræft s8, crīsten [V]2, crūc s3, cwide s1, cyning s10, cyrtel s2, dæg s12, dǣl s5 [n]3, dēaþ s2, dēofol s2 [n]11, disc s2, discipul s21, dōm s4, drēam s3, drinc s5 [n]1, dynt s5, earm s20, engel s29, eorl s3, fǣtels s1, finger s3, fisc s2, fox s3, frosc s1 [V]1, fugel s10, gāst s6, gimm s2, glǣm s4, god s17, gylt s9, hǣþen [V]2, hamor s2, hearm s1, helm s1, heofon s1, heorot s3, hlāford s1, hlīep s3, hrēam s1, hund s2, hyll s12, list [n]1, lust s14, mǣg s1, magister s11, martyr s6, mete s6, mūþ s2, nægl s8, pening s1, pīc s3, pīl s2, prēon s1, prēost s1, rǣd s3, sang s2, sceacel s1, scilling s1, scōh s1 [n]2, scop s1, sealm s9, sice s2, sīþ s2 [n]11 [V]9, snǣd s1, spring s1, stæf s11, stǣpe s1, stān s5, stede [n]2, stenc s1, stice [n]2, storm s2, strēam s3, sweng s6, tægel s3, tapor s1, tēar s19, tind s3, titt s9, tramet [V]1, tūsc s1, þanc s2, þearm s3, þēaw s29, þegn s1, þōht s11, þorn s9, þrǣl s2, þrēat s2, wæg s7 [n]1, wāg s6, wamm s1, weall s2, wer s1, wiell s1 (n)1, wind s1, wine s4, wrenc s8, wulf s1, wyrm s5

Masc-N assa n1, besma [s]1, cnotta n1, draca n1, drōsna [V]2, ēaca n1, efeta n1 [V]1, fāh n7, fēolaga [s]6, fēra n3 [V]1, frogga n2, hālga n9, hīwan n13, ieldra n2 [V]1, impa n6, lama n5, lēo [s]1, līchama [s]3, lippa n2, lōma n1, maþa n1, nama n77 [V]2, oxa n1, plega n1, prica [s]1, rēfa n1, scanca n1, scucca n1, snaca n2, spāca n1, spearca [s]1, stela n9, stēora n1, steorra n1, swica [V]1, tēona n1, twisa n1, þēowa [s]2 [ø]1, wā [s]5, wana [s]1, wela [s]2 n3, willa [s]2, winna [s]2, wita n1, wrǣcca [s]8 n2 [V]5

Neut-N ēage n35 [V]2, ēare n21 [V]1

Fem-N āncre [s]7 n11, arwe n3, asce n1, belle n1, bīeme n1, blǣse n1, cēace n3, eorþe n1, gristle [s]2, heorte n3, hlǣfdige [s]4, lilie [s]1, mǣsse n1, māge n1, nǣdre n5, sīde n6, tāde n2, tunge n3, wīse n1 [V]1, wuduwe n2

Masc-V hād [s]9, sculdor [s]1 [n]1, sunu [s]1

Neut-V andgiet V3, bæþ [s]3, bed [n]3, bod V1, dǣl [ø]5, fæt [n]1, flit [s]1, gamen [s]3, geat [s]4 [n]4, hnesce [s]1, hof [n]1, lim [s]1 [n]7, liþ V1, lor [n]1, lot [s]3, mǣgden [s]23, met V2, sceap V2, spere [n]1, stycce [s]1, tæl [ø]4, trod [n]7, þyrel [s]9, wēofod (s)1, wigle [s]1, writ [s]2 V1, yfel [s]5 V2

Fem-V -ing [s]3 V1, -ness [s]11 [n]1 V4, -ung [s]34, -waru (n)1 V2, ǣht V1, andswaru [s]1, bēn [n]7, bend (s)11, bliss [n]7 V2, clufu [s]1, dǣd [s]1 [n]9 V4, dūn [s]22, ēst (s)4, felg (n)1, fierd [s]1, fȳlþ [n]1, fȳst [s]2, fyrmþ V1, giefu [s]1 [n]3, gierd [n]1, glēd [n]3, grāp [s]1, hǣs [s]6 [n]3 V2, hand [n]28, healf [s]1 [ø]3, heord V2, hwīl [s]1, lār V1, lagu [s]1 [n]9 V3, lēode [n]4, lufu (n)6 V2, mēd [n]4, mearc [n]9, miht [s]3 [n]1, myrgþ [s]4 [n]3, nīed V1, pīn [n]13, rūn [s]5, sagu (n)4 V1, sāwol [n]3 V2, sceaft (s)1 [n]2 V1, sealf [n]1, siht [n]2, sorg [s]1, sprǣc [n]1, stǣger [n]1, strengþ [n]2, stund V1, synn [n]25 V2, talu [n]1, tīd V4, trēowþ [s]1 [n]1, þēod V1, wǣd V1, weard [n]1, wiht [s]6 V1, wund [n]6, wynn [n]1, wyrd [s]1

Masc-Ø brōþor [n]1, fæder [s]5

Neut-Ø anginn [s]1, bān [s]6 ø2, bearn ø4, bedd [s]1, bodig [s]3, bold [s]3, cnēow [n]2, cynd [s]1 (V)1, cynn [s]2 [V]1 ø4, cynrēd [s]2, dēor ø3, fēg [V]1, fers (s)2, flǣsc [s]1, gēar [s]6 ø7, gift [s]1 (V)3, gōd [n]1 ø2, hīw [s]1 ø1, hlēor [s]1, hocor [s]4, hors ø1, hrīþer [n]1, hūs [s]9, hwēol [s]14 ø2, īsen [s]1, lāc [s]1, lǣden [s]2, land [s]3, lēaf [s]1, lēoht [V]1, līc [s]1, limp ø2, marc [s]1, mōd [s]1, mōt [s]2, nebb [s]4, pund [s]1, rād [V]1, riht [V]1, sǣd [s]1, sār [s]1, scēap ø2, scrūd [s]1, searo [n]1, spell [s]1, swinc [s]10 ø1, ticcen [s]6, tintreg (n)1, trēow [n]14, tungol [n]1, þing [s]67 ø58, wǣpen [s]1 [n]6 [V]3, wǣter [s]14, weder [s]1, weorc [s]25 ø1, werod [s]1, wīf [s]1, wīl [s]1, wīn [s]3, winter (V)4, witt [s]24 ø1, wōh [V]1, word [s]57 ø83, wundor [s]15

Fem-Ø dohtor [n]3, sweostor [n]64

Masc-M -ende [V]2 M2, fēond (s)3 [ø]7, fōt M15, frēond (s)1 [ø]14, mann M187, tōþ M5

Masc-M cild [n]9

Fem-M bōc [s]6 M4, brōc M1, burg [s]1, gāt M6

B.5.6 PFP 290000 (C13b South-West Midland)

TEXT INFO TEXT: ##2, 3, 10, 126, 158, 187, 214, 218, 220, 222, 229, 238, 246, 247, 248, 249, 264, 271, 278, 1100, 2002

TOKENS Nominative/Accusative Plurals 980 (165), Syncretised Dative/Prepositional Plurals 159 (40), Unsyncretised Dative/Prepositional Plurals 172 (185), Syncretism Rate 0.48 (0.18), Genitive Plurals 75 (26), Total of Plurals 1386 (416)

TYPES AND RATES

	s	n	V	ø	M	TOTAL
TYPES	160 (193)	54 (60)	29 (32)	23 (23)	3 (3)	269 (311)
RATE	0.59 (0.62)	0.2 (0.19)	0.11 (0.1)	0.086 (0.074)	0.011 (0.0097)	1 (1)
SPREAD RATE	1.7 (2.1)	1.4 (1.5)	0.41 (0.46)	0.43 (0.43)	0.23 (0.23)	—

Masc-S -ere s9, -ing s7, -ling s4, æcer s1, apostol s6, beorn s2, biscop s1, blōstm [n]2 (V)4, brand s1, bridd s12, Bryttas s5, castel s1, cēap s1, ceorl s4, clāþ s4, cleric s3, clifer s10, clūd s2, cniht s9 [V]2, cræft s7, cwide s1, cyning s16, dæg s7, dēaw s1, dēofol s1 [n]6, disc s3, dōm s7, dynt s3, earm s9, engel s17, eorl s2, finger s1, fisc s2, flocc s4, forst s2, fox s2, fugel s10, gār [n]1, gāst s2, gylt s9, hafoc s2, heorot s2, hierde s2, horn s9, hund s8, lēc s2, locc s1, lust s8, munuc s3, nægl s3, pæþ s6, pening s4, pic s2, pīc s2, post s1, prēost s3, pytt s3, ræd s3, sang s7, scield s2, sīþ s1 [V]1, smiþ s2, snægl s2, solor s1, sott s3, stæf s3, stān s6, stede (V)2, storm s1, stot s2, strēam s1, swān s1, sweng s2, tēar s11, top s2, tūr s2, þēaw s6, þegn s6, þēof s5, þōht s5, þorn s5, þræl s2, wæg s4, wāg s3, weall s4 [V]1, wine s1, wrenc s2, wulf s2, wyrm s17

Masc-N assa n2, bera [s]1, cempa n1, crāwa [V]4, dropa n1, fēra n2 [V]1, frogga n1, hunta n1, ieldra n2 [V]1, lēo [s]2, mūga n1, nama [s]1, oxa [V]2, rēfa n1, snaca n4, spāca n1, steorra n1 [V]2, swica n1 [V]1, wræcca [s]3

Neut-N ēage n13 [V]1, ēare [s]1 n2, wange n1

Fem-N bīeme n2, hielde [s]1, hlǣfdige [s]9, mæsse [s]4 n5, mȳderce [s]1, nǣdre n4, sīde [s]1, tunne n2, ūle [s]1, wīce [V]4

Masc-V feld [s]1, sunu [s]1 [n]1

Neut-V bed [s]2, bod [s]1 [n]1, geat [s]3, græf [s]1, lim [s]1, mægden [s]10, rīce [s]1, scip [s]2 [n]2, slæd [s]1, spere [s]1 [n]1, þyrel [s]3

Fem-V -ing [s]2, -ung [s]3, -waru (n)1, bend (s)5, bliss [n]2, caru [s]1, dǣd [s]5 [n]2 V4, duru [n]1, gierd [s]1, glōf [n]1, grīn [s]1 V1, hǣs [s]2 V1, hand [s]1 [n]6 V1, healf [ø]1, henn [n]2, heord [s]1, hind [s]1, lagu [n]4 V4, lār [s]1, lēode [n]1, lufu (n)1, mearc [n]1, miht [n]1, mīl V1, myrgþ [s]2, pīn [s]4 [n]3, rūn V2, sagu [s]1, sāwol [s]3 [n]11 V6, sceaft (s)1, seono [s]1, sorg [s]1 [n]3, synn [s]15 [n]14, talu [s]1, þēod [s]1, wǣd [n]2, wiht [s]6 V2, wund [s]3 [n]4, ȳþ [n]2

Masc-Ø brōþor [n]6

Neut-Ø bān [s]2 ø2, bearn [s]1, bereærn [s]1, brēost [V]1, būr [s]1, cnēow [s]1, corn [s]1 ø1, dēor ø2, dor ø1, gēar [V]1 ø4, gift [s]2, gōd [V]4, hors ø4, hrīs [s]1 ø1, hūs [s]3, lac ø1, land [s]1 ø1, lēaf [s]6, līf [s]1, sǣd [s]4, scēap ø4, spell [s]1, sweord [s]1 ø1, swinc ø1, tācen [n]1, trēow [n]5, tron [n]1, þēoh [s]1, þing [s]2 [V]1 ø6, wǣpen [n]2 [V]2, wedd [s]1, weder [s]1, wēod [n]1, weorc [s]17 ø1, wīf [s]4 ø1, winter [s]1 (V)2 ø4, word [s]34 [n]1 ø9

Masc-M fēond (s)14 [ø]8, fōt M7, frēond (s)5 [ø]17, mann [ø]1 M169, tōþ M4

Masc-M cild [n]18 [V]1

Fem-M mūs [ø]4, niht [s]2 [ø]2

B.5.7 PFP 300000 (C14a South-West Midland)

TEXT INFO TEXT: ##125, 27000

TOKENS Nominative/Accusative Plurals 72 (19), Syncretised Dative/Prepositional Plurals 33 (5), Unsyncretised Dative/Prepositional Plurals 1 (16), Syncretism Rate 0.97 (0.24), Genitive Plurals 2 (0), Total of Plurals 108 (40)

TYPES AND RATES

	s	n	V	ø	M	TOTAL
TYPES	28 (32)	2 (2)	3 (3)	1 (1)	2 (2)	36 (40)
RATE	0.78 (0.8)	0.056 (0.05)	0.083 (0.075)	0.028 (0.025)	0.056 (0.05)	1 (1)
SPREAD RATE	1.9 (2.1)	0.5 (0.5)	0.27 (0.27)	0.33 (0.33)	0.67 (0.67)	—

Masc-S -ere $s1$, āþ $s1$, cleric $s1$, cnīf $s1$, cniht $s11$, dæg $s3$, dynt $s2$, earm $s7$, fugel $s1$, hring $s1$, hund $s2$, nægl $s1$, prēost $s1$, tēar $s3$, þegn $s1$
Masc-N fēolaga $[s]1$, fēra $n9$, tīma $[V]1$
Fem-N belle $[V]1$
Masc-V Saracene $[s]4$, sunu $[s]4$
Neut-V dæl $[s]2$, geat $[s]1$, græs $[s]1$, mægden $[s]3$, rib $[s]1$, scip $[s]1$
Fem-V hand $[s]1$ $V1$, wund $[s]1$
Neut-Ø cnēow $[s]1$, winter $ø1$, word $[s]6$
Masc-M fōt $M1$, mann $M5$
Masc-M cild $[n]4$

B.6 PFPs of Southwestern Text Group

B.6.1 PFP 310000 (C12b Southwestern)

TEXT INFO TEXT: #63
TOKENS Nominative/Accusative Plurals 8 (0), Syncretised Dative/Prepositional Plurals 2 (0), Unsyncretised Dative/Prepositional Plurals 1 (0), Syncretism Rate 0.67 (NA), Genitive Plurals 1 (0), Total of Plurals 12 (0)

TYPES AND RATES

	s	n	V	ø	M	TOTAL
TYPES	1 (1)	3 (3)	2 (2)	2 (2)	0 (0)	8 (8)
RATE	0.13 (0.13)	0.38 (0.38)	0.25 (0.25)	0.25 (0.25)	0 (0)	1 (1)
SPREAD RATE	NA (NA)	1.5 (1.5)	NA (NA)	0.4 (0.4)	0 (0)	—

Masc-N ǣrendraca $[V]1$, ieldra $n1$
Masc-Ø brōþor $[n]1$
Neut-Ø þing $[s]1$, winter $(V)1$, word $ø3$
Fem-Ø sweostor $[n]1$
Masc-M mann $[ø]1$

B.6.2 PFP 320000 (C13a Southwestern)

TEXT INFO TEXT: ##144, 156, 157, 26000
TOKENS Nominative/Accusative Plurals 83 (22), Syncretised Dative/Prepositional Plurals 33 (8), Unsyncretised Dative/Prepositional Plurals 12 (12), Syncretism Rate 0.73 (0.4), Genitive Plurals 15 (0), Total of Plurals 143 (42)

Appendix B 211

TYPES AND RATES

	s	n	V	ø	M	TOTAL
TYPES	30 (33)	4 (4)	4 (4)	3 (3)	1 (1)	42 (45)
RATE	0.71 (0.73)	0.095 (0.089)	0.095 (0.089)	0.071 (0.067)	0.024 (0.022)	1 (1)
SPREAD RATE	1.9 (2.1)	0.67 (0.67)	0.36 (0.36)	0.5 (0.5)	0.33 (0.33)	—

Masc-S -ere s1, āþ s1, clāþ s1, cniht s15, cyning s1, dæg s3, dynt s3, earm s5, finger s1, fugel s1, hund s2, nægl s1, stān s1, tēar s4, þegn s6 [V]1

Masc-N fēolaga [s]3, fēra n7, tīma [V]1

Fem-N belle [s]1, cirice n1, mæsse [s]1

Masc-V Saracene [s]3, sunu [s]2

Neut-V dæl [s]2, geat [s]1, mægden [s]3, rib [s]1, scip [s]2, spere [s]1, writ [s]1

Fem-V hand V1, wund [s]1

Neut-Ø cnēow [s]2, gēar ø1, riht [n]1 [V]1, þing ø1, word [s]5

Masc-M mann [ø]1 M10

Masc-M cild [n]4

B.6.3 PFP 330000 (C13b Southwestern)

TEXT INFO TEXT: ##163, 263

TOKENS Nominative/Accusative Plurals 3 (1), Syncretised Dative/Prepositional Plurals 1 (0), Unsyncretised Dative/Prepositional Plurals 1 (1), Syncretism Rate 0.5 (0), Genitive Plurals 1 (0), Total of Plurals 6 (2)

TYPES AND RATES

	s	n	V	ø	M	TOTAL
TYPES	2 (2)	1 (1)	0 (0)	0 (0)	1 (1)	4 (4)
RATE	0.5 (0.5)	0.25 (0.25)	0 (0)	0 (0)	0.25 (0.25)	1 (1)
SPREAD RATE	2 (2)	1 (1)	0 (0)	NA (NA)	1 (1)	—

Masc-S nægl s1
Masc-N fāh n1
Fem-V synn [s]1
Masc-M fōt M1

B.6.4 PFP 340000 (C14a Southwestern)

TEXT INFO TEXT: ##140, 258, 286

TOKENS Nominative/Accusative Plurals 430 (14), Syncretised Dative/Prepositional Plurals 134 (4), Unsyncretised Dative/Prepositional Plurals 27 (15), Syncretism Rate 0.83 (0.21), Genitive Plurals 16 (0), Total of Plurals 607 (33)

TYPES AND RATES

	s	n	V	ø	M	TOTAL
TYPES	69 (100)	24 (26)	9 (11)	9 (9)	3 (3)	114 (149)
RATE	0.6 (0.67)	0.21 (0.17)	0.079 (0.074)	0.079 (0.06)	0.026 (0.02)	1 (1)
SPREAD RATE	1.5 (2.2)	1.6 (1.7)	0.38 (0.46)	0.43 (0.43)	0.38 (0.38)	—

Masc-S -ere s2, -ing s2, æppel [n]1, apostol s6, belg s1, bōg s1, bulluc s3, canon s2, clāþ s2, cleric s6, clūd [n]1, cniht s12, crūc [ø]2, cyrnel s4, dæg s24, dēofol [n]10, discipul s7, earm s2, engel s7, fēfer s1, fisc s2 [ø]4, fugel s7, gimm s1, god s5, gylt s2, gyrdel s1, hamor s1, harm s1, hlāf s2, læce s1, magister s5, munuc s39, nægl s3, pening s5, prēost s1, sīþ [V]1, smiþ s1, stæf s1, stæpe s3, stān s3, stede s2, tapor s14, þēof s3, þorn s1, wiell (n)1

Masc-N bula n1, fāh n2, fēolaga [s]7, hālga [V]1, oxa n1, scrēawa n9, stēora [s]1, tīma [V]1, wræcca [s]2

Neut-N ēage n5

Fem-N āncre [s]1, mæsse n2, more n1, tunge n1, ūle [s]2

Masc-V sunu [s]3

Neut-V bed [s]1 [n]3, geat [s]1, lim [s]5, scip [s]1

Fem-V bend (s)1, brēr [s]1, dǣd V1, gierd [n]8, glōf [n]1, grāp [s]5, hǣs [s]1, hand [n]4 V1, mīl V1, rōd [n]1, sāwol [n]1, segen [n]1, seono [n]1, strǣt [s]1, synn [s]1, þrāg [s]1, wund [n]1

Masc-Ø mōnaþ [s]1

Neut-Ø bān [s]4, cnēow [n]1, fers (s)1 ø1, gēar ø20, gōd [V]1, lēaf [s]1, līc [s]1, riht [V]1, scēap ø7, spell [s]2, trēow [n]2, þing [s]1, wæter [s]1, wēod [s]1, weorc [s]1, wīc (V)2, winter ø1, word [s]3 ø2

Masc-M fōt M17, frēond (s)1 [ø]2, mann M104, tōþ M1

Masc-M cild [n]2

Fem-M bōc [s]2, niht [ø]2

B.6.5 PFP 350000 (C14b Southwestern)

TEXT INFO TEXT: #24000

TOKENS Nominative/Accusative Plurals 576 (22), Syncretised Dative/Prepositional Plurals 258 (25), Unsyncretised Dative/Prepositional Plurals 16 (15), Syncretism Rate 0.94 (0.63), Genitive Plurals 0 (1), Total of Plurals 850 (63)

TYPES AND RATES

	s	n	V	ø	M	TOTAL
TYPES	112 (178)	6 (7)	2 (2)	8 (9)	4 (4)	132 (200)
RATE	0.85 (0.89)	0.045 (0.035)	0.015 (0.01)	0.061 (0.045)	0.03 (0.02)	1 (1)
SPREAD RATE	2.2 (3.6)	0.24 (0.28)	0.065 (0.065)	0.4 (0.45)	0.67 (0.67)	—

Masc-S -ere s1, -ling s3, abbod s1, brǣw s1, capun s2, circul s1, clāþ s5, cleric s1, cniht s27 [ø]1, cocc s1, cyning s16, dæg s9, disc s1, dynt s3, earm s7, fæþm [V]1, finger s1, god s5, guttas s6, hearm s1, helm s15, heorot s1 [ø]1, hlāf s1, hlāford s26, hōc s1, horn s6, hrycg s1, hund s1, hyll s2, læce s1, magister s1, munuc s1, nægl s10, prior s1, ræfter s1, scield s10, scōh [n]1, sīþ s1, stæf s1, stān s4, stede s1, tūn s2, þearm s1, þēof s2, wæg s3, weall s2, wulf s1, wyrm s1

Masc-N boga [s]1, fāh [s]8 n2, fēolaga [s]18, freca [s]1, gealga [s]5, hnecca [s]1, hosa n1, lēo [s]4, lippa n1, nama [s]1, scrēawa [s]1, spearca [s]2, spura [s]1, stēda [s]7, tīma [s]1, winna [s]1

Neut-N ēage n3

Fem-N cēace [s]1, cuppe [s]1, force [s]2, heorte [s]2, hlǣfdige [s]1, nunne [s]1, sīde [s]2

Masc-V feld [s]5, Saracene [s]85, sculdor [s]3, sumor [s]3

Neut-V bed [s]2, gamen [s]1, geat [s]3, hēafod [s]10, mægden [s]5, rib [s]1, spere [s]5

Fem-V -ing [s]1, -ung [s]1 [ø]1, brū [s]1, byrd [s]3, cǣg [s]2, dǣd [s]7, fetor [s]1, glōf [s]1, hand [s]9 V1 [ø]1, miht [s]2, mīl [n]1, pīn [s]1, sagu [s]2, talu [s]2, wǣd [s]1, weard (s)2, wund [s]1

Masc-Ø mōnaþ [s]3

Neut-Ø bān [s]1, bodig [s]1, brēost (s)1, folc [s]1, gēar [s]1 ø2, hundred [s]1 ø2, land [s]1, lēaf [s]1, līf [s]2, pund ø1, sweord [s]9, trēow [s]1, þing ø6, wǣpen [s]1, weorc [s]1, witt [s]1, word [s]7

Masc-M fōt M15, frēond (s)2, mann M80, tōþ M4

Fem-M furh [s]1, gōs M1

B.6.6 PFP 360000 (C15a Southwestern)

TEXT INFO TEXT: #23000

TOKENS Nominative/Accusative Plurals 290 (16), Syncretised Dative/Prepositional Plurals 90 (4), Unsyncretised Dative/Prepositional Plurals 13 (3), Syncretism Rate 0.87 (0.57), Genitive Plurals 0 (0), Total of Plurals 393 (23)

TYPES AND RATES

	s	n	V	ø	M	TOTAL
TYPES	67 (112)	5 (5)	4 (4)	2 (3)	2 (2)	80 (126)
RATE	0.84 (0.89)	0.063 (0.04)	0.05 (0.032)	0.025 (0.024)	0.025 (0.016)	1 (1)
SPREAD RATE	2.2 (3.6)	1 (1)	0.18 (0.18)	0.12 (0.18)	0.4 (0.4)	—

Masc-S -dōm s3, -ere s2, æppel [n]3, alter s1, biscop s3, bridd s1, Bryttas s4, castel s1, clāþ s13, cleric s2, cniht s1, crūc s1, cyning s7, dæg s2, earm s2, engel s9, eorl s4, finger s1, fugel s1, hlāford s12, hwelp s5, Iotas s2, martyr s1, munuc s3, Pehtas s1, prēost s3, scilling s1, Scottas s1, tūn s1, þēof s2, þrǣl s1

Masc-N nama [s]1, tīma [s]2

Fem-N cirice [s]2, hlǣfdige [s]15, mæsse [s]2

Masc-V Dene [s]6, Engle [s]1, Seaxe [s]7, sunu [s]4

Neut-V bed [s]1, geat [s]1, lim [s]3, mægden [s]8

Fem-V -ung [s]2, candel [s]2, culfer (n)2, dǣd [s]2, glēd [s]2, hand [s]1 V1, lagu [s]2, miht [s]1, myrgþ [s]1, synn [s]2, witnes V1, wucu [s]1, wund [s]3

Masc-Ø mōnaþ [s]1

Neut-Ø gēar [s]2 [V]19, hūs [s]1, land [s]7, mynster [s]1, þing [s]3 ø5, weorc [s]2, wīf [s]1, winter (V)2 ø4, witt [s]1, word [s]5, wrang [s]1

Fem-Ø dohtor [n]1, sweostor [n]8

Masc-M frēond (s)2, mann M42, tōþ M1

Masc-M cild [n]4

Fem-M niht [s]2

B.7 PFPs of Southeastern Text Group

B.7.1 PFP 370000 (C13a Southeastern)

TEXT INFO TEXT: ##8, 17, 67, 142

TOKENS Nominative/Accusative Plurals 146 (17), Syncretised Dative/Prepositional Plurals 38 (3), Unsyncretised Dative/Prepositional Plurals 12 (11), Syncretism Rate 0.76 (0.21), Genitive Plurals 6 (1), Total of Plurals 202 (32)

TYPES AND RATES

	s	n	V	ø	M	TOTAL
TYPES	38 (46)	14 (14)	7 (8)	7 (7)	1 (1)	67 (76)
RATE	0.57 (0.6)	0.21 (0.18)	0.1 (0.11)	0.1 (0.092)	0.015 (0.013)	1 (1)
SPREAD RATE	1.7 (2)	1.4 (1.4)	0.3 (0.35)	0.88 (0.88)	0.33 (0.33)	—

Masc-S -ere s4, -ing s6, -ling s1, apostol s2, cleric s1, crōg s1, cyning s6, dæg s2, dēofol [n]1, discipul s4, earm s1, engel s2, eorl s1, fisc [ø]1, fugel s1, manslieht s1, nægl s1, strēam s1, tēar s2, þorn s1, wæg s1, weall s1, wine s1
Masc-N efeta n1, fēolaga [s]1, ieldra n1, offerenda [s]2, snaca n1, steorra n1
Neut-N ēage n2
Fem-N heorte [s]1, hlǣfdige [s]1, nǣdre n1
Neut-V fæt [n]2, writ [s]1, yfel [s]1
Fem-V -ung [s]2 V1, bend (s)1, dǣd [n]2, hǣs [n]2, lagu [n]1 V1, lufu V1, mēd [s]1, nīed [s]2, pīn [n]1, sāwol [n]1 V1, stund V1, synn [s]1 [n]7 V2, tīd [s]1 V1, woruld [s]1
Neut-Ø gēar ø2, gōd [s]1, land [s]2, þing [s]6 ø2, weorc [s]14 ø1, word ø1
Masc-M fēond [ø]2, frēond [ø]2, mann M40

B.7.2 PFP 380000 (C14a Southeastern)

TEXT INFO TEXT: ##291, 21000
TOKENS Nominative/Accusative Plurals 334 (0), Syncretised Dative/Prepositional Plurals 201 (0), Unsyncretised Dative/Prepositional Plurals 23 (0), Syncretism Rate 0.9 (NA), Genitive Plurals 14 (0), Total of Plurals 572 (0)

TYPES AND RATES

	s	n	V	ø	M	TOTAL
TYPES	86 (157)	11 (12)	2 (3)	6 (6)	2 (2)	107 (180)
RATE	0.8 (0.87)	0.1 (0.067)	0.019 (0.017)	0.056 (0.033)	0.019 (0.011)	1 (1)
SPREAD RATE	2 (3.6)	1.1 (1.2)	0.087 (0.13)	0.24 (0.24)	0.4 (0.4)	—

Masc-S -ere s16, -hād s3, -ing s1, -ling s2, apostol s2, bōg s16, bydel s2, capun s1, castel s1, cleric s2, cniht s1, cwide s1, cyning s1, dæg s3, dǣl s2, discipul s2, earm s1, engel s3, god s1, gylt s1, harm s2, healh s1, healoc s1, hearm s1, hlāford s4, horn s4, hyll s1, lust s2, nēahgebūr s4, pening s7, pott s1, prafost s1, scipe s1, sīþ [V]5, stæpe s5, stīpel s1, tūn s1, tūr s1, þanc s1, þēaw s1, þēof s5, þōht s4, wind s1, wulf s1
Masc-N hālga n2, rēfa n1, willa [s]1, wræcca [s]1, wuna [s]2
Fem-N bēce [s]1, cirice n1, cuppe [s]2, mæsse n1, wicce n1
Masc-V wudu [s]1
Neut-V fær V1, hēafod [s]5, twig [s]1
Fem-V -ing [s]26, -ness [s]3, bēn [s]2, dǣd [s]6, giefu [s]3, hǣs [s]8, hand [n]1, healf [s]1, henn [n]1, hīehþ [s]1, mēd [s]1, nīed [s]5, sāwol [s]3 [n]1, scamu [s]1, sorg [s]1, synn [s]18 [n]2, witnes [s]2
Masc-Ø fæder [s]5
Neut-Ø bereærn [s]1, bodig [s]1, corn [s]1, cwēad [s]3, gēar ø1, gift [s]4, gōd [s]46 ø2, hors ø3, lāc [s]2, lǣn [s]1, land [s]4, scēap ø1, swīn ø1, tācen [n]3, trēow [s]1, þing [s]18 ø1, weorc [s]15, weorþ [s]2, wīf [s]1, witt [s]1, word [s]2, wrang [s]1
Masc-M fēond (s)1, fōt M5, frēond (s)2, mann M29
Masc-M cild [n]3

B.7.3 PFP 390000 (C15a Southeastern)

TEXT INFO TEXT: #20000

TOKENS Nominative/Accusative Plurals 38 (0), Syncretised Dative/Prepositional Plurals 12 (0), Unsyncretised Dative/Prepositional Plurals 14 (0), Syncretism Rate 0.46 (NA), Genitive Plurals 0 (0), Total of Plurals 64 (0)

TYPES AND RATES

	s	n	V	$\emptyset$	M	TOTAL
TYPES	12 (21)	2 (2)	2 (2)	0 (0)	0 (0)	16 (25)
RATE	0.75 (0.84)	0.13 (0.08)	0.13 (0.08)	0 (0)	0 (0)	1 (1)
SPREAD RATE	2 (3.5)	1 (1)	0.5 (0.5)	0 (0)	NA (NA)	—

Masc-S -ere s3, abbod s1, hund s1, pening s2, sīþ s1 [V]4

Masc-N tīma [s]2 [V]2

Neut-V bed [s]1, col [s]1

Fem-V cǣg [s]1, sāwol [s]1

Masc-Ø brōþor [n]6

Neut-Ø gōd [s]5, þing [s]2

Fem-Ø sweostor [n]7

Appendix C Panchronic Summary of Plural Formation Transfer

The tables and graphs below provide a panchronic summary of the text groups examined in Section 3.2. The first five pages give the TYPE RATES of the five plural types (s, n, V, $\emptyset$, and M in this order), while the second five pages give the SPREAD RATES. Discussion related to the summary given here is found in Section 3.2.9.

Table C.1: Rate for -s

	C9a	C9b	C10a	C10b	C11a	C11b	C12a	C12b	C13a	C13b	C14a	C14b	C15a
N	—	—	0.36	—	—	—	—	—	0.91	0.84	0.8	—	—
NEM	—	—	—	—	—	—	—	0.82	—	0.75	1	—	—
SEM	—	—	—	—	—	—	0.6	0.58	0.75	0.74	0.77	—	—
NWM	—	—	—	—	—	—	—	—	0.8	0.95	—	—	—
SWM	0.3	0.34	0.32	—	—	—	—	0.38	0.53	0.59	0.78	—	—
SW	—	—	—	—	—	—	—	0.13	0.71	0.5	0.6	0.85	0.84
SE	—	—	—	—	—	—	—	—	0.57	—	0.8	—	0.75

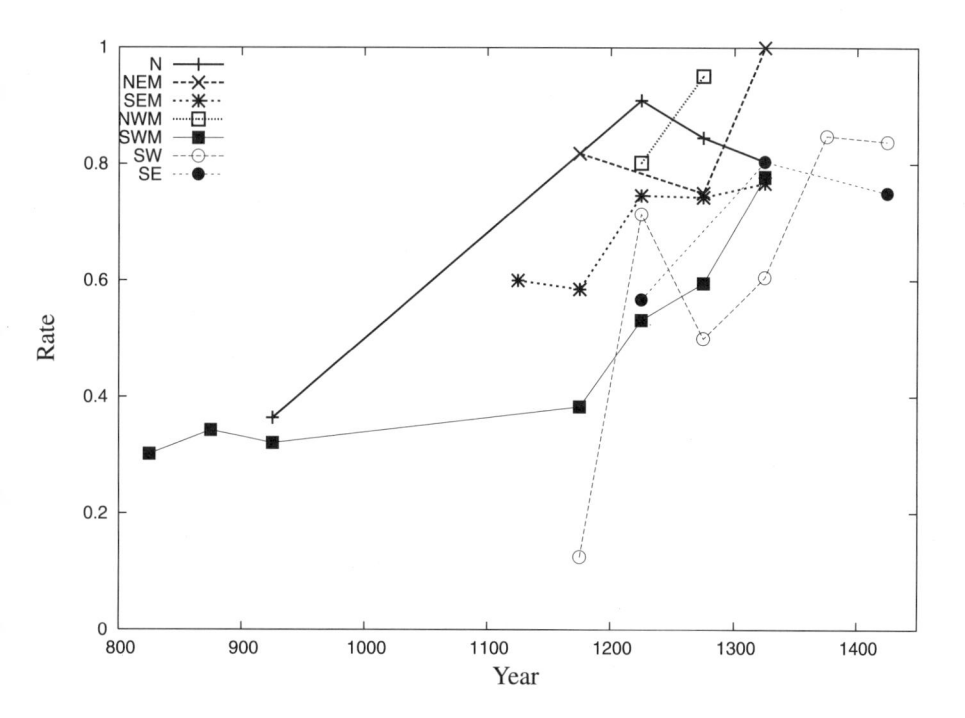

Figure C.1: Rate for -s

Table C.2: Rate for -n

	C9a	C9b	C10a	C10b	C11a	C11b	C12a	C12b	C13a	C13b	C14a	C14b	C15a
N	—	—	0.0051	—	—	—	—	—	0	0.019	0.01	—	—
NEM	—	—	—	—	—	—	—	0.021	—	0	0	—	—
SEM	—	—	—	—	—	—	0.027	0.14	0.16	0.086	0.047	—	—
NWM	—	—	—	—	—	—	—	—	0.03	0	—	—	—
SWM	0.13	0.11	0.068	—	—	—	—	0.24	0.27	0.2	0.056	—	—
SW	—	—	—	—	—	—	—	0.38	0.095	0.25	0.21	0.045	0.063
SE	—	—	—	—	—	—	—	—	0.21	—	0.1	—	0.13

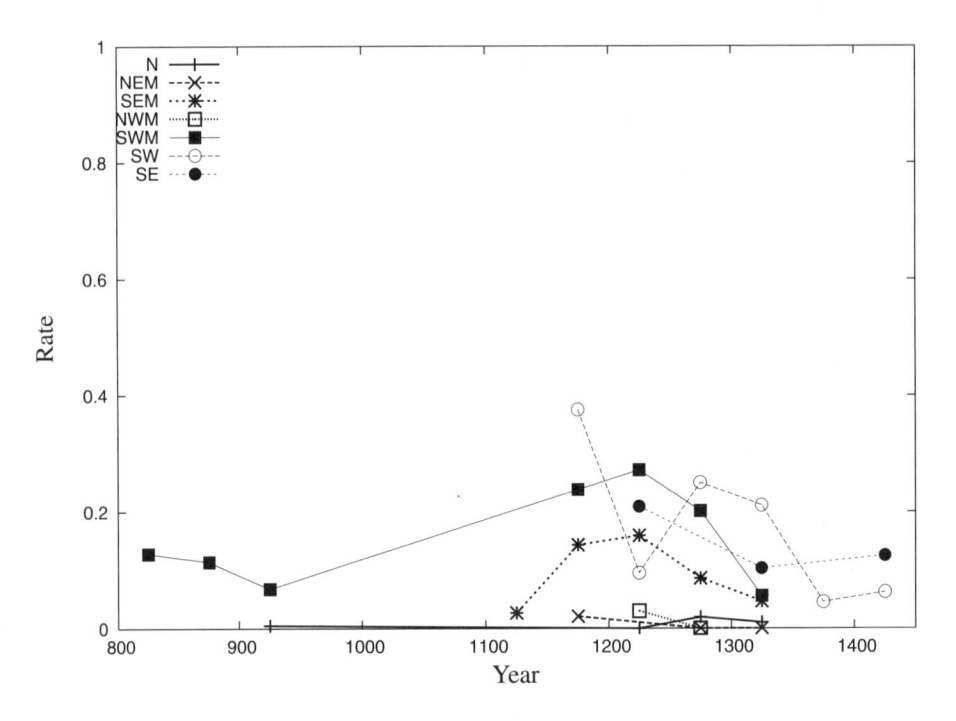

Figure C.2: Rate for -n

Table C.3: Rate for -V

	C9a	C9b	C10a	C10b	C11a	C11b	C12a	C12b	C13a	C13b	C14a	C14b	C15a
N	—	—	0.5	—	—	—	—	—	0	0.039	0.041	—	—
NEM	—	—	—	—	—	—	—	0.078	—	0	0	—	—
SEM	—	—	—	—	—	—	0.2	0.19	0.048	0.089	0.047	—	—
NWM	—	—	—	—	—	—	—	—	0.084	0.024	—	—	—
SWM	0.28	0.37	0.36	—	—	—	—	0.23	0.13	0.11	0.083	—	—
SW	—	—	—	—	—	—	—	0.25	0.095	0	0.079	0.015	0.05
SE	—	—	—	—	—	—	—	—	0.1	—	0.019	—	0.13

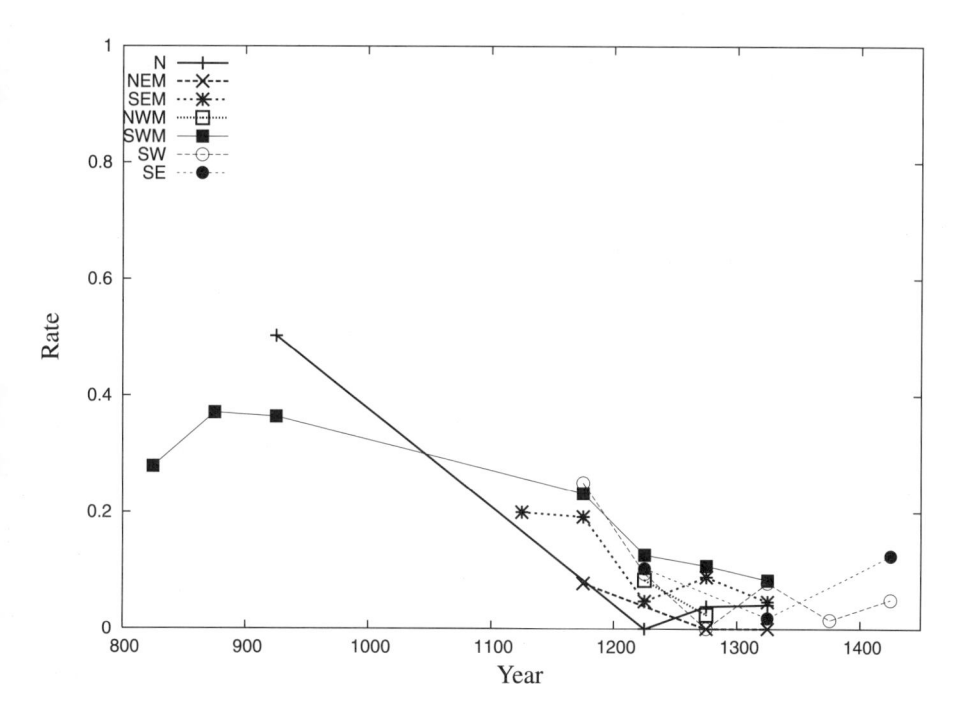

Figure C.3: Rate for -V

Table C.4: Rate for -∅

	C9a	C9b	C10a	C10b	C11a	C11b	C12a	C12b	C13a	C13b	C14a	C14b	C15a
N	—	—	0.12	—	—	—	—	—	0	0.065	0.1	—	—
NEM	—	—	—	—	—	—	—	0.063	—	0	0	—	—
SEM	—	—	—	—	—	—	0.13	0.066	0.016	0.064	0.07	—	—
NWM	—	—	—	—	—	—	—	—	0.06	0	—	—	—
SWM	0.22	0.11	0.22	—	—	—	—	0.11	0.053	0.086	0.028	—	—
SW	—	—	—	—	—	—	—	0.25	0.071	0	0.079	0.061	0.025
SE	—	—	—	—	—	—	—	—	0.1	—	0.056	—	0

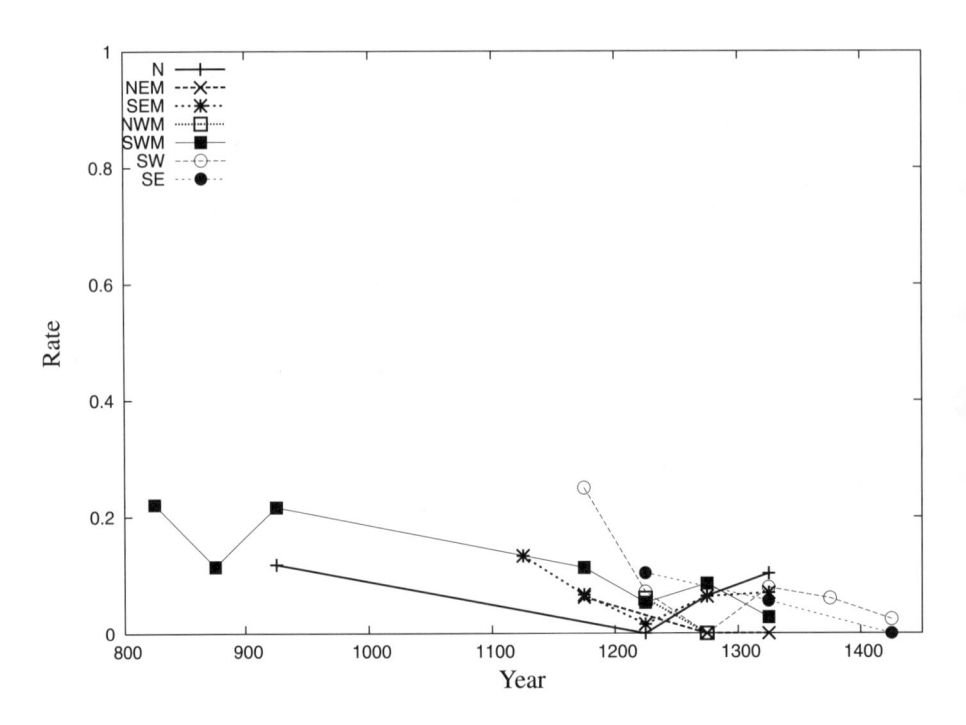

Figure C.4: Rate for -∅

Table C.5: Rate for Minor Plural Types

	C9a	C9b	C10a	C10b	C11a	C11b	C12a	C12b	C13a	C13b	C14a	C14b	C15a
N	—	—	0.01	—	—	—	—	—	0.091	0.032	0.041	—	—
NEM	—	—	—	—	—	—	—	0.021	—	0.25	0	—	—
SEM	—	—	—	—	—	—	0.04	0.014	0.032	0.019	0.07	—	—
NWM	—	—	—	—	—	—	—	—	0.024	0.024	—	—	—
SWM	0.07	0.057	0.031	—	—	—	—	0.035	0.016	0.011	0.056	—	—
SW	—	—	—	—	—	—	—	0	0.024	0.25	0.026	0.03	0.025
SE	—	—	—	—	—	—	—	—	0.015	—	0.019	—	0

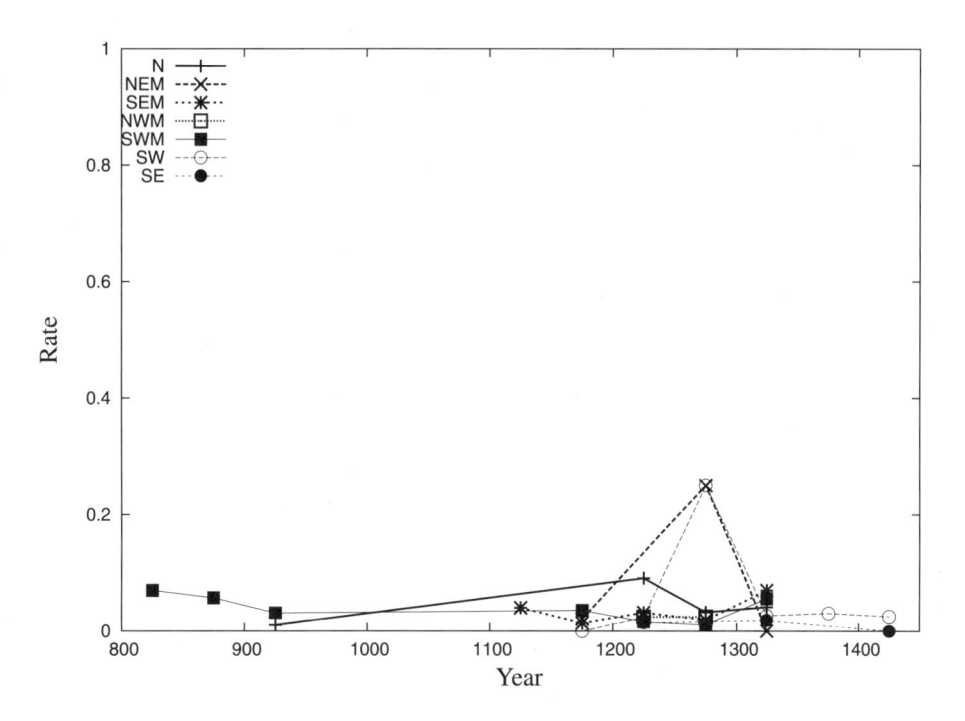

Figure C.5: Rate for Minor Plural Types

Table C.6: Spread Rate for -s

	C9a	C9b	C10a	C10b	C11a	C11b	C12a	C12b	C13a	C13b	C14a	C14b	C15a
N	—	—	1.1	—	—	—	—	—	—	2.5	2.3	—	—
NEM	—	—	—	—	—	—	—	2.5	—	3	1	—	—
SEM	—	—	—	—	—	—	1.3	1.8	2	2.1	1.6	—	—
NWM	—	—	—	—	—	—	—	—	2.7	2	—	—	—
SWM	0.93	1	1.1	—	—	—	—	1.1	1.7	1.7	1.9	—	—
SW	—	—	—	—	—	—	—	—	1.8	2	1.5	2.2	2.2
SE	—	—	—	—	—	—	—	—	1.6	—	2	—	2

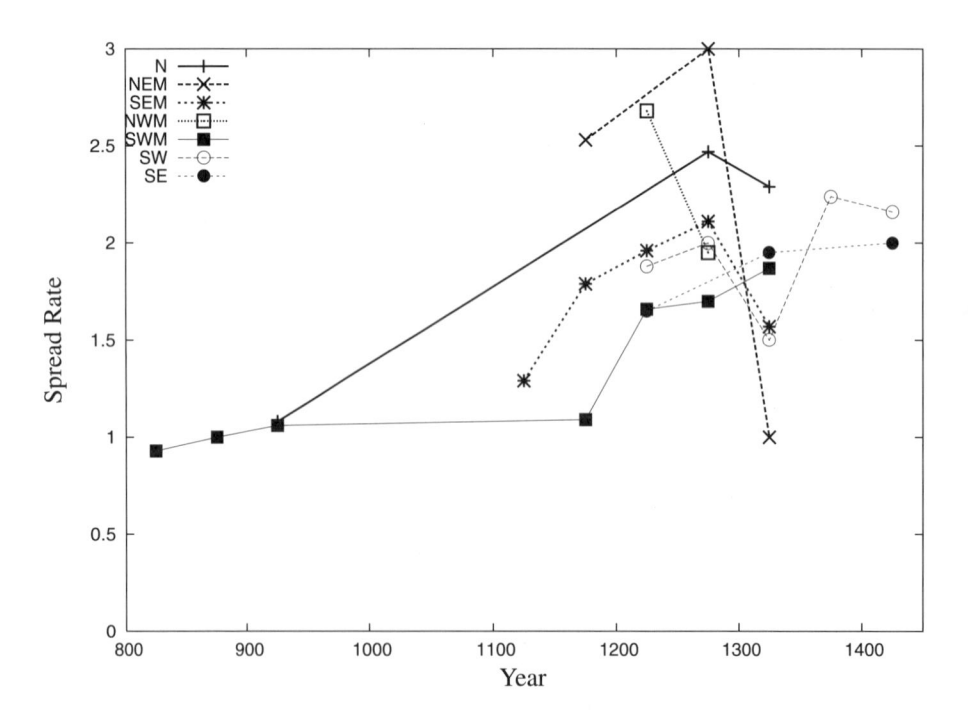

Figure C.6: Spread Rate for -s

Table C.7: Spread Rate for -n

	C9a	C9b	C10a	C10b	C11a	C11b	C12a	C12b	C13a	C13b	C14a	C14b	C15a
N	—	—	0.05	—	—	—	—	—	0	0.14	0.077	—	—
NEM	—	—	—	—	—	—	—	0.15	—	—	—	—	—
SEM	—	—	—	—	—	—	0.25	0.76	3.3	0.47	0.5	—	—
NWM	—	—	—	—	—	—	—	—	0.19	0	—	—	—
SWM	1.2	0.8	0.42	—	—	—	—	1.5	1.5	1.4	0.5	—	—
SW	—	—	—	—	—	—	—	1.5	0.67	1	1.6	0.24	1
SE	—	—	—	—	—	—	—	—	1.4	—	1.1	—	1

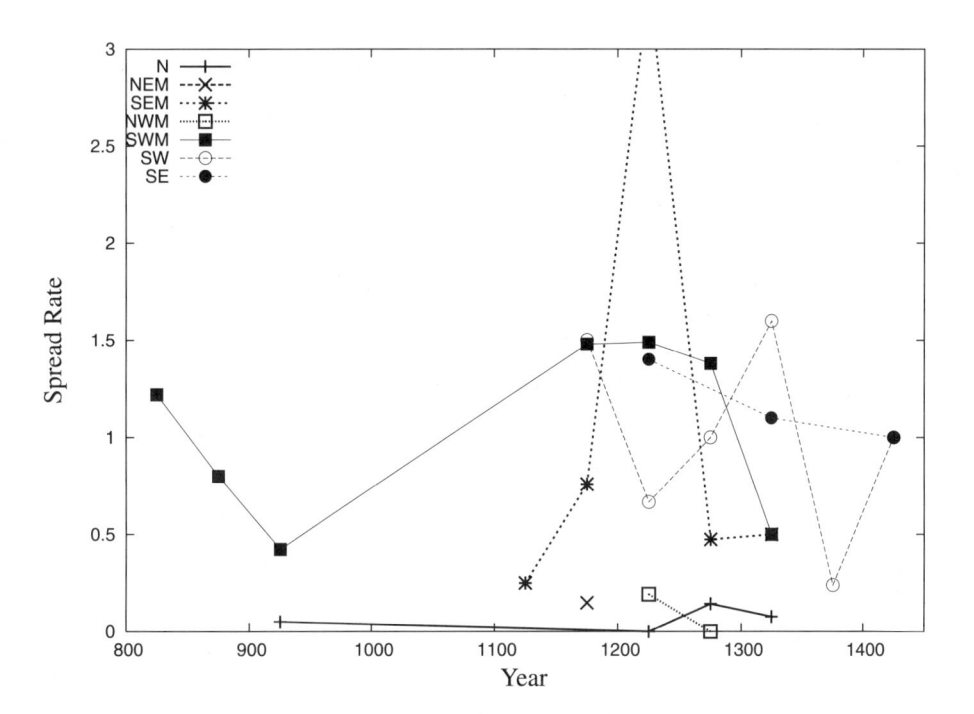

Figure C.7: Spread Rate for -n

Table C.8: Spread Rate for -V

	C9a	C9b	C10a	C10b	C11a	C11b	C12a	C12b	C13a	C13b	C14a	C14b	C15a
N	—	—	1.7	—	—	—	—	—	0	0.14	0.17	—	—
NEM	—	—	—	—	—	—	—	0.3	—	0	—	—	—
SEM	—	—	—	—	—	—	1.1	0.69	0.17	0.38	0.33	—	—
NWM	—	—	—	—	—	—	—	—	0.26	0.2	—	—	—
SWM	1	1.2	1.3	—	—	—	—	0.91	0.47	0.41	0.27	—	—
SW	—	—	—	—	—	—	—	—	0.36	0	0.38	0.065	0.18
SE	—	—	—	—	—	—	—	—	0.3	—	0.087	—	0.5

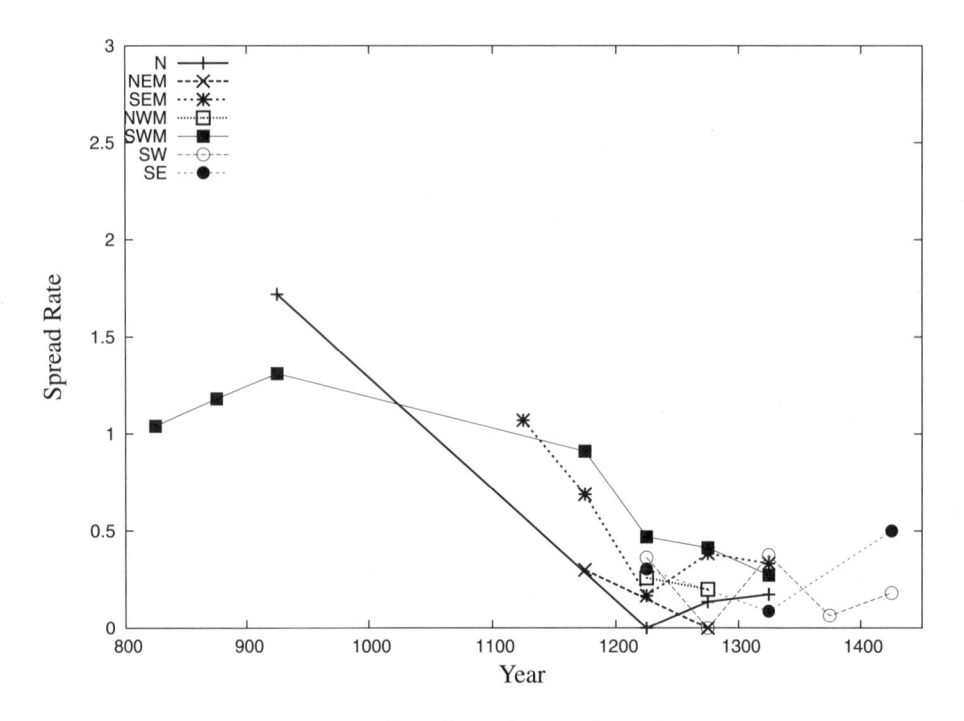

Figure C.8: Spread Rate for -V

Table C.9: Spread Rate for -ø

	C9a	C9b	C10a	C10b	C11a	C11b	C12a	C12b	C13a	C13b	C14a	C14b	C15a
N	—	—	0.5	—	—	—	—	—	0	0.34	0.53	—	—
NEM	—	—	—	—	—	—	—	0.28	—	0	—	—	—
SEM	—	—	—	—	—	—	0.71	0.41	0.071	0.34	0.33	—	—
NWM	—	—	—	—	—	—	—	—	0.34	0	—	—	—
SWM	1	0.8	1	—	—	—	—	0.58	0.27	0.43	0.33	—	—
SW	—	—	—	—	—	—	—	0.4	0.5	—	0.43	0.4	0.12
SE	—	—	—	—	—	—	—	—	0.88	—	0.24	—	0

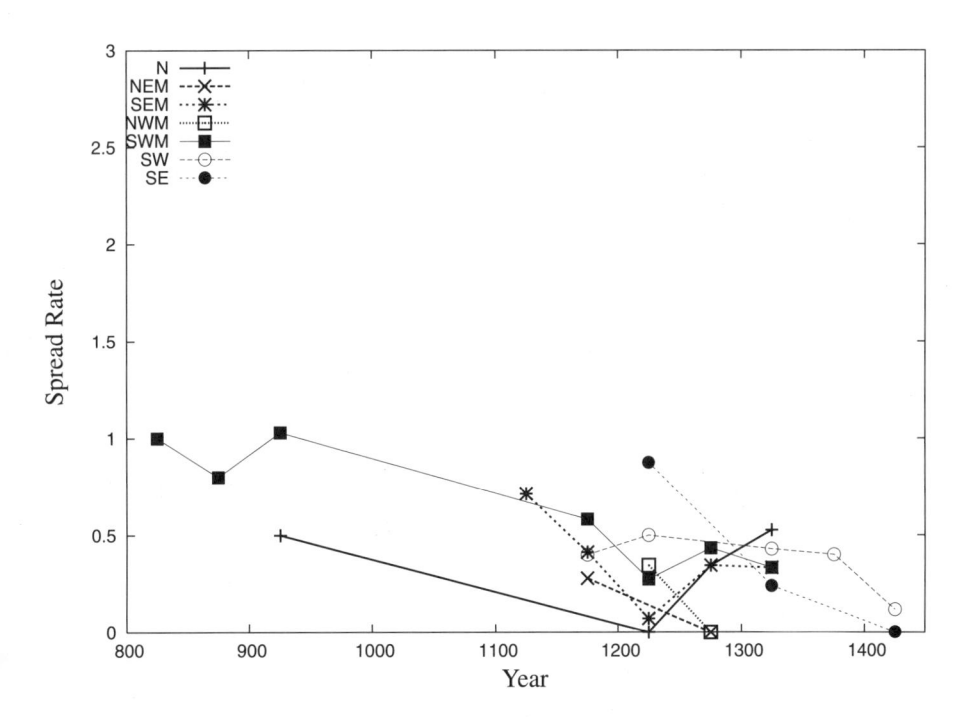

Figure C.9: Spread Rate for -ø

Table C.10: Spread Rate for Minor Plural Types

	C9a	C9b	C10a	C10b	C11a	C11b	C12a	C12b	C13a	C13b	C14a	C14b	C15a
N	—	—	0.33	—	—	—	—	—	1	0.63	0.5	—	—
NEM	—	—	—	—	—	—	—	0.4	—	1	—	—	—
SEM	—	—	—	—	—	—	0.75	0.31	0.5	0.38	1	—	—
NWM	—	—	—	—	—	—	—	—	0.5	1	—	—	—
SWM	0.83	1	0.63	—	—	—	—	0.85	0.47	0.23	0.67	—	—
SW	—	—	—	—	—	—	—	0	0.33	1	0.38	0.67	0.4
SE	—	—	—	—	—	—	—	—	0.33	—	0.4	—	—

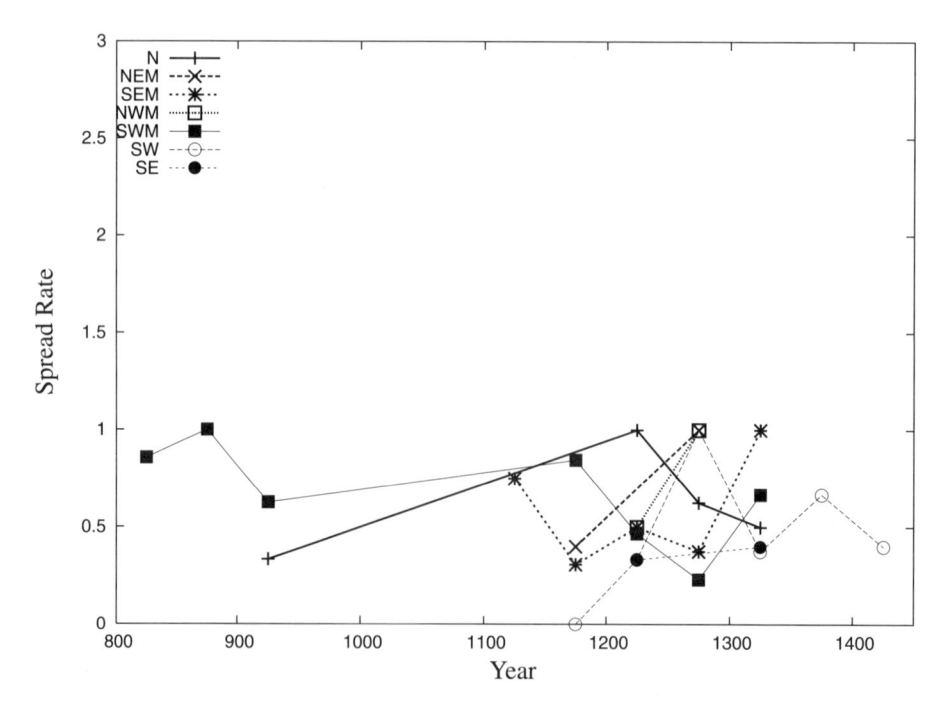

Figure C.10: Spread Rate for Minor Plural Types

Appendix D   PFPs of Selected Texts

The PFPs presented in the following pages are those for the selected texts examined in Chapter 4: the *Lambeth Homilies*, *The Owl and the Nightingale*, the *Ancrene Wisse/Riwle*, the *Poema Morale*, and *The Peterborough Chronicle*.

The notations and abbreviations in the PFPs in this Appendix are practically the same as those in Appendix B, where there are explanatory notes. The only difference is that the PFPs in this section gives various kinds of information about the text in the TEXT INFO part, such as manuscript reference, text reference, consulted edition(s)/corpus, period, and dialect (grid reference where available).

D.1   PFPs of the *Lambeth Homilies*

D.1.1   PFP 2000 (Lang 1)

TEXT INFO   MS: Lambeth Palace Library 487; TEXT: Lambeth Homilies, hand A, lang 1 (cited as Lang 1), conflating ##190, 191, 192, 193, 194, 198, 199, 200, 201, 202; SOURCE: Morris (*Homilies*, 1st ser., Part 1, Texts I-V, IX-XIII); PERIOD: C12b2 (c1200); DIALECT: South-West Midland (Worcestershire); GRID REF: 372 262

TOKENS   Nominative/Accusative Plurals 477 (0), Syncretised Dative/Prepositional Plurals 63 (0), Unsyncretised Dative/Prepositional Plurals 173 (0), Syncretism Rate 0.27 (NA), Genitive Plurals 56 (0), Total of Plurals 769 (0)

TYPES AND RATES

	s	n	V	ø	M	TOTAL
TYPES	58 (64)	42 (43)	44 (44)	14 (14)	9 (9)	167 (174)
RATE	0.35 (0.37)	0.25 (0.25)	0.26 (0.25)	0.084 (0.081)	0.054 (0.052)	1 (1)
SPREAD RATE	1 (1.1)	1.4 (1.5)	1 (1)	0.47 (0.47)	1 (1)	—

Masc-S   -ere s15, apostol s20, biscop s1, blōstm [n]1 (V)1, castel s1, cierr s1, clāþ s8, cniht s2, cost s1, cyning s1, dæg s13, dēofol s1 [n]2 (V)1, dōm s3, drinc [n]2, engel s5, ent s1, finger [M]1, fisc s2, fugel s2, giest s1, gylt s1, hafoc s1, hlāford s2, hund s1, līeg s1, lust s3, mānāþ s1, manslieht s1, māþum s1, mete (V)1, posl s1, prēost s1, rāp s7, sang s1, scōh s1, scyttel s1, sealm s1, slege [n]1, sott s1, stān s1, strēam s1, tēar s2, tūn s1, þēaw s8, þēof s3, þōht s1, þrǣl s1, wǣg s3, wæstm s2 (V)1, wer [M]1, wine s1, wyrm s1

Masc-N   crabba n1, fāh n1, frogga n1 [V]1, gelēafa n1, līchama [V]2, loca n1, slaga [V]1, steorra n2, wela n1, wītega n1 [V]1, wrǣcca n2 [V]2, wyrhta n1

Neut-N   ēage n4, ēare n3

Fem-N bīeme n1, heorte n5 [V]1, mæsse n1, nǣdre n2 [V]2, tāde n2 [V]1, tunge n2 [V]1, wīce n1, wuduwe n1

Neut-V bed [n]1 V1, bod [n]3 V9, geat V3, lim [n]3, nīeten V2, oferslege [M]1, twig V1, writ [n]1, yfel [s]2 [$ø$]2

Fem-V -ing V2, -ness V2, -ung V1, ǣht [n]2, ælmesse [n]3, bend (s)1, bisen V1, bōt V1, dǣd V9, duru [n]1, giefu V3, glēd [n]1, hǣs V5, hand [n]4, lagu [n]2 V10, miht [n]2 V1, myrgþ V1, nīed V1, pīn [n]1 V1, renc [s]1, sāwol [n]7 V8, sprǣc [n]3, stīg (s)2, synn [n]19 V26, tīd V1, ȳþ V1

Masc-Ø brōþor [n]2 [V]8, mōnaþ $ø$1

Neut-Ø bearn $ø$9, dēor $ø$3, gōd $ø$1, hām [s]1, hors $ø$1, hūs [s]1, lēaf $ø$1, līf $ø$1, mǣl [s]1, mynster [V]1, swīn $ø$1, tācen [V]1, trēow [n]1, þing [s]3 [V]1 $ø$17, wǣpen [V]1, weder [s]2, weorc [s]6, wīf [s]1 [M]1, winter (V)1, word [s]8 [V]1 $ø$6, wundor $ø$1

Fem-Ø sweostor [V]3

Masc-M fēond [$ø$]5, fōt M7, frēond [$ø$]1, mann [V]6 M83

Masc-M cild [n]2

Fem-M bōc M1, mūs M1, niht M1

D.1.2 PFP 2001 (Lang 2)

TEXT INFO MS: Lambeth Palace Library 487; TEXT: Lambeth Homilies, hand A, lang 2 (cited as Lang 2), conflating ##195, 196, 197, 203, 204, 205, 206; SOURCE: Morris (*Homilies*, 1st ser., Part 1, Texts VI-VIII, XIV-XVII); PERIOD: C12b2 (c1200); DIALECT: South-West Midland (Worcestershire); GRID REF: 372 262

TOKENS Nominative/Accusative Plurals 152 (9), Syncretised Dative/Prepositional Plurals 34 (1), Unsyncretised Dative/Prepositional Plurals 45 (12), Syncretism Rate 0.43 (0.077), Genitive Plurals 10 (1), Total of Plurals 241 (23)

TYPES AND RATES

	s	n	V	$ø$	M	TOTAL
TYPES	33 (37)	12 (14)	17 (17)	7 (7)	2 (2)	71 (77)
RATE	0.47 (0.48)	0.17 (0.18)	0.24 (0.22)	0.099 (0.091)	0.028 (0.026)	1 (1)
SPREAD RATE	1.4 (1.5)	2.4 (2.8)	0.81 (0.81)	0.41 (0.41)	0.5 (0.5)	—

Masc-S apostol s3, borg s1, brand s2, cniht s1, dæg s2, discipul s1, dynt s1, engel s8 [$ø$]1, fisc s1, fugel s1, gāst s1, gylt s3, lust s1, munuc s1, nægl s1, pening s2, sang s1, tēar s13, þēof s4, wæg s1, wielm s1, wine s1, wyrm s1

Masc-N fāh n2, līchama [V]1, steorra n2, wā [V]1

Fem-N sīde [V]1

Masc-V sunu [s]1

Neut-V bed [n]1 V1, bod [s]1 V2, geat [n]2, mægden V1

Fem-V -rǣden [$ø$]1, -waru V2, dǣd [n]1, hǣs [n]2 V2, lagu [n]1, mōdor [s]2, rōd [n]1, sāwol V1, sceaft V1, synn [n]6 V9, wund [n]2 V1

Masc-Ø fæder [s]2

Neut-Ø cynn [s]1, dēor $ø$2, fers $ø$1, lāst [s]1, þing [V]1 $ø$15, wǣpen [n]1 [V]3, wæter [s]1, weorc [s]2, wīf [s]1, word [s]3 [V]1 $ø$5, wundor [V]1

Fem-Ø sweostor [n]1

Masc-M fōt M3, frēond [$ø$]1, mann M30

Masc-M cild [V]2

D.1.3 PFP 5 (L)

See Section D.4.1 below for the *Poema Morale* part.

D.2 PFPs of *The Owl and the Nightingale*

D.2.1 PFP 1 (J)

TEXT INFO MS: Oxford, Jesus College 29, fols. 156r-168v; TEXT: The Owl and the Nightingale (cited as J), conflated as #1100 with ##9, 145, 250, 251, 252, 253, 254, 255; SOURCE: Grattan and Sykes, Wells, and Atkins; PERIOD: C13b2; DIALECT: South-West Midland (Herefordshire); GRID REF: 372 244

TOKENS Nominative/Accusative Plurals 145 (30), Syncretised Dative/Prepositional Plurals 10 (3), Unsyncretised Dative/Prepositional Plurals 35 (59), Syncretism Rate 0.22 (0.048), Genitive Plurals 17 (5), Total of Plurals 207 (97)

TYPES AND RATES

	s	n	V	ø	M	TOTAL
TYPES	47 (50)	4 (4)	12 (13)	7 (7)	1 (1)	71 (75)
RATE	0.66 (0.67)	0.056 (0.053)	0.17 (0.17)	0.099 (0.093)	0.014 (0.013)	1 (1)
SPREAD RATE	1.2 (1.3)	0.57 (0.57)	1.7 (1.9)	0.54 (0.54)	0.17 (0.17)	—

Masc-S blōstm (V)2, bridd s6, ceorl s2, cleric s1, clifer s5, clūd s1, cniht [V]1, cræft s3, dynt s1, engel s1, flocc s2, forst s1, fox s1, fugel s2, hierde s1, hund s2, lēc s1, lust s3, pæþ s3, prēost s1, rǣd s1, sang s3, smiþ s1, snægl s1, sott s1, stān s1, stede (V)1, stot s1, sweng s1, tēar s2, top s1, þēof s1, þorn s1, wāg s1, weall s1, wrenc s1, wulf s1, wyrm s1

Masc-N crāwa [V]2, oxa [V]1, steorra [V]1

Neut-N ēage n3, ēare n1

Fem-N hlǣfdige [s]2, wīce [V]2

Neut-V mægden [s]1, scip [s]1

Fem-V bend (s)1, grīn V1, rūn V1, wiht [s]3 V1

Neut-Ø bān ø1, corn ø1, dēor ø1, hors ø2, hrīs [s]1, hūs [s]1, lēaf [s]2, sǣd [s]2, trēow [n]3, wǣpen [V]1, wīf [s]1, word [s]5 ø2

Masc-M frēond [ø]1, mann M38

Masc-M cild [n]1 [V]1

Fem-M mūs [ø]2, niht [s]1

D.2.2 PFP 2 (C1)

TEXT INFO MS: London, British Library, Cotton Caligula A ix, fols. 233r-239v l13, 240r l6-241v l15; TEXT: The Owl and the Nightingale, language 1 (cited as C1); SOURCE: Grattan and Sykes, Wells, and Atkins; PERIOD: C13b2; DIALECT: South-West Midland (Worcestershire); GRID REF: 390 262

TOKENS Nominative/Accusative Plurals 108 (27), Syncretised Dative/Prepositional Plurals 9 (1), Unsyncretised Dative/Prepositional Plurals 21 (46), Syncretism Rate 0.3 (0.021), Genitive Plurals 14 (3), Total of Plurals 152 (77)

TYPES AND RATES

	s	n	V	ø	M	TOTAL
TYPES	36 (39)	5 (5)	9 (10)	6 (6)	1 (1)	57 (61)
RATE	0.63 (0.64)	0.088 (0.082)	0.16 (0.16)	0.11 (0.098)	0.018 (0.016)	1 (1)
SPREAD RATE	1.1 (1.2)	0.83 (0.83)	2.3 (2.5)	0.67 (0.67)	0.2 (0.2)	—

Masc-S blōstm (V)2, bridd s5, ceorl s2, cleric s2, clifer s3, clūd s1, cniht s1, cræft s3, engel s1, flocc s2, forst s1, fox s1, fugel s1, hierde s1, hund s2, lēc s1, munuc s1, pæþ s3, prēost s1, sang s2, snægl s1, sott s1, stān s1, stede (V)1, stot s1, sweng s1, tēar s2, top s1, þorn s1, weall [V]1, wrenc s1, wulf s1, wyrm s1

Masc-N crāwa [V]2, oxa [V]1

Neut-N ēage n2 [V]1, ēare n1

Fem-N wīce [V]2

Fem-V grīn [s]1, rūn V1, wiht [s]3 V1

Neut-Ø bān ø1, hors ø1, hrīs ø1, lēaf [s]1, sǣd [s]2, trēow [n]1, tron [n]1, word [s]5 ø1

Masc-M frēond [ø]1, mann M28

Masc-M cild [n]2

Fem-M mūs [ø]2, niht [s]1

D.2.3 PFP 3 (C2)

TEXT INFO MS: London, British Library, Cotton Caligula A ix, fols. 239v l14-240r l5, 241v l16-246r; TEXT: The Owl and the Nightingale, language 2 (cited as C2); SOURCE: Grattan and Sykes, Wells, and Atkins; PERIOD: C13b2; DIALECT: South-West Midland (Worcestershire); GRID REF: 379 267

TOKENS Nominative/Accusative Plurals 40 (3), Syncretised Dative/Prepositional Plurals 1 (1), Unsyncretised Dative/Prepositional Plurals 14 (15), Syncretism Rate 0.067 (0.063), Genitive Plurals 3 (3), Total of Plurals 58 (22)

TYPES AND RATES

	s	n	V	ø	M	TOTAL
TYPES	18 (19)	1 (1)	2 (3)	3 (3)	1 (1)	25 (27)
RATE	0.72 (0.7)	0.04 (0.037)	0.08 (0.11)	0.12 (0.11)	0.04 (0.037)	1 (1)
SPREAD RATE	1.8 (1.9)	0.5 (0.5)	0.67 (1)	0.33 (0.33)	1 (1)	—

Masc-S bridd s1, clifer s2, dynt s1, fugel s1, lust s3, rǣd s1, sang s1, smiþ s1, þeof s1, wāg s1

Masc-N steorra [V]1

Fem-N hlǣfdige [s]3

Neut-V mægden [s]1, scip [s]1

Fem-V bend (s)1

Neut-Ø corn [s]1, dor ø1, hūs [s]1, lēaf [s]1, trēow [n]1, wǣpen [V]1, wīf [s]1 ø1, word ø1

Masc-M mann M10

D.3 PFPs of the *Ancrene Wisse/Riwle*

D.3.1 PFP 272 (A)

TEXT INFO MS: Cambridge, Corpus Christi College 402, fols. 1r-117v; TEXT: Ancrene Wisse (cited as A); SOURCE: Tolkien, and Bennett and Smithers (Text XVIII); analysed for Parts 6 and 7 only; PERIOD: C13a2 (c1230); DIALECT: South-West Midland (Shropshire); GRID REF: 352 275

TOKENS Nominative/Accusative Plurals 234 (1), Syncretised Dative/Prepositional Plurals 101 (0), Unsyncretised Dative/Prepositional Plurals 47 (3), Syncretism Rate 0.68 (0), Genitive Plurals 18 (0), Total of Plurals 400 (4)

TYPES AND RATES

	s	n	V	ø	M	TOTAL
TYPES	77 (105)	29 (29)	2 (3)	5 (6)	2 (2)	115 (145)
RATE	0.67 (0.72)	0.25 (0.2)	0.017 (0.021)	0.043 (0.041)	0.017 (0.014)	1 (1)
SPREAD RATE	1.6 (2.2)	1.9 (1.9)	0.071 (0.11)	0.24 (0.29)	0.5 (0.5)	—

Masc-S -dōm s1, -ere s1, -scipe s3, belg s2, brand s1, cāsere s1, castel s1, clāþ s2, cleric s1, cniht s2, coss s1, cyning s1, cyrtel s1, dæg s2, dēofol [n]1, disc s1, discipul s8, drinc s2, dynt s1, earm s4, finger s2, fox s3, fugel s1, glǣm s1, gylt s1, hamor s2, hearm s1, heorot s1, hlīep s1, hyll s2, lust s1, magister s1, mete s2, scōh s1, sice s1, sweng s1, tægel s3, tēar s9, tind s1, titt s2, þēaw s6, þōht s4, þorn s2, wæg s1, wāg s2, weall s1, wine s1

Masc-N fāh n1, fēolaga [s]2, hālga n3, impa n2, lama n1, stela n3, wā [s]1, wræcca [s]2 [V]1

Neut-N ēage n2

Fem-N āncre [s]2 n2, blǣse n1, heorte n1, sīde n2

Neut-V bæþ [s]1, bed [n]2, gamen [s]1, lim [n]1, mægden [s]3, trod [n]2, þyrel [s]1, yfel [s]1

Fem-V -ness [s]3, -ung [s]11, -waru V2, bēn [n]2, bliss [n]1, clufu [s]1, dūn [s]7, fierd [s]1, gierd [n]1, glēd [n]1, hǣs [s]1, hand [n]5, healf [ø]1, lufu (n)2, mearc [n]3, myrgþ [s]1, sealf [n]1, stǣger [n]1, synn [n]3, wund [n]1

Masc-Ø fæder [s]1

Neut-Ø bān [s]1, cnēow [n]1, gēar [s]1 ø1, hūs [s]3, hwēol [s]4, land [s]1, nebb [s]2, swinc [s]4, trēow [n]4, þing [s]14 ø7, wǣpen [n]1, wæter [s]3, weorc [s]6, wīn [s]1, word [s]6 ø2, wundor [s]2

Fem-Ø sweostor [n]15

Masc-M fōt M1, frēond [ø]2, mann M20

Fem-M burg [s]1

D.3.2 PFP 273 (C)

TEXT INFO MS: London, British Library, Cotton Cleopatra C.vi, fols. 4r–194r, hand A; TEXT: Ancrene Riwle (cited as C); SOURCE: Dobson (*Ancrene*); analysed for Parts 6 and 7 only; PERIOD: C13a2 (1225-1230); DIALECT: South-West Midland (Herefordshire); GRID REF: 349 258

TOKENS Nominative/Accusative Plurals 432 (0), Syncretised Dative/Prepositional Plurals 188 (0), Unsyncretised Dative/Prepositional Plurals 101 (0), Syncretism Rate 0.65 (NA), Genitive Plurals 24 (0), Total of Plurals 745 (0)

TYPES AND RATES

	s	n	V	ø	M	TOTAL
TYPES	104 (154)	47 (50)	9 (9)	5 (6)	3 (4)	168 (223)
RATE	0.62 (0.69)	0.28 (0.22)	0.054 (0.04)	0.03 (0.027)	0.018 (0.018)	1 (1)
SPREAD RATE	1.8 (2.6)	1.7 (1.8)	0.21 (0.21)	0.15 (0.18)	0.6 (0.8)	—

Masc-S -dōm s2, -ere s5, -scipe s3, apostol s1, bōg s1, brand s1, cāsere s1, castel s1, clāþ s6, cleric s1, cniht s3, coss s1, cræft s1, crūc s3, cyning s1, cyrtel s1, dæg s2, dǣl [n]3, dēofol [n]1, discipul s7, dōm s1, drinc s1, earm s5, engel s3, fugel s3, glǣm s2, gylt s1, heorot s1, hlīep s1, hyll s4, lust s5, magister s2, martyr s1, mete s2, mūþ s2, nægl s1, pening s1, prēost s1, sceacel s1, scilling s1, scōh [n]1, sealm s9, sīþ [n]7, snǣd s1, stān s1, stice [n]2, strēam s1, sweng s2, tēar s4, tind s1, titt s2, þēaw s6, þōht s3, þorn s2, wæg s2, wāg s1, wamm s1, wrenc s1, wulf s1

Masc-N assa n1, fāh n1, fēolaga [s]1, fera n1, hālga n2, impa n2, lama n2, līchama [s]1, oxa n1, prica [s]1, stela n3, wā [s]1, wræcca [s]1 [V]2

Neut-N ēage n12, ēare n12 [V]1

Fem-N āncre [s]5 n7, arwe n3, cēace n3, heorte n2, hlæfdige [s]1, mæsse n1, nædre n1, sīde n2, tunge n1, wuduwe n2

Masc-V hād [s]1

Neut-V bæþ [s]1, gamen [s]1, geat [s]1 [n]2, lim [n]1, mægden [s]4, spere [n]1, trod [n]2, þyrel [s]7, wēofod (s)1, yfel [s]1

Fem-V -ing V1, -ness [s]2 [n]1, -ung [s]12, andswaru [s]1, bēn [n]2, bliss [n]2 V1, dǣd [n]2, dūn [s]8, fȳst [s]2, giefu [n]2, glēd [n]1, hǣs [s]4, hand [n]8, healf [s]1 [ø]1, heord V2, lagu [n]1, lufu (n)2, mearc [n]3, myrgþ [s]1, rūn [s]1, siht [n]1, sprǣc [n]1, synn [n]6, talu [n]1, trēowþ [s]1 [n]1, þēod V1

Masc-Ø fæder [s]1

Neut-Ø anginn [s]1, bān [s]1, cynd (V)1, cynn [s]1 [V]1, fers (s)1, flǣsc [s]1, gēar [s]1 ø2, hūs [s]3, hwēol [s]4, īsen [s]1, land [s]1, lēaf [s]1, riht [V]1, sǣd [s]1, sār [s]1, spell [s]1, swinc [s]3, ticcen [s]6, trēow [n]4, þing [s]28 ø11, wǣpen [s]1, wæter [s]2, weorc [s]5, wīn [s]1, witt [s]16, word [s]22 ø4, wundor [s]2

Fem-Ø dohtor [n]1, sweostor [n]33

Masc-M fōt M2, frēond [ø]4, mann M39

Masc-M cild [n]2

Fem-M gāt M6

D.3.3 PFP 245 (N)

TEXT INFO MS: London, British Library, Cotton Nero A xiv, fols. 1r–120v, hand A; TEXT: Ancrene Riwle (cited as N); SOURCE: Day; analysed for Parts 6 and 7 only; PERIOD: C13a2; DIALECT: South-West Midland (Worcestershire); GRID REF: 378 253

TOKENS Nominative/Accusative Plurals 171 (0), Syncretised Dative/Prepositional Plurals 81 (0), Unsyncretised Dative/Prepositional Plurals 27 (0), Syncretism Rate 0.75 (NA), Genitive Plurals 13 (0), Total of Plurals 292 (0)

TYPES AND RATES

	s	n	V	ø	M	TOTAL
TYPES	58 (80)	26 (26)	1 (2)	3 (4)	2 (2)	90 (114)
RATE	0.64 (0.7)	0.29 (0.23)	0.011 (0.018)	0.033 (0.035)	0.022 (0.018)	1 (1)
SPREAD RATE	1.7 (2.3)	2.2 (2.2)	0.045 (0.091)	0.17 (0.22)	0.67 (0.67)	—

Masc-S -dōm s1, -scipe s4, brand s1, cāsere s1, castel s1, clāþ s2, cleric s1, cniht s2, cyning s1, dæg s1, dēofol [n]1, disc s1, discipul s5, drinc s2 [n]1, dynt s2, earm s4, fugel s1, glǣm s1, gylt s1, heorot s1, hlīep s1, hyll s5, lust s2, magister s1, mete s2, scōh [n]1, sweng s1, tēar s2, tind s1, titt s2, þēaw s4, þorn s2, wæg [n]1, wāg s1

Masc-N fāh n1, fēolaga [s]1, hālga n2, impa n2, lama n2, stela n3, wā [s]1, wræcca [s]1 [V]2

Neut-N ēage n1

Fem-N āncre n2, sīde n2

Neut-V bæþ [s]1, gamen [s]1, geat [s]1, lim [s]1, mægden [s]3, trod [n]3, yfel [s]1

Fem-V -ness [s]3, -ung [s]5, bend (s)1, bliss [n]1, dūn [s]7, giefu [n]1, glēd [n]1, hǣs [n]1, hand [n]2, lufu (n)2, mearc [n]3, miht [n]1, myrgþ [s]1, pīn [n]3, synn [n]3

Masc-Ø fæder [s]1

Neut-Ø bān [s]1, gēar [s]1 ø1, hūs [s]3, hwēol [s]4, land [s]1, swinc [s]3, trēow [n]4, þing [s]18 ø3, wǣpen [n]1, wæter [s]2, weorc [s]3, wīn [s]1, word [s]3, wundor [s]2

Fem-Ø sweostor [n]11
Masc-M fōt M1, frēond [ø]1, mann M18

D.3.4 PFP 118 (T)

TEXT INFO MS: London, British Library, Cotton Titus D xviii, fols. 14r–105r (except T2 sections); TEXT: Ancrene Riwle, language T1 (cited as T); SOURCE: *LAEME* text database and Mack; analysed for the tagged part only (fols. 14r–40ra1); PERIOD: C13a1; DIALECT: North-West Midland (Cheshire); GRID REF: 370 349

TOKENS Nominative/Accusative Plurals 285 (0), Syncretised Dative/Prepositional Plurals 152 (0), Unsyncretised Dative/Prepositional Plurals 24 (0), Syncretism Rate 0.86 (NA), Genitive Plurals 17 (0), Total of Plurals 478 (0)

TYPES AND RATES

	s	n	V	ø	M	TOTAL
TYPES	108 (150)	4 (4)	14 (14)	6 (6)	4 (4)	136 (178)
RATE	0.79 (0.84)	0.029 (0.022)	0.1 (0.079)	0.044 (0.034)	0.029 (0.022)	1 (1)
SPREAD RATE	2.8 (3.8)	0.2 (0.2)	0.3 (0.3)	0.26 (0.26)	0.57 (0.57)	—

Masc-S -ere s5, -scipe s1, bōg s1, bridd s21, coss s1, crūc s2, cyrnel s1, dæg s1, discipul s2, dōm s1, dynt s1, engel s2, fox s6, fugel s1, glǣm s1, hamm s1, lust s6, magister s1, martyr s1, mūþ s3, nægl s1, pening s1, sceacel s1, sealm s1, sīþ [V]1, stān s3, stede s1, stice s1, storm s1, strēam s1, sweng s1, tēar s3, þēaw s4, þōht s3, þorn s1, þrǣl s1, wǣg s2, wulf s1, wyrm s1

Masc-N fēra [s]1, hālga [s]1, līchama [s]1, lippa [s]1, prica [s]1, ūtlaga [s]1, wræcca [s]1

Neut-N ēage n9, ēare [s]13 n1 [V]1

Fem-N āncre [s]17 [V]1 [ø]1, arwe [s]3, cēace [s]3, heorte [s]1, molde [s]1, nǣdre [s]1, tunge [s]1

Masc-V sunu [s]1

Neut-V bed [s]1, dǣl [s]1, geat [s]2, hol [s]3 [n]1, lim [s]3, mægden [s]1, spere [s]1, þyrel [s]4, yfel [s]1

Fem-V -ung [s]12, andswaru [s]1, bliss [s]3, bōt [s]1, clūs [s]1, dǣd [s]1 V1, feþer [s]2, fȳlþ [s]2, fȳst [s]1, giefu [s]1, glēd [s]1, grīn [s]1, hand [s]2 [n]1 V4, healf [ø]1, henn [s]1, heord [s]2 V1, hulu [s]1, lǣs [s]1, miht [s]1, pīn [s]4, rūn [s]1, sāwol [s]1, siht [s]1, sprǣc [s]3, synn [s]10, talu [s]1, tīd [s]2, trēowþ [s]1, wæcc V1, wucu [s]1, wund [s]2, ȳþ [s]1

Masc-Ø brōþor [V]2

Neut-Ø cnēow [s]1, cynn [s]2, dēor [V]1, flǣsc [s]1, gēar ø1, hǣr [s]1, lēaf [s]1, mǣl ø1, nest [s]4, sǣd [s]1, spell [s]1, ticcen [s]5, þing [s]10 [V]1, wǣpen [s]1, weorc [s]6, witt [s]14, word [s]19 ø1, wundor [s]2

Fem-Ø dohtor [V]1, sweostor [V]5

Masc-M fōt M2, frēond [ø]2, mann M25

Masc-M ǣg [V]1, cild [V]4

Fem-M gāt M6, gōs M1

D.4 PFPs of the *Poema Morale*

D.4.1 PFP 5 (L)

TEXT INFO MS: London, Lambeth Palace Library 487, fols. 59v–65r; TEXT: Poema Morale (cited as L); SOURCE: Hall (*Selections*, Text VIII) and Morris (*Homilies*,

1st ser., Part 1: 159–83); PERIOD: C12b2 (C12b2, c1200); DIALECT: South-West Midland (Worcestershire); GRID REF: 372 262

TOKENS Nominative/Accusative Plurals 43 (12), Syncretised Dative/Prepositional Plurals 3 (1), Unsyncretised Dative/Prepositional Plurals 8 (3), Syncretism Rate 0.27 (0.25), Genitive Plurals 3 (1), Total of Plurals 57 (17)

TYPES AND RATES

	s	n	V	ø	M	TOTAL
TYPES	9 (9)	2 (2)	11 (11)	6 (7)	1 (1)	29 (30)
RATE	0.31 (0.3)	0.069 (0.067)	0.38 (0.37)	0.21 (0.23)	0.035 (0.033)	1 (1)
SPREAD RATE	1.3 (1.3)	0.67 (0.67)	1.1 (1.1)	0.86 (1)	0.5 (0.5)	—

Masc-S -ing s2, -ling s1, engel s1, fisc s1, fugel s1, þræl s1, wæg s1
Masc-N ieldra [V]1, swica n1
Neut-N ēage n1
Neut-V geat V1
Fem-V bend (s)1, bliss V1, dǣd V1, gesǣlþ V1, hǣs V1, lagu V1, sāwol V1, stund V1, synn V1
Neut-Ø gēar ø1, līf ø1, swinc ø1, þing ø1, weorc [s]3, winter (V)1, word ø2
Masc-M frēond [ø]3, mann M10

D.4.2 PFP 6 (e)

TEXT INFO MS: London, British Library, Egerton 613, fols. 64r–70v (e); TEXT: Poema Morale (cited as e); SOURCE: Zupitza and Schipper; PERIOD: C13a; DIALECT: South-West Midland (Worcestershire); GRID REF: 385 239

TOKENS Nominative/Accusative Plurals 58 (15), Syncretised Dative/Prepositional Plurals 6 (2), Unsyncretised Dative/Prepositional Plurals 6 (11), Syncretism Rate 0.5 (0.15), Genitive Plurals 5 (1), Total of Plurals 75 (29)

TYPES AND RATES

	s	n	V	ø	M	TOTAL
TYPES	14 (14)	3 (3)	13 (14)	6 (6)	1 (1)	37 (38)
RATE	0.38 (0.37)	0.081 (0.079)	0.35 (0.37)	0.16 (0.16)	0.027 (0.026)	1 (1)
SPREAD RATE	1.3 (1.3)	0.38 (0.38)	1.4 (1.6)	1 (1)	0.33 (0.33)	—

Masc-S -ere s1, -ing s3, dēofol s1, engel s1, eorl s1, fisc s1, fugel s1, gylt s2, þræl s1, wæg s1, wine s1
Masc-N efeta [V]1, fēra [V]1, ieldra [V]1, snaca n1, swica [V]1
Neut-N ēage n1 [V]1
Fem-N nǣdre n1
Fem-V -ung [s]1, bend (s)1, dǣd V2, hǣs V1, lagu V2, lufu V1, sāwol V2, stund V1, synn V1
Neut-Ø gēar ø1, þing ø2, weorc [s]2 ø1, winter (V)2, word ø2
Masc-M fēond [ø]2, frēond [ø]3, mann M13

D.4.3 PFP 7 (E)

TEXT INFO MS: London, British Library, Egerton 613, fols. 7r-12v; TEXT: Poema Morale (cited as E); SOURCE: Morris (*Old English Homilies*, 1st ser., Part 1, 288-95, 175-83); PERIOD: C13a; DIALECT: South-West Midland (Worcestershire); GRID REF: 378 246

TOKENS Nominative/Accusative Plurals 55 (15), Syncretised Dative/Prepositional Plurals 9 (1), Unsyncretised Dative/Prepositional Plurals 7 (8), Syncretism Rate 0.56 (0.11), Genitive Plurals 6 (2), Total of Plurals 77 (26)

TYPES AND RATES

	s	n	V	ø	M	TOTAL
TYPES	18 (18)	7 (7)	6 (7)	6 (6)	1 (1)	38 (39)
RATE	0.47 (0.46)	0.18 (0.18)	0.16 (0.18)	0.16 (0.15)	0.026 (0.026)	1 (1)
SPREAD RATE	1.4 (1.4)	0.88 (0.88)	0.75 (0.88)	1 (1)	0.33 (0.33)	—

Masc-S -ere s1, -ing s3, -ling s1, dēofol s1, engel s1, eorl s1, fisc s1, fugel s1, gylt s2, þræl s1, wæg s1, weall s1, wine s1

Masc-N efeta n1, ieldra n1, snaca n1, willa [s]1, wræcca n1

Neut-N ēage n1 [V]1

Fem-N nǣdre n1

Fem-V -ung [s]1, bend (s)1, dǣd [n]2, hǣs V1, lagu [s]1 V1, lufu V1, synn V1

Neut-Ø gēar $ø$1, swinc $ø$1, þing $ø$2, weorc [s]3, winter (V)2, word $ø$2

Masc-M fēond [$ø$]2, frēond [$ø$]3, mann M13

D.4.4 PFP 9 (J)

TEXT INFO MS: Oxford, Jesus College 29, fols. 169r-174v; TEXT: Poema Morale (cited as J), conflated as #1100 with ##1, 145, 250, 251, 252, 253, 254, 255; SOURCE: Morris (*Miscellany* 58-71); PERIOD: C13b2; DIALECT: South-West Midland (Herefordshire); GRID REF: 372 244

TOKENS Nominative/Accusative Plurals 61 (11), Syncretised Dative/Prepositional Plurals 8 (3), Unsyncretised Dative/Prepositional Plurals 9 (5), Syncretism Rate 0.47 (0.38), Genitive Plurals 7 (2), Total of Plurals 85 (21)

TYPES AND RATES

	s	n	V	ø	M	TOTAL
TYPES	17 (17)	10 (11)	3 (4)	8 (8)	1 (1)	39 (41)
RATE	0.44 (0.41)	0.26 (0.27)	0.077 (0.098)	0.2 (0.2)	0.026 (0.024)	1 (1)
SPREAD RATE	1.5 (1.5)	1.7 (1.8)	0.33 (0.44)	0.89 (0.89)	0.25 (0.25)	—

Masc-S -ere s1, -ing s2, -ling s1, dēofol [n]1, engel s1, eorl s1, fisc s1, fugel s1, gylt s1, þræl s1, weall s1

Masc-N ieldra [V]1, rēfa n1, snaca n1, swica n1

Neut-N ēage n1

Fem-N nǣdre n1

Fem-V -ung [s]1, bend (s)1, dǣd [n]1 V1, hǣs [s]1, lagu V2, lufu (n)1, sāwol [n]1, synn [n]1

Neut-Ø gēar $ø$1, gift [s]1, swinc $ø$1, þing [s]1 $ø$3, weorc [s]4 $ø$1, winter $ø$1, word $ø$2

Masc-M fēond (s)2 [$ø$]1, frēond [$ø$]3, mann M17

D.4.5 PFP 10 (M)

TEXT INFO MS: Cambridge, Fitzwilliam Museum, McClean 123, fols. 115r–120r; TEXT: Poema Morale (cited as M); SOURCE: Paues; PERIOD: C13b2 (C13b2–C14a1, c1300); DIALECT: South-West Midland (Gloucestershire); GRID REF: 394 213

TOKENS Nominative/Accusative Plurals 44 (12), Syncretised Dative/Prepositional Plurals 10 (0), Unsyncretised Dative/Prepositional Plurals 5 (10), Syncretism Rate 0.67 (0), Genitive Plurals 4 (1), Total of Plurals 63 (23)

TYPES AND RATES

	s	n	V	ø	M	TOTAL
TYPES	17 (17)	1 (1)	6 (7)	4 (4)	1 (1)	29 (30)
RATE	0.59 (0.57)	0.035 (0.033)	0.21 (0.23)	0.14 (0.13)	0.035 (0.033)	1 (1)
SPREAD RATE	1.7 (1.7)	0.5 (0.5)	0.86 (1)	0.57 (0.57)	0.33 (0.33)	—

Masc-S -ere $s1$, -ing $s4$, -ling $s1$, dēofol $s1$, engel $s1$, gylt $s1$, þrǣl $s1$, wæg $s1$, weall $s1$, wine $s1$

Masc-N swica $[V]1$

Neut-N ēage $n2$

Fem-V -ung $[s]1$, bend $(s)1$, dǣd $V1$, hǣs $V1$, lagu $V2$, sāwol $V2$, synn $[s]1$

Neut-Ø gēar $ø1$, þing $ø1$, weorc $[s]8$, wīf $[s]1$, winter $[s]1$ $(V)2$, word $[s]2$

Masc-M fēond $[ø]2$, frēond $[ø]2$, mann $M8$

D.4.6 PFP 4 (T)

TEXT INFO MS: Cambridge, Trinity College B. 14. 52, fols. 2r–9v; TEXT: Poema Morale (cited as T); SOURCE: Hall (*Selections*, Text VIII); PERIOD: C12b; DIALECT: South-East Midland (Essex); GRID REF: 557 222

TOKENS Nominative/Accusative Plurals 61 (14), Syncretised Dative/Prepositional Plurals 11 (2), Unsyncretised Dative/Prepositional Plurals 8 (8), Syncretism Rate 0.58 (0.2), Genitive Plurals 7 (3), Total of Plurals 87 (27)

TYPES AND RATES

	s	n	V	ø	M	TOTAL
TYPES	17 (17)	7 (7)	7 (8)	7 (8)	1 (1)	39 (41)
RATE	0.44 (0.41)	0.18 (0.17)	0.18 (0.2)	0.18 (0.2)	0.026 (0.024)	1 (1)
SPREAD RATE	1.4 (1.4)	1 (1)	0.78 (0.89)	0.88 (1)	0.33 (0.33)	—

Masc-S -ere $s1$, -ing $s2$, -ling $s2$, dēofol $[n]1$, engel $s2$, eorl $s1$, fisc $s1$, fugel $s1$, gylt $s2$, þrǣl $s1$, wæg $s1$, wine $s1$

Masc-N efeta $n1$, ieldra $[V]1$, snaca $n1$, swica $n1$

Neut-N ēage $n2$

Fem-N nǣdre $n1$, wicce $n1$

Neut-V bed $V1$

Fem-V -ung $[s]1$, bend $(s)1$, dǣd $V1$, lagu $[s]1$ $V1$, lufu $[s]1$, stund $V1$, synn $V1$

Neut-Ø gēar $ø1$, swinc $ø1$, þing $[s]1$ $ø3$, weorc $[s]5$, winter $(V)2$ $ø1$, word $ø2$

Masc-M fēond $[ø]2$, frēond $[ø]3$, mann $M16$

D.4.7 PFP 8 (D)

TEXT INFO MS: Oxford, Bodley Digby 4, fols. 97r–110v; TEXT: Poema Morale (cited as T); SOURCE: Zupitza; PERIOD: C13a; DIALECT: Southeastern (Kent); GRID REF: 568 157

TOKENS Nominative/Accusative Plurals 63 (16), Syncretised Dative/Prepositional Plurals 7 (3), Unsyncretised Dative/Prepositional Plurals 6 (10), Syncretism Rate 0.54 (0.23), Genitive Plurals 5 (1), Total of Plurals 81 (30)

TYPES AND RATES

	s	n	V	ø	M	TOTAL
TYPES	13 (13)	12 (12)	6 (7)	7 (7)	1 (1)	39 (40)
RATE	0.33 (0.33)	0.31 (0.3)	0.15 (0.17)	0.18 (0.17)	0.026 (0.025)	1 (1)
SPREAD RATE	1.2 (1.2)	2 (2)	0.43 (0.5)	1.4 (1.4)	0.33 (0.33)	—

Masc-S -ere $s1$, -ing $s2$, -ling $s1$, dēofol $[n]1$, engel $s1$, eorl $s1$, fisc $[ø]1$, fugel $s1$, wæg $s1$, weall $s1$, wine $s1$

Masc-N efeta $n1$, ieldra $n1$, snaca $n1$, steorra $n1$

Neut-N ēage $n2$

Fem-N nǣdre $n1$

Fem-V -ung $V1$, bend $(s)1$, dǣd $[n]1$, hǣs $[n]2$, lagu $[n]1$ $V1$, lufu $V1$, mēd $[s]1$, pīn $[n]1$, sāwol $V1$, stund $V1$, synn $[s]1$ $[n]2$, tīd $V1$

Neut-Ø gēar $ø2$, þing $ø2$, weorc $[s]5$ $ø1$, word $ø1$

Masc-M fēond $[ø]2$, frēond $[ø]2$, mann $M18$

D.5 PFPs of *The Peterborough Chronicle*

D.5.1 PFP 15000 (CA)

TEXT INFO MS: Oxford, Bodleian Library, Laud Misc 636, fols. 58v–81r; TEXT: Peterborough Chronicle, Copied Annals (1070–1121) (cited as CA); SOURCE: Earle and Plummer, and Clark; PERIOD: Late Old English; DIALECT: Close to the standard Late West-Saxon but with a tint of Southern peculiarities

TOKENS Nominative/Accusative Plurals 458 (0), Syncretised Dative/Prepositional Plurals 1 (0), Unsyncretised Dative/Prepositional Plurals 124 (0), Syncretism Rate 0.008 (NA), Genitive Plurals 81 (0), Total of Plurals 664 (0)

TYPES AND RATES

	s	n	V	ø	M	TOTAL
TYPES	62 (62)	31 (31)	41 (41)	20 (20)	2 (2)	156 (156)
RATE	0.4 (0.4)	0.2 (0.2)	0.26 (0.26)	0.13 (0.13)	0.013 (0.013)	1 (1)
SPREAD RATE	1.2 (1.2)	1.7 (1.7)	0.98 (0.98)	0.54 (0.54)	0.25 (0.25)	—

Masc-S -ere $s1$, -gengel $s3$, abbod $s6$, āþ $s7$, biscop $s13$, calic $[n]1$, cantelcāp $s1$, castel $s13$, ceorl $s1$, circul $s1$, cleric $s1$ $[V]1$, cniht $s4$, cyning $s5$, dæg $s3$, dǣl $[ø]1$, ealdor $s2$, eorl $s5$, gærsum $s2$ $[n]3$ $[V]6$, geard $s1$, gīsl $s3$, hearm $s1$, heorot $s1$, hlāf $s1$, lāttēow $s1$, manslieht $s1$, mere $s3$, munuc $s24$ $[V]3$, nēahgebūr $s1$, rǣd $s1$, regn $s3$, sceatt $s2$, Scottas $s3$, seht $(V)1$, sīþ $[V]1$, stæf $s1$, stīweard $s1$, toll $s1$, tūn $s1$, tūr $s1$, þegn $s4$, þēof $s1$, þorp $s1$, wæstm $s2$, Wēalas $[n]1$, weall $s1$, wer $s2$, wind $s1$

Masc-N byrla [s]1, hālga n2, here-toga [s]1, līchama n1, mitta n1, mōna n1, rēfa n1, steorra n2, sticca n1, swica n1, tēona n1, wita n4
Neut-N ēage n1
Fem-N arwe n2, cirice n1, hacele [s]1, nunne [V]2, tunne n1
Masc-V feld V1, Norþhymbre [n]1, sunu [s]1 [n]3, wudu [s]1 V3
Neut-V abbodrīce [s]3 [n]1 V1, biscoprīce [s]1 [n]1, bod [n]1 V1, fæsten V1, foþor [ø]2, lim V1, scip V5, writ [s]1 V10 [ø]1
Fem-V -ness V2, -ung V4, æht V1, byrþen [s]1, duru [n]1 V1, earmþu V1, foreweard V2, hand V4, lagu [s]2 [n]1 V7, lēode [n]1, mīl V5, rōd [n]3, scīr [n]1, synn V1, tilþ V1, trēowþ V1, witnes [s]1 V2, wucu [n]1
Masc-Ø brōþor [V]3
Neut-Ø -ett [V]2, corn ø2, cotlīf ø1, dēor ø1, fenn (s)4, gēar ø3, gield [V]1 ø9, hām [s]1, hors ø1, hūs [s]4, hund ø3, hundred ø6, land [s]6 ø5, marc ø4, mōt ø1, mynster [s]3 [V]4, rād ø1, rēaf [s]1, riht [n]1 [V]2 ø3, scrīn [s]1 [V]1, scrūd ø1, tācen [V]1, þing ø9, þūsend [n]2, wæpen [V]1, wæter [s]2, weder [V]3, winn [n]2, word [V]2
Fem-Ø sweostor [V]3
Masc-M -ende [V]1, fēond [ø]2, mann [V]2 [ø]1 M92
Fem-M bōc [s]1 M1, burg [V]1

D.5.2 PFP 16000 (1C)

TEXT INFO MS: Oxford, Bodleian Library, Laud Misc 636, fols. 81r-91v; TEXT: Peterborough Chronicle, First Continuation (1122–1131) with later interpolations (cited as 1C); SOURCE: Earle and Plummer, and Clark; PERIOD: C12a2 (c1132); DIALECT: South-East Midland (Peterborough); GRID REF: 519 298

TOKENS Nominative/Accusative Plurals 146 (0), Syncretised Dative/Prepositional Plurals 0 (0), Unsyncretised Dative/Prepositional Plurals 5 (0), Syncretism Rate 0 (NA), Genitive Plurals 9 (0), Total of Plurals 160 (0)

TYPES AND RATES

	s	n	V	ø	M	TOTAL
TYPES	45 (45)	2 (2)	15 (15)	10 (10)	3 (3)	75 (75)
RATE	0.6 (0.6)	0.027 (0.027)	0.2 (0.2)	0.13 (0.13)	0.04 (0.04)	1 (1)
SPREAD RATE	1.3 (1.3)	0.25 (0.25)	1.1 (1.1)	0.71 (0.71)	0.75 (0.75)	—

Masc-S -ere s1 [V]1, abbod s4, æcer s1, āþ s1 [ø]1, biscop s14, būc s1, canon s1, castel s4, cell s1, cniht s2, cræft s1, dæg s5, dīacon s1, earm s1, eorl s3, fugel s1, gærsum s2 [V]1, hæþen [V]1, horn [ø]2, hund s1, munt s1, munuc s11, pening s1, plōg s1, prior s1, ræd [V]1, scilling s3, stān s2, tūn s1, þegn s5, þēof s1, wrenc s1
Masc-N hunta [s]2, pāpa [s]1, tīma [V]1, winna [s]1
Fem-N āte n1, belle [V]1, bēo n1, hacele [s]1
Masc-V wudu [s]1
Neut-V abbodrīce [s]2, hēafod [ø]1, rīce [s]1, writ V1
Fem-V æht V2, bend (s)1, brycg [s]1, drān V2, giefu V2, hand V1, lagu [s]1, mīl V1, sibb V1
Neut-Ø -lac [s]1, dwild ø1, gēar ø1, gield [s]1, hors ø1, hundred ø2, mōt [s]1, riht [s]1 [V]1, swīn ø1, tācen [V]1, þing ø2, wīf [s]3, wīl [s]1
Masc-M fēond [ø]1, frēond M2, mann M17
Fem-M bōc M1

D.5.3 PFP 149 (FC)

TEXT INFO MS: Oxford, Bodleian Library, Laud Misc 636, fols. 88v–91v; TEXT: Peterborough Chronicle final continuation (cited as FC); SOURCE: Earle and Plummer, and Clark; PERIOD: C12b1 (c1154); DIALECT: South-East Midland (Peterborough); GRID REF: 519 298

TOKENS Nominative/Accusative Plurals 109 (0), Syncretised Dative/Prepositional Plurals 0 (0), Unsyncretised Dative/Prepositional Plurals 2 (0), Syncretism Rate 0 (NA), Genitive Plurals 4 (0), Total of Plurals 115 (0)

TYPES AND RATES

	s	n	V	ø	M	TOTAL
TYPES	36 (39)	3 (3)	0 (0)	3 (3)	2 (2)	44 (47)
RATE	0.82 (0.83)	0.068 (0.064)	0 (0)	0.068 (0.064)	0.045 (0.043)	1 (1)
SPREAD RATE	2.1 (2.3)	0.33 (0.33)	0 (0)	0.5 (0.5)	0.67 (0.67)	—

Masc-S -ere s1, āþ s3, biscop s1, castel s9, cleric s1, dæg s1, dēofol s1, eorl s2, gīsl s1, giest s1, martyr s1, munuc s8, rāp s1, sand s1, stān s1, streng s1, tūn s2

Masc-N hālga n1, nefa [s]1, snaca [s]1, steorra [s]1, swica [s]2, þūma [s]1

Fem-N nǣdre [s]1, padde [s]1, wīce n1

Neut-V lim [s]1

Fem-V candel [s]1, dǣd [s]1, fetor [s]1, foreweard [s]1, hǣrn [s]1, racen-tēah [s]1, synn [s]1, trēowþ [s]2

Neut-Ø dēor ø1, gield [s]2, land [s]7, þūsend [n]1, weorc [s]2, wundor ø2

Masc-M fōt M2, frēond [ø]3, mann M30

Appendix E Item Profiles

In the following, sixty-six Item Profiles are printed in tabular format. They are arranged by the Old English reference class of the key item, as it was introduced in Section 3.1.4 (i.e. Masc-S, Masc-N, Neut-N, Fem-N, Masc-V, Neut-V, Fem-V, Masc-Ø, Neut-Ø, Fem-Ø, Masc-M, Neut-M, and Fem-M). Discussion about the key items is found in Section 3.3.

The special notations in Item Profiles are the same as those in Plural Forms Profiles. Parentheses around a plural type designate that it was an alternative type in Old English, while square brackets designate that the type was impossible in Old English (therefore a case of plural formation transfer). The frequency is based on token counting.

Appendix E   241

Table E.1: Item Profile for *blōstm* (Masc-S)

	C9a	C9b	C10a	C10b	C11a	C11b	C12a	C12b	C13a	C13b	C14a	C14b	C15a	TOTAL
N										$s1$				1
NEM														
SEM								$s8\,[n]2\,(V)4$							14
NWM										$s2$				2
SWM								$[n]2\,(V)2$	$[n]4$	$[n]3\,(V)7$				18
SW														
SE														
TOTAL								18	4	13				35

Table E.2: Item Profile for *dēofol* (Masc-S)

	C9a	C9b	C10a	C10b	C11a	C11b	C12a	C12b	C13a	C13b	C14a	C14b	C15a	TOTAL
N		$s12$								$s2$				14
NEM								$s6$						6
SEM								$s11\,[n]13$	$s1$						25
NWM									$s1$					1
SWM			$[\emptyset]6$					$s3\,[n]5\,(V)2$	$s2\,[n]14$	$s1\,[n]8$				41
SW												$[n]10$		10
SE										$[n]1$				1
TOTAL			18					40	19	11	10			98

Table E.3: Item Profile for *sīþ* (Masc-S)

	C9a	C9b	C10a	C10b	C11a	C11b	C12a	C12b	C13a	C13b	C14a	C14b	C15a	TOTAL
N										$s1\,[V]1$				2
NEM								$s7$						7
SEM								$s14$	$s1$	$s6\,[V]4$				25
NWM									$[V]1$					1
SWM								$s1$	$s3\,[n]15\,[V]13$	$s2\,[V]1$				35
SW												$[V]1$	$s1$	2
SE												$[V]5$		$s1\,[V]4$	10
TOTAL								22	33	15	6	1	5	82

Table E.4: Item Profile for *fāh* (Masc-N)

	C9a	C9b	C10a	C10b	C11a	C11b	C12a	C12b	C13a	C13b	C14a	C14b	C15a	TOTAL
N												$[s]2$		2
NEM														
SEM								$n4$	$n4$						8
NWM									$n4$					4
SWM								$n7\,[\emptyset]4$	$n8$						19
SW										$n1$	$n2$	$[s]8\,n2$		13
SE														
TOTAL								15	12	5	4	10		46

Table E.5: Item Profile for *fēolaga* (Masc-N)

	C9a	C9b	C10a	C10b	C11a	C11b	C12a	C12b	C13a	C13b	C14a	C14b	C15a	TOTAL
N										[s]1	[s]9			10
NEM														
SEM										[s]1				1
NWM														
SWM									[s]6		[s]1			7
SW									[s]3		[s]7	[s]18		28
SE									[s]1					1
TOTAL									10	2	17	18		47

Table E.6: Item Profile for *fēra* (Masc-N)

	C9a	C9b	C10a	C10b	C11a	C11b	C12a	C12b	C13a	C13b	C14a	C14b	C15a	TOTAL
N										[s]1				1
NEM								[s]2						2
SEM									n1	[s]3 n2				6
NWM									[s]1	[s]1				2
SWM			n1					n3	n3 [V]1	n3 [V]1	n9			21
SW									n7					7
SE														
TOTAL			1					5	13	11	9			39

Table E.7: Item Profile for *hālga* (Masc-N)

	C9a	C9b	C10a	C10b	C11a	C11b	C12a	C12b	C13a	C13b	C14a	C14b	C15a	TOTAL
N									[s]1					1
NEM														
SEM								n5	n1	n2				8
NWM									[s]2					2
SWM								n9 [V]1	n11					21
SW											[V]1			1
SE											n2			2
TOTAL								15	15	2	3			35

Table E.8: Item Profile for *hīwan* (Masc-N)

	C9a	C9b	C10a	C10b	C11a	C11b	C12a	C12b	C13a	C13b	C14a	C14b	C15a	TOTAL
N											n1 [V]1			2
NEM								n2						2
SEM								n2						2
NWM														
SWM			n1						n20					21
SW														
SE														
TOTAL			1					4	20		2			27

Appendix E   243

Table E.9: Item Profile for *nama* (Masc-N)

	C9a	C9b	C10a	C10b	C11a	C11b	C12a	C12b	C13a	C13b	C14a	C14b	C15a	TOTAL
N										[s]1	[s]2			3
NEM								[s]3 [V]3						6
SEM								[s]4		[s]3				7
NWM														
SWM			[V]1					n2	n154 [V]3	[s]2				162
SW												[s]1	[s]1	2
SE														
TOTAL			1					12	157	6	2	1	1	180

Table E.10: Item Profile for *steorra* (Masc-N)

	C9a	C9b	C10a	C10b	C11a	C11b	C12a	C12b	C13a	C13b	C14a	C14b	C15a	TOTAL
N			[V]1							[s]1	[s]2			4
NEM								[s]6						6
SEM								[s]9		[s]1				10
NWM														
SWM	n1		n1					n10	n1	n2 [V]3				18
SW														
SE									n1					1
TOTAL	1		2					25	2	7	2			39

Table E.11: Item Profile for *tīma* (Masc-N)

	C9a	C9b	C10a	C10b	C11a	C11b	C12a	C12b	C13a	C13b	C14a	C14b	C15a	TOTAL
N														
NEM								[s]2						2
SEM							[V]1	[s]2 [V]2		[s]2				7
NWM														
SWM											[V]1			1
SW									[V]1		[V]1	[s]1	[s]2	5
SE													[s]2 [V]2	4
TOTAL							1	6	1	2	2	1	6	19

Table E.12: Item Profile for *wrœcca* (Masc-N)

	C9a	C9b	C10a	C10b	C11a	C11b	C12a	C12b	C13a	C13b	C14a	C14b	C15a	TOTAL
N										[s]6				6
NEM								[s]1						1
SEM								[s]10		[s]2				12
NWM									[s]1					1
SWM								[s]1 n5 [V]4	[s]10 n3 [V]5	[s]4				32
SW											[s]2			2
SE											[s]1			1
TOTAL								21	19	12	3			55

Table E.13: Item Profile for *ēage* (Neut-N)

	C9a	C9b	C10a	C10b	C11a	C11b	C12a	C12b	C13a	C13b	C14a	C14b	C15a	TOTAL
N			[V]8							n3				11
NEM								n1						1
SEM								n20		n3	n1			24
NWM									n10					10
SWM	n9		n6 [V]2					n21	n45 [V]2	n18 [V]1				104
SW												n5	n3	8
SE									n2					2
TOTAL	9		16					42	59	25	6	3		160

Table E.14: Item Profile for *ēare* (Neut-N)

	C9a	C9b	C10a	C10b	C11a	C11b	C12a	C12b	C13a	C13b	C14a	C14b	C15a	TOTAL
N			[V]2							n1				3
NEM														
SEM								n4 [V]2						6
NWM									[s]13 n1 [V]1					15
SWM			n3 [V]1					n6	n26 [V]1	[s]1 n3				41
SW														
SE														
TOTAL			6					12	42	5				65

Table E.15: Item Profile for *cirice* (Fem-N)

	C9a	C9b	C10a	C10b	C11a	C11b	C12a	C12b	C13a	C13b	C14a	C14b	C15a	TOTAL
N										[s]1				1
NEM														
SEM								[s]2		[s]3				5
NWM														
SWM								n1						1
SW									n1				[s]2	3
SE											n1			1
TOTAL								3	1	4	1		2	11

Table E.16: Item Profile for *heorte* (Fem-N)

	C9a	C9b	C10a	C10b	C11a	C11b	C12a	C12b	C13a	C13b	C14a	C14b	C15a	TOTAL
N										[s]6				6
NEM								[s]9						9
SEM								[s]6 [V]8		[s]1				15
NWM									[s]1					1
SWM		n1						n10 [V]2	n3					16
SW												[s]2		2
SE									[s]1					1
TOTAL		1						35	5	7		2		50

Appendix E   245

Table E.17: Item Profile for *hlǣfdige* (Fem-N)

	C9a	C9b	C10a	C10b	C11a	C11b	C12a	C12b	C13a	C13b	C14a	C14b	C15a	TOTAL
N										[s]1				1
NEM														
SEM										[s]1	[s]8			9
NWM														
SWM									[s]4	[s]15				19
SW												[s]1	[s]15	16
SE									[s]1					1
TOTAL									5	17	8	1	15	46

Table E.18: Item Profile for *mæsse* (Fem-N)

	C9a	C9b	C10a	C10b	C11a	C11b	C12a	C12b	C13a	C13b	C14a	C14b	C15a	TOTAL
N														
NEM								[s]1						1
SEM														
NWM														
SWM								n2	n1	[s]6 n9				18
SW									[s]1		n2		[s]2	5
SE											n1			1
TOTAL								3	2	15	3		2	25

Table E.19: Item Profile for *nǣdre* (Fem-N)

	C9a	C9b	C10a	C10b	C11a	C11b	C12a	C12b	C13a	C13b	C14a	C14b	C15a	TOTAL
N			[V]2							[s]2	[s]1			5
NEM								[s]4						4
SEM								[s]1 n1		[s]1				3
NWM									[s]1					1
SWM			[V]1					n4 [V]4	n6	n5				20
SW														
SE									n1					1
TOTAL			3					14	8	8	1			34

Table E.20: Item Profile for *sunu* (Masc-V)

	C9a	C9b	C10a	C10b	C11a	C11b	C12a	C12b	C13a	C13b	C14a	C14b	C15a	TOTAL
N			V17							[s]1	[s]1 [ø]1			20
NEM								[s]14						14
SEM								[s]4		[s]25 [n]2				31
NWM									[s]1					1
SWM			[s]2 V2					[s]5 [n]1	[s]1	[s]2 [n]2	[s]4			19
SW								[s]2			[s]3		[s]4	9
SE														
TOTAL			21					24	4	32	9		4	94

Table E.21: Item Profile for *bed* (Neut-V)

	C9a	C9b	C10a	C10b	C11a	C11b	C12a	C12b	C13a	C13b	C14a	C14b	C15a	TOTAL
N											V1			1
NEM								$[s]$11						11
SEM								$[s]$6 $[n]$2 V9		$[s]$2				19
NWM									$[s]$1					1
SWM								$[n]$4 V5	$[n]$3	$[s]$4				16
SW											$[s]$1 $[n]$3	$[s]$2	$[s]$1	7
SE												$[s]$1		1
TOTAL								37	4	6	5	2	2	56

Table E.22: Item Profile for *bod* (Neut-V)

	C9a	C9b	C10a	C10b	C11a	C11b	C12a	C12b	C13a	C13b	C14a	C14b	C15a	TOTAL
N			V2							$[s]$4				6
NEM														
SEM									V2	$[s]$2				4
NWM														
SWM			V1 $[ø]$1					$[s]$2 $[n]$7 V28	V2	$[s]$1 $[n]$1				43
SW														
SE														
TOTAL			4					37	4	8				53

Table E.23: Item Profile for *geat* (Neut-V)

	C9a	C9b	C10a	C10b	C11a	C11b	C12a	C12b	C13a	C13b	C14a	C14b	C15a	TOTAL
N			$[ø]$1								$[s]$4			5
NEM														
SEM								$[n]$10	$[n]$2	$[s]$1				13
NWM									$[s]$2					2
SWM	V4							$[n]$4 V7	$[s]$5 $[n]$4	$[s]$6	$[s]$1			31
SW									$[s]$1		$[s]$1	$[s]$3	$[s]$1	6
SE														
TOTAL	4		1					21	14	7	6	3	1	57

Table E.24: Item Profile for *lim* (Neut-V)

	C9a	C9b	C10a	C10b	C11a	C11b	C12a	C12b	C13a	C13b	C14a	C14b	C15a	TOTAL
N										$[s]$4 $[ø]$1	$[s]$1			6
NEM								$[s]$4						4
SEM								$[s]$11 $[n]$6	$[n]$1	$[s]$5	$[s]$1			24
NWM								$[s]$5						5
SWM								$[n]$9	$[s]$1 $[n]$8	$[s]$1				19
SW											$[s]$5		$[s]$3	8
SE														
TOTAL								30	15	11	7		3	66

Appendix E   247

Table E.25: Item Profile for *mægden* (Neut-V)

	C9a	C9b	C10a	C10b	C11a	C11b	C12a	C12b	C13a	C13b	C14a	C14b	C15a	TOTAL
N											$[s]1$			1
NEM														
SEM									$[s]9$	$[s]3$				12
NWM								$[s]1$						1
SWM							$V2$	$[s]25$	$[s]17$	$[s]3$				47
SW								$[s]3$				$[s]5$	$[s]8$	16
SE														
TOTAL							2	29	26	7	5	8		77

Table E.26: Item Profile for *writ* (Neut-V)

	C9a	C9b	C10a	C10b	C11a	C11b	C12a	C12b	C13a	C13b	C14a	C14b	C15a	TOTAL
N			$V3$											3
NEM								$[s]6$						6
SEM							$V1$	$[s]2$	$[s]1$	$[s]3\ V16$				23
NWM														
SWM			$V3$					$[n]2$	$[s]2\ V2$					9
SW								$[s]1$						1
SE								$[s]1$						1
TOTAL			6				1	10	7	19				43

Table E.27: Item Profile for *yfel* (Neut-V)

	C9a	C9b	C10a	C10b	C11a	C11b	C12a	C12b	C13a	C13b	C14a	C14b	C15a	TOTAL
N			$V4$							$[s]1$				5
NEM														
SEM								$[ø]2$	$[s]1$					3
NWM									$[s]1$					1
SWM	$[ø]4$		$V1\ [ø]2$					$[s]4\ [ø]4$	$[s]6\ V3$					24
SW														
SE									$[s]1$					1
TOTAL	4		7					10	12	1				34

Table E.28: Item Profile for *-ung* (Fem-V)

	C9a	C9b	C10a	C10b	C11a	C11b	C12a	C12b	C13a	C13b	C14a	C14b	C15a	TOTAL
N			$V5\ [ø]1$											6
NEM														
SEM								$[s]7\ V2$	$[s]1$	$[s]1$				11
NWM								$[s]12$						12
SWM	$V1$		$V3$				$V4$	$[s]34$	$[s]5$					47
SW											$[s]1\ [ø]1$	$[s]2$		4
SE								$[s]2\ V1$						3
TOTAL	1		9				13	49	6	1	2	2		83

Table E.29: Item Profile for *bēn* (Fem-V)

	C9a	C9b	C10a	C10b	C11a	C11b	C12a	C12b	C13a	C13b	C14a	C14b	C15a	TOTAL
N														
NEM								[s]7						7
SEM								V2		[s]2				4
NWM														
SWM	V1								[n]10					11
SW														
SE											[s]2			2
TOTAL	1							9	10	2	2			24

Table E.30: Item Profile for *bliss* (Fem-V)

	C9a	C9b	C10a	C10b	C11a	C11b	C12a	C12b	C13a	C13b	C14a	C14b	C15a	TOTAL
N										[ø]1				1
NEM														
SEM										[s]1				1
NWM								[s]4						4
SWM								[n]1 V1	[n]8 V3	[n]4				17
SW														
SE														
TOTAL								2	15	6				23

Table E.31: Item Profile for *dǣd* (Fem-V)

	C9a	C9b	C10a	C10b	C11a	C11b	C12a	C12b	C13a	C13b	C14a	C14b	C15a	TOTAL
N									[s]1	[s]4	[s]14			19
NEM								[s]55						55
SEM								[s]13 [n]12 V27	[s]2	[s]2				56
NWM									[s]1 V1					2
SWM								[n]2 V21	[s]2 [n]12 V6	[s]8 [n]3 V7				61
SW											V1	[s]7	[s]2	10
SE									[n]2		[s]6			8
TOTAL								130	27	24	21	7	2	211

Table E.32: Item Profile for *giefu* (Fem-V)

	C9a	C9b	C10a	C10b	C11a	C11b	C12a	C12b	C13a	C13b	C14a	C14b	C15a	TOTAL
N														
NEM								[s]7						7
SEM							V2							2
NWM									[s]1					1
SWM								V6	[s]1 [n]3					10
SW														
SE											[s]3			3
TOTAL							2	13	5		3			23

Table E.33: Item Profile for *hǣs* (Fem-V)

	C9a	C9b	C10a	C10b	C11a	C11b	C12a	C12b	C13a	C13b	C14a	C14b	C15a	TOTAL
N														
NEM														
SEM								*V*6						6
NWM														
SWM								[*n*]5 *V*16	[*s*]6 [*n*]3 *V*2	[*s*]3 *V*1				36
SW											[*s*]1			1
SE									[*n*]2		[*s*]8			10
TOTAL								27	13	4	9			53

Table E.34: Item Profile for *hand* (Fem-V)

	C9a	C9b	C10a	C10b	C11a	C11b	C12a	C12b	C13a	C13b	C14a	C14b	C15a	TOTAL
N			*V*1							[*s*]3 *V*6 [*M*]3	[*s*]1 [*ø*]1 [*M*]1			16
NEM								[*s*]1 *V*3						4
SEM							*V*1	[*n*]10 *V*2 [*ø*]2		[*s*]13 [*n*]1 [*M*]1	[*n*]1			31
NWM									[*s*]3 [*n*]1 *V*4					8
SWM	*V*4	*V*2	*V*2					[*n*]8	[*n*]31	[*s*]1 [*n*]8 *V*2	[*s*]1 *V*1			60
SW									*V*1		[*n*]4 *V*1	[*s*]9 *V*1 [*ø*]1	[*s*]1 *V*1	19
SE											[*n*]1			1
TOTAL	4	2	3				1	26	40	38	12	11	2	139

Table E.35: Item Profile for *lagu* (Fem-V)

	C9a	C9b	C10a	C10b	C11a	C11b	C12a	C12b	C13a	C13b	C14a	C14b	C15a	TOTAL
N										[*s*]3				3
NEM								[*s*]45						45
SEM							[*s*]1	[*s*]1 *V*1		[*s*]2				5
NWM														
SWM								[*n*]7 *V*24	[*s*]1 [*n*]11 *V*3	[*n*]6 *V*6				58
SW													[*s*]2	2
SE									[*n*]1 *V*1					2
TOTAL							1	78	17	17			2	115

Table E.36: Item Profile for *lufu* (Fem-V)

	C9a	C9b	C10a	C10b	C11a	C11b	C12a	C12b	C13a	C13b	C14a	C14b	C15a	TOTAL
N														
NEM														
SEM								[*s*]1	[*s*]1					2
NWM														
SWM									(*n*)6 *V*2	(*n*)2				10
SW														
SE									*V*1					1
TOTAL								1	10	2				13

Table E.37: Item Profile for *miht* (Fem-V)

	C9a	C9b	C10a	C10b	C11a	C11b	C12a	C12b	C13a	C13b	C14a	C14b	C15a	TOTAL
N			V5 [ø]1							[s]3				9
NEM								[s]23						23
SEM								[s]10 [n]2 V2	[s]4					18
NWM									[s]1					1
SWM								[n]4 V4	[s]3 [n]1	[n]1				13
SW											[s]2		[s]1	3
SE														
TOTAL			6					45	9	4		2	1	67

Table E.38: Item Profile for *pīn* (Fem-V)

	C9a	C9b	C10a	C10b	C11a	C11b	C12a	C12b	C13a	C13b	C14a	C14b	C15a	TOTAL
N										[s]4	[s]2			6
NEM														
SEM								[n]2 V6	[s]1 [n]2					11
NWM									[s]5					5
SWM								[n]2 V3	[n]15	[s]5 [n]5				30
SW												[s]1		1
SE									[n]1					1
TOTAL								13	24	14	2	1		54

Table E.39: Item Profile for *sāwol* (Fem-V)

	C9a	C9b	C10a	C10b	C11a	C11b	C12a	C12b	C13a	C13b	C14a	C14b	C15a	TOTAL
N										[s]2	[s]1 [ø]1			4
NEM								[s]25						25
SEM								[s]2 V8	[s]2	[s]1				13
NWM									[s]1					1
SWM	V1							[n]15 V19	[n]4 V2	[s]6 [n]12 V9				68
SW											[n]1			1
SE									[n]1 V1		[s]3 [n]1		[s]1	7
TOTAL	1							69	11	30	7		1	119

Table E.40: Item Profile for *synn* (Fem-V)

	C9a	C9b	C10a	C10b	C11a	C11b	C12a	C12b	C13a	C13b	C14a	C14b	C15a	TOTAL
N			V7						[s]2	[s]5 [ø]1	[s]7			22
NEM								[s]126		[s]2				128
SEM								[s]233 [n]24 V21	[s]15 [n]2	[s]5				300
NWM									[s]11					11
SWM	V2		V7					[n]59 V75	[n]33 V2	[s]17 [n]24				219
SW										[s]1	[s]1		[s]2	4
SE									[s]1 [n]7 V2		[s]18 [n]2			30
TOTAL	2		14					538	75	55	28		2	714

Table E.41: Item Profile for *wund* (Fem-V)

	C9a	C9b	C10a	C10b	C11a	C11b	C12a	C12b	C13a	C13b	C14a	C14b	C15a	TOTAL
N									[s]2	[s]1				3
NEM								[s]2						2
SEM								[s]6 [n]6		[s]9				21
NWM								[s]4						4
SWM								[n]7 V2	[n]9	[s]5 [n]4	[s]1			28
SW									[s]1		[n]1	[s]1	[s]3	6
SE														
TOTAL								23	16	19	2	1	3	64

Table E.42: Item Profile for *brōþor* (Masc-Ø)

	C9a	C9b	C10a	C10b	C11a	C11b	C12a	C12b	C13a	C13b	C14a	C14b	C15a	TOTAL
N			[V]8 ø1											9
NEM								[V]12						12
SEM								[n]4		[s]1 [n]1 [V]17				23
NWM									[V]3					3
SWM		[V]4	[V]4 ø6					[n]4 [V]18	[n]1	[n]6				43
SW								[n]1						1
SE													[n]6	6
TOTAL		4	19					39	4	25			6	97

Table E.43: Item Profile for *bān* (Neut-Ø)

	C9a	C9b	C10a	C10b	C11a	C11b	C12a	C12b	C13a	C13b	C14a	C14b	C15a	TOTAL
N										[s]5				5
NEM								[s]2						2
SEM										[s]6				6
NWM									[s]1	[s]1				2
SWM	ø5								ø5	[s]7 ø3	[s]3 ø3			26
SW											[s]4	[s]1		5
SE														
TOTAL	5							7	11	13	9	1		46

Table E.44: Item Profile for *bearn* (Neut-Ø)

	C9a	C9b	C10a	C10b	C11a	C11b	C12a	C12b	C13a	C13b	C14a	C14b	C15a	TOTAL
N										[s]1				1
NEM								[s]2 ø1						3
SEM								[s]4		ø8				12
NWM									[s]2					2
SWM	ø8		ø15					ø22	ø8	[s]1				54
SW														
SE														
TOTAL	8		15					29	10	10				72

Table E.45: Item Profile for *cynn* (Neut-Ø)

	C9a	C9b	C10a	C10b	C11a	C11b	C12a	C12b	C13a	C13b	C14a	C14b	C15a	TOTAL
N			[V]4											4
NEM														
SEM								[s]2 [V]12	[s]1					15
NWM									[s]2					2
SWM			ø2					[s]2 ø2	[s]3 [V]1 ø8					18
SW														
SE														
TOTAL			6					18	15					39

Table E.46: Item Profile for *dēor* (Neut-Ø)

	C9a	C9b	C10a	C10b	C11a	C11b	C12a	C12b	C13a	C13b	C14a	C14b	C15a	TOTAL
N														
NEM								[s]1 ø8						9
SEM								ø19		[s]1 ø2				22
NWM									[V]1					1
SWM								ø10	ø3	ø3				16
SW														
SE														
TOTAL								38	4	6				48

Table E.47: Item Profile for *gēar* (Neut-Ø)

	C9a	C9b	C10a	C10b	C11a	C11b	C12a	C12b	C13a	C13b	C14a	C14b	C15a	TOTAL
N			ø1							ø7	ø1			9
NEM								[s]10 ø7						17
SEM							ø1	[s]14 ø3		[s]1 [V]1 ø41	[V]2 ø1			64
NWM									ø1					1
SWM	ø1							[V]2 ø1	[s]7 ø7	[V]1 ø7				26
SW									ø1		ø20	[s]1 ø2	[s]2 [V]19	45
SE									ø2		ø1			3
TOTAL	1		1				1	37	18	58	25	3	21	165

Table E.48: Item Profile for *gōd* (Neut-Ø)

	C9a	C9b	C10a	C10b	C11a	C11b	C12a	C12b	C13a	C13b	C14a	C14b	C15a	TOTAL
N			[V]1											4
NEM														
SEM								[V]1						1
NWM														
SWM	ø3		ø5					ø3	[n]2 ø4	[V]8				25
SW											[V]1			1
SE								[s]1			[s]46 ø2		[s]5	54
TOTAL	3		9					3	8	8	49		5	85

Appendix E   253

Table E.49: Item Profile for *hors* (Neut-Ø)

	C9a	C9b	C10a	C10b	C11a	C11b	C12a	C12b	C13a	C13b	C14a	C14b	C15a	TOTAL
N														
NEM								ø1						1
SEM							ø1	ø2		ø12	ø2			17
NWM														
SWM								ø2	ø2	ø7				11
SW														
SE											ø3			3
TOTAL							1	5	2	19	5			32

Table E.50: Item Profile for *hundred* (Neut-Ø)

	C9a	C9b	C10a	C10b	C11a	C11b	C12a	C12b	C13a	C13b	C14a	C14b	C15a	TOTAL
N														
NEM								ø4						4
SEM							ø2			ø8				10
NWM														
SWM														
SW												[s]1 ø2		3
SE														
TOTAL							2	4		8		3		17

Table E.51: Item Profile for *land* (Neut-Ø)

	C9a	C9b	C10a	C10b	C11a	C11b	C12a	C12b	C13a	C13b	C14a	C14b	C15a	TOTAL
N		[V]1								[s]2				3
NEM								[s]2						2
SEM								[s]7		[s]9 [V]8 ø12	[s]1			37
NWM														
SWM	ø1	ø1							[s]3	[s]1 ø1				7
SW												[s]1	[s]7	8
SE								[s]2		[s]4				6
TOTAL		1	2					9	5	33	5	1	7	63

Table E.52: Item Profile for *scēap* (Neut-Ø)

	C9a	C9b	C10a	C10b	C11a	C11b	C12a	C12b	C13a	C13b	C14a	C14b	C15a	TOTAL
N														
NEM								ø10						10
SEM								ø14		[s]1 ø8				23
NWM														
SWM	ø1		ø5					ø1	ø3	ø7				17
SW												ø7		7
SE												ø1		1
TOTAL	1		5					25	3	16		8		58

Table E.53: Item Profile for *trēow* (Neut-Ø)

	C9a	C9b	C10a	C10b	C11a	C11b	C12a	C12b	C13a	C13b	C14a	C14b	C15a	TOTAL
N										[s]4	[s]1			5
NEM								[s]6						6
SEM								[s]8 [n]2		[s]1 [n]2				13
NWM														
SWM								[n]2	[n]14	[n]8				24
SW											[n]2	[s]1		3
SE										[s]1				1
TOTAL								18	14	15	4	1		52

Table E.54: Item Profile for *þing* (Neut-Ø)

	C9a	C9b	C10a	C10b	C11a	C11b	C12a	C12b	C13a	C13b	C14a	C14b	C15a	TOTAL
N									[s]1	[s]4 ø7	[s]4 [V]1 ø5			22
NEM								[s]19 [V]1						20
SEM							ø2	[s]11 [V]2 ø97	[s]1 ø7	[s]1 [V]17 ø4	[s]2 ø3			147
NWM									[s]16 [V]1 ø2	[s]1				20
SWM		ø2						[s]6 [V]4 ø84	[s]70 ø81	[s]3 [V]2 ø9				261
SW								[s]1	ø1		[s]1	ø6	[s]3 ø5	17
SE									[s]6 ø2		[s]18 ø1		[s]2	29
TOTAL		2					2	225	188	48	35	6	10	516

Table E.55: Item Profile for *wǣpen* (Neut-Ø)

	C9a	C9b	C10a	C10b	C11a	C11b	C12a	C12b	C13a	C13b	C14a	C14b	C15a	TOTAL
N														
NEM								[n]2						2
SEM								[s]10 [V]6		ø1				17
NWM									[s]1					1
SWM								[n]2 [V]10	[s]1 [n]7 [V]6	[n]2 [V]3				31
SW												[s]1		1
SE														
TOTAL								30	15	6		1		52

Table E.56: Item Profile for *wæter* (Neut-Ø)

	C9a	C9b	C10a	C10b	C11a	C11b	C12a	C12b	C13a	C13b	C14a	C14b	C15a	TOTAL
N									[s]2	[s]2				2
NEM								[s]2						2
SEM								[s]6		[s]6				12
NWM										[s]2				2
SWM		ø2						[s]2	[s]15					19
SW											[s]1			1
SE														
TOTAL		2						10	15	10	1			38

Table E.57: Item Profile for *weorc* (Neut-Ø)

	C9a	C9b	C10a	C10b	C11a	C11b	C12a	C12b	C13a	C13b	C14a	C14b	C15a	TOTAL
N			[s]1 [V]3 ø2							[s]5	[s]2			13
NEM								[s]14						14
SEM								[s]19 ø2	[s]14	[s]1				36
NWM								[s]6						6
SWM	ø6		ø3					[s]21 ø3	[s]27 ø1	[s]22 ø2				85
SW											[s]1	[s]1	[s]2	4
SE									[s]14 ø1		[s]15			30
TOTAL	6		9					59	63	30	18	1	2	188

Table E.58: Item Profile for *wīf* (Neut-Ø)

	C9a	C9b	C10a	C10b	C11a	C11b	C12a	C12b	C13a	C13b	C14a	C14b	C15a	TOTAL
N			[V]2 ø1											3
NEM								[s]5						5
SEM						[s]3				[s]15	[s]1			19
NWM														
SWM			ø2					[s]4 ø1 [M]2	[s]2	[s]6 ø1				18
SW													[s]1	1
SE											[s]1			1
TOTAL			5			3		12	2	22	2		1	47

Table E.59: Item Profile for *winter* (Neut-Ø)

	C9a	C9b	C10a	C10b	C11a	C11b	C12a	C12b	C13a	C13b	C14a	C14b	C15a	TOTAL
N			ø1							[s]1 ø3	ø1			6
NEM														
SEM								(V)16 ø1	(V)1	[s]1 ø19				38
NWM														
SWM			ø1					(V)6	(V)4	[s]1 (V)2 ø8	ø1			23
SW								(V)1			ø1		(V)2 ø4	8
SE														
TOTAL			2					24	5	35	3		6	75

Table E.60: Item Profile for *witt* (Neut-Ø)

	C9a	C9b	C10a	C10b	C11a	C11b	C12a	C12b	C13a	C13b	C14a	C14b	C15a	TOTAL
N										[s]2				2
NEM														
SEM									[s]5					5
NWM									[s]14					14
SWM							[s]1	[s]29 ø2						32
SW											[s]1		[s]1	2
SE										[s]1				1
TOTAL							1	50	2	1	1		1	56

256

Table E.61: Item Profile for *word* (Neut-Ø)

	C9a	C9b	C10a	C10b	C11a	C11b	C12a	C12b	C13a	C13b	C14a	C14b	C15a	TOTAL
N			[V]6 ø3							[s]5	[s]11			25
NEM								[s]49		[s]1				50
SEM								[s]34 ø60	[s]13	[s]6 ø1	[s]1			115
NWM									[s]22 ø1	[s]1				24
SWM	ø5		ø9					[s]24 [V]4 ø26	[s]65 ø156	[s]50 [n]1 ø13	[s]6			359
SW								ø3	[s]5		[s]3 ø2	[s]7	[s]5	25
SE									ø1		[s]2			3
TOTAL	5		18					200	263	78	25	7	5	601

Table E.62: Item Profile for *sweostor* (Fem-Ø)

	C9a	C9b	C10a	C10b	C11a	C11b	C12a	C12b	C13a	C13b	C14a	C14b	C15a	TOTAL
N			[V]1 ø1											2
NEM								[s]4						4
SEM								[s]2		[s]6				8
NWM									[V]5					5
SWM			ø2					[n]2 [V]6	[n]66					76
SW								[n]1					[n]8	9
SE													[n]7	7
TOTAL			4					15	71	6			15	111

Table E.63: Item Profile for *fēond* (Masc-M)

	C9a	C9b	C10a	C10b	C11a	C11b	C12a	C12b	C13a	C13b	C14a	C14b	C15a	TOTAL
N			(s)3								(s)3			6
NEM														
SEM							[ø]1	[ø]2		(s)4				7
NWM									[ø]1					1
SWM	[ø]7 M4		(s)3					(s)1 [ø]13	(s)4 [ø]10	(s)22 [ø]10				74
SW														
SE									[ø]2		(s)1			3
TOTAL	11		6				1	16	17	36	4			91

Table E.64: Item Profile for *frēond* (Masc-M)

	C9a	C9b	C10a	C10b	C11a	C11b	C12a	C12b	C13a	C13b	C14a	C14b	C15a	TOTAL
N			(s)1							(s)5	(s)3			9
NEM								[ø]4						4
SEM							M2	[ø]12		[ø]8				22
NWM									[ø]5					5
SWM								[ø]14	(s)2 [ø]14	(s)9 [ø]29				68
SW											(s)1 [ø]2	(s)2	(s)2	7
SE								[ø]2		(s)2				4
TOTAL			1				2	30	23	51	8	2	2	119

Table E.65: Item Profile for *cild* (Neut-M)

	C9a	C9b	C10a	C10b	C11a	C11b	C12a	C12b	C13a	C13b	C14a	C14b	C15a	TOTAL
N			[s]1							M4	M1			6
NEM								[V]24						24
SEM								[n]12 [V]4	[n]1	[n]16 [V]20 M1				54
NWM									[V]4					4
SWM			[ø]2					[n]6 [V]4	[n]12	[n]30 [V]2	[n]4			60
SW									[n]4		[n]2		[n]4	10
SE											[n]3			3
TOTAL			3					50	21	73	10		4	161

Table E.66: Item Profile for *niht* (Fem-M)

	C9a	C9b	C10a	C10b	C11a	C11b	C12a	C12b	C13a	C13b	C14a	C14b	C15a	TOTAL
N														
NEM								[s]5 [ø]1						6
SEM									[s]1	[s]4 [ø]6				11
NWM														
SWM	M1		M2					[ø]2 M2		[s]3 [ø]2				12
SW											[ø]2		[s]2	4
SE														
TOTAL	1		2					10	1	15	2		2	33

Appendix F Old Norse Declensions

a-stem masc. (str.)	sg.	pl.
nom.	armr	armar
acc.	arm	arma
gen.	arms	arma
dat.	arme	örmum

a-stem neut. (str.)	sg.	pl.
nom.	barn	börn
acc.	barn	börn
gen.	barns	barna
dat.	barne	börnum

i-stem masc. (str.)	sg.	pl.
nom.	bekkr	bekkir
acc.	bekk	bekki
gen.	bekks, -iar	bekkia
dat.	bekk	bekkium

ja-stem neut. (str.)	sg.	pl.
nom.	kuǣþi	kuǣþi
acc.	kuǣþi	kuǣþi
gen.	kuǣþis	kuǣþa
dat.	kuǣþi	kuǣþum

u-stem masc. (str.)	sg.	pl.
nom.	völdr	vendir
acc.	vönd	völdo
gen.	vandar	vanda
dat.	vende	völdum

ō-stem fem. (str.)	sg.	pl.
nom.	sög	sagar
acc.	sög	sagar
gen.	sagar	saga
dat.	sög	sögum

n-stem masc. (wk.)	sg.	pl.
nom.	hani	hanar
acc.	hana	hana
gen.	hana	hana
dat.	hana	hönum

jō-stem fem. (str.)	sg.	pl.
nom.	ben	beniar
acc.	ben	beniar
gen.	beniar	benia
dat.	ben	benium

nd-stem masc. (minor)	sg.	pl.
nom.	gefandi	gefendr
acc.	gefanda	gefendr
gen.	gefanda	gefanda
dat.	gefanda	geföndum

i-stem fem. (str.)	sg.	pl.
nom.	öxl	axlir
acc.	öxl	axlir
gen.	axlar	axla
dat.	öxl	öxlum

	n-stem fem. (wk.)			athematic fem. (minor)	
	sg.	pl.		sg.	pl.
nom.	gata	götur	nom.	röng	rengr
acc.	götu	götur	acc.	röng	rengr
gen.	götu	gatna	gen.	rangar	ranga
dat.	götu	götum	dat.	röng	röngum

Notes

1. When I conducted this research before 2005, *LAEME* was not publicly available; but when the draft of this book came to completion in August, 2008, the online *LAEME* Version 1.1 was available at http://www.lel.ed.ac.uk/ihd/laeme1/laeme1.html.
2. The map in Figure 2.1 on page 8 has been adapted for the present purpose from maps available in such references as *Plan and Bibliography* (ed. Kurath, Ogden, Palmer, and McKelvey) and *LALME* (ed. McIntosh, Samuels, and Benskin). It is to be noted that the labels given to the dialects vary across reference books. Some label Southwestern and Southeastern as Southern and Kentish respectively, for example.

    The reader might wonder why the more rough and common division into five dialects should not do (i.e. Northern, East Midland, West Midland, Southern, and Kentish); in the present book, however, I adopt the finer division not only to concord with Roedler's division but also with a view to uncovering any subtle differences between neighbouring dialects which might be left hidden if the rougher dialect division were adopted.
3. For example, the South-East Midland dialect shows both northern and southern dialectal characteristics and may be included in either depending on what features to look at.
4. In examining *The Peterborough Chronicle* in Section 4.5, I divide the text into three parts rather than two.
5. The present study assigns *The Peterborough Chronicle* and the *Havelok* to South-East Midland and the *Harrowing of Hell* to South-West Midland, while the localisation of the *Debate between Body and Soul* is left open.
6. The following is the original passage in German: ". . . im nordöstl. mittelland schon gegen 1200—vielleicht schon in der 2. häfte des 12. j.'s, je nachdem man die aus dem 2. teil der P. C. [Peterborough Chronicle] gewonnenen resultate verallgemeinern will oder nicht—die ausbreitung des plural-*s* principiell den neuenglischen standpunkt erreicht hat."
7. The following is the original passage in German: "Vielleicht aber hat die entwicklung im nordwestlichen mittelland denselben verlauf genommen wie im nordöstlichen nachbardialekt, sodass wir sogar bis 1200 zurückgehen können."
8. I must admit that my decision to take the more traditional dialect division is only conventionally motivated. I should mention that the reason for Kurath et al. to dismiss the traditional approach is that in distinguishing South-West Midland from Southwestern it gives more importance, from a structural point of view, to the contrast between -*en* and -*eth* in the present plural ending of the verb than to the *mon/man* contrast.
9. The B-text of Laȝamon's *Brut* is now normally dated around 1275.
10. It is to be noted that Roedler used the distribution of the plurals to propose a text

localisation rather than predict a distribution of the plurals by the known localisation of a text.

11   Although Roedler assigned all these texts to what is traditionally defined as the Southwestern dialect, most of them should really be assigned to South-West Midland in accord with the *LALME-* and *LAEME*-proposed localisations.

12   The following is the original passage in German: "Die endung *-es* ist die regel bei der grossen masse der starken masculina und neutra; doch finden sich noch zahlreiche reste anderer bildungsarten auch in diesen klassen. In den übrigen klassen herrscht noch starkes schwanken zwischen den endungen *-en* und *-es*, wenn auch bei den starken fem. und den masc. *n*-stämmen der *s*-plural in grösserem umfange eingang gefunden hat. Am zähesten scheinen die schwachen feminina die alte bildung beibehalten zu haben."

13   Roedler's dialectal assignment of these texts is dubious. According to *LAEME*, *Vices and Virtues*, the *Poema Morale*, and the *Trinity Homilies* are assigned to South-East Midland instead of Southeastern; on the other hand, the *Vespasian Homilies* may be assigned, though with little uncertainty, to South-West Midland.

14   There are different views on the chronology of the phonological levelling. The issue will be discussed in Section 6.2.

15   His assumption about the relative quantity of weak nouns is poorly grounded. I will come back to this issue when I discuss the Old Norse contact hypothesis in Section 7.4.

16   For the recent discussion on this topic, see Hoad (21) and his bibliography.

17   To quote Prokosch's words:

> It is perhaps more than mere coincidence that Old English and Old Saxon have the same form as Gothic: Originally, the Goths and other East Germanic tribes were the neighbours of the (later) Anglo-Frisian group; it may well be that of the two available forms, nom. *wulfō* and acc. *wulfans* > *wulfōs(s)*, bilingual speakers gave the preference to that form which their East Germanic neighbours used for the nominative.

18   R. Keller illustrated the confusion by showing it to be common practice that the plural form of the word *tag* could be either *tag*, *täg*, or *tage*.

19   The palatal *R* was merged with alveolar *r* by 1100 in East Scandinavian.

20   Haugen explains the loss of *R* as due to a combination of factors such as assimilation to a following consonant and linguistic contact with neighbouring Low German (*Scandinavian* 280).

21   For further discussion on this issue, see Roedler (2: 471–81). He devoted one chapter to enquiry into the *s*-plurals of non-substantives. Mustanoja also provides general background for nominally used adjectives (643–48).

22 Here and throughout the discussion of case syncretism I define the dative environment either as a syntactic position after verbs or adjectives which would require the dative case form to occur in the traditional West-Saxon grammar or as a syntactic position after any preposition. In Old English there were prepositions like *ofer*, *būtan*, and *betweox* which could govern either a dative or an accusative according to usage, but as the distinction in usage was blurred in the process of case syncretism itself, separate treatment would practically make no sense. This is why I regard a position after any preposition as effectively a dative environment. The dative case as I define it is close to d'Ardenne's "Case 3" in the AB language (205–07).

23 Uncertainty might arise where a plural in a dative environment is ø-ending. A ø-ending can be interpreted either as a form which has come to take the same form as its ø-ending nominative/accusative or a maximally reduced reflex of -*um*. Evidence shows, however, that the former is typically the case while the latter is too rare to be a problem.

The following example could be counted among the rare instances of -*um* being reduced to -ø. In the *Lambeth Homilies*, Sermon XIV, there appears the phrase "bi-tweone engel *and* monne." Here *engel* might be considered an innovative ø-plural which could be used in the nominative/accusative as well as the dative environments, but this view seems almost unlikely since all of the other eight instances for "angels" in the text occur with -*s*. It is more reasonable to see this *engel* as a fully reduced reflex of the older dative plural with -*um* rather than as an innovative ø-plural. This interpretation is also supported by the following *monne*, which is clearly a reduced reflex of an older dative plural.

24 The "difficult judgement" I have discussed in the preceding and present sections does not apply, however, to the AB language. According to d'Ardenne (205–07), in the AB language, *en*-plurals occurring after prepositions can safely be interpreted not as the reflexes of the old dative plural endings but as "genuine" *en*-plurals, that is, as plural forms that can also occur in common case environments. Thus, when we see an *en*-plural after a preposition, we can safely count it among suitable examples. Interestingly enough, the same cannot be said of the *es*-plurals. Thus, when we see an *es*-plural after a preposition, e.g. "under hire fotes," we cannot assume at once that "fotes" represents an unmarked plural that could occur in any syntactic environment. In fact, as we expect, "fet" occurs as the common variant in the nominative/accusative case position. The case/number subsystem in the AB language is thus unique, and should deserve careful treatment, but the "difficult judgement" arising from case syncretism remains a general problem that students of Early Middle English must tackle.

25 For a detailed description of the traditional stem-types, see Campbell (Chapter 11).

26 Historically, the Germanic ō-stem feminine noun had developed its *n*-plural by the Old

English period and continued this innovation into Early Middle English.

27 The type rate is easier to read but more text-dependent than the spread rate. This is because it is likely affected by the unique set of vocabulary used in the text. For example, if the analysed text happens to contain more than the average share of the Masc-S nouns, the type rate for the *s*-plural will appear higher than in average texts. This can happen, for example, if the text is too short to be representative of the underlying language. In contrast, the spread rate is a less text-dependent index because the assumption is that the frequency of, say, the Old English Masc-S nouns in the text is set to 1.0 and the spread rate of the *s*-plural is calculated in proportion to this preset base. The spread rate is also a diachronic index in that it represents the difference of the plural distribution from the Old English West-Saxon to the Early Middle English text language.

28 The periodisation by the half century is admittedly arbitrary. It could be by decade or by century. I believe, however, that half a century is the best possible interval I can think of in light of the text availability for each period and the speed of linguistic change in Early Middle English.

29 I discuss the three Old English texts under the section on the South-West Midland dialect, but it should not be assumed that the Mercian dialects they represent are in any sense direct predecessors of the SWM dialect of Early Middle English. In Old English the dialectal boundaries within the Midlands were more obscure than in Middle English, so any localisation of the Old English texts in Middle English dialectological terms is potentially anachronistic.

There is disagreement particularly on the localisation of the dialect that *Ru1* represents. The traditional placing wavers between Harewood in the West Riding of Yorkshire, as the closest Mercian Harewood to Northumbria, and Harewood in Herefordshire (Kitson, "Margins"); on the other hand, Coates recently proposed as an alternative Stowe near Lichfield. Since there is much uncertainty about this issue, we should for the moment understand that *Ru1* might represent a predecessor of a variety of Early Middle English localised broadly in the Midlands.

30 My collected data being underrepresented, I am exaggerating here the rarity of the *n*-plural. In fact Roedler enumerated a few dozen surviving *n*-plurals taken from the C14 South-West Midland texts, the Harley Lyrics and Robert of Gloucester's *Chronicle of England* (1: 68–71).

31 For the term "panchronic" see the following quotation from Lass: "The view I take here, then, is neither synchronic (the language seen in the snapshot at a given moment), nor diachronic (historical): rather 'panchronic'. . . ." (*Shape* xii).

32 If an Old English word can be inflected in more than one way, as if belonging to more than one morphological class, it is assigned to one of the possible classes, as I discussed

on page 48.

33   Another example is *hīwan*, occurring only in -*n* or -*V* even in Northern.

34   This item, derived from the Old Norse weak masculine *fēlagi*, always pluralised with -*s*. In Old Norse the nominative plural was *fēlagar*, and the *s*-ending for the English word was perhaps inspired by the Old Norse *r*-ending via language contact.

35   For a diachronic study of the plural forms for "eye," see Hotta (*Historical*).

36   The most common West-Saxon nominative/accusative plural forms of these nouns were *i*-mutated *fīend* and *frīend* respectively, so they are counted in the Masc-M class rather than in the Masc-Ø class despite their possibly taking uninflected plural forms. However, the Early Middle English forms may effectively be regarded as ø-plurals because the effect of *i*-mutation in these words was blurred in Early Middle English.

37   What is implicit in the Item Profile for *cild* is that every instance of the plural has an -*r*- infix in the stem except a few instances of the ø-plural *cild*. Accordingly, the plural types [*n*] and [*V*] should be understood to represent forms like *children* and *childre* respectively. The plural type *M*, on the other hand, is meant to represent forms that end in -*r*, e.g. *childer*. See a related explanation on page 51 in Section 3.1.4.

38   For general discussion about the significance of studying different versions of text, see Laing ("Linguistic").

39   For that matter, Sermon VI, *Pater Noster*, is also rhyming verse and might as well be separately handled. However, there is little evidence that rhyming affected plural forms in this sermon. Accordingly, I decided to treat it together with the other Lang 2 sermons.

40   There are six sermons in the Lang 1 part which certainly go back to Old English (Sermons I-III and IX-XI). Sisam notes that Sermons IX, X, and part of XI are derived from Ælfric's works, while Sermon II contains most of a short discourse by Wulfstan (105–06).

41   At the time of the analysis only this part for T was grammatically tagged in the *LAEME* text database.

42   See Smith's "Tradition," "Linguistic," and "Standard."

43   The dating of A in C13a, as I adopt it, represents a traditional view, whereas, according to Millett (xi), Malcolm Parkes recently proposed a later date, "probably 1270s or early 1280s." This could have wide implications when we interpret the data.

44   For related arguments, see Sisam (113), Benskin and Laing (65), Laing ("Anchor" 38), and Smith ("Tradition" 54).

45   It may be possible to read this *swikene* (preceded by *þe* in line 103) as an inflected adjective rather as a plural noun.

46   As was mentioned earlier in the section, localisation of M has not been well established. It was once localised to Kent, Essex, or the Central South Midlands. It is now localised

to the South-West Midlands—still provisionally.

47 Although there are no "pure" *n*-ending plurals, there are in fact two *ne*-ending plural forms derived from *n*-plurals, that is, *eʒene* (OE Neut-N *ēage*) and *hesne* (OE Fem-V *hǣs*). The form *hesne*, occurring three times in the D text as well, is referred to in *Middle English Dictionary* as perhaps a variant of the *en*-plural.

48 Here the assumption is that the pattern form in the exemplar was *e*-ending and that the scribe turned it into *-es* or *-en* as he copied. The opposite interpretation can be held logically, but it is unlikely because *V*-plurals far outnumber *n*-plurals in rhyming positions.

49 It is known that some Early Middle English scribes practised archaising by convention or deliberately. Stanley explains how the scribes of Laʒamon's *Brut* (BL Cotton Caligula A ix) generated an archaic air:

> . . . the scribes were following a tradition of orthographic archaizing, which is a product of retaining conventional spellings rather than a manifestation of a deliberate antiquarianism. Orthographic conventions, derived from OE spelling practice, were retained even in cases where they had long ceased to have a direct relation to the spoken language. It may well be that the origins of this retention of Anglo-Saxonisms in e.ME manuscripts (written at a time when the last copies of OE tests were being made) are to be sought in the strict scriptorial discipline required of those non-West Saxon scribes who were made to write West Saxon outside the area of West-Saxon speech. Spelling is of course always artificial and conventional; nevertheless, it is perhaps permissible to speak of the exceptional artificiality of e.ME orthography and of the possibly even greater artificiality of very late OE orthography on which it is based. ("Laʒamon's" 26)

The Peterborough scribe's archaising was possibly a result of both deliberate antiquarianism and a "wrongly" practised West-Saxon spelling convention.

50 Many studies have contributed to the theoretical refinement of Lexical Diffusion. The reader may find the following references departure points exploring the theory: Aitchison ("Missing"; *Language*, Chapter 6), Chen and Wang, Chen ("Time"; "Relative"), Chen and Hsieh, Kiparsky, McMahon (Chapter 3), Ogura, Ogura and Wang ("Snowball"; "Evolution"), Sturtevant (page 82 in particular), Wang ("Measurement"; "Competing"), and Wang and Lien.

51 All of the four patterns have been known to exist in actual language change. Although the original model of Lexical Diffusion only assumed Type 2, the latest version of Lexical Diffusion would be capable of all types.

52 The S-curve is sometimes also called a logistic curve, which typically explains the pattern of changing populations.

53   It is not necessarily clear, however, whether it is for their high or low frequency that words are first affected by change. Aitchison, for example, counts high frequency as a determinant of the first environments to be affected ("Missing" 13), whereas Anttila is of the opinion that infrequent forms tend to be changed earlier because analogy kicks in where memory fails (101). In the meantime, Phillips is of the opinion that either direction is possible, hypothesising that "[p]hysiologically motivated sound changes affect the most frequent words first; other sound changes affect the least frequent words first" ("Word" 336).

54   For the concept of "double diffusion," see also Aitchison (*Language* 85), Chambers and Trudgill (160), Hudson (169), McMahon (50–51), and Wang ("Competing" 82).

55   As for dialect-to-dialect change, the wave model was once proposed to describe the geographical diffusion of linguistic innovation. Then some geographically aware linguists developed an extended theory on linguistic diffusion over space. Chambers and Trudgill, for example, advanced the gravity model against the traditional wave model to account for the path along which innovation diffuses in space (166). In this model, a linguistic innovation is likened to a stone skipping across a pond since it spreads not necessarily from a speaker or place to its immediate adjacent but jumps from one speaker or place to another which may be geographically apart but socially connected. For example, linguistic innovation can spread from one big city to another, skipping small towns in between.

Opposition was recently raised against the gravity model. For example, G. Bailey et al. show that some diffusions proceed counterhierarchically, that is, from small towns to big cities. On the other hand, Boberg emphasises that beside the social hierarchy, we should take account of factors such as border effect, social prestige, and subjective evaluation in geographical diffusion (23).

Linguists have thus become aware of various geographical aspects of language change. The concept of S-diffusion in Lexical Diffusion should be understood in line with this development in geolinguistics.

56   For bibliographic references to the recent theoretical expansion of Lexical Diffusion, see Wang and Lien (385). More recently, the following studies have appeared: Ogura ("Development"), and Ogura and Wang ("Snowball"; "Evolution"). The first of these is a syntactic application of Lexical Diffusion, the second a morphological one, and the third an attempt to build an extended theory of Lexical Diffusion.

57   It may be questioned whether syllable weight rules such as High Vowel Deletion (see Lass, *Old* 100), which controlled the strong neuter nominative/accusative plural forms in Old English, could still be functional in Early Middle English. Insights into the issue can be gained when we refer to Ritt, who proposed that the incidence of Middle English

Open Syllable Lengthening varied according to the syllable weight of words (30–31). This suggests that syllable weight was still a synchronic category in C12 and C13, when the lengthening was taking place.

58 The figures were calculated on all my data by type counting. The period and dialect for each data point were not taken account of, so the results should be read as a rough summary. I also tried token counting but it pointed to much the same tendency. By type counting, the heavy-syllabic neuters were over twice as many as the light-syllabic neuters.

59 The figures are again calculated on all my data by type counting. Token counting points to a similar tendency. By type counting, heavy-syllabics were over four times as numerous as light-syllabics.

60 I cannot discuss the whole issue of inorganic -e in this study, but the following is a short introduction to inorganic -e. As Early Middle English began, inorganic -e was introduced to a varying extent to the nominative singular inflections of nouns. Various strong feminines and strong neuters (especially light-syllabic ones) accepted it, and in time merged into weak nouns.

The way inorganic -e was actually added differed from noun to noun, but as a rule in the nominative singular more feminines took inorganic -e than masculines or neuters (Minkova 57). In *The Ormulum*, for example, most heavy-syllabic ō-stem feminines take inorganic -e in the nominative singular, e.g. *are*, *blisse*, *gerrde*, *helle*, *lade*, *lare*, *millce*, and *sinne* (Minkova 57). Likewise, the *Genesis and Exodus* provides instances of inorganic -e primarily in the feminines, e.g. *agte*, *bene*, *blisse*, *burge*, *dede*, *drugte*, *froure*, *liknesse*, *meðe*, *migte*, *safte*, *selðe*, *sigte*, *sinne*, *sorge*, and *sowle* (Minkova 60).

61 Possibly relevant to this point is Sundby's observation that *Gibben*, the genitive form of a person's name, had a more "colloquial ring" than the alternative genitive form *Gibbes*, with the *en*-suffix associated with a French diminutive suffix (226). Here Sundby speaks of the genitive singular inflection rather than the nominative plural, but we may think of the "colloquial ring" perhaps carried by the *n*-plural.

62 Euphonic liaison is common in language. In some varieties of Present-Day English /r/ is sometimes heard as in "law(r) and order" or in "the idea(r) is . . ." /n/ may also be heard in "India(n) and Pakistan."

63 Lehnert makes interesting points on this matter (60). German feminine nouns with -*el* and -*er* tend to take plural forms distinct from singular forms since the definite article alone may not serve as a reliable number marker. Compare singulars such as *die Nadel*, *Windel*, *Regel*, *Wimper*, *Leiter*, and *Steuer* with their plurals *die Nadeln*, *Windeln*, *Regeln*, *Wimpern*, *Leitern*, and *Steuern*. In these examples, the nominal *n*-ending, not the definite article, serves as a number marker.

64 I addressed the topic of this section in more detail in my article "Language Changes Walking Hand in Hand."

65 Multiple causation of language change has been assumed in modern historical linguistics. To the quotations from Thomason given in the text, the following may be added: ". . . the multi-factorial causation of events needs to be an accepted part of the methodology of historical linguistics" (Smith, *Historical* 111); "Linguistic and social factors are closely interrelated in the development of language change. Explanations which are confined to one or the other aspect, no matter how well constructed, will fail to account for the rich body of regularities that can be observed in empirical studies of language behaviour" (Weinreich, Labov, and Herzog 188).

66 For the reasons why Old French could not be relevant, refer to Jespersen (*Chapters* 33). To summarise the main grounds against the hypothesis of Old French influence on the English *s*-plural:

   1. Considering that the genitive singular -*s* spread earlier and faster than the nominative plural -*s*, French should first have influenced genitive singular forms, which is however impossible because Old French had no *s*-ending for the genitive singular.

   2. The extension of the *s*-plural started before the Norman Conquest, making it unnecessary to propose French influence.

   3. The fact that -*s* prevailed earlier in the northern dialects than in the southern is against the expectation if French influence was assumed. Such French influence would have been felt first and foremost in the South.

   4. The *s*-ending was just one of the various plural endings available in Old French, and it was usually an accusative plural ending instead of a nominative plural.

   5. In English, adjectives rarely took the *s*-plural after the Old French model. If French influence had been at work, not only nouns but also adjectives might have been affected.

   6. The English *s*-ending was usually preceded by a vowel typically spelt *e*, while in Old French such a vowel spelling never occurred. We might note that the forms -*es* and -*s* were kept distinct well into Late Middle English.

67 For the phonological implication of Norse-English contact, see Geipel (20–23) and Knowles (41–42).

68 See W. Keller (85–86); Baugh and Cable (101); Stein ("OE" 637–38). For a different view, see Holmqvist (Chapter 1 particularly).

69 See Holmqvist (46); W. Keller (87); Baugh and Cable (101).

70 See Baugh and Cable (101).

71 See Jespersen (*Growth* 75).

72 See Jespersen (*Growth* 75).
73 See B. Hansen (61).
74 See B. Hansen (62). A related mention is found in Holmqvist (193).
75 See Menner 239–40; Clark (lxix).
76 See Jespersen (*Growth* 76); Baugh and Cable (102); Nist (103); this is however argued against by Einenkel (121–24) and Kirch (503–06).
77 See Jespersen (*Growth* 76–77); Baugh and Cable (102); this is however argued against by Kirch (507–08).
78 See Baugh and Cable (102).
79 See Jespersen (*Growth* 77); Curme (472); Visser (2034–40).
80 See Jespersen (*Growth* 77) and Nist (103); this is however argued against by Kirch (508–09).
81 According to Thomason, the parameters are either social or linguistic (60). Social factors include: 1) intensity of contact (duration of contact, population size, and socioeconomic dominance); 2) presence vs. absence of imperfect learning; 3) speakers' attitudes toward the languages. On the other hand, linguistics factors include: 4) universal markedness; 5) degree to which features are integrated into the linguistic system; 6) typological distance between source and recipient languages.
82 Norwegian varieties are relevant in the northwestern part of England. In the present study, however, I will leave them out of account because my interest is first and foremost in language contact in the more eastern Danelaw.
83 The following general points may be made on this issue. Differences between several Old Norse dialects developed only after around 1000 and even afterwards the differences in inflectional paradigms generally remained insignificant among Old Norse dialects (Gordon 265; Flom 7–8). For inflectional paradigms in different Old Norse dialects, we may refer to Noreen (*Altisländische* and *Altschwedische*).
84 One of the inscriptions is the dial at Kirkdale, Yorkshire, printed in Gordon (327).
85 The table is summarily adapted from Classen's with reference to Noreen (*Altisländische* 276–82). The paradigms shown here are those of Old Icelandic and West-Saxon, not of Old Danish and the Eastern variety of Old English.
86 Some may wonder why we should need such an account of correspondence between Old English -*s* and Old Norse -*r* to explain the spread of the *s*-plural over to historically non-*s*-plural nouns. Is it not enough to ascribe the generalisation of the *s*-plural simply to what has traditionally been proposed, as by Bradley, as a utilitarian practice of substituting the most obvious endings for ambiguous ones which could mislead both Old English and Old Norse speakers in contact situations? I am not opposed to the view that general inflectional levelling, encouraged by Norse

contact, played an important role in pushing forward the spread of -*s* into historically unexpected nouns. I would rather ask why -*s* in particular was chosen as the most representative and the least misleading of the plural endings.

One reason is, as I discussed earlier, its high frequency; but another, more specific and more direct, reason is, in my opinion, that the Old Norse *r*-ending corresponded to the Old English *s*-ending and that the former was more widely (i.e. both in strong and weak declensions and both for the masculine and the feminine) used in Old Norse than the latter was in Old English. Under these circumstances, the explanation of the spread of -*s* as due to the conspicuous frequency of its corresponding Old Norse -*r* may be proposed with reason.

To discuss the issue from another point of view, let us take Townend's view. He takes the traditional position, saying "that . . . inflexions were largely non-functional in Anglo-Norse communication, and that therefore Anglo-Norse contact was indeed an important factor in the atrophy and loss of inflexions not only in the English language but also in the Norse language in general" (201). The quotation above is, however, preceded by "with a few exceptions such as the dominant forms of the genitive singular and nominative/accusative plural." To put it another way, in his opinion, Old Norse -*r* and Old English -*s* as plural endings were among the few functional inflections on either side even in the time of general inflectional levelling. Old Norse and Old English speakers were evidently conscious of the correspondence.

While the traditional view that contact situations brought about inflectional levelling is undoubtedly attractive, it is too general an explanation to make particular contact-induced language changes worthy of study. I believe that it is more constructive in historical linguistics to propose as many causes as possible that lead to language change, whether particular or general.

87 The following are examples from *The Peterborough Chronicle*: *feonlandes, geoldes/gæildes, huses, landes, mynstres/mynstras, reafes, abbotrices/biscoprices, scrines, wateres/watres, castelweorces/weorkes, wiles, wifes,* and *writes*. More from *The Ormulum*: *barrness, bordess, brestess, cnes/cnewwess, deoress, fetless, ȝæress/ȝeress/gæress, ȝeldess, Goddspelless, gresess, wheless/wheoless/Goddspellwheless, innseȝȝless, landess, lifess, minnstress, wordess, sætess, spelless, tacness, treos/þreos, þingess, wattress, weorrkess/werrkess, wifess, bodewordess, writess,* and *scaldess*.

88 Referring to Sawyer (*Age* 174–75), Thomason and Kaufman remark:

> . . . there was a great growth of quite profitable sheep-farming at the hands of Norse-origin or even Norse-speaking entrepreneurs in the eleventh century in the Lincolnshire Wolds (which lie in Lindsey, the major town being Louth) and in the Yorkshire Wolds

(which lie in the East Riding of Yorkshire part of Deira, the major town being Bridlington), which lie right across the Humber from each other. (289)

Bibliography

Primary Sources

Arngart, Olof, ed. *The Middle English Genesis and Exodus.* Lund Studies in English. 36. Lund: Gleerup, 1968.

Atkins, J. W. H., ed. *The Owl and the Nightingale.* 1922. New York: Russell, 1971.

Bennett, J. A. W. and G. V. Smithers, eds. *Early Middle English Verse and Prose.* 2nd ed. Oxford: Clarendon, 1968.

Bliss, Alan Joseph, ed. *Sir Orfeo.* London: OUP, 1954.

Böddeker, K., ed. *Altenglische Dichtungen des MS. Harl. 2253.* Berlin: Weidmannsche, 1878.

Brown, Carleton, ed. *English Lyrics of the XIIIth Century.* Oxford: Clarendon, 1932.

Brown, Carleton, ed. *Religious Lyrics of the XIVth Century.* 2nd ed. Rev. G. V. Smithers. Oxford: Clarendon, 1970.

Buehler, Philip G., ed. *Middle English* Genesis and Exodus*: A Running Commentary on the Text of the Poem.* The Hague: Mouton, 1974.

Cartlidge, Neil, ed. *The Owl and the Nightingale: Text and Translation.* Exeter: U of Exeter P, 2001.

Clark, Cecily, ed. *The Peterborough Chronicle 1070–1154.* Oxford: Clarendon, 1970.

d'Ardenne, S. R. T. O., ed. *Þe Liflade ant te Passiun of Seinte Iuliene.* EETS os 248. 1961.

Day, Mabel, ed. *The English Text of the Ancrene Riwle Edited from Cotton MS. Nero A. XIV.* EETS os 225. 1952.

Dickins, Bruce and R. M. Wilson, eds. *Early Middle English Texts.* London: Bowes, 1951.

Dobson, Eric John, ed. *The English Text of the Ancrene Riwle Edited from B. M. Cotton MS. Cleopatra C. vi.* EETS os 267. 1972.

Dobson, Eric John and F. Ll. Harrison, eds. *Medieval English Songs.* London: Faber, 1979.

Earle, John and Charles Plummer, eds. *Two of the Saxon Chronicles Parallel with Supplementary Extracts from the Others.* 2 vols. Oxford: Clarendon, 1892.

Furnivall, Frederick James. *Early English Poems and Lives of Saints.* Berlin: Asher, 1862.

Gradon, Pamela, ed. *Dan Michel's Ayenbite of Inwyt.* Rev. ed. Vol. 1. EETS os 23. 1965. Vol. 2. EETS os 278. 1979

Grattan, J. H. G. and G. F. H. Sykes, eds. *The Owl and the Nightingale*. EETS es 119. 1935.

Hall, Joseph, ed. *King Horn: A Middle English Romance*. Oxford: Clarendon, 1901.

Hall, Joseph, ed. *Selections from Early Middle English 1130–1250*. 2 vols. Oxford: Clarendon, 1920.

Herrtage, Sidney J., ed. *Sir Ferumbras*. EETS es 34. 1879.

Holt, Robert, ed. *The Ormulum*. 2 vols. Oxford: Clarendon, 1878.

Holthausen, Ferd., ed. *Vices and Virtues, Being a Soul's Confession of Its Sins, with Reason's Description of the Virtues*. Part 1. EETS os 89. 1888. Part 2. EETS os 159. 1921.

Horobin, Simon and Jeremy J. Smith. "The English Ordinance and Custom in the Cartulary of the Hospital of St Laurence, Canterbury." *Anglia* 120 (2002): 488–507.

Horstmann, Carl, ed. *Altenglische Legenden*. Neue Folge. 1881. Hildesheim: Olms, 1969.

Horstmann, Carl, ed. *S. Editha sive Chronicon Vilodunense im Wiltshire Dialekt aus MS. Cotton. Faustina B III*. Heilbronn: Henninger, 1883.

Irvine, Susan, ed. *Old English Homilies from MS Bodley 343*. EETS os 302. 1993.

Irvine, Susan, ed. *MS. E: A Semi-Diplomatic Edition with Introduction and Indices*. Cambridge: Brewer, 2004. Vol. 7 of *The Anglo-Saxon Chronicle: A Collaborative Edition*.

Kubouchi, Tadao and Keiko Ikegami, eds. *The* Ancrene Wisse*: A Four-Manuscript Parallel Text: Preface and Parts 1–4*. Studies in English Medieval language and Literature. 7. Frankfurt am Main: Peter Lang, 2003.

Kubouchi, Tadao and Keiko Ikegami, eds. *The* Ancrene Wisse*: A Four-Manuscript Parallel Text: Parts 5–8 with Wordlists*. Studies in English Medieval Language and Literature. 11. Frankfurt am Main: Peter Lang, 2003.

Logeman, H., ed. *The Rule of St Benet*. EETS os 90. 1888.

Lumby, J. Rawson, ed. *King Horn, Floriz and Blauncheflur, The Assumption of Our Lady*. EETS os 14. 1866. Rev. George Harley McKnight. 1901.

Mack, Frances M., ed. *The English Text of the Ancrene Riwle Edited from Cotton MS. Titus D. XVIII*. EETS os 252. 1963.

McKnight, George Harley, ed. *Middle English Humorous Tales in Verse*. Boston: Heath, 1913.

Morris, Richard, ed. *Old English Homilies and Homiletic Treatises of the Twelfth and Thirteenth Centuries*. 1st ser. Part 1. EETS os 29. 1868. Part 2. EETS os 34. 1868.

Morris, Richard, ed. *An Old English Miscellany Containing A Bestiary, Kentish Sermons, Proverbs of Alfred, Religious Poems of the Thirteenth Century*. EETS os 49.

1872.

Morris, Richard, ed. *Old English Homilies and Homiletic Treatises of the Twelfth and Thirteenth Centuries*. 2nd ser. EETS os 53. 1873.

Morris, Richard, ed. *Cursor Mundi*. 7 vols. EETS os 57, 59, 62, 66, 68, 99, and 101. 1874–93.

Paues, Anna C. "A Newly Discovered Manuscript of the Poema Morale." *Anglia* 30 (1907): 217–37.

Person, Henry A., ed. *Cambridge Middle English Lyrics*. Seattle: U of Washington P, 1953.

Shepherd, Geoffrey, ed. *Ancrene Wisse: Parts Six and Seven*. Rev. ed. Exeter: U of Exeter P, 1991.

Skeat, Walter William, ed. *The Holy Gospels in Anglo-Saxon, Northumbrian, and Old Mercian Versions*. Cambridge: CUP, 1871–87.

Skeat, Walter William and Kenneth Sisam, eds. *The Lay of Havelok the Dane*. Rev. ed. Oxford: Clarendon, 1915.

Small, John, ed. *English Metrical Homilies*. Edinburgh: Paterson, 1862.

Smithers, G. V., ed. *Havelok*. Oxford: Clarendon, 1987.

Stanley, Eric Gerald, ed. *The Owl and the Nightingale*. London: Nelson, 1960.

Sweet, Henry, ed. *The Oldest English Texts*. EETS os 83. 1885.

Thompson, W. Meredith, ed. *Þe Wohunge of Ure Lauerd*. EETS os 241. 1958.

Tolkien, John Ronald Reuel, ed. *Ancrene Wisse*. EETS os 249. 1962.

Vleeskruyer, R., ed. *The Life of St. Chad: An Old English Homily*. Amsterdam: North-Holland, 1953.

Wells, John Edwin, ed. *The Owl and the Nightingale*. Boston: Heath, 1907.

Wilson, R. M., ed. *Sawles Warde: An Early Middle English Homily Edited from the Bodley, Royal and Cotton MSS*. Leeds School of English Texts and Monographs. 3. Kendal: Wilson, 1938.

Zupitza, Julius. "Zum Poema Morale." *Anglia* 1 (1878): 5–38.

Zupitza, Julius and J. Schipper. "Poema Morale." *Alt- und Mittelenglisches Übungsbuch*. Wien: Braumüller, 1910. 58–69.

Secondary Sources

Aitchison, Jean. "The Missing Link: The Role of the Lexicon." *Historical Linguistics and Philology*. Ed. J. Fisiak. Berlin: Walter de Gruyter, 1990. 11–28.

Aitchison, Jean. *Language Change: Progress or Decay*. 3rd ed. Cambridge: CUP, 2001.

Allen, Cynthia L. *Case Marking and Reanalysis: Grammatical Relations from Old to Early Modern English*. Oxford: Clarendon, 1995.

Andersen, Henning. "Abductive and Deductive Change." *Language* 49 (1973): 765–93.

Anttila, Raimo. *Historical and Comparative Linguistics.* Rev. ed. Amsterdam: John Benjamins, 1989.

Arngart, Olof. "Some Aspects of the Relation between the English and the Danish Element in the Danelaw." *Studia Neophilologica* 20 (1947): 73–87.

Bailey, Charles-James N. *Variation and Linguistic Theory.* Arlington: Center for Applied Linguistics, 1973.

Bailey, Guy, Tom Wikle, Jan Tillery, and Lori Sand. "Some Patterns of Linguistic Diffusion." *Language Variation and Change* 5 (1993): 359–90.

Baugh, Albert C. and Thomas Cable. *A History of the English Language.* 4th ed. London: Routledge, 1993.

Behm, O. P. *The Language of the Later Part of the Peterborough Chronicle.* Gothenburgh: Goteborg, 1884.

Benskin, Michael and Margaret Laing. "Translations and *Mischsprachen* in Middle English Manuscripts." *So Meny People Longages and Tonges: Philological Essays in Scots and Mediaeval English Presented to Angus McIntosh.* Ed. Michael Benskin and Michael Louis Samuels. Edinburgh: Middle English Dialect Project, 1981. 55–106.

Björkman, Erik. *Scandinavian Loan-Words in Middle English.* Part 1. Studien zur englischen Philologie. 7. Halle: Niemeyer, 1900. New York: Greenwood, 1969.

Black, Merja Ritta. *Studies in the Dialect Materials of Medieval Herefordshire.* Diss. U of Glasgow, 1997.

Boberg, Charles. "Geolinguistic Diffusion and the U.S.-Canada Border." *Language Variation and Change* 12 (2000): 1–24.

Bosworth, Joseph and T. Northcote Toller, eds. *An Anglo-Saxon Dictionary.* Oxford: OUP, 1898.

Bradley, Henry. *The Making of English.* London: Macmillan, 1904.

Britain, Dave. "Geolinguistics and Linguistic Diffusion." *Sociolinguistics: International Handbook of the Science of Language and Society.* Ed. U. Ammon et al. Berlin: Mouton de Gruyter, 2004.

Bynon, Theodora. *Historical Linguistics.* Cambridge: CUP, 1977.

Campbell, A. *Old English Grammar.* Oxford: Clarendon, 1959.

Carpenter, H. C. A. *Die Deklination in der nordhumbrischen Evangelien-Übersetzung der Lindisfarner hs.* Bonner Studien zur englischen Philologie. 2. Bonn: Hanstein, 1910.

Chambers, J. K. and Peter Trudgill. *Dialectology.* 2nd ed. Cambridge: CUP, 1998.

Chen, Matthew Y. "The Time Dimension: Contribution toward a Theory of Sound Change."

Foundations of Language: International Journal of Language and Philosophy 8 (1972): 457–98.

Chen, Matthew Y. "Relative Chronology: Three Methods of Reconstruction." *Journal of Linguistics* 12 (1976): 209–58.

Chen, Matthew Y. and Hsin-I Hsieh. "The Time Variable in Phonological Change." *Journal of Linguistics* 7 (1971): 1–13.

Chen, Matthew Y. and William S-Y. Wang. "Sound Change: Actuation and Implementation." *Language* 51 (1975): 255–81.

Classen, E. "-s and -n Plurals in Middle English." *Modern Language Review* 14 (1918): 94–96.

Classen, E. *Outlines of the History of the English Language*. London: Macmillan, 1919.

Coates, Richard. "The Scriptorium of the Mercian Rushworth Gloss: A Bilingual Perspective." *Notes and Queries* 44 (1997): 453–58.

Curme, George O. *Syntax*. Boston: Heath, 1931.

diPaolo, Healey Antoinette, Joan Holland, Ian McDougall, and Peter Mielke, eds. *The Dictionary of Old English Corpus in Electronic Form*. TEI-P3 conformant version. CD-ROM. Toronto: DOE Project 2000, 2000.

Dobson, Eric John. *English Pronunciation 1500–1700*. 2nd ed. 2 vols. Oxford: Clarendon, 1968.

Einenkel, E. "Die dänischen Elemente in der Syntax der englischen Sprache." *Anglia* 29 (1906): 120–28.

Fidelholz, James. "Word Frequency and Vowel Reduction in English." *Papers from the 11th Regional Meeting of the Chicago Linguistic Society*. Ed. Robin E. Grossman, L. James San, and Timothy J. Vance. Chicago: Chicago Linguistic Society, 1975. 200–13.

Fischer, R. "Zur Sprache und Autorschaft der mittelengl. Legenden St. Editha und St. Etheldreda." *Anglia* 11 (1889): 175–218.

Flom, George Tobias. *Scandinavian Influence on Southern Lowland Scotch: A Contribution to the Study of the Linguistic Relations of English and Scandinavian*. New York: AMS, 1966.

Garmonsway, G. N., trans. *The Anglo-Saxon Chronicle*. London: Dent, 1953.

Geipel, John. *The Viking Legacy: The Scandinavian Influence on the English and Gaelic Languages*. Newton Abbot: David and Charles, 1971.

Glauser, Beat. *The Scottish-English Linguistic Border: Lexical Aspects*. English Dialect Series. 20. Bern: Francke, 1974.

Gordon, Eric Valentine. *An Introduction to Old Norse*. 2nd ed. Rev. A. R. Taylor. Oxford: Clarendon, 1957.

Görlach, Manfred. "Middle English—a Creole?" *Linguistics across Historical and Geographical Boundaries*. Ed. Dieter Kastovsky and Aleksander Szwedek. Berlin: Mouton de Gruyter, 1986. 329–44.

Hall, John Richard Clark, ed. *A Concise Anglo-Saxon Dictionary*. 4th ed. Cambridge: CUP, 1960.

Hansen, Anita Berit. "Lexical Diffusion as a Factor of Phonetic Change: The Case of Modern French Nasal Vowels." *Language Variation and Change* 13 (2001): 209–52.

Hansen, B. H. "The Historical Implications of the Scandinavian Linguistic Element in English." *North-Western European Language Evolution* 4 (1984): 53–95.

Hashimoto, Mantaro J. "Review of the Lexicon in Phonological Change." *Language* 37 (1981): 183–91.

Haugen, Einar. "The Analysis of Linguistic Borrowing." *Language* 26 (1950): 210–31.

Haugen, Einar. *The Scandinavian Languages: An Introduction to Their History*. London: Faber, 1976.

Hill, Betty. "Notes on the Egerton *e* Text of the *Poema Morale*." *Neophilologus* 50 (1966): 353–59.

Hill, Betty. "Twelfth-Century *Conduct of Life*, Formerly the *Poema Morale* or *A Moral Ode*." *Leeds Studies in English* ns 9 (1977): 97–144.

Hoad, Terry. "Preliminaries: Before English." *The Oxford History of English*. Ed. Lynda Mugglestone. Oxford: OUP, 2006. 1–31.

Holmqvist, Erik. *On the History of the English Present Inflections Particularly -th and -s*. Heidelberg: Winter, 1922.

Hooper, Joan. "Word Frequency in Lexical Diffusion and the Source of Morphophonological Change." *Current Progress in Historical Linguistics*. Ed. William M. Christie, Jr. Amsterdam: North-Holland, 1976. 95–105.

Hotta, Ryuichi. "The Spread of the *s*-Plural in Early Middle English: Its Origin and Development." *Studies in English Literature* 79.2 (2002): 123–42.

Hotta, Ryuichi. "A Historical Study on 'eyes' in English from a Panchronic Point of View." *Studies in Medieval English Language and Literature* 20 (2005): 75–100.

Hotta, Ryuichi. "The Development of the Nominal Plural Forms in Early Middle English." Diss. U of Glasgow, 2005.

Hotta, Ryuichi. "Language Changes Walking Hand in Hand: The Spread of the *s*-Plural and Case Syncretism in Early Middle English." *Individual Languages and Language Universals*. Special Issue. Ed. Michiko Takeuchi. Yokohama: Center for Language Studies at Kanagawa U, 2008. 95–124.

Hudson, Richard Anthony. *Sociolinguistics*. Cambridge: CUP, 1980.

Ihalainen, Ossi. "The Dialects of England Since 1776.". *The Cambridge History of the English Language.* 5. Ed. Robert Burchfield. Cambridge: CUP, 1994. 197–274.

Jack, George B. "The Prepositional Plural in the AB Language." *Neuphilologische Mitteilungen* 82 (1981): 175–80.

Jespersen, Otto. *Chapters on English.* London: Allen, 1918. Rpt. of *Progress in Language.* 1894.

Jespersen, Otto. *Language: Its Nature, Development and Origin.* London: Allen, 1922.

Jespersen, Otto. *A Modern English Grammar on Historical Principles.* 6 vols. Copenhagen: Munksgaard, 1961–65.

Jespersen, Otto. *Growth and Structure of the English Language.* 10th ed. Chicago: U of Chicago, 1982.

Jones, Charles. "The Functional Motivation of Linguistic Change." *English Studies* 48 (1967): 97–111.

Jones, Charles. *Grammatical Gender in English: 950 to 1250.* London: Croom Helm, 1988.

Jordan, Richard. "Der Dialekt der Lambeth-Handschrift des Poema Morale." *Englische Studien* 42 (1910): 38–42.

Kishida, Takayuki. *A Study of the Case Syncretism in English.* Tokyo: Gakushuin U, 2001. [in Japanese]

Keller, R. E. *The German Language.* London: Faber, 1978.

Keller, Wolfgang. "Skandinavischer Einfluss in der englischen Flexion." *Probleme der englischen Sprache und Kultur.* Heidelberg: Winter, 1925. 80–87.

Keyser, Samuel Jay and Wayne O'Neil. "The Simplification of the Old English Strong Nominal Paradigms." *Papers from the 4th International Conference on English Historical Linguistics.* Ed. Roger Eaton et al. Amsterdam: Benjamins, 1985. 85–107.

Kiparsky, Paul. "The Phonological Basis of Sound Change." *The Handbook of Phonological Theory.* Ed. John A. Goldsmith. Oxford: Blackwell, 1995. 640–70.

Kirch, M. S. "Scandinavian Influence on English Syntax." *Publications of the Modern Language Association of America* 74 (1959): 503–10.

Kirk, John M., Stewart Sanderson, and J. D. A. Widdowson, eds. *Studies in Linguistic Geography: The Dialects of English in Britain and Ireland.* London: Croom Helm, 1985.

Kitson, Peter R. "When Did Middle English Begin? Later than You Think!" *Studies in Middle English Linguistics.* Ed. Jacek Fisiak. Berlin: Mouton de Gruyter, 1997. 221–69.

Kitson, Peter R. "On Margins of Error in Placing Old English Literary Dialects." *Methods and Data in English Historical Dialectology.* Ed. Marina Dossena and Roger

Lass. Bern: Peter Lang, 2004. 221–39.

Knowles, Gerry. *A Cultural History of the English Language.* London: Arnold, 1997.

Kubouchi, Tadao and Keiko Ikegami, eds. *Language of Peterborough Chronicle 1066–1154.* Tokyo: Gakushobo, 1984. [in Japanese]

Kurath, Hans, Margaret S. Ogden, Charles E. Palmer, and Richard L. McKelvey. *Plan and Bibliography.* Ann Arbor: U of Michigan P, 1954.

Kurath, Hans, Sherman M. Kuhn, and John Reidy, eds. *Middle English Dictionary.* Ann Arbor: U of Michigan P, 1952–2001.

Labov, William. "The Overestimation of Functionalism." *Functionalism in Linguistics.* Ed. René Dirven and Vilém Fried. Amsterdam: Benjamins, 1987. 311–32.

Labov, William. *Internal Factors.* Cambridge, Mass.: Blackwell, 1994. Vol. 1 of *Principles of Linguistic Change.* 2 vols. 1994–2001.

Labov, William. *Social Factors.* Maldon: Blackwell, 2001. Vol. 2 of *Principles of Linguistic Change.* 2 vols. 1994–2001.

Laing, Margaret, ed. *Middle English Dialectology: Essays on Some Principles and Problems.* Aberdeen: Aberdeen UP, 1989.

Laing, Margaret. "Anchor Texts and Literary Manuscripts in Early Middle English." *Regionalism in Late Medieval Manuscripts and Texts.* Ed. Felicity Riddy. Cambridge: Brewer, 1991. 27–52.

Laing, Margaret. "A Linguistic Atlas of Early Middle English: The Value of Texts Surviving in More than One Version." *History of Englishes.* Ed. Matti Rissanen et al. Berlin: Mouton de Gruyter, 1992. 566–81.

Laing, Margaret, ed. *Catalogue of Sources for a Linguistic Atlas of Early Medieval English.* Cambridge: Brewer, 1993.

Laing, Margaret. *"Never the twain shall meet*: Early Middle English—The East-West Divide." *Placing Middle English in Context.* Ed. Irma Taavitsainen et al. Berlin: Mouton de Gruyter, 2000. 97–124.

Laing, Margaret and Roger Lass, eds. *A Linguistic Atlas of Early Middle English, 1150–1325.* http://www.lel.ed.ac.uk/ihd/laeme1/laeme1.html. Online. Edinburgh: U of Edinburgh, 2007. (The version I used for the study is one that was still under preparation in 2003.)

Lass, Roger. *The Shape of English: Structure and History.* London: Dent, 1987.

Lass, Roger. "Phonology and Morphology." *The Cambridge History of the English Language.* 2. Ed. Norman Blake. Cambridge: CUP, 1992. 23–154.

Lass, Roger. *Old English: A Historical Linguistic Companion.* Cambridge: CUP, 1994.

Lehnert, Martin. *Sprachform und Sprachfunktion im "Ormulum."* Berlin: Deutscher Verlag der Wissenschaften, 1953.

Lightfoot, David W. *Principles of Diachronic Syntax.* Cambridge: CUP, 1979.

Lyons, John. *Introduction to Theoretical Linguistics.* London: CUP, 1968.

McClure, J. Derrick. "English in Scotland." *The Cambridge History of the English Language.* 5. Ed. Robert Burchfield. Cambridge: CUP, 1994. 23–93.

McIntosh, Angus. "The Analysis of Written Middle English." *Transactions of the Philological Society* (1956): 26–55. Rpt. in *Middle English Dialectology.* Ed. Margaret Laing. 1–21. 1989.

McIntosh, Angus. "A New Approach to Middle English Dialectology." *English Studies* 44 (1964): 1–11. Rpt. in *Middle English Dialectology.* Ed. Margaret Laing. 22–31. 1989

McIntosh, Angus. "Word Geography in the Lexicography of Mediaeval English." *Annals of the New York Academy of Sciences* 211 (1973): 55–66. Rpt. in *Middle English Dialectology.* Ed. Margaret Laing. 86–97. 1989.

McIntosh, Angus. "Scribal Profiles from Middle English Texts." *Neuphilologische Mitteilungen* 76 (1975): 218–35. Rpt. in *Middle English Dialectology.* Ed. Margaret Laing. 32–45. 1989.

McIntosh, Angus, Michael Louis Samuels, Michael Benskin, eds. *A Linguistic Atlas of Late Mediaeval English.* 4 vols. Aberdeen: Aberdeen UP, 1986.

McMahon, April M. S. *Understanding Language Change.* Cambridge: CUP, 1994.

Menger, Louis Emil. *The Anglo-Norman Dialect: A Manual of Its Phonology and Morphology with Illustrative Specimens of the Literature.* New York: Columbia UP, 1904.

Menner, Robert J. "The Conflict of Homonyms in English." *Language* 12 (1936): 229–44.

Meyer, H. *Zur Sprache der jüngeren Teile der Chronik von Peterborough.* Diss. Freiburg U, 1889.

Meyer-Lübke, Wilhelm. *Grammaire des langues romanes.* Trans. Eugene Rabiet, Auguste Doutrepont, and Georges Doutrepont. 4 vols. Geneve: Slatkine, 1974.

Millar, Robert McColl. *System Collapse System Rebirth: The Demonstrative Pronouns of English 900–1350 and the Birth of the Definite Article.* New York: Peter Lang, 2000.

Millett, Bella, ed. *Ancrene Wisse: A Corrected Edition of the Text in Cambridge, Corpus Christi College MS 402, with Variants from Other Manuscripts.* Vol. 1. EETS os 325. 2005.

Milroy, James. *Linguistic Variation and Change: On the Historical Sociolinguistics of English.* Oxford: Blackwell, 1992.

Milroy, James. "Middle English Dialectology." *The Cambridge History of the English Language.* 2. Ed. Norman Blake. Cambridge: CUP, 1992. 156–206.

Milroy, James. "A Social Model for the Interpretation of Language Change." *History of Englishes*. Ed. Matti Rissanen et al. Berlin: Mouton de Gruyter, 1992. 72–91.

Minkova, Donka. *The History of Final Vowels in English: The Sound of Muting*. Berlin: Mouton de Gruyter, 1991.

Mitchell, Bruce. *Old English Syntax*. 2 vols. Oxford: Clarendon, 1985.

Moore, Samuel. "Loss of Final *n* in Inflectional Syllables of Middle English." *Language* 3 (1927): 232–59.

Moore, Samuel. "Earliest Morphological Changes in Middle English." *Language* 4 (1928): 238–66.

Moore, Samuel. *Historical Outlines of English Sounds and Inflections*. Rev. Albert Marckwardt. Ann Arbor: Wahr, 1951.

Mossé, Fernand. *A Handbook of Middle English*. Trans. James A. Walker. Baltimore: Johns Hopkins, 1952.

Mustanoja, Tauno F. *A Middle English Syntax*. Part 1. Helsinki: Société Néophilologique, 1960.

Nahkola, Kari and Marja Saanilahti. "Mapping Language Changes in Real Time: A Panel Study on Finnish." *Language Variation and Change* 16 (2004): 75–91.

Nakao, Toshio, ed. *History of English II*. Outline of English Linguistics. 9. Tokyo: Taishukan, 1972. [in Japanese]

Napier, A. "Ein altenglisches Leben des Heiligen Chad." *Anglia* 10 (1888): 131–56.

Newman, John G. "The Spread of the *S*-Plural in Middle English (1150–1420): A Corpus Study." *Studia Anglica Posnaniensia* 34 (1999): 73–89.

Nielsen, Hans Frede. *The Germanic Languages: Origins and Early Dialectal Interrelations*. Tuscaloosa: U of Alabama P, 1989.

Nist, John. *A Structural History of English*. New York: St Martin's, 1966.

Noreen, Adolf. *Altschwedische Grammatik mit Einschluss des Altgutnischen*. Halle: Niemeyer, 1904. Vol. 2 of Atlnordische Grammatik.

Noreen, Adolf. *Geschichte der nordischen Sprachen: Besonders in altnordischer Zeit*. Strassburg: Trübner, 1913.

Noreen, Adolf. *Altisländische und altnorwegische Grammatik (Laut- und Flexionslehre) unter Berücksichtigung des Urnordischen*. 5th ed. Tübingen: Niemeyer, 1970. Vol. 1 of Atlnordische Grammatik.

Ogura, Mieko. "The Development of Periphrastic *Do* in English: A Case of Lexical Diffusion in Syntax." *Diachronica* 10 (1993): 51–85.

Ogura, Mieko and William S-Y. Wang. "Snowball Effect in Lexical Diffusion: The Development of -*s* in the Third Person Singular Present Indicative in English." *Papers from the 8th International Conference on English Historical Linguistics.* Ed. Derek Britton. Amsterdam: Benjamins, 1994. 119–41.

Ogura, Mieko and William S-Y. Wang. "Evolution Theory and Lexical Diffusion." *Advances in English Historical Linguistics.* Ed. Jacek Fisiak and Marcin Krygier. Berlin: Mouton de Gruyter, 1998. 315–43.

Ono, Shigeru and Toshio Nakao, eds. *History of English I.* Outline of English Linguistics. 8. Tokyo: Taishukan, 1980. [in Japanese]

The Oxford English Dictionary. 2nd ed. CD-ROM. Version 3.1. Oxford: OUP, 2004.

Phillips, Betty S. "Lexical Diffusion and Southern *tune, duke, new.*" *American Speech* 56 (1981): 72–78.

Phillips, Betty S. "Word Frequency and the Actuation of Sound Change." *Language* 60 (1984): 320–42.

Preusler, W. *Syntax in Poema Morale.* Breslau: Korn, 1914.

Prokosch, Eduard. *The Sounds and History of the German Language.* New York: Holt, 1916.

Prokosch, Eduard. *A Comparative Germanic Grammar.* Philadelphia: Linguistic Society of America, 1939.

Pyles, Thomas. *The Origins and Development of the English Language.* New York: Harcourt, 1964.

Quirk, Randolph. and C. L. Wrenn. *An Old English Grammar.* 2nd ed. London: Methuen, 1957.

Ralf, Bo. "Phonological and Graphematic Developments from Ancient Nordic to Old Nordic." *The Nordic Languages: An International Handbook of the History of the North Germanic Languages.* Vol. 1. Ed. Oskar Bandle et al. Berlin: Walter de Gruyter, 2002. 703–19.

Rissanen, Matti, Merja Kytö, and Minna Palander-Collin, eds. *Early English in the Computer Age: Explorations through the Helsinki Corpus.* Berlin: Mouton de Gruyter, 1993.

Ritt, Nikolaus. *Quantity Adjustment: Vowel Lengthening and Shortening in Early Middle English.* Cambridge: CUP, 1994.

Robinson, Orrin W. *Old English and Its Closest Relatives: A Survey of the Earliest Germanic Languages.* London: Routledge, 1992.

Roedler, Eduard. "Die Ausbreitung des 's'-Plurals im Englischen." Vol. 1. Diss. Christian-Albrechts U, 1911. Vol. 2. *Anglia* 40 (1916): 420–502.

Ross, Alan S. C. "Sex and Gender in the Lindisfarne Gospels." *Journal of English and Germanic Philology.* 35 (1936): 321–30.

Rynell, Alarik. *The Rivalry of Scandinavian and Native Synonyms in Middle English Especially* taken *and* nimen. Lund: Gleerup, 1948.

Samuels, Michael Louis. *Linguistic Evolution with Special Reference to English.* Cambridge: CUP, 1972.

Samuels, Michael Louis. "The Dialect of the Scribe of the Harley Lyrics." *Poetica* (1984): 39–47. Rpt. in *Middle English Dialectology.* Ed. Margaret Laing. 256–63. 1989.

Samuels, Michael Louis. "The Great Scandinavian Belt." *Papers from the 4th International Conference on English Historical Linguistics.* Ed. Roger Eaton et al. Amsterdam: Benjamins, 1985. 269–81.

Sandred, Karl Inge. "The Study of Scandinavian in England: A Survey of Swedish Contributions Including Ongoing Research in East Anglia." *Language Contact in the British Isles: Proceedings of the Eighth International Symposium on Language Contact in Europe, Douglas, Isle of Man, 1988.* Ed. P. Sture Ureland and George Broderick. Tübingen: Niemeyer, 1991. 317–36.

Sawyer, P. H., ed. *Anglo-Saxon Charters: An Annotated List and Bibliography.* London: Royal Historical Society, 1968.

Sawyer, P. H. *The Age of the Vikings.* 2nd ed. London: Arnold, 1971.

Sayce, A. H. *Introduction to the Science of Language.* 2 vols. London: Kegan Paul, 1883.

Sievers, Eduard and Karl Brunner. *Abriss der Altenglischen Grammatik.* Tübingen: Niemeyer, 1963.

Sisam, C. "The Scribal Tradition of the *Lambeth Homilies.*" *Review of English Studies* ns 2 (1951): 105–13.

Smith, Jeremy J. "Tradition and Innovation in South-West-Midland Middle English." *Regionalism in Late Medieval Manuscripts and Texts.* Cambridge: Brewer, 1991. 53–65.

Smith, Jeremy J. "A Linguistic Atlas of Early Middle English: Tradition and Typology." *History of Englishes.* Ed. Matti Rissanen et al. Berlin: Mouton de Gruyter, 1992. 582–91.

Smith, Jeremy J. *An Historical Study of English: Function, Form and Change.* London: Routledge, 1996.

Smith, Jeremy J. "Standard Language in Early Middle English?" *Placing Middle English in Context.* Ed. Irma Taavitsainen et al. Berlin: Mouton de Gruyter, 2000. 125–39.

Stanley, Eric Gerald. "Laȝamon's Antiquarian Sentiments." *Medium Ævum* 38 (1969): 23–37.

Stein, Dieter. "OE Northumbrian Verb Inflection Revisited." *Linguistic Theory and Historical Linguistics.* Ed. Dieter Kastovsky and Aleksander Szwedek. Berlin: Gruyter,

1986. 637–50.

Stein, Dieter. "At the Crossroads of Philology, Linguistics and Semiotics: Notes on the Replacement of *th* by *s* in the Third Person Singular in English." *English Studies* 68 (1987): 406–31.

Stein, Dieter. *The Semantics of Syntactic Change: Aspects of the Evolution of 'do' in English*. Berlin: Mouton de Gruyter, 1990.

Stevenson, W. H. "Yorkshire Surveys and Other Eleventh-Century Documents in the York Gospels." *The English Historical Review* 27 (1912): 1–25.

Strang, Barbara M. H. *A History of English*. London: Methuen, 1970.

Sturtevant, Edward H. *Linguistic Change*. 1917. New York: Stechert, 1942.

Sundby, Bertil. *The Dialect and Provenance of the Middle English Poem* The Owl and the Nightingale. Lund: Gleerup, 1950.

Szemerényi, Oswald John Louis. *Introduction to Indo-European Linguistics*. Oxford: Clarendon, 1996.

Tesnière, Lucien. "Phonologie et mélange de langues." *Études phonologiques*. Prague: Jednota ceskych matematiku a fysiku, 1939.

Thomason, Sarah Grey. *Language Contact*. Edinburgh: Edinburgh UP, 2001.

Thomason, Sarah Grey and Terrence Kaufman. *Language Contact, Creolization, and Genetic Linguistics*. Berkeley: U of California P, 1988.

Thomson, S. Harrison. "The Date of the Early English Translation of the *Candet Nudatum Pectus*." *Medium Ævum* 4 (1935): 100–05.

Toller, T. Northcote, ed. *An Anglo-Saxon Dictionary: Supplement*. Oxford: Clarendon, 1921.

Toon, Thomas E. "Old English Dialects." *The Cambridge History of the English Language*. 1. Ed. Richard M. Hogg. Cambridge: CUP, 1992. 409–51.

Townend, Matthew. *Language and History in Viking Age England: Linguistic Relations Between Speakers of Old Norse and Old English*. Turnhout: Brepols, 2002.

Trudgill, Peter. "Linguistic Change and Diffusion: Description and Explanation in Sociolinguistic Dialect Geography." *Language in Society* 3 (1974): 215–46.

Visser, Frederik Theodoor. *An Historical Syntax of the English Language*. 4 vols. Leiden: Brill, 1963–73.

Vogt, Hans. "Contact of Languages." *Word* 10 (1954): 365–74.

Voyles, Joseph B. *Early Germanic Grammar: Pre-, Proto-, and Post-Germanic Languages*. San Diego: Academic P, 1992.

Wang, William S-Y. "The Measurement of Functional Load." *Phonetica* 16 (1967): 36–54.

Wang, William S-Y. "Competing Changes as a Cause of Residue." *Readings in Historical Phonology: Chapters in the Theory of Sound Change*. Ed. Philip Baldi and

Ronald N. Werth. University Park: Pennsylvania State UP, 1978. 236–57.

Wang, William S-Y. "Language Change—A Lexical Perspective." *Annual Review of Anthropology* 8 (1979): 353–71.

Wang, William S-Y. and Chinfa Lien. "Bidirectional Diffusion in Sound Change." *Historical Linguistics: Problems and Perspectives.* Ed. Charles Jones. London: Longman, 1993. 345–400.

Wardale, E. E. *An Introduction to Middle English.* London: Routledge and Kegan Paul, 1937.

Weinreich, Uriel, William Labov, and Marvin I. Herzog. "Empirical Foundations for a Theory of Language Change." *Directions for Historical Linguistics.* Ed. Winfred Philipp Lehmann and Yakov Malkiel. Autsin: U of Texas P, 1968. 95–188.

Wells, John Edwin. "Accidence in 'The Owl and the Nightingale.'" *Anglia* 33 (1910): 252–69.

Whitelock, Dorothy, trans. *The Anglo-Saxon Chronicle: A Revised Translation.* London: Eyre, 1961.

Whitney, William Dwight. *Language and the Study of Language: Twelve Lectures of the Principles of Linguistic Science.* 5th ed. New York: Scribner, 1872.

Wright, Joseph. *The English Dialect Dictionary.* 6 vols. London: Henry Frowde, 1896–1905.

Wyld, Henry Cecil. *A History of Modern Colloquial English.* London: Unwin, 1920.

Wyld, Henry Cecil. *A Short History of English with a Bibliography and Lists of Texts and Editions.* 3rd ed. London: Murray, 1927.

Zoëga, Geir T., ed. *A Concise Dictionary of Old Icelandic.* Oxford: Clarendon, 1910.

Index

a

abductive 3
AB group 11, 13, 105
AB language 84, 90, 93, 104, 145, 262
ablative 22
absolute cause 2
academic modesty 2
actuation 118
adjectival 38
adjective 38, 47, 268
Ælfric 264
agreement 28, 29, 141, 144, 149, 150, 178
analogical 15, 19, 25, 134, 137
analogy 31, 36, 78, 117, 119, 123, 133, 145, 266
anchor 108
Ancrene Riwle 11, 12, 97, 104
Ancrene Wisse/Riwle 91, 92, 94–96, 146
-and 155
Anglicisation 160
Anglo-Frisian 24
animacy 29, 146, 149
animate 28, 146
apocopy 27
archaism 101, 103
assimilation 15, 261
assonance 112
Assumption of Our Lady 10
availability of texts 6
Ayenbite of Inwyt 14

b

bān 77, 251
bearn 77, 251
bed 75, 246
Bede 63–65
bēn 77, 248
Bestiary 10
bilingual 159
bliss 77, 248
blōstm 74, 241
bod 75, 246
borrowing 117, 159
brōþor 77, 78, 251
Brut 12, 13, 260, 265
bundling 54, 179

c

Canticum de Creatione 10
carry-over 111, 114
case syncretism 39–43, 65, 147, 262
centripetal force 33, 134, 148
children 51, 88, 264
cild 78, 257
cirice 75, 244
Classen 19, 20, 154, 161–163, 173
cognate 168
cognate languages 20, 21
common case 39, 40
Common Scandinavian 29, 31–33
comparative linguistics 44
compensatory lengthening 31
compound 46, 47, 51, 52
conditioning factor 2, 120
conflated 37, 181
conspiracy 119, 150
constrained 88, 89, 103, 104, 107
contact-induced 122, 153
contact linguistics 4, 173
countable unit 143, 145, 149
cross-dialectal contact 79, 80, 154
cross-gender transfer 16
Cursor Mundi 9
cynn 77, 252

d

dǣd 77, 128, 248
Danelaw 18, 20, 159, 160, 269
Danish 33, 35, 160, 167
Dan Michel 14
dating 17, 37
dative environment 41–43, 262
Debate between Body and Soul 10, 12, 13, 260
definite article 28, 29, 142, 143, 147, 267
dēofol 74, 241
dēor 77, 252
derivative 46, 51
determiner 28, 113, 114, 141
diachronic comparability 39
dialect map 6, 8
dialectology 11, 17

diffusion 4, 18, 41, 118, 120–122, 126, 128–130, 266
disyllabic 35
double assignment 133, 134
double diffusion 120, 266
double plural 10, 50
drift 21, 35, 36, 130, 162
Durham Ritual 160

e

ēage 75, 244
ēare 75, 244
Earliest Complete English Prose Psalter 11
Early New High German 24, 27, 28, 146
East Germanic 22, 24
English historical linguistics 5
-*en*/-*eth* line 11
epidemics 120
-*er* 156
-*ere* 47
etymological identity 160
euphony 140, 141

f

fāh 74, 241
false archaism 111, 115
fēolaga 74, 242
fēond 78, 256
fēra 74, 242
fit technique 37
Floris and Blauncheflur 10
fluctuation 35, 50, 63, 65, 66, 75–77, 92, 103, 107, 113
French 18, 28, 142, 155, 158, 267
frēond 78, 256
functional correspondence 168
functionalistic 15, 17, 18, 142, 144, 178
functional motivation 78, 111, 144
functional word 155, 158

g

ge- 156
gēar 77, 129, 252
geat 75, 76, 79, 246
gender 15, 16, 44, 45, 137, 138
gender barrier 27, 138
Genesis and Exodus 10, 267
genitive singular 34, 36, 165, 167, 268, 270
geolinguistics 266
German 142
Germanic 20–22, 35, 36, 44, 163
giefu 77, 248
gōd 78, 79, 130, 252
Gothic 22–24, 36, 261
gravity model 266

h

hǣs 77, 249
hālga 74, 242
Hali Meiðhad 12
hand 77, 249
Harrowing of Hell 10, 17, 260
Havelok 10, 17, 260
heavy-syllabic 138, 139, 267
heorte 75, 244

High German 24, 25, 27, 28
High Vowel Deletion 266
Historia 64
historical linguistics 2, 3, 17, 179, 268
History 63–65
hīwan 242
hlǣfdige 75, 245
hors 77, 253
how 2–4, 117, 133, 178, 179
hundred 77, 253
hunting animal 143, 145, 149
hyperadaptation 105

i

imperfect learner 159
implementation 117, 118, 122, 123
inanimacy 29, 146, 149
inanimate 93, 123
independent development 79, 80
inertia 85
infectious disease 120
-*ing* 13
inorganic -*e* 16, 137–139, 267
instrumental 22
isogloss 21
item enumeration 107, 145, 149
item-internal diffusion 122, 128–130
Item Profile 73, 240, 264
i-mutation 25, 27–29, 42, 264

j

Japanese 150
Jespersen 20

k

Kentish Gospels 14
Kentish Sermons 14
key item 73, 240
kinship noun 13, 145, 173

l

LAEME 3, 5, 17, 37, 38, 92, 179, 181, 260, 261, 264
Laȝamon 12, 13, 140, 260, 265
lagu 77, 249
LALME 3, 37, 260, 261
Lambeth Homilies 12, 13, 51, 65, 82, 83, 102, 142, 146, 262
land 77, 253
language contact 122, 133, 153, 156, 159, 168
language-external 18, 19, 21, 120, 133, 153, 162, 173, 174, 178, 179
language-internal 18, 19, 21, 120, 133, 148, 150, 153, 173, 174, 178
language mixture 101
Late Middle English 5–7, 13, 14
Late Old English 6, 7, 40, 47, 57, 65, 160
Latin 155, 158
levelling 15, 16, 27, 33, 36, 40, 134–136, 261

Lexical Diffusion 4, 117–126, 178, 179, 265, 266
lexicon 4, 118, 120, 122
Life of St Chad 63
Life of St Juliana 13
Life of St Katherine 13
light-syllabic 137–139, 267
lim 76, 246
Lindisfarne Gospels 9, 157, 158, 160, 169, 170
linguistic change 20
linguistic contact 19, 21
Linguistic Profile 37, 38
literary text 37
literatim 101
loanword 35, 47, 141, 149, 154, 155, 158, 160, 174
localisation 17, 37, 54, 55, 106, 108, 179, 181, 263, 264
locative 22
Lofsong of ure Louerde 13
logistic curve 265
long-syllabic 9, 10, 13, 15, 16, 92
loss of *n* 15, 16, 137
Low German 28, 29, 36, 261
lufu 77, 249

m

mægden 247
mæsse 75, 245
Magdalenen-legende 10
maȝden 76
-*man* 47
mechanical copying 12
mechanical copyist 83, 87, 89, 104, 106
memory 99, 101, 106
-*men* 51
Mercian 63, 64, 263
merger 15, 34, 134, 136, 178
metathesis 51
Middle Danish 35
Middle English Innovation 47
Middle English Open Syllable Lengthening 266
Middle High German 24, 25, 28
Middle Scandinavian 29
Midlands 11, 263
miht 77, 250
mind ear 101
minor declension 50
Mischsprache 40
Modern Danish 29, 35
Modern English 5–7
Modern Scandinavian 29
momentum 118, 119, 122
mon/man line 11
monosyllabic 35, 74, 140
morphological change 123, 125
morphological device 27, 28
morphological process 40, 117
multi-factorial 18, 174, 268

n

nǣdre 75, 245
nama 74, 243
Neogrammarian 117, 118, 121, 123
ne-plural 50

Index 289

New High German 24, 25, 28
niht 79, 257
-nis 13, 92
normal development 19, 161
Norsified English 175
North English Legendary 9
northern dialects 9, 36, 71, 74, 75, 77–79, 128, 147, 150, 162, 174, 178, 179
North Germanic 29
North-South divide 150
Northumbrian 57
North-West Germanic 25
Norwegian 269
number category 150
number distinction 15, 16, 27, 31, 35, 135, 137, 150
numeral 38, 123, 129, 143
nunnation 140, 141, 149
n-plural 10, 12–14, 16, 19, 27, 28, 39, 41, 50, 57, 58, 60, 66, 84, 105–107, 126, 128, 136–138, 140, 141, 145, 146, 149, 162, 263

O

Octavian 14
Old Danish 33–36
Old French 154, 268
Old High German 24–26, 29
Old Icelandic 160
Old Norse 36
Old Norse contact hypothesis 19, 35, 154, 161, 163, 169, 173, 179, 261
Old Saxon 24, 25, 29, 30, 36, 261
Old Scandinavian 29, 33
On God Ureison of ure Lefdi 13
Ormulum 10, 58, 169, 171, 173, 267, 270
Owl and the Nightingale 86, 87, 104

P

panchronic 70, 72, 216, 263
parallelism 79, 130, 174, 178
Pater Noster 264
Peterborough Chronicle 9, 10, 17, 43, 109, 110, 114, 145, 158, 160, 169, 170, 260, 270
PFP 38, 51, 54, 194, 227
philology 17
phonological process 27
Piers Plowman 12
pīn 77, 250
place name 155
plural formation transfer 46, 47
Plural Forms Profile 38, 51
plural type 44, 45, 51, 70
Poema Morale 12–14, 17, 51, 83, 84, 98–100, 261
Polychronicon 13
polysyllabic 140
present participle 155
Pre-Old English 36
pronominal 38
pronominal reference 141, 144
Proto-Germanic 5, 7, 21–23, 25, 27, 29
Proto-Scandinavian 29, 30

q

quantifier 129, 141, 143–145, 149

r

r-coloured [z] 29, 168
reconstruction 21
reference class 46, 50, 194, 240
reference form 46, 47, 50, 51, 194
reference system 43, 44, 47, 50
reflexive 156
relative pronoun 156
R-ending 31, 33, 34
r-ending 27, 31, 165, 167, 169, 170, 173, 264, 270
repertoire 89, 96, 102, 104, 111
residue 121
rhyming 40, 51, 83, 104, 194, 264
Robert of Gloucester's Chronicle 13
Roedler 2, 5, 7, 9–11, 13–15, 17, 18, 87, 92, 139, 260, 261, 263
rule generalisation 124
Rushworth Gospels 160

S

saturated 66
Sawles Warde 13

sāwol   77, 250
-sc   160
Scandinavian   29
scēap   77, 253
Schriftsprache   10, 111, 158
schwa   135, 136, 163
scope   5, 6
scribal diglossia   40
scribal text   37, 38, 181
S-curve   4, 67, 118–120, 122, 124–126, 129, 130, 174, 178, 179, 265
S-diffusion   120, 126, 128–130, 266
semantic association   93, 125, 178
semantic borrowing   155
Seven Sins   10
shift-induced interference   159
short-syllabic   13, 14, 16, 92
sibilant   124, 141, 149
simplification   34, 36, 40, 156–158
Sir Gawain and the Green Knight   11
sīþ   74, 241
-sk   156, 160
slip   64, 65
slow-quick-quick-slow   4
s/n-dichotomic system   84, 90, 92, 105–108
snowball   118, 119
sociolinguistic   18, 34, 154, 173, 175
sound change   117, 119, 121, 123, 266
southern dialects   9, 19, 36, 61, 74–79, 136–138, 150, 162, 174, 178

spelling system   83, 87
spoken variety   67, 90
spontaneous   87–90, 96, 101–104, 106, 107, 111, 115
spread rate   52, 70, 97, 194, 263
Stabat iuxta crucem Christi   17
standard   90
standardisation   27
stemma   106
stem-type   45, 262
steorra   74, 243
sunu   75, 245
survival of the fittest   15
sweostor   78, 256
syllable weight   44, 45, 50, 138, 139, 149, 266, 267
syncope   31
syncretism rate   52, 194
synn   77, 128, 250
synonym   93, 145, 149
systemic change   147
systemic optimisation   66
systemic regulation   15, 18, 133, 137

t

-t   155
text database   5, 17, 37
text group   54, 56
textual evidence   6, 37
þing   77, 129, 254
tīma   74, 243
time range   5, 6
token counting   51, 240, 267
Tok Pisin   123, 124
traditional grouping   11

transitional period   7
translator   83, 89, 104, 106
trēow   78, 254
Trevisa   13
trigger   157
Trinity Homilies   14, 17, 261
type counting   52, 267
type rate   52, 70, 263
typological sequence   95, 96
typological similarity   159, 160

u

-um   39, 41, 42, 74, 135, 165, 262
-ung   13, 47, 76, 77, 92, 247
universal   3

v

variation   5, 18, 27, 47, 48, 50, 73–75, 85, 88, 93, 95, 96, 101, 112, 121, 122, 124, 141
variationist   18, 48
Vespasian Homilies   14, 261
Vespasian Psalter   63, 64
Vices and Virtues   14, 17, 261
V-plural   42, 43, 58, 60, 84, 105, 136, 137

w

wǣpen   78, 254
wæter   77, 254
wave model   266

W-diffusion   120, 122, 126, 128, 130
Wel swuþe god Ureison of God Almihti   83, 102
weorc   77, 129, 255
West Germanic   22, 24, 25
West-Saxon   43–45, 50, 63, 64, 110, 114, 160, 194
why   2–4, 18, 133, 178, 179
wīf   77, 255
William of Shoreham   14
winter   78, 255
witt   78, 255
word   77, 129, 256
wrœcca   74, 243
writ   76, 247

written variety   90
Wulfstan   264
wund   77, 251

y

yfel   76, 79, 130, 247
York   175

【著者紹介】

堀田 隆一（ほった りゅういち）

1975 年東京都生まれ。

〈学歴〉東京外国語大学外国語学部英米語学科（学士），東京大学大学院総合文化研究科言語情報科学専攻（修士），英国グラスゴー大学大学院英語学研究科（博士）。

〈職歴〉神奈川大学経営学部助教を経て，現在，中央大学文学部助教。

〈主な著書・論文〉"The Spread of the *s*-Plural in Early Middle English: Its Origin and Development." *Studies in English Literature* 79.2 (2002): 123–42. "A Historical Study on 'eyes' in English from a Panchronic Point of View." *Studies in Medieval English Language and Literature* 20 (2005): 75–100. "The Development of the Nominal Plural Forms in Early Middle English." Diss. U of Glasgow, 2005.

Hituzi Linguistics in English No. 10

The Development of the Nominal Plural Forms in Early Middle English

発行	2009 年 2 月 14 日　初版 1 刷
定価	13000 円 + 税
著者	ⓒ 堀田隆一
発行者	松本　功
装丁	向井裕一（glyph）
印刷所	三美印刷株式会社
製本所	田中製本印刷株式会社
発行所	株式会社 ひつじ書房

〒 112-0011 東京都文京区千石 2-1-2 大和ビル 2F
Tel.03-5319-4916　Fax 03-5319-4917
郵便振替 00120-8-142852
toiawase@hituzi.co.jp　http://www.hituzi.co.jp/

ISBN978-4-89476-403-3　C3080

造本には充分注意しておりますが，落丁・乱丁などがございましたら，小社かお買上げ書店にておとりかえいたします．ご意見，ご感想など，小社までお寄せ下されば幸いです。